LEND ME YOUR EARS

THE ESSENTIAL
BORIS JOHNSON
LEND ME YOUR EARS

HarperCollinsPublishers

HarperCollins*Publishers*
77–85 Fulham Palace Road,
Hammersmith, London W6 8JB

www.harpercollins.co.uk

Published by HarperCollins*Publishers* 2003
1 3 5 7 9 8 6 4 2

A catalogue record for this book
is available from the British Library

ISBN 0 00 717224 9

Set in Sabon and Frutiger Bold Condensed by
Rowland Phototypesetting Ltd,
Bury St Edmunds, Suffolk

Printed and bound in Great Britain by
Clays Ltd, St Ives plc

CONTENTS

INTRODUCTION
When History Speeded Up

Crumbs, I thought, as I stood on the edge of the crater. Crumbs was the word. Or perhaps that should be fragments, little fist-sized fragments of house. Whatever explosive the US Air Force use in their bunkerbusters, it is powerful stuff. I was standing in the posh al-Mansour district of Baghdad, looking at the place where the Americans thought, in the last days of the war, that they had located Saddam Hussein.

It is hard to imagine the detonation that creates such a hole *from above*, not just destroying four houses, but somehow sucking up the earth beneath them, or blowing it down and out. They may not have hit Saddam, who was allegedly noshing in a nearby chicken and chip joint. But that hole nicely expresses what America did to his reign, and it sums up the range and irresistibility of America. When I first became a journalist fifteen years ago, America had not yet reached this pitch of technological virtuosity, of being able to drop a bomb on any house in any third world capital, at a time of her choosing. And she certainly did not have the licence to do so.

It was mesmerising, in April 2003, to stand in Baghdad and look at the contrast between the Americans and the people they had liberated. The Iraqis were skinny and dark, badly dressed and fed. The Americans rode in their Humvees (a vehicle that is eloquently bigger than our Land Rover: more slouching, bigger tyred, cooler). The marines had the shades with the slick little nick in the corner. They were taller and squarer than the indigenous people, with heavier chins and better dentition. They looked like a master race from outer space, or something from the pages of Judge Dredd. It would be fair to say that Baghdad was not yet perfectly under their control. Everywhere there was shooting and looting, and a pall of smoke from the myriad bonfires, where Iraqis where barbecuing the street cables to get at the copper.

But as I looked at the American effort, at the vast caravanserai of victualling lorries, I felt a real sense of awe. Saddam may have turned out to be a papier mache dictator. But it was still an astonishing military achievement to remove him with so few casualties on either side; and the political achievement was greater still. Whatever the anti-war brigade say – and they will continue to protest that the operation was not worth the finger of a single child – Iraq is now free.

As many people there told me, they genuinely believe they have the prospect of a better future. America achieved this with the support of only one significant ally, and in the teeth of opposition from Russia and the two most traditionally influential nations of the European Union. The French tried to use the UN to veto the operation. The French, and the UN, were brushed aside.

The conquest of Baghdad was made politically possible by the military reality. American spends more on defence than the next twenty-eight countries combined. We are left with a unipolar world, in which the Pentagon can not only call upon bases in Britain, and Turkey, and Cuba, but in the former Soviet republic of Uzbekistan, a place which, fifteen years ago, had missiles trained on the west. No, when I started out as a journalist, I didn't see any of this coming; any more than the residents of al-Mansour saw the bunkerbuster.

Perhaps there were some wise owls, like Francis Fukuyama, who had some intimation of how things would go, back in 1987, the year when I left university and looked for a job. Perhaps there were thinkers who could predict that Communism was about to collapse, that European integration would surge and then falter, that the anti-globalisation movement would arise, and then disappear up the spout of its own fundamental contradictions. Maybe someone foresaw the emergence of Tony Blair, the hobbling of the Tory party, and Islamic terror.

Perhaps you, clever reader, were among those who had already sussed out that the country would want to move on from the harsh vocabulary of Thatcherism, and that Britain would one day be suffused by the Age of Diana. Perhaps you even predicted that the apparently happily married young Sloane would one day be transformed into a martyr and icon of sentimental values. If you did have any such inklings, you were well ahead of me. Because in 1987, aged twenty-three, newly married and full up to the gills with the finest education England can provide, I didn't have the faintest idea what was going on. I am writing this on a delayed service to Paddington, late at night, staring at the darkened windows. I could no more have predicted the future than I could tell you what is out there in the night or when South West trains will get this blasted thing moving again.

My journalistic career began in the basement of a Mayfair hotel, where some plucky management consultants were trying to teach me their arts. Try as I might, I could not look at an overhead projection of a growth-profit matrix, and stay conscious. After I had sunk for the fourth time into a coma, and then jerked all too obviously awake, one of my fellow-trainees, a young thruster in a grey suit, could take no more. He was my age, and had also just signed on at the absurd (then) rate of £18,000 p.a. He nudged me and spoke in tones of disgust. 'Listen,' he said, 'if you continue to take this attitude I don't think you are going to get very far.'

I thought, and think, that he was a pompous squit, and I hope that he was an early victim of the management consultancy shake-out that followed. But as my ears burned, I knew he was right. I tiptoed to the telephone, rang a man called Peter Stothard, and found myself hired by the *Times*. To begin with, journalism was almost as confusing and depressing as management consultancy. Most journalists seemed just to sit in front of their Atex computer screens sending each other romantic messages, and then getting in a terrible state when they found they'd sent them to the wrong person.

Work consisted of placing a call, being told X was in a meeting, waiting half an hour, and then trying again. Looking back through the articles I wrote, I can find nothing of any merit whatever. The only half-decent contribution was a kind of threnody for the Yuppie, written after Meltdown Monday 1987, when there was not only a stock market crash but also a hurricane. Apart from anything else, this sent boughs crashing through the windscreens of Porsches, which many people found a consoling sight. I composed a sprightly meditation, and handed it to Foreign Editor George Brock, who had the misfortune to be my trainer. 'Well,' he said, handing it back, 'it's a fourth leader – if it's anything.'

Like many of what we fancy to be our better articles, it was never published. But the crash was ominous for a chap on a short-term contract. And though Nigel Lawson reacted by slashing interest rates – for which we were all

4

to pay later – I could not help wondering how long the *Times* could afford to employ such a heroically unproductive hack. In an attempt to step up my output, I started trawling the agency wires. All Atex users were able to call up Reuters or AP, and I soon noticed that there seemed to be big things afoot in Russia and Eastern Europe. And because the *Times* did not have staff correspondents all over Eastern Europe, I started to take a proprietorial interest in these stories.

It seemed to be one of the rules that you could rewrite agency copy, and claim it as your own, if you made at least one phone call to show that you had 'added value' to the story. With the help of the beleaguered Brock, I soon built up a network of dons, at places like the London School for Slavonic and East European Studies, who would happily give a 'quote' about the matter in hand. There might be a shoe shortage in Bulgaria, or a tractor factory strike in Brasov, or some rum doings in the Ukrainian Uniate Church. I blush now to look at these stories, which were not really original to me, though almost every reporter will have thousands of such pieces in his cuttings book. Poor Brock was so overwhelmed by the effort of rewriting my rewritten version of some story about Gorbachev that at one stage he retired to his little glass box. Hearing a high-pitched noise, I peeked at him. He had his head in his hands and appeared to be screaming.

Had I the wit to see it, back in later '87 and '88, I might have detected a pattern in all this rubbish I was producing. I might have realised that not only was state socialism an inadequate means of satisfying material wants, but that it was about to implode. Everybody says that history started to accelerate in the late '80s. I am ashamed to say that I watched it without really grasping what was happening. I was too busy trying to get my byline on the story to wonder what the story might signify. It was only a year later, after

I had left the *Times* in inglorious circumstances, that the process became obvious, even to me. The miserable members of the Warsaw Pact had not only been technologically out-generalled by Ronald Reagan. They were finally waking up to the reality that socialism, and the state enforcement of equality, is not only corrupting but inequitable: the *nomenklatura* will always get the shoes that are withheld from the masses. Yearly, almost monthly, they could see how they were falling behind the west.

When I joined the *Times*, editor Charlie Wilson – a man straight from a Britflick gangster movie – told me a long story about how he used to thwart rivals. He would unscrew the telephone headset and remove the diaphragm, so they couldn't dictate their copy. This tip was already a bit hoary in 1987, but look how fast communications have moved on. When I first arrived in Brussels, as the Common Market Correspondent of the *Daily Telegraph*, Nigel Wade or Frank Taylor would send us messages by telex. Mobile telephones had not been invented, and correspondents had only just acquired the means of transmitting their copy electronically. You had a pair of 'acoustic couplers', a bit like a rubber fetish bra, which you had to clamp over the phone receiver as soon as you heard the right high-pitched whistle, and your little Tandy 200 then gibbered your text over in gobbets of electronic morse. No one who has done it can forget the semi-sexual sense of release when the electronic moaning and squeaking indicated that the article had arrived.

Such equipment seems palaeolithic to us now; but the east Europeans had televisions, and they could see the consumerist, technological miracle that was taking place.

That's why the Ossies started driving their Trabants to the west. That's why the Berlin Wall fell, in November '89, six months after I had arrived in Brussels. And even then, in spite of all the indications they might have picked up in the foreign pages of the *Times*, the event was greeted in other European capitals with amazement and consternation. Thatcher seemed to try to stop German unification, and held a reactionary seminar at Chequers. The conclusion was that the Hun was either at your feet or at your throat. Mitterrand flew to Kiev for a mysterious meeting with Gorbachev, at which they tried, abortively, to think of a way of impeding the inevitable. One of the few European statesmen to grasp immediately the magnitude and irreversibility of the change was a Christian Lacroix-wearing, pipe-puffing former French socialist prime minister called Jacques Delors.

The other day I asked a twenty-five year old *Spectator* colleague whether she knew who he was. 'I know the name' she said cautiously. There, my friends, you have the glow-worm transience of journalism. Who knows how much of my life I have consecrated to writing up the doings of Jaques Delors? Months, years. Young people these days (pause to go purple) can't remember who he is!

Delors realised that the thing we all used to worry about – the Soviet threat – was over. The KGB, the gulags, Smersh, the ICBMs trained on London – they had all gone west with the evil empire. But he also saw that German unification was a profoundly unsettling event. Across Europe, people started to mutter about the lessons of history, and revanchism, and a German colossus of 81 million people which would 'dominate' Europe. A means had to be found to control Germany, to moderate her new strength, to make sure in the phrase of Thomas Mann, that there would be a European Germany and not a German Europe. In the view of Paris the answer was to build up the institutions of the EEC, to the point where Germany was 'locked in' to a federal economic and political union. Delors hoped this glorious new entity would in some sense fill the vacuum left by the collapse of the Soviet Union.

Europe would not be adversarial to America, or certainly not hostile; but she would supply the other pole of influence in a bipolar world.

As Chou En-Lai said of the French revolution, it is too early to say whether this Delors plan for monetary and political union can be counted a success. But if you want an illustration of how far short the EU has so far fallen, as a counterweight to America, consider a cartoon published in the *Financial Times* in November 1990, at the time of the first discussions of the Common Foreign and Security Policy. The cartoon imagines some kind of rumpus in the Middle East. I seem to think Israel is involved. Washington is thowing its weight around, as usual, when suddenly the phone jangles off the hook! It's the EU, speaking as one, and the Common Foreign and Security Policy is 'Non/Nein/No' to whatever Washington had planned! What a joke, eh. Here we are, thirteen years after that futuristic cartoon, and the EU is so divided over Iraq that the subject cannot even be discussed at summits of EU leaders.

Why is Europe so feeble? Why can't Brussels pull the skin off a rice pudding? The answer is that Europe is not a natural political unit. As Delors was to discover, the people of Europe do not vote as one, think as one or speak as one. To put the problem in its crudest terms: I was once at a friend's house in Brussels, and the television happened to be showing that flower of English comic genius, *Fawlty Towers*. Life must have been getting me down at the time, because I found the pratfalls of Manuel, from Barcelona, almost unbearably funny. I howled and retched with laughter. I then looked up to see that my friend's husband was staring at me with an expression of real pain. He was an intelligent and proud Castilian.

The longer I stayed in Brussels – and I served five happy years – the more obvious it was that it would never work.

The Germans had German dinner parties, the French had French dinner parties. The British sent their children to play cricket at the British School in Tervuren. The Danes were so keen on remaining Danes that they inserted a special clause in the Maastricht Treaty, on monetary and political union, ensuring that Germans could not buy holiday homes on the coast of Jutland. And in spite of this protection, on June 2nd 1992, the Danes threw the programme into chaos.

All journalists probably delude themselves that they may have influenced the history they are paid to observe; that their butterfly-flap triggered the storm. My boast, and I make it in the confidence that no one gives a monkey's, is that I probably did contribute to the Danish rejection of Maastricht. It was May 2nd 1992, and I was at one of those agreeable jaunts which punctuate the life of the Brussels correspondent: an informal meeting of foreign ministers at a scenic place called Guimaraes in Portugal. I remember going to a payphone at teatime that Saturday, standing in the dusty square and watching the dogs lying in the sun, and ringing Frank Taylor, the foreign editor of the *Sunday Telegraph*, to find out what had happened to my story. I thought it was quite good stuff, all about plans being incubated by Delors to create a European President, and centralise yet more power in Brussels, once the Maastricht treaty had been ratified. Frank thought it positively tremendous.

'We've made it the splash,' he said with his beardy chuckle, 'and I've called it "Delors Plans to Rule Europe".' Cor, I thought. That was a bold way of expressing it, and I wasn't sure that my chums in the EC commission would be thrilled. But the splash was the splash – the main article on the front page – and I happily consented. That story went down big. It may not have caused the dropping of marmalade over the breakfast tables of England, but it was huge in Denmark. With less than a month until their referendum, and with mounting paranoia about the erosion of Danish independence, the story was seized on by the No campaign. They photocopied it a thousandfold. They marched the streets of Copenhagen with my story fixed to their banners. And on June 2nd, a spectacularly sunny day, they joyously rejected the Treaty and derailed the project. Jacques Delors was not the only victim of the disaster; the aftershocks were felt across Europe, and above all in Britain.

I first stood in the physical presence of Margaret Thatcher when she swept past me in her twin-set, at the Madrid summit in 1989. Not only was she really rather beautiful, with a sort of glow about her. She was also very cross. Perhaps she looks beautiful when she is cross. At any rate, she said something like 'Pfoogh', as well she might, since she had just been ambushed by Nigel Lawson and Geoffrey Howe and forced to agree on a timetable for British membership of the European Exchange Rate Mechanism.

Lawson wanted to go into the ERM, because he thought it would help him contain the inflation he had unleashed by cutting interest rates after meltdown Monday in 1987. Howe liked the ERM mainly because it was the Europhile thing to do, a step on the road to scrapping the pound and enjoying the single currency. Thatcher thought both motives were utterly wet. From then on the split in the Tory party became an indispensable cliché of British journalism.

Day after day I would sit in my wonderful office in Brussels, looking out at the ponds, the Art Nouveau buildings of square Marie-Louise, and I would marvel, in a horrified way, at the impact of news from Brussels. It was like chucking a crust into the water, and watching the fish boil and thrash to get it. This was the era of harmonisation, and the creation of the single market. The idea was partly a noble one: to encourage the free movement of goods, people, services and capital. But at every turn, it seemed, the commission officials found themselves treading on the sceptics' ingrown toenails. It looked at one stage as if a directive on bus safety would banish the double decker the very emblem of Britain from London. They said our chocolate didn't have enough cocoa solids, and would have to be called vegelate. They decided how many fishing vessels Britain could put to sea, and whether it was all right for children to do paper rounds.

Sometimes I would look up from my desk, and survey the extraordinary events going on in other *Telegraph* bureaux. The Soviet Union was collapsing with dizzying speed. Yeltsin fought off a coup. The end of the Cold War kicked the legs out from beneath the apartheid regime in South Africa, and the whole planet watched Mandela walk from Robben Island. In the Middle East the Palestinians were engaged in the first *intifada*, and both sides were sowing the seeds of hatred and recrimination. And in Brussels, whatever convulsion racked the world, the response of the bureaucrats was the same: we must build Europe!

No detail seemed to escape their regulatory lust. There really is European legislation on the weight, dimensions and composition of your coffin; and there really is a regulation about the minimum width of a condom. The Italians made a bit of fuss (or so I was told by a Belgian spokesman) because the regulation seemed to put their own minima in a bad light. By now the great George Brock, my put-upon former mentor, had arrived in Brussels as my rival correspondent, he for the *Times*, I for the *Telegraph*. One of my keenest pleasures was to hunt for scoops, exclusive stories that might cause the *Times* to ring Brock up, long after he was tucked up in bed. 'Stand by your phone, George', I would say, tapping my nose. I like to think that Mr and Mrs Brock had several interrupted nights on my account; and at least once, annoyingly, I was rung by the *Telegraph* and asked to chase up one of his.

We would all sit for hours in the smoke-filled press rooms in Brussels or Luxembourg, drinking beer or eating steak tartare sandwiches, and waiting for the council of twelve national ministers to agree some regulation – piffling to us, but no doubt poisonous to someone. Once, at the end of some marathon council negotiation, there was a breakthrough about border controls. In some excitement, I dictated a 500 word piece, and was thrilled to find the following day that the story had been printed in full. Except that the copytakers had enigmatically changed the words 'border controls' to 'water controls' throughout. It says something about the way eyes glaze over when they come to Common Market news, that not a single person complained. But as Thatcher's long reign grew more fretful, the Brussels story was moving ever higher up the agenda.

I was told that Denis Skinner had stood up in the Commons and cited one of my pieces. Brussels had decided for the sake of a 'level playing-field' that no farmer should be able to make use of a farmyard seriously smellier than his neighbour's. In trying to fix the norms for the maximum permissible odour of farmyard compounds, the commission's agriculture directorate had contracted teams of dung-sniffers, to inhale the various concentrations of vapour, and to decide what was acceptable. That story, said Skinner, showed that this whole Europe business was out of control. Thatcher agreed.

The trouble was, many in her party did not; and her vulgar and chauvinistic views on Europe as they saw them became the focus for discontent. A year after she had been ambushed at Madrid, Mrs Thatcher was set upon again. This time her assailants were the other eleven EC leaders, who decided to set an ambitious target for monetary union, and the fusing of their currencies into one. It was Thatcher's response to the Rome summit, on October 28th 1990, which gave her enemies the pretext for assassination. The programme for monetary union was 'cloudcuckooland', she told a TV interviewer. In the Commons, the following week, she denounced Delors' plans for a European senate and other federalist advances. 'No! No! No!'

There is no need here to rehearse the steps of the matricide. Howe pounced. Heseltine did his stuff. After it was all over, my wife, Marina, claimed that she came upon me, stumbling down a street in Brussels, tears in my eyes, and claiming that it was as if someone had shot Nanny.

I dispute this, naturally; but what is certain is that the defenestration of Thatch triggered a cycle of reprisals in the Tory party which has taken years to abate. The Eurosceptics wanted revenge. The harder John Major tried to make peace between Brussels and London, the more truculent they became. Other European leaders were delighted by his frank and open style, his stroking with his pink-palmed, paddle-like hands. He called journalists by their first names, which always makes us preen. But Major's economic inheritance was cursed. The Lawson boom had turned to slump; mortgage interest rates were causing pain to millions of Tory voters, and to make matters worse, it seemed as though European institutions were intensifying the recession.

Early one morning in the summer of 1991, I was driving in the dark from Brussels to Noordwijk in Holland, for a breakfast meeting with the Chancellor, Norman Lamont. On the 'Today' programme came Ruth Lea, the economist from the Institute of Directors, who made a good point about Britain's membership of the ERM. The trouble with the Ostmark-Deutschemark conversion rate of one to one, she pointed out, was that it pushed up German interest rates. And since we had to track German interest rates in

order to maintain our parity within the ERM, British interest rates were likely to be higher than we required for our
domestic needs. This struck me as a sound analysis, and I
put it to Norman Lamont, who was looking, as ever, like
an inscrutable human badger. 'I did not hear that interview,' he said. Huh, I thought. A year later, when disaster
had overtaken him, I am sure he would have publicly
endorsed every word. For a while, though, Major's honey-
moon continued. In December 1991 he compromised at
Maastricht, and secured about as good a deal as Britain
could hope to get. He excluded Britain from the social
chapter and from the single currency. 'Game, set and
match', he crowed; or was said to have crowed.

In the last minutes of the summit my friend David
Usborne of the *Independent* went to the British briefing
room in search of a quotation. He found the nice girl with
blonde hair who organised the microphones. What would
you call it, asked Usborne. 'Oooh', she said, 'I'd say it
was game, set and match, wouldn't you?' This Usborne
attributed to 'British sources', who evolved into John
Major. Labour made a great song and dance about this
attitude at the time, claiming that it showed our 'isolation'
in Europe. It hasn't stopped the Labour party from making
use of that opt-out, has it? But then there's no gratitude
in politics.

The Maastricht deal could be sold to party and to the
public, and in April '92 Major won the election. It was an
astonishing fourth win for the Tories; but their majority
was only twenty-one. The Euro-sceptics had become math-
ematically important.

In May 1992 I went to Guimaraes and wrote my stunning, historic and now wholly forgotten article. In June
the Danes were so scandalised by this piece that they threw
out the Treaty, and the Eurosceptics went wild. We were
told that anti-marketeers, Labour and Tory alike, rolled

around the Commons singing 'wonderful, wonderful Copenhagen'. They demanded that Britain halt the ratification process. The Major government panicked and the Bill was shelved. And the panic was shared in Brussels, Paris and Bonn, because the Danish rejection meant that the Treaty was legally dead. Without approval by all twelve countries, the plan for monetary and political union could not go ahead. Choc! Horreur!

Mitterrand then compounded the problem by calling for a French referendum, to efface the Danish No, to be held on September 20th. What no one had foreseen was how all this uncertainty would affect the markets. Before the Danish No the money markets had more or less assumed that the ERM was on a glide path towards the single currency. Bond yields and interest rates had converged. After the Danish No it was all up in the air. The single currency might not happen. The parities were open to challenge. The money men could see the problem that Ruth Lea had described: German interest rates were too high for the rest of Europe. Some currencies would benefit from an interest rate cut and a realignment. But since a realignment had been expressly ruled out, and since governments were prepared to spend fantastic sums to protect their ERM parity, the men in teddy bear braces saw an opportunity to get rich. They started to bet that the weaker currencies would devalue.

They gang-banged the peseta, the escudo, the lira, and as the summer went on, they turned their fire on sterling. Britain was in a terrible hole. Homes were being repossessed. Every week Lamont or Major was forced to issue a stout defence of our ERM membership, and the absolute inviolability of our parity. And the louder they protested that these interest rates were necessary, the more the thrusters chuckled and sold sterling short. On Black Wednesday, September 16th, 1992, the hedge funds moved in for the kill. All day long George Soros and other New York titans were selling sterling to the UK government, in the sure knowledge that they could buy it back more cheaply later on, in a myriad series of one-way bets. It was beautiful, and ruthless. It was hugely expensive for the taxpayer, and humiliating for the government. Who can forget Norman Lamont, emerging from the Treasury after raising interest rates, at one stage, to fifteen per cent, flicking the hair out of his eyes, and saying, 'This has been a very difficult and turbulent day'? I watched Lamont from Strasbourg, and flew to Brussels that night, in time to see Sir Nigel Wicks, the Treasury Mandarin, walk mayonnaise-faced into the meeting of the EC monetary committee and beg that the whole ERM be suspended. The committee refused. Britain's misery was complete.

Black Wednesday was politically catastrophic because it appeared that the outcome forced on the Government, the outcome Major tried might and main to resist, the devaluation of sterling and the attendant cutting of interest rates was the very outcome which enabled the economic recovery to begin. That may be unfair on the Major government, in the sense that the beginnings of the recovery probably predated Black Wednesday. But the public could see that it was an economic cock-up on an intergalactic scale. The Tories lost, at a stroke, their single most important advantage over Labour: their reputation as the party of economic competence. Ever since, for more than ten years, they have roughly flatlined in the polls, bobbing gently along at thirty per cent. For Bill Cash, Iain Duncan Smith and the rest of the Tory Euro-sceptics, Black Wednesday was a crashing vindication. 'Maastricht had met mortgages' in the way they had always predicted. They proceeded for the dying years of the Major government and it spent the next five years dying to torture their poor Prime Minister.

They rebelled scores of times over Maastricht, and in an effort to placate them Mr Major was forced into such quixotic enterprises as the Beef War. By the time of the election on May 1st 1997, and the first Blair landslide, Tory ministers had long been sitting in their offices, clutching their heads and waiting for the end, like Marlon Brando in the final reel of Apocalypse Now.

When I came back from Brussels in 1994, to write columns for the *Daily Telegraph* and the *Spectator*, I found myself endlessly dissecting some ministerial indiscretion, usually served up on a platter, beautifully garnished, by Labour propagandists. No sooner had he been caught out doing something mysterious in the Paris Ritz than Jonathan Aitken summoned me for a private briefing. I was inwardly appalled that a Cabinet minister should wish to confide in me in this way, but I heard him out. He gave some muttered explanation of what he was up to, and why there was this confusion about the presence or absence of his wife. But I cannot for the life of me remember what it was all about. Can you? Can you remember exactly what crime it was Aitken was supposed to have committed in the Paris Ritz, and what made him lie about it in this bone-headed way? I bet you can't. Sleaze washed over the Major government, obliterating many good things, the foundation of peace in Ulster, for instance, and the end of the Tories was superabundantly overdetermined.

I would like to pretend, in a babyish way, that my despatch from Guimaraes was the root of it all. Someone from the *Sydney Morning Herald* did once argue that if I had not filed my piece about the 'Delors Plan to Rule Europe' the Danes would not have thrown out Maastricht; the ERM crisis would not have happened; and John Major's government would not have been thrown into chaos, and so on. It's all nonsense, of course. The Tories

17

had plenty of other problems; and the difficulties of the ERM were not solely a function of the Danish No.

The reason I became a sceptic about integration was that it continually involved a Procrustean squeezing or chopping of national interests. The one-size-fits-all ERM didn't suit us, which is why I have the gravest doubts about the single currency. And the same point can be made, in spades, about the plans for political union. Europe has been catastrophically disunited over Iraq. But people forget that she was catastrophically disunited over the first Gulf War, too. Not only did the Belgians refuse to send any troops. They even refused to sell us ammunition, a product Belgium has traditionally made in quantity. Chirac has been criticised for breaking with the Anglo-American coalition. But Mitterrand was almost as creepy in the first Gulf War, and this time round I have little doubt that he would have done the same. The wonder is that anyone still expects unity from Europe, on any really difficult issue of foreign policy.

Just as the Maastricht negotiations reached their mid-point, in June 1991, there was worrying news from the Balkans. Here we all were trying to forge a federal state, *e pluribus unum*, and the Serbs and the Croats were on the point of destroying federal Yugoslavia. In a dada-ist diplomatic venture, the EC decided to send a special 'troika' mission from the Luxembourg summit, to see if they could knock heads together. There was Gianni de Michelis, the eighteen stone disco-dancing Italian Foreign Minister, later indicted for corruption. There was Hans Van den Broek, the Dutchman, and the man in the hotseat, the serving President of the Council of Ministers, that international titan, the Luxembourg foreign minister, M Jacques Poos, a waiterish fellow with a fine quiff of white hair.

On the plane out the journalists tried to tempt M Poos into a quotation. 'Would you say, M Poos, that this was the hour of Europe?' we asked. Plainly delighted, he replied, 'Yes, this is the hour of Europe.' That remark has lived on, as a fine example of bathos. The mission was a total farce. I seem to remember pitching up in Zagreb at about midnight, and meeting Franjo Tudjman, the jefe of Croatia, before going to meet Milosevic in Belgrade. We all sat for hours while Gianni and Hans and Jacques jawed away with the Slavs. I remember Misha Glenny, the Balkans expert, sitting next to me in the press room and being pretty acid about our mission. 'It's all about the Serbs and the Croats', he briefed us Brussels correspondents, who knew not much of Balkan politics. 'They hate each other'. So it seemed.

The trouble was, the European countries couldn't work out which was the more detestable of the two. The Germans seemed to like the Croats, on the slightly worrying grounds that they had been good solid Nazis during the war. The British and the French had a certain symmetrical philoserbism. Endless conferences were convened under the auspices of the EU, usually in the Hague, chaired by Lord Carrington. I remember almost nothing about the negotiations, except that they were abortive. Mainly I remember the disgusting deep-fried cheese patties we were given. It is a wonder that the Dutch look so tall and healthy, when you consider what they eat. It might have been comical to watch the EU's bungling efforts to stop the crisis, had the Americans not decided to take Poos seriously. It was the hour of Europe, and the massacres were taking place in Europe's backyard. Go ahead, guys, said Bush the Elder's administration: you solve it.

For three years the problem was left to Europe, and it was a disaster. There was a stage, right at the beginning, when they did consider sending an expeditionary force to oppose the Milosevic purges. Hurd argued vehemently against any such intervention; and from then on the strategy was pretty much to let the warlords get on with it, while doing what we could to alleviate the humanitarian disaster. Only after the siege of Sarajevo, and the appalling humiliation of the UN operation at Srebrenica, did the US decide that enough was enough. The Hour of Europe was over, and the Clinton administration implemented the policy of 'Lift and Strike', lifting the arms embargo against the Bosnian Muslims, and bombing the Serbs.

The lesson of Bosnia seemed pretty clear. Europe supplied dithering and appeasement. The Pentagon supplied violence, and a solution. Not that I saw any of the action myself, being mainly condemned to report the conferences and summits and nonsensical communiques. Feeling a bit of a wuss, I rang the Foreign Desk during the first Gulf War, and begged to be sent out, along with Pat Bishop and Robert Fox, and all the other macho characters with their special Kate Adie warzone waistcoats. 'Hur hur', said the Foreign Desk. 'Nah, Boris, we reckon you're too valuable where you are.' Then I rang up during the Yugoslav crisis, being particularly jealous of Alec Russell, Tim Butcher and other reporters who had done some really gripping stuff. What do you think? I asked. Did our heroes perhaps need some assistance, from someone well-versed in pointless multinational negotiations? There was some cackling. 'Nah, Boris', the Foreign News Editor eventually returned, 'if you go to Yugoslavia you'll just take them all out to lunch.' This seemed to be some sort of reference to my expenses claims. 'You just stick in Brussels,' they chortled, 'and make sure you don't get hit by any profiteroles!'

This rankled, as you can imagine; and so when the next war came, I was determined not to be caught out. As Nato began to bomb Belgrade, with a view to driving the Serbs out of Kosovo, I went to see what it was like. This was now 1999, and a new concept was emerging in international relations: liberal imperialism. Gone was the old Hurdian instinct for appeasement and compromise. This was Blair and Clinton, the two uber-yuppies determined to create a better world, and to use smart bombs to do so. Before going to Serbia, I had decided that the methods were cowardly, and likely to prove ineffective. How could we justify bombing from 30,000 feet, when we were bound to kill innocent civilians, and would simply entrench Milosevic in power? I opposed the war partly, I suppose, because I mistrusted and opposed the Blair government. Indeed, Conrad Black tells me, which makes me very proud, that Blair told him: 'When I heard Boris was going to Belgrade, I rang up SACEUR (the Strategic Allied Commander in Europe) and told him to step up the bombing!'

The truth is, though proper war reporters will bust their pants with laughter at this, that there were moments in Serbia, and Kosovo, that were faintly worrying. As I drove down through Vojvodina to Belgrade, huge plumes of smoke went up, only a couple of hundred yards away, from bombs dropped on either side. I couldn't work out what they were trying to hit, but I hoped it wasn't the road. Every night I would lie awake in the Hyatt Belgrade, listening to the bombing and rebombing of deserted barracks and empty government buildings. At one stage I crept out of bed to see a Yugoil building go kerrump next door. Then I drew the curtains and continued to watch that brilliant John Woo movie 'Face/Off', starring Nicholas Cage and John Travolta in scenes of hyperkinetic violence. It seemed somehow more realistic than what was happening outside.

In the morning, if the smart bombs had been dumber than intended, we would be taken to see the collateral damage. It was particularly sad, walking up a suburban street, where dead and injured were being taken out of their houses, to find a pair of artists keening and wailing.

21

They specialised in very large plaster objects, and everywhere the shrapnel had ripped through their house, narrowly missing their son, but tearing into their sculptures. I did wonder fleetingly, with that cynical detachment which must afflict all journalists, whether these artefacts were better or worse for the attentions of Nato. But somehow, though the joke was a good one, it was suddenly irrelevant. These things were treasured by a pair of civilised and bohemian artists. I felt a surge of anger that my taxpayer's money was being used to fund this destruction, and I am afraid that pathetically, in a mumbled way, I apologised. It is difficult to be in an ancient European capital, under bombing, and not to oppose the bombardment.

I wrote what I hoped were some caustic pieces – not in defence of Milosevic, of course not, but against this manner of removing him. I was not against the war. I was all in favour of military action against Slobbo. But it would be fair to say that I was so critical of the methods, that a casual reader might have concluded that I did not support the ends. In so far as that made me 'anti-war', I now think I was wrong. Whatever the problems of modern Serbia – and they are huge – the Serbs no longer have an autocratic ruler whose method of retaining power is to whip up ethnic hatreds, and to set one group murderously against another. Whatever the troubles of Kosovo, they do not include hideous pogroms and massacres. I think, in retrospect, that I failed to see the wood for the trees; and that has made me approach the second Gulf War with a more open mind.

There are many good conservatives and decent socialists who deeply dislike the New World Order/liberal imperialism business. They believe, like Enoch Powell, that Britain should avoid all foreign entanglements save where her interests are directly threatened. I am not so sure. They say we cannot do everything, cannot go around the world fighting every fire. That is true, but it is no reason to do nothing. I supported, and support, the second Gulf War on a strictly utilitarian calculation. The world is better for removing Saddam from power than keeping him there and allowing the Iraqis to suffer another twelve years of tyranny and economic sanctions. You can say what you like about Blair – and I have said and will continue to say some disobliging things – but he has participated in the toppling of two tyrants, Milosevic and Saddam, whom Major had left in power. And unlike the supposedly Euro-sceptic Tories, Blair took not the blindest notice of European opinion, or the need to adhere to a common European position. The Kosovo enterprise was wildly unpopular in some parts of the Community, notably Greece. As for the second Gulf War, the split is the most sensational I have seen: France, Germany, Belgium, directly opposing an action supported by the governments of Britain, Italy, Spain, Holland, Denmark, and a comet tail of 'new European' states.

Confronted with a cold, hard choice, Blair went with the country that had the power and the money to do what he thought was right. He went with America, and with the Pentagon. And he won. All of which, of course, makes it much harder for mainstream Atlanticist Tories. How, we ask ourselves, are we meant to oppose the blighter? We thought Blair cosied up to Clinton just because Bill was a Democrat, and a fellow exponent of the aromatherapy mysteries of the Third Way. One of the joys of the first Blair term was going out to Washington, at the height of the Monica Lewinsky business, and watching him rally round the great philanderer.

By some mistake I was admitted to the Oval Office when they were posing for the cameras, and bunged a cheeky (and pathetic) question about Monica. Alastair Campbell later chided me, saying that this was no way to treat a head of state. 'How would you feel if an American said that to the Queen?' he asked, preposterously. Actually, I rather supported Clinton over Monica; I simply wanted to dissipate some of the glutinous mutual congratulation between Blair and Clinton.

And yet such is Blair's protean political personality that five years later he seems to have forged an equally close relationship with the teetotal, hot-dang, Bible-reading G Dubya Bush. Of course his own party, Robin Cook and other backbenchers, hate it like poison. But what are we Tories supposed to make of it?

I began my journalistic efforts as the Cold War was ending. Those shoe shortages in Bulgaria; those wrathful Hungarian housewives who could find nothing in the shops but pickles; those stories which I furtively and uncomprehendingly plagiarised from the wires, were full of meaning. But fifteen years later, with the Cold War long buried, the winners and losers are, as I say, unexpected.

You might have thought the Tories would be triumphant, since the transformation was a spectacular ideological vindication. It proved what we had argued all along: that socialism was a hopelessly inept system for satisfying human desires. For years the Tories had been calling for freedom, and democracy, and free markets in eastern Europe and suddenly it all happened! What did Labour do in the Cold War? They turned their fire on Ronald Reagan, and Margaret Thatcher. They went on CND marches, ignored the Gulags, and took fraternal junkets to Moscow. And yet fifteen years later it is Labour which has adapted far more effectively to the New Order. With the end of the Soviet menace, the Tories were left still looking beetle-browed, and paranoid, and alarmist; but alarmist about what? Europe? Yes, the public was broadly Euro-sceptic, but with the best will in the world, it wasn't possible to turn Delors, and EU integration, into a threat to national security.

24

Where was the external threat to replace communism, against which the Tories had put up such yeoman resistance? China? Asylum-seekers? It didn't work. The Tories had lost a high card, and Blair followed Clinton in developing a new formula, that was attractive to an increasingly affluent country. He took the yuppyish Thatcherite values, which characterised the 1980s, and sanded off the rougher edges. You could still be a free-market liberal, he said; you could still be basically acquisitive and materialist. But under New Labour you could have it all in a caring, quivering-lip sort of way. And meanwhile Gordon Brown's enormous stealth taxes not only rewarded Labour's public sector heartlands, but greatly expanded their numbers.

If you need evidence of Blair's sensitivity to the national mood, and his skill in manipulating it, remember his handling of the death of the Princess of Wales. During that amazing, Latin American carnival of grief that followed, one Tory MP said: 'I just don't recognise my own country'. Which of course explained precisely why his own country had rejected him so vigorously at the polls, and would do so again. That is one tentative conclusion that we can draw about the world fifteen years on. Our culture has probably become gentler, more touchy-feely, more politically correct, more *American* if you like, and that may of course be partly because we are richer. Per capita GDP has increased, at today's rates, from £12,637 to £17,096. The world has also broadly improved, in the sense that there were one hundred and fifteen countries which were classed 'free or partly free' in 1987. There are now one hundred and forty-five, though it should be noted that the number of unfree countries remains roughly the same. The wheels of capitalism turn ever faster and more productively. The House of Commons Library tells me that of the 2.7 million *Daily Telegraph* readers who might have read my first articles, it is likely that about 700,000 have now died. One or two of them, who knows, may even have kicked the bucket over breakfast, apoplectically choking on their toast as they read the latest news from Brussels. Amazingly, their ranks have been replenished by just as many others, who recognise the range and genius of that publication.

It is to the reader that all journalists owe the biggest debt: that huge, silent interlocutor with whom we feel we can converse on terms of such intimacy, and who sits in patient judgment over our babble. To those few, those faithful few who have reached this stage in the argument, I wish to leave this final, repetitive thought. Fifteen years after the collapse of communism, the biggest and most salient political fact in the world is American dominance. Japan was meant to eclipse her economically; and Japan, along with the other Asian economies, has been in serious difficulties. Russia is in a bad way. China grows fast, but shows no interest yet in impinging on the rest of the world. It is obvious that this American dominance is producing, and will continue to produce, a reaction; or rather a spectrum of reaction. Even in the Arab world, attitudes to America range from support and approval to the demented attacks of bin Laden's networks. America's performance in Iraq was formidable, and made Europe look ridiculous. But in the hearts of many moderate people, the very lopsidedness of the world demands some sort of compensation. The Iraq war not only undermines the case for Euro-federalism; it is also, paradoxically, a recruiting-sergeant for Europeanism.

Already, in Brussels, the kindly and charming bureaucrats are no doubt pushing aside their moules frites and doodling new plans on their napkins. Indeed, as I write these words, they are preparing for a new constitution of Europe. And good Lord Tony Blair proposes that there should be a new 'President of Europe', who should be, no doubt, a charismatic, glistering-toothed and straight sort of guy, with four children and an interest in rock music.

Where have I read that story before? Yes, at the risk of flogging a dead horse, it was 'Delors Plan to Rule Europe', my path-breaking despatch from Guimaraes.

This time I have no idea how it will all turn out, though I stick to my central point: that it is very difficult to make a single political unit out of fifteen – now twenty-five – countries; and it is no use expecting to rival America, if you will only spend a relatively tiny amount on defence. All I will predict is that whoever comes to power in Britain, this country will continue to try to have it both ways; pretending a unique allegiance to both Europe and America, not because we are especially duplicitous, but because it is the sensible thing to do. We will stick with America while contriving to remain on the European 'train'.

And talking of trains, the Totnes to Paddington is finally pulling in. Don't ask how I could have written so much on one journey. We were diverted to Newbury, if you must know, because of something to do with signals. What do you expect? It's a Labour government, isn't it?

POLITICS
From Thatcher to Blair

There was a time when we Tories used to call ourselves the oldest and most successful political party in the world. Where did it all go wrong? What caused the Tory ruin in the 1990s? Many things, but Europe was among them.

The following is the kind of revelation that started the Eurosceptics snorting, including Margaret Thatcher. I have a feeling this story was originally longer, but it has been much improved by the sub-editors of the Daily Telegraph. In so far as I have learned to write English, it is thanks to them.

Snails are fish

After five months' study the EEC Commission has decided snails should be categorised as fish, not meat. It was in April that the then Tory Euro-MP for Cheshire West, Mr Andrew Pearce, put the poser to the Irish Agriculture Commissioner, Mr Ray McSharry.

A parliamentary question of this kind, involving

translation into the nine languages of the EEC, involves spending about £1,000, and in the interim Mr Pearce lost his seat. Yesterday in Liverpool he said he was interested to hear the news but was now unsure why he had asked the question.

Brussels officials believed their plans were entirely reasonable. They were in despair at Mrs Thatcher's attitude, and began scouring the Tory ranks for someone more amenable.

Heseltine catches EEC's eye

'Ah yes, the member for Henley-on-Thames,' said a learned EEC official from Luxembourg. 'We liked his book.'

As Mrs Thatcher faces record unpopularity in the polls, it is slowly dawning on the Brussels bureaucracy that she could be replaced in the not too distant future by a potentially more palatable successor.

'We look carefully at what is happening on the political scene in all the big member states,' said a highly-placed source responsible for commission strategy. 'Heseltine is looked on with interest.'

It would be an exaggeration to say the bureaucrats are mouthing his name in unison, as the man to save the European dream from what many regard as the curmudgeonliness of the Prime Minister.

But even allowing for the bias of Euro-federalists, there is unanimity in Brussels that Mrs Thatcher's unwavering stance has caused Britain's voice to become, frankly, ignored.

'Britain doesn't count in the discussions any more. If a new leader could convince people they were committed to the same goal, it might be different,' said one official.

Another bureaucrat puts the blame squarely on the Prime Minister: 'There was respect for her in the past, but there is now exasperation at the narrowness of her analysis.'

The pessimists say EEC leaders last took Britain seriously at the Madrid European council nine months ago, when all attention was fixed on its response to plans for a single Euro-bank and currency.

And they were thrilled when John Major first showed his famous suppleness.

Major signals softer stance on EU unity

Mr Major, the Chancellor, left western Ireland yesterday having created the impression of a sea change in the Government's attitude towards European union. He startled other EEC finance ministers by engaging in detailed discussion of how to give the Common Market greater control over fiscal and monetary policy.

This is something that has been utterly rejected in principle by Mrs Thatcher.

The EEC Finance Commissioner, Mr Henning Christophersen, described Mr Major's stance as 'much more positive and constructive', while a Dutch official said his change of tack was 'amazing'.

An Irish diplomat said Mr Major had 'moved as far as he could without incurring the wrath of Mrs Thatcher'.

But the Chancellor later insisted that he had not given ground, saying: 'The substance of the British position remains what it was before.'

Mr Major delighted his colleagues at the informal talks

in Ashford Castle, Co Mayo, on a single European bank and currency, by agreeing that monetary union would involve limitations on national budgetary policy.

The Government has previously argued that any EEC interference in budgets – including control over taxation – would 'go to the jugular' of parliamentary sovereignty.

On Saturday, Mr Major consented that Brussels could have explicit powers to police national budget deficits. He also agreed that countries should not be allowed to take advantage of any future European central bank by 'printing money' to finance deficits.

However, he cast grave doubts over the democratic accountability of such a bank.

All other EEC countries are committed to a single bank and currency, and the Government's new spirit of co-operation may be intended to avoid complete isolation when full-scale talks begin in December. Britain may also have calculated that, now the discussion has turned to practicalities, the advantage may swing its way.

But Thatcher was having none of it. She went to the Rome summit on October 28th 1990, and told them where to get off.

Thatcher alone as EU votes for single currency

Sweeping aside objections from Mrs Thatcher, European leaders yesterday unexpectedly set a deadline of January 1, 1994, for the creation of an EC central bank with powers over domestic monetary policy, and paved the way for a single European currency by the end of the decade. The Prime Minister immediately denounced the plan as being in 'cloud cuckoo land' and served notice that she was prepared to use Britain's veto to stop it. She stressed: 'We shall block things which are not in Britain's interests. Of course we shall.'

Within minutes of the ending of the EC summit in Rome, the Prime Minister underlined her hatred of the plan to sweep away national currencies. 'If anyone is suggesting that I would go to Parliament and suggest the abolition of the pound sterling – no,' she said.

She also criticised the way business at the summit had been handled and the way Signor Andreotti, the Italian Prime Minister and host for the conference, loaded the agenda. The Italian presidency of the EC was not competent, she said. 'It is a mess.'

Of the summit decisions, she said: 'They have set a date for Stage Two, but they have not decided what the substance of the next stage is. It seems to be putting the cart before the horse.

'People who get on a train like that deserve to get taken for a ride.

'We are in the silly position where we could not reach a decision on the urgent things and the presidency curtailed discussion on the urgent things, but took refuge on non-urgent and distant things, cloaked in grand and vague words because we have not got round to the nitty-gritty of negotiation.'

Mrs Thatcher commented: 'It seems like cloud cuckoo land to give a date for the beginning of Stage Two and we don't know what it is going to be.'

In the Common Market's most decisive step towards integrated monetary and economic policy, British reservations were relegated to a solitary paragraph in the conclusions of the summit.

The move has entrenched divisions in Europe with seven weeks before the start of the treaty-changing conferences in Rome on monetary and political union. Although all countries except Britain approved the changes involved, some were furious that Mrs Thatcher had been placed in such dramatic and calculated isolation.

The Danish Foreign Minister, Mr Uffe Ellman-Jensen, said: 'The Italian presidency has pressed far too much. Ditches have been dug which will be very difficult to fill in later on.'

Similar concern was expressed by Chancellor Kohl of Germany, who said he was against 'crystallising positions' before the December conference.

Mrs Thatcher had hoped to go to the conference on Dec 14 armed with Britain's counter-proposals for a 'hard ecu' – a parallel currency which would not replace the pound.

That hope seemed to have evaporated yesterday when leaders called for 1994 to see the birth of 'a new monetary institution, comprising member states' central banks, and a central organ, exercising full responsibility for monetary policy'.

M Delors, president of the Brussels Commission, hailed the surprise timetable for considering a move to the final stage by 1997, saying, 'We will have a single currency before 2000.' Mrs Thatcher countered that the British Parliament would never agree to abolish the pound, which she described as the 'most powerful expression of sovereignty you can have. It is against the feeling of the people.'

In a dissenting statement, Britain said decisions on the substance of the second stage of monetary union should be taken before setting a timetable.

The summit decisions appear to have created an unbridgeable gulf between Britain and its partners. Mrs Thatcher will face the choice in December of agreeing to the deadlines for the Euro-bank and the currency or exercising the Government's right to veto any changes to the Treaty of Rome.

Such a veto would precipitate an immediate crisis in the community which could confront Britain with the option of breaking away from the EC's most important programme of integration.

A 'two-tier Europe' would be greeted with horror by London financial institutions. Bankers fear the City's earnings would drain away to Frankfurt and other European centres.

But were the Prime Minister to accept such a programme, she would be flying in the face of her most deeply-held political convictions. 'Each parliament would have to put up a proposal to terminate its own currency,' she said, adding that she would never put such a plan before the Commons.

The choice between abandoning control of monetary sovereignty and being cut adrift from EC integration will leave the Tory party more riven on Europe than ever before.

Sir Geoffrey Howe, the Deputy Prime Minister, conceded yesterday that there were differences of opinion in the Cabinet over Europe's long-term future. But he insisted that there was unanimity that a single currency should not be imposed.

Sir Geoffrey's view that decisions on the single currency were 'far in the future' seemed immediately overtaken yesterday.

The Government had hoped that its decision to enter the ERM would be taken as a signal of its good intentions and relieve the pressure for rapid monetary union. But the framework envisaged in yesterday's conclusions involves irrevocably fixed exchange rates, a new single currency as 'an expression of the EC's identity and unity', and an independent Bank of England as the agent of a Euro-bank.

Despite yesterday's unpredicted acceleration, Mrs Thatcher appeared ready to continue the fight to December and beyond. Drawing a parallel with the EC's deepening disarray over proposed cuts in farming subsidies, which must now be urgently agreed, she said, 'The nearer things get to decisions, the more difficult things become.'

Agriculture ministers will this week make their eighth attempt to end the stalemate on farm subsidies caused by French and German objections.

Mrs Thatcher and her Dutch colleague, Mr Lubbers, failed to commit the summit to the commission's programme of 30 per cent cuts, which M Mitterrand said France could not accept. She accused the French of blocking an agreement that was ready for signing in the early hours of Saturday.

'It is clear that some members openly take the view that the community is protectionist and will remain protectionist. That is not my ideal of the community,' she said.

Mrs Thatcher used the collapse of the farm talks to throw back the criticism of M Mitterrand who had earlier said: It is not for the slowest in Europe to dictate the pace of the rest.'

British officials were dismayed that the Government was also forced into isolation over long-term plans for 'political union'. Britain's objections were recorded against four suggestions contained in what Mrs Thatcher referred to as a rag-bag of ideas.

Without full discussion at the inter-governmental conference, the Government refuses to endorse the general consensus in favour of:

- An extension of EC powers into more areas such as employment law.
- Giving the European Parliament the ability to initiate legislation.
- Introducing new European citizenship.
- Development of a common security policy.

Mr Hurd, Foreign Secretary, won a notable success in knocking out references to decreasing the use of the veto by one country.

Signor Andreotti tried to dismiss suggestions that Britain had been prematurely isolated as a result of his decision to put such far-reaching items on the agenda. But he added, 'At moments of importance, countries need political inspiration for choices that must be made. Let us hope that this happens in the future in Britain.'

The Italian leader failed to dispel the impression that he had raised the stakes far beyond what even members of his own government had expected, in order to justify calling an emergency summit.

The EC leaders demanded Iraq's withdrawal from Kuwait and said 'additional steps' would be considered on top of economic sanctions. They told Israel that the situation in the occupied territories was 'unsustainable'.

They promised to study an international package to help East Europe weather economic storms caused by the Gulf crisis, and said they would act on any Soviet request for emergency food aid during the winter.

And that was the end of Thatcher. Heseltine, Howe and the rest of the Europhiles retaliated. The Tories had their fateful spasm, the leadership election, and clever Mr Major emerged on top. Did his nice-guy strategy slow down the drive to a harmonised Europe? You must be joking.

Eurocondoms

The Italian rubber industry has fallen foul of EC rules by making undersized condoms.

Brussels bureaucrats have shown their legendary attention to detail by rejecting new specifications for condom dimensions proposed by the Italian government on March 19, 1990.

Under EC law, all standard weights, measures and sizes introduced at a national level must first be approved by the European Commission. All 12 member states have agreed that an unstretched condom should be 16 centimetres long.

However, the EC has dismissed Italian plans for a maximum condom width of 54 millimetres.

M Willy Helin, spokesman for the commission's industrial standards division, said: 'This is a very serious business. We have conducted a long analysis of condom sizes throughout the community, including in other Mediterranean countries.'

Experts had determined that the maximum permitted width for a condom should be 55 mm. 'One millimetre either way can make all the difference,' said M Helin. 'To be blunt, it is either too tight or it comes off.'

The commissioner responsible, Herr Martin Bangemann, has taken the view that different standard sizes in different countries could pose barriers to free trade in the Single Market. Herr Bangemann was most recently in the public eye over his efforts to abolish prawn cocktail flavour crisps.

Italian egos smarting over this decision will be consoled by the fact that their minimum proposed width of 50 mm was deemed too large. The EC survey has concluded that the minimum diameter should be 49 mm.

And what gave European integration this urgency? Why was the Commission pushing so hard? Because the end of the Cold War meant that Germany would be reunited, and suddenly all of Eastern Europe could be joined with Western Europe. The French wanted to create a tight European federation in which Germany could be controlled. The trouble was, and is, that Europe is not a natural political unit.

Wider still and wider, but where will Europe stop?

In the chancelleries of Europe, it is nothing short of an identity crisis. The mandarins mutter over their atlases; the ministers are stumped. In the few short weeks since the final collapse of the Soviet Union, a glaring hole has been uncovered in the diplomatic lexicon.

'What is the eventual size of Europe?' one EC ambassador asked last week after the Brussels commission announced delphicly that it would propose varying relations with the ex-Soviet countries according to whether or not they were 'European'. 'Who is a European?' he asked querulously. 'Where does Europe end?'

Britain knows, as it prepares to take over the EC presidency in July, that the question is central. Being 'European' gives a country the right, eventually, to participate in the Community institutions in Brussels. After years of chafing at the introversion of the 'little Europeans' such as the French government and M Jacques Delors, Downing Street is signposting the 'wider Common Market' as the key advance of the British presidency. The Foreign Office has been asked to produce a position paper.

But while it is one thing to accommodate Poland, Hungary, even the Baltic states, where does one stop? Mr Major has proclaimed a new, wider European Community 'from the Atlantic to the Urals'. Does he really mean it – that the EC will one day embrace most of the 150 million people of the new Russia? And if so, what about the Russians on the other side of the Urals?

39

The reference books do not help. The Treaty of Rome, article 237, says only that 'Each European country may apply for membership', with no attempt to define what Europe is. Hesiod said she was a girl raped by a bull; the Homeric Hymn to Apollo describes it as the Greek mainland; Herodotus, getting warmer, says it is one of the three continents, with Asia and Libya.

Europe is not really a distinctive racial or linguistic community, or even a cultural one. The spirit of European culture is as alive in Podunk, Massachusetts, as it is in Florence. Spanish and English, market leaders in the Indo-European family of languages, are spoken around the world; and even if we confine the test to this side of the Atlantic, no one would exclude Hungary and Finland because their language is Finno-Ugrian.

Even geography has proved a poor means of discriminating. In about AD 800, when Charlemagne was described as the 'venerable head of Europe' by the poet Angilbert, 'Europe' did not refer to Britain, any more than it did in the following century. To this day, English people talk casually of 'travelling to Europe', and only on close interrogation will they admit that in reality they are already there.

The confusion extends to the Mediterranean, where Morocco (in Africa) and Turkey (partly in Asia) have applied to join the EC; where even Israel is a member of the UN Economic Commission for Europe, and is favoured for Community membership by Gianni de Michelis, Italy's creative foreign minister. It is true that Leptis Magna is the ruin of a European civilisation. But no one has ever regarded Libya, though once ruled by fair Dido, as a European country.

These conundrums pale, however, in comparison with the problems being thrown up now by the 19th-century Russian conquest of Asia. The best the Foreign Office can come up with, as it stares at the map, is that the Baltics,

Belarus, Ukraine and Moldova are the most 'European' portions of the ex-Soviet Union and would, if they so desired, enjoy the 'more intimate' relations with the Community reserved for their kind. But on what principle, exactly, do we exclude Azerbaijan, Armenia and Georgia, all within Mr Major's boundary of the Urals, if the line is drawn down to the Caspian? Most of all, can Russia, birthplace of Tchaikovsky and Tolstoy, seriously be held to be a non-European civilisation?

There can certainly be no religious or ethnic excuse for shutting out the Islamic republics. After all, Albania, Bosnia and Bulgaria have large Muslim populations, and no one questions their Europeanness. Not even M Delors, whose beliefs, it is known, privately lead him to identify Europe with Christendom, has blocked their faltering progress up the ladder towards EC membership.

Perhaps some flimsy justification, to do with democracy and human rights, will be found to keep out the Muslims of the Commonwealth of Independent States. Some EC politicians say that Islam is incompatible with article 119 of the Treaty of Rome, which insists on equal treatment of men and women. But that is a figleaf, no more.

The strongest reason for excluding these countries is nothing to do with their supposed Europeanness but with practical self-interest. Any overture to Armenia, for instance, would make admission of Turkey inescapable. The EC's original commitment to admit the Turks was made in 1963, and has, in the words of one diplomat last week, 'bugged us ever since'. With a population nearing 60 million, still largely Anatolian peasants, free movement of Turkish labour within the EC is not something that our politicians can contemplate. And even though Russia is as European as Chekhov, it will never join the EC. It would destroy us if it collapsed; it would dominate us if it did not. For if Europe is nothing else, it is now an economic

41

power bloc, ruled by Germany, France, Britain and maybe Italy, and that is how we want it to remain.

For any disconsolate Russians, Azerbaijanis, Turks, Israelis or Moroccans, however, the Maastricht EC summit has provided unexpected grounds for hope. In what seems to be a genuine accident, the weird, last-minute solution to Britain's problems with the Social Chapter has opened the way for what is known as a 'multi-speed Europe'. Just as Britain can opt out of the EC 'Social Community', so perhaps Turkey might be excluded from the Common Agricultural Policy and the free-movement zone, but included in other areas, such as trade in manufactured goods and political cooperation.

In the meantime, though, Mr Major should perhaps drop the phrase 'from the Atlantic to the Urals'. Herodotus, who had never heard of the Urals, had a much better eastern boundary for Europe, at the Don and the Sea of Azov. That leaves out almost all of Russia and the worrying Middle Easterners, but keeps Ukraine, Moldova, Belarus and the Baltics. The Foreign Office should go with Herodotus.

The French answer was to 'deepen' the Community's institutions as fast as possible, and French officials were brilliant in their methods.

The French empire of Europe

On the 28th of this month, in a solitary wind-shaken skyscraper on the Luxembourg plateau, big, bad things will happen. Mr John Major will glumly finger the draft of an EEC treaty which will begin the effacement of the vestiges of this country's national sovereignty.

42

To judge by the way the inter-governmental negotiations are proceeding, the 12 will this year sign a treaty to establish a European monetary bloc some time towards the end of the decade. Mr Lamont last week accepted that Britain will benefit from a saving clause enabling 'a future parliament' to take the final decision on the abolition of sterling. Our leverage stops there. We cannot prevent the others going ahead outside the Treaty of Rome; when the time comes, one suspects, it will be difficult to stay aloof. How have we been so cornered? How is it that our ministers and their mandarins seem so – well – impotent?

The European Community, alas, is ruled by France. French control has increased, is increasing, and shows no sign of being diminished. As the pressure tightens on our monetary jugular, we should realise that a Euro-bank controlling the supply of money in Europe, were it to happen, would be just the latest, if the most decisive, triumph of the French civil servants, in particular those who went to the Ecole Nationale d'Administration, the 'Enarques'. To speak of 'conspiracy' is not quite right. It is a chess-like genius for thinking ahead, and dressing up French national interest as the European dream.

So far from being a committed cell of homogenised Euromaniacs, the EEC Commission is deeply riven on national lines. For instance, Sir Leon Brittan's 'cabinet', or team of six political advisers, is in continuous social and professional intercourse with the 25 emollient characters of 'Ukrep', the permanent British government representatives led by Sir John Kerr.

But take that gentlemanly little liaison, square it, cube it, and you have something approaching the swollen, throbbing umbilicus between Brussels and Paris. It was widely remarked that Edith Cresson's new government contains Martine Aubry, daughter of M. Delors, the President of the EEC Commission. But did you know that

Pascal Lamy, M. Delors' *chef de cabinet* (or chief political fixer), has just been offered the same job in the French government? Or that an identical offer was made to M. Francois Lamoureux, his deputy *chef de cabinet*?

They call it the 'Pink Tide'. They are all somewhere in their early forties; they are French; many of them went to the Ecole Nationale d'Administration; they are members of the Socialist Party; they see France's destiny in asserting itself through Europe. They include the minister for European affairs, Elizabeth Guigou, with her Cannes starlet looks, and Hubert Vedrine, Mitterrand's supercilious spokesman. But the most important in Brussels is Pascal Lamy. With his virtually shaven head and parade-ground manner, Lamy runs the upper echelons of the Commission like a Saharan camp of the French Foreign Legion. 'I like Pascal,' says another *chef de cabinet* in a quavery sort of voice. 'His mind works like a beautiful machine. There are so many idiots running about this place that you have to be rude sometimes.'

When Delors and Lamy arrived at the Commission in 1985, it was already a profoundly French organisation. It is not just that the everyday language is French: the structure, the 'cabinet' system, even the budgetary procedures are French. At the daily noon briefing, when cyclostyled pap is distributed to the obedient hacks, etiquette still demands that Danish journalists use French to talk to Dutch spokesmen.

After eight years in power, Delors and Lamy now have a dense network of gauleiters at the pressure points of the Commission: Legras at agriculture, Pons in the monetary division, Dewost in the legal department. But these are just the most obvious fluttering *tricolores*. The real pervasiveness of French influence, involving even the most junior officials reporting straight back to the Quai d'Orsay, became apparent at a party thrown by Lamy to celebrate his award of the

Légion d'Honneur. 'I suddenly realised how it all worked,' remembers one British official. 'There they all were.'

There is no British counter-network. The *locus classicus* of British limp-wristedness is a former Treasury official who came to hold a position of potentially sweeping influence in the personnel department. At the leaving ceremony of another British Eurocrat, he produced a gold watch and made a farewell speech – in French. 'British officials have been trained to think they should be politically impartial,' says one man. With their shy grins and corrugated-soled shoes, they are no match for the intellectual brutality of Lamy and his stooges.

Nor do the Germans have any taste for this kind of institutional guerrilla warfare. The understanding, almost 40 years after the war, is that it would be bad form for Germany to throw its weight around. By now it would, in any event, be difficult.

They say that Sir Leon is the only one who can go the distance with Delors, dialectically, when the 17 commissioners meet on Wednesdays. But it may be doubted how successful he has in fact been in curbing the nationalist, protectionist impulses of the President of the Commission. Sir Leon's department wanted Renault to pay back £1.2 billion in illegal state subsidies to the French state. Delors demurred. Finally the Commission settled on £600 million, most of which the French government appeared to pump straight back in about two weeks later.

Then Sir Leon hailed a great triumph for competition in the skies as Air France, the state-owned carrier, gobbled up its only two domestic rivals, Air Inter and UTA. Sir Leon had extracted a promise from Air France that it would expose itself to competition from domestic rivals, glossing over the detail that they were now non-existent. Others thought it was difficult to see the value of a competition policy if it merely eliminated competitors.

In the Commission's overseas development division, one eurocrat freely concedes: 'This department has never not been masterminded by France. My basic function is to provide outdoor relief for French African ex-colonies.' What makes the British Eurocrat sometimes bitter is that he is marooned by Whitehall, his career forgotten, on the assumption that he has 'gone native'. But his French colleagues are no loony federasts. They are out and out nationalists.

Nothing can be done to the £22 billion agricultural subsidy system without French approval, down to the tiniest detail. Why should it be that even EEC legislation on cider presses is based wholly on practice in Brittany, as if no cider-making took place in Devon and Somerset?

And now, as we near the endgame of the argument on monetary union, is it really right to see it as nothing but the logical extension of the 1992 Single Market? Would it be too cynical to look for a French plot in this too?

This, at least, is how it appears to have happened. The idea of a central Euro-bank mysteriously resurfaced, after a long spell on the shelf, in a speech in January 1988 by the Gaullist finance minister, M. Edouard Balladur. He had a list of grievances against the way the European Monetary System was loaded against the potentially weak, inflationary currencies, such as the franc and the lira, and in favour of the strong currencies, namely the deutsch-mark. One of Balladur's aides says: 'We thought it essential that our government should have some tools to define its own economic policy.'

As the French explain it, ever since the birth of the EMS in 1979, they had been labouring under the tyranny of the Bundesbank. Whenever they wanted to go for growth, the gnomes of Frankfurt said 'nein'. It was bad enough to be in hock to the low-inflation, low-growth policies of that worldly, suntanned former soccer writer, Dr Pöhl. More galling still was the importance assumed by the provincial bankers on the Bundesbank council, the maddening little Poloniuses from Hamburg, Bavaria and North-Rhine Westphalia. These men controlled German, and therefore French, interest rates.

What Balladur was proposing in the 'European Central Bank' was effectively a French seat on the Bundesbank. After ten years of knuckling under, France wanted to mount a rescue operation for its monetary sovereignty. Not all Germans were delighted but Herr Genscher, the foreign minister, was unquestionably forewarned of the Balladur speech, and chimed in with a five-page memorandum of support.

Genscher has the reputation of being a 'Euro-nut', determined to enmesh his country so deeply in the EEC that it can never again appear adversarial towards Paris. Dr Kohl (whose private office contains one of Lamy's contemporaries at ENA) went along with it, almost as if out of habit. Not so the finance ministry, under Gerhard Stoltenberg, which noted the suggestion, through gritted teeth, only after several weeks.

Balladur had made his move at a highly significant point: Delors had just been reconfirmed in his second four-year term as President of the EEC Commission. No sooner had Balladur spoken than it turned out Delors had a plan for a committee of 'wise men' to examine the whole problem of a central bank and currency. Was it all a French conspiracy? My own working hypothesis is that in January 1985 Delors had been deliberately planted in Brussels by Mitterrand, with the acquiescence of Dr Kohl, to avenge the humiliations of the franc.

One has to remember that the finance minister at the time of the most painful franc-deutschmark realignments, in 1981, 1982, and 1983, was Jacques Delors (and his *chef de cabinet*, incidentally, was Pascal Lamy). Almost as soon as

Delors left government in 1984, Mitterrand began negotiations with Kohl over placing him in the Commission on the retirement of the ineffectual Luxembourger, Gaston Thorn. It is certainly plausible that even at that stage Mitterrand and Delors recognised, that some form of 'European union' would give them a lever over German monetary policy, and so end the economic servitude they had experienced.

From Balladur's speech onwards, the plot takes on a Sophoclean inevitability. The June 1988 Hanover summit did indeed mandate the Delors committee of wise men to produce a report on moves to monetary union. It was unveiled in April 1989, adopted by all except Mrs Thatcher at the Madrid summit in June. Now we are five months into the intergovernmental conference which was called, overruling Mrs Thatcher, in Strasbourg in December 1989.

Whatever happens, it seems clear that the 12 will agree to set up some kind of European monetary institution, possibly leading to a single currency. The Germans, in the end, will consent. Delors will be able to campaign for the 1995 French presidential election as the man who united Europe and recovered French monetary sovereignty. The Enarques will have triumphed. It shows what national governments can pull off if they use their Eurocrats in their own national interests.

Maastricht was a triumph for Delors.

The making of a president

Jacques Delors was drawing a picture. Unprecedented! While Mr Wim Kok, the Dutch finance minister, burbled on about the latest semi-ritual humiliation of the British Government, the Commission President's blue fountain pen skittered over the page. He held it up to the press conference, obviously much pleased, beaming and making a thumbs-up gesture.

Some kind of cylinder, bulging at the top? A lavatory bowl? Non, non, explained M. Delors' aide and propagandist (and art critic), M. Bruno de Thomas, a *champagne* glass. For Mr Lamont, the Chancellor, had just been cruelly ambushed over Britain's plan to allow all Common Market countries to opt out of monetary union, and Delors was feeling festive.

Who knows, then, what doodles he will flash us next Tuesday or Wednesday, when he sits, haloed in the 12 stars of Europe, next to Mr Ruud Lubbers at the final 'presidential' press conference of the Maastricht summit. An ecu coin? A French cockerel? And how has it become so obviously *his* triumph?

M. Delors, it has been said with technical accuracy, has no more standing in the negotiations on monetary and political union than the Emperor of Patagonia. Inter-Governmental Conferences are, properly, the business of sovereign governments.

The protagonists are presidents and prime ministers of big, ancient countries; he 'presides' over 16 fellow senior bureaucrats and about 13,000 junior functionaries. To call him 'President Delors', then, in the manner of some English newspapers and CNN, is a misnomer, a silly equivocation.

And yet, and yet. When Mr Major triumphantly excises one word 'federal' for the treaty on 10 December, it will be dismissed as an Aunt Sally, a mere turnip-ghost, just shoved in there as an afterthought to scarify the Brits. Alas, no amount of scholiastic twiddling with a single word will alter the basic direction of this and earlier EEC treaties.

We are locked into a federation, in the most simple sense. By deciding ever more in common, the 12 countries have created a supranational federal authority in Brussels.

And the exact status of Delors, homo foederalis, has become ever more mysterious.

Muddled television producers have occasionally given him the subtitle 'European President'. Absurd, yes; but this is the future. You could say it is the fuzzy chrysalis that will, some time soon, produce a yet greater political imago.

By the end of next year, it won't even be possible to say he is an 'unelected bureaucrat'. An unnoticed clause in the political union treaty provides for 'approval' by the Euro-parliament. Blissful, infinite cunning: a just about serviceable democratic figleaf for a job which already has all the trappings of a world leader.

Now, when M. Delors speaks at press conferences, the 12-star blue and gold Euro-flag is invariably part of the backdrop, just as Mr Bush always speaks on a podium with the Seal of the President of the United States.

As social climbing, it has been long and slow. To seek the origins of his wailing police escorts, and the presence of M. Delors' dapper form in the summiteers' 'family photos', one has to dig back in Brussels lore to the time of Roy Jenkins. In the dreary, sodden spring of 1977, the newly appointed and, by his own account, rather depressed British president of the commission found himself embroiled in an undignified protocol war with President Giscard D'Estaing of France.

'The British weren't very helpful, either,' Lord Jenkins now says, before referring one, very properly, to his recently published autobiography (Macmillan, £20). In late 1975 Giscard and his buddy Helmut Schmidt had started an informal gathering of the leaders of the six largest Western economies at Rambouillet. By the following year, with the addition of Canada, the G7 was born at Puerto Rico, amid furious resentment from the excluded.

The Common Market's 'little five' – Benelux, Ireland, Denmark – felt, with Jenkins, that the economic summits were arrogantly despatching questions falling directly within EEC competence: mainly external trade. They wanted a voice, but in the interests of cosiness they could not all go. Roy Jenkins was to be their – federal – representative.

Giscard objected, on the not unreasonable grounds that, in spite of everything, Mr Jenkins was not really a world leader. 'Giscard's central syllogism was that the summit was a meeting of sovereign governments, and the Commission was not a sovereign government . . .' he says. 'This, apart from being nonsense, as subsequent events have shown, struck deep at the heart of community doctrine.'

So the Commission is a 'sovereign government', eh? That he got his way (though, just as ladies rise for the port, he was barred from the summit dinner) was the first triumph of the hitherto unheard-of notion of 'EEC sovereignty'. It implanted the notion, most strongly in Brussels but also elsewhere, that the Commission was in its soul a kind of government and its head was . . . a supranational, *federal* president.

Now, almost 15 years later, the signs are everywhere. Look at the photograph of the CSCE summit in November last year, taken on the fateful evening when so many Tories betrayed Mrs Thatcher, in the leadership election, over Europe. She stands in an exactly symmetrical position to M. Delors, she at the far left of the second row, he at the far right. Delors has become so grand that when he and his theoretical superior, M. Jacques Santer, prime minister of Luxembourg, visited President Bush earlier this year, the White House was clearly baffled about who should take precedence over whom.

And do not think that he sits silently at the summits and meetings of foreign ministers, taking notes with his Mont Blanc pen, like an EEC version of Sir Robin Butler. As we know, he makes tempestuous, percussive interjections. At his final press conference in Rome last December, when

51

events seemed to have gone smoothly for Mr Major, he seemed to be challenging the British government to a fight.

How, bluntly, does he have the cheek? Partly it is to do with the French tradition on which the Commission is organised. It is a civil service, but not as the British understand it, with blameless, faceless mandarins murmuring impartially to their political leaders. In Brussels, as in Paris, there is a continuum between ministerial posts and senior officialdom. French Sir Humphreys are politically engaged, wearing their party badges on their sleeves.

Partly it is to do with his vague but genuine mandate to be the 'guardian' of the Treaty of Rome, giving him the right, one supposes, to victimise anyone, such as Mrs Thatcher, who appears to be standing in the path of 'European union'.

But mainly, surely, the enormous advance in the dignity of his office, even since the time of Jenkins, is due to the character of M. Delors. He is a modest and charming man, and funny not just because of his extreme Clouseau-ish accent when attempting English. If you speak to the manager of Au Poux Qui Tousse, the Sardinian restaurant in the centre of Brussels where he has been lunching for years, he will tell you of a sparing, diet-conscious, generous man, with a Jeevesian enthusiasm for fish.

Yet there is something about him – probably a mixture of brilliance and lust for power – which has propelled him to the centre of the international stage. What single fact do you know about Delors' predecessor for four years, M. Gaston Thorn (1981–85)? Do you even know which country he came from? Up to a point, Delors is important because of who he is, not what he is.

For most EEC countries, there is an appetite to go the whole way. Remember the EEC is an equalising system: within the club of 12, the big, proud states find themselves pinned like Gulliver; the small states, one the size of Wolverhampton, have a quite disproportionate voice. For the *petits pays*, and to a lesser extent Italy, the Commission is a protector. For the Germans, so they insist, the federal system protects them from themselves.

They would be quite happy, in the present conferences, to see an expanded road for Delors and the Commission, and they will largely succeed. The Italians want him to run their economy, the Germans want him to solve their immigration problems. To a very great extent, this issue has been at the heart of the whole 11-month war over 'political union' between Britain and the rest.

It was what prompted M. Delors' *cri de coeur* in Strasbourg two weeks ago, a richly disingenuous intervention. Do not trust too much this mumbo-jumbo about 'pillars', 'temples' and 'trees'. It is in Mr Hurd's interest to play up his success in keeping some things, such as foreign policy and the police, temporarily out of the Commission's clutches. It is up to M Delors to cry foul. Whatever happens at Maastricht, the power of the Brussels Commission will be more, not less.

There have been setbacks, of course, and snubs. Sometimes the cuckoo-like EEC proto-government is rumbled, as when poor Henning Christophersen, the finance commissioner, was ejected from a G7 meeting in Bangkok. But the chutzpah of Brussels is bottomless.

On the Monday before the Middle East peace conference opened in Madrid, foreign ministers spent two hours in Brussels arguing over how they should be represented. M. Delors wanted Abel Matutes, the bald-headed, cigar-chewing multi-millionaire Spanish commissioner who owns most of Ibiza, and controls the EEC Commission's 'Middle East policy', to be at the table. That would mean being co-equal not just with Mr Hans van den Broek, Dutch foreign minister, but with James A. Baker III.

'We asked the Americans,' says a Dutch official, 'and Baker said fuck off.'

Tolerance of the upstart's antics depends, naturally, on France – and Britain, the other strongly nationalistic big country. Do not forget that it was the French foreign minister who stormed out in 1965, largely expressing de Gaulle's irritation at the self-aggrandisement of the first holder of the office, Herr Walter Hallstein. He liked to receive national plenipotentiaries, apparently, with subtly chalked crosses on the red carpet to show where they should stand.

But by the time of the Single European Act in 1986, the French had got their man on the 13th floor of the Berlaymont, and they were content to enshrine his role in treaty language. Article 1 of the SEA explicitly provides for the president of the Commission to attend EEC summits as an equal.

For the time being, presumably as long as the president of the Commission is French, Paris is prepared to leave the objections to the British. A very senior government official once told me that Britain would veto it if M. Delors stuck by his current plan to stay on at the Commission for an extra two years, until the end of 1994. Now I am not so sure. Onward and upward will be the course, for man and office alike. In a recent Gallup poll, 25 per cent of Britons said they would favour a 'European president'.

And then he overreached himself.

Delors plan to rule Europe

European Community foreign ministers were stunned yesterday to learn of a plan by Jacques Delors to transform the Brussels Commission into a 'European government', with himself or his successor becoming a fully fledged, elected 'President of the European Community' with executive powers.

British officials were appalled by the plan, which they believe could inflame Tory backbench suspicions about the ambitions of Brussels just as the Commons faces ratification of the Maastricht Treaty.

Douglas Hurd, the Foreign Secretary, refused to discuss the plan, news of which spread like wildfire at an informal EC meeting in Portugal. But he said the Government would fight Mr Delors and other governments which want to make radical changes to the EC Treaty – perhaps as early as next year.

'We can't even think about this,' said one senior British source. 'How can you start making more changes when you have only just finished Maastricht?'

Britain had vociferous support from the Danes, with Mr Uffe Ellmann-Jensen, the Foreign Minister, describing the Delors ideas as 'absurd'. 'No one will agree to this,' he said. But France and Germany said Brussels' powers should be boosted to cope with 20 members or more.

Close aides of Mr Delors disclosed some of the plans which the Commission president will formally table at the Lisbon summit on June 26.

He will suggest:

• Transforming the role of EC Commission president (now the appointee of the 12 governments) into a 'European President', possibly elected by the 518 members of the European Parliament;
• Putting the new 'European President' in charge of at least some regular meetings in Brussels of national cabinet ministers, where Community law is decided;
• Scrapping the system whereby the 12 national leaders and their governments take it in six-monthly turns to run the Community, centralising power in Brussels;
• Abolishing remaining national rights of veto, so Britain could be drowned out by a majority vote on even the most sensitive issues.

Mr Delors said such reforms were inescapable if the EC was not to become unmanageable 'with 15 to 17 or even 20–30 members'.

'For those who know the Community, it is evident that for efficiency and democratic accountability, profound institutional changes are needed,' he said.

In the past month he has hinted that his germinating ideas would 'shock' certain countries – namely Britain – when they were unveiled. He said yesterday that he expected preliminary discussions by foreign ministers on May 12 in Strasbourg.

The audacity of his plan led some diplomats yesterday to divine that he intended to set out a bargaining position, accepting that full-scale federalism might not be achievable in the short term. But his commitment to greater integration is undoubted.

Britain and Denmark were vehemently opposed to any changes. One Danish source said that, with feelings running high, Mr Delors risked a 'No' vote at the Danish referendum on Maastricht on June 2. That could cause the whole treaty to be dropped across Europe.

Mr Major will be aghast at re-entering negotiations on European union before 1996, the date he accepted at Maastricht for a review.

But Mr Delors knows that one or two countries alone cannot stop a new Treaty-changing conference from being convened.

The Dutch government said it had always been in favour of boosting the EC Commission, and could well imagine a new inter-governmental conference in 1993 or 1994.

Above all, Hans-Dietrich Genscher, the outgoing German Foreign Minister and architect of his country's Euro-federalist stance, said after his valedictory EC meeting: 'We can fulfil the Maastricht obligations only with reform, but enlargement makes it more necessary than ever.'

Roland Dumas, the French Foreign Minister, said he supported Mr Delors.

Even British officials said that Mr Delors's thinking – while completely unacceptable – was an attempt to respond to a real problem.

A morose Douglas Hurd, Foreign Secretary, told journalists that the preceding article was responsible for provoking the next event.

Danes vote to scupper Maastricht

The five million Danes last night delivered a devastating rebuke to the European leaders who, six months ago, agreed the Maastricht treaty for European union by throwing out the far-reaching plans for a monetary, economic and political union in their national referendum. With 90 per cent of the votes counted, 50.7 per cent of Danes were against the treaty while 49.3 per cent were in favour.

The Prime Minister Mr Poul Schlueter conceded that a 'no' now seemed inevitable.

He said that it was a 'sad day' and that he will be calling an emergency meeting of the Cabinet this morning.

The Danish decision has incalculable consequences for the project of European integration. At the very least, it will force the 12 governments to re-enter negotiations on Maastricht, at a time when suspicion against the treaty has been mounting in almost every EC country.

Under Article R.2 of the treaty, the blueprints for a 'united states of Europe' cannot come into force unless they have received ratification by all 12 countries.

Denmark could now be forced to take a massive 'opt out' from the ambitious plans sketched out by Maastricht, though Brussels legal experts said last night it would be a nightmare to disentangle the Danes from their obligations without effectively asking them to leave the Community.

'It is a complete catastrophe,' said one senior source.

Mr Uffe Ellemann Jensen, the pro-federalist Danish Foreign Minister whose career last night appeared to be over, said the vote was a 'fist in the face'.

The shockwaves will be felt around the Community and deal a deep psychological blow to Mr Jacques Delors, Commission President, and his colleagues who were instrumental in drawing up the Maastricht plans.

In Britain, it will once more propel anti-European Tory backbenchers to the centre of the political stage and greatly strengthen the pressure for a British national referendum.

It comes at a crucial time in Britain's own ratification process, with the treaty facing detailed and hostile scrutiny in the committee stage in the House of Commons.

Mr Major and Mr Hurd, who led the negotiations at Maastricht, will now have to return to inter-governmental talks, at least to write in a protocol to allow the Danes to opt out; but it may be impossible to restrain the pressure for further changes from governments of countries where the electorate has been taken aback at the scale of the changes involved by Maastricht.

Above all, the Germans may wish to insert an 'opt out' clause into the plan for a single European currency, allowing them – like Britain – to choose not to scrap their national money in favour of the ecu.

That would be completely to undermine the federalists' gains at Maastricht which nationally binds the Germans to abandoning the Deutschmark by 1999 at the latest.

In Denmark, it has been a roller-coaster campaign in which the unspoken issue has been resentment at German dominance, past and future, of Europe. Copenhagen has been festooned with posters saying both Ja and Nej and Danes have covered the issues in a depth and detail not seen in any other EC country.

The only other national referendum, in Ireland on June 18, was expected to give a handsome majority in favour of the treaty with opposition currently running at only 10 per cent; but Denmark last night did the work of Euro-sceptics throughout the Community.

France may call a national referendum and even Luxembourg has shown an interest in renegotiating the Maastricht treaty.

The Danish 'no' springs from a deep Euro-scepticism which has already led them almost to throw out the single European Act in 1986. They have insisted that Maastricht contains the right for them to hold a further referendum if they are ever to adopt the single European currency – which now looks unlikely.

The Danes have now served notice that any further programme of EC integration will be received with extreme scepticism.

In particular, Denmark has its doubts about the plans dear to M Delors and the French Government to convert the EC, in short order, into a defence pact possibly supplanting Nato. This was due to be the main topic of discussion at the next inter-governmental talks in 1996.

The 12 EC countries will now be forced to re-assemble at the negotiating table in the hope of finding some amendment which could appease the Danes.

The mixture of Far Left, Far Right and environmentalist groups who opposed the treaty argued that Brussels was forcing Denmark to adopt standards of environmental and social protection which were too low, in contrast to Britain where Tory Eurosceptics say the EC intervenes too much.

More generally, the Danes feel their country is just too small to be swallowed in a European superstate, an emotion felt especially strongly by women.

The strength of the 'no' vote was attributed partly to the high turn-out as doubters resolved to counteract opinion polls showing a strong 'yes' at the weekend.

And as soon as the markets thought that Maastricht was in danger, they started attacking the ERM, which was meant to be the precursor to the single currency.

Lamont fails to save pound

A sombre Mr Lamont, the Chancellor, last night effectively conceded that the pound would be devalued after a day of unprecedented and costly turmoil on the foreign exchanges. The sterling crisis intensified dramatically when the Government abandoned its battle to defend the pound and announced it was suspending Britain's membership of the Exchange Rate Mechanism.

But Mr Lamont reversed an earlier decision to push up interest rates to 15 per cent to defend sterling. Base rates will stay at 12 per cent – two points higher – and a further three per cent increase will not take effect today as planned.

Parliament is to be recalled next Thursday to discuss the crisis.

There was considerable bitterness in Downing Street last night against Germany, with Mr Major holding the Bundesbank responsible for initiating the run on sterling.

Downing Street listed five separate occasions on which officials or council members of the Bundesbank had been reported making statements that put the pound under pressure.

Mr Major yesterday telephoned Chancellor Kohl to complain about the Bundesbank's behaviour.

Last night Sir Norman Fowler, Tory party chairman, said: 'Frankly, if anyone should resign it should be the president of the Bundesbank.'

Sir Marcus Fox, Chairman of the backbench 1922 Committee, said: 'The guilty men are not in Downing St. It is the president of the Bundesbank who has caused all this turmoil.'

Britain's decision to suspend membership of the ERM, rather than remain within the system and seek a devaluation, was being seen by EC experts last night as a hardening of the Government's position towards the rest of the Community. They said it might have been triggered by irritation at 'unhelpful' statements from the Frankfurt Bundesbank yesterday morning.

Comments by Herr Helmut Schlesinger, Bundesbank president, appeared to be calling directly for a devaluation of sterling and so almost certainly precipitated the markets' rush to sell.

The most dramatic U-turn in Government economic policy since the devaluation crisis of 1967 represented a humiliation for Mr Major and Mr Lamont.

Tory MPs, stunned by the climbdown, predicted that the Maastricht treaty would be the next casualty. They said that the unravelling of the ERM had dealt a fatal blow to the controversial blueprint for closer European economic union and there was now little chance of securing a parliamentary majority for the treaty.

The Prime Minister, however, is determined to keep Mr Lamont at the Treasury and is ready to share the criticism for the failure of a central plank of the Government's strategy.

Both had staked their authority on resisting a devaluation. But their gamble – which involved spending billions of pounds of foreign exchange reserves and a double increase in interest rates – failed to halt the slide in sterling's value. As the pound sank further in overnight trading, the Government called for the whole ERM to be suspended until after Sunday's French referendum on the Maastricht treaty.

As Mr Lamont made a brief statement in the courtyard of the Treasury building in Whitehall, the pound was three pfennigs below its floor within the European Exchange Rate Mechanism.

'Today has been an extremely turbulent and difficult day,' Mr Lamont said.

'Massive speculative fluctuations continue to disrupt the function of the Exchange Rate Mechanism. As chairman of the European council of finance ministers, I have called a meeting of the Monetary committee in Brussels tonight to consider how stability can be restored to the Exchange Rate Market.

'In the meantime the Government has concluded that Britain's best interests would be served by suspending our exchange rate membership. As a result the second of the two interest rate increases which I sanctioned will not take place. The minimum lending rate will be at 12 per cent until conditions become calmer.

'I will be reporting to Cabinet, discussing the situation with colleagues tomorrow and may make futher statements then. But until then I have nothing further to say. Thank you very much.'

The EC's monetary committee met in Brussels last night to discuss new arrangements, which may involve a devaluation of the lira and other southern European currencies.

One prediction was that the committee was negotiating a possible further cut in German rates of one per cent, in exchange for a revaluation of the Deutschmark-zone currencies and a devaluation of the rest, with the pound out of the system.

This would mean that the D-mark, the Belgian franc, the Luxembourg franc, the Dutch guilder and the Danish kroner would all increase by four per cent in value, while the rest fell by four per cent.

Downing Street officials refused to concede that the Chancellor's statement amounted to a devaluation. 'What happens to market rates is something we have to see. There is likely to be a lot of volatility in the run-up to the French referendum. It is a suspension and not a withdrawal from the ERM.'

They said there was 'absolutely no question' of either the Chancellor or the Prime Minister's resignation.

However, many Conservatives doubt whether Mr Lamont can survive long term.

Mr Andrew Hunter, Conservative MP for Basingstoke, said Mr Lamont should resign as his whole strategy had failed. 'Even now he must acknowledge that his policies are likely to turn recession into depression,' he added.

Mr William Cash, Tory MP for Stafford and a leading critic of the Government's European policy, said the Chancellor's position was 'extremely precarious'.

He added: 'We are in a state of political shambles and people will have to answer a lot of questions.'

If the pound is devalued – as now seems inevitable – Mr Lamont will be the first Chancellor for 25 years to preside over a formal lowering of the pound's international value. In 1967, the then Labour Chancellor, Mr James Callaghan, resigned after devaluing the pound by 14 per cent – following an unsuccessful battle to defend its parity which had many parallels with the present crisis.

The Chancellor's statement came at the end of a day of high drama in Whitehall and the exchange markets. Mr Major, who last week described devaluation as a 'betrayal' of the nation's future, authorised deployment of all the Treasury's weapons to defend sterling.

But the Government was overwhelmed by the most serious economic crisis since 1976, when the then Chancellor, Mr Denis Healey, was forced to turn back from London Airport because of a run on the pound.

What MPs are calling Mr Major's 'Black Wednesday' began with massive intervention by the Bank of England, and later by other European Central Banks, to prop up the pound.

By mid-morning it was clear this was not enough. Mr Lamont, after talks with the Governor of the Bank of England, Mr Robin Leigh Pemberton, sanctioned a two per cent rise in base rates and said he hoped it would be possible to bring them down when the present uncertainties abated.

But the pressure on sterling continued, and the Treasury played its final card: an unprecented second interest rate rise of three per cent, taking base rates back to 15 per cent, where they stood when Mr Major, as Chancellor, took Britain into the ERM almost two years ago.

This decision sent shockwaves through the Conservative Party and industry.

When this further rise in interest rates failed to dissuade the currency speculators, it became clear that the Government's policy was politically unsustainable. Senior Tory MPs warned the Government that it would split the party and deepen the already serious divisions over Europe.

Critics of the Maastricht Treaty described the Chancellor's policy as 'insanity', while normally loyal backbenchers acknowledged that defence of the pound within the ERM was placing intolerable strains on the economy and should be abandoned.

The decision to suspend sterling's membership of the exchange rate mechanism was taken by Mr Major and senior Cabinet colleagues after the money markets closed, with the pound still under pressure.

Mr John Smith, Labour leader, said last night that the crisis was 'the direct, unavoidable result of Conservative mismanagement of the economy'. He added: 'I think it represents an almost total defeat for the strategy that has been followed for a number of years, not just by the Chancellor, but by the present Prime Minister.'

Mr Lamont is already facing growing criticism over the failure to deliver the economic recovery promised by the Conservatives at the election. When the immediate shockwaves subside, there are still likely to be angry protests over the impact of the two per cent increase in interest rates, particularly if it leads to a rise in home loan rates and pushes more businesses into liquidation.

It was an epic disaster for the Tories. Still, it is just about conceivable that they could have recovered, had John Smith not died . . .

Labour leadership contenders – Blair ahead

Tony Blair's smile lurks permanently upon his face. Whenever he is called upon to speak of his ambitions, his lips twitch upwards, waiting to burst open in a glistening crescent of confidence.

On Thursday July 21 the ballots will be finally counted in the Labour leadership race, and his anointment is seen as inevitable. The latest poll puts him 20 points ahead of Margaret Beckett.

But the Labour electorate is vast, unknowable. It must be wooed even by a runaway front-runner, whose authority will depend on the extent of his victory; and it must be wooed by the candidates for deputy leader.

Today in Sheffield, tomorrow in Stirling, and then in Darlington and Birmingham next week, all three candidates will be perspiring under the arc lights at hustings of a kind unknown to the Tory Party.

And as the ballot papers land on the mats of 4.2 million trades union levy-payers, 270,000 Labour Party members, as well as the 331 Labour MPs and MEPs, even hustings are not enough. This is a television election.

By now the slogans are tiring. How many times will Margaret Beckett joke that she is 'uniquely able to offer the prospect of Tories in Downing Street, shouting "Maggie, Maggie, Maggie, out! out! out!"'?

Viewers will be familiar with Mr Blair's belief that Labour should take power 'not just for a parliament, not just for a term of office, but for a generation'.

Labour's political culture is more florid than the Tories'. Rhetoric consists of key words such as people, hope, values, principles, change – endlessly repeated in varying combinations. It produces virtual gibberish such as Mrs Beckett's uplifting 'We must bind together the people of Britain to light a beacon of hope'.

Charged with a lack of substance, each candidate takes refuge in Labour doctrine that the party leader cannot 'make policy on the hoof' while subtle attempts are made to mark themselves out.

Mr Blair the barrister has appeared as the wholesome urban professional, kicking a ball amid the pink roses of a public park with his son: the kind of man disillusioned Tories across Britain could embrace.

Asked how he could contemplate the leap, at 41, to party leadership and, who knows, Prime Minister, he has formulated a simple, manly answer to do with 'a time and a tide in the affairs of men', while stressing the consultation he has taken with his wife Cherie.

Mr Prescott has been seen at the wheel of his sailing craft on the Humber, a salty tar, chaffing political correspondents about his days as a Cunard waiter. He tells us slyly how he met a Tory voter who pledged his vote because 'he liked the cut of my jib'.

Mrs Beckett makes no attempt to present herself as an outdoor type, trading on feminine calm, and the success of the Labour campaign during the Euro-elections. Mr Prescott and Mrs Beckett are both pitching for the Left-wing vote.

But even here there are shades. Mr Prescott styles himself as the commonsense trades unionist, accepting a need to re-write some of Lady Thatcher's 1980s union reform without a wholesale evisceration of the statute book.

Mrs Beckett's approach is harder-Left, apparently favouring a root-and-branch reform and perhaps even the restoration of secondary picketing. And as the man who will almost certainly be leader, and who must pitch for those Tory voters, Mr Blair is the most evasive, giving the impression that the Thatcher reforms would essentially persist under Labour.

On jobs, too, there are differences of nuance. Mr Prescott has isolated the weak word in Mr Blair's slogan. 'It's not enough to talk about the goal of full employment,' he says. 'We need to show there is something beneath the rhetoric'. After all, as he implies, Labour and Tories alike now endorse that goal. What matters are the steps taken to achieve it.

On one matter dear to the electorate's heart, all three are mute. None will give any hostage to fortune on taxation.

One Labour MP said: 'I don't believe a word any of them says. I suspect whichever wins will put tax at 60 per cent for earnings over £50,000 and have some form of taxation in the City to reduce dividends and increase investment.' If there is any suspense when the announcement is made, it will surround the deputy leadership.

Women will unquestionably tend to vote for Mrs Beckett, even though she has come out second-best in Commons exchanges with Mr Major.

But several MPs from both parties have suggested that Mr Prescott is, despite his glowering persona, the more sensitive of the two.

Some of Mrs Beckett's supporters imagine that she could run Mr Blair very close if Mr Prescott were to be eliminated first in the single transferable vote system. They believe his second preference votes would pass substantially to Mrs Beckett.

But it is a faint hope. If there is one reason why the party is set to vote for Mr Blair in such numbers, it is because they think he is the most likely to put Labour feet under the desk in Downing Street.

His slogan, 'Principle, Purpose, Power', seems designed

to be read aloud as a statement of motives. His principal purpose is power.

And as Tory problems deepened, there was feuding – or alleged feuding – between those who were thought likely to take over from Mr Major. Michael Portillo was in those days thought to be on the Right of the party.

Heseltine v Portillo

Anyone in the Department of Trade and Industry who thinks Britain's space programme is the definition of pouring money into a black hole must be secretly cursing Michael Portillo. Just as the nation was quietly scaling down its contribution to the European Space Agency, opting out of Ariane Cinq, the new French firecracker, refusing to pay a penny to Hermes, Europe's doomed retort to the Space Shuttle, doing its best to head off the impending fiasco of a European manned flight, known as operation *homme sur la lune*; just as things were going so nicely, in fact, along comes the messiah of the Right and makes life more difficult.

Before Mr Portillo's pungent demand that Mr Heseltine abandon the DTI's funding for space research, among other things, Britain had already been whittling away its annual subventions to the European Space Agency from £100 million to £77 million. While France and Germany pump billions of ecus into the upper air, Britain's effort accounts for a mere 7.5 per cent of the ESA budget, and has been sped on its downward path, Mr Portillo will be pleased to note, by the collapse of the pound on Black Wednesday. This year, the DTI has even opted out of Festip (Future European Space Transportation Investi-

69

gations Programme), a new breed of smaller, sleeker interplanetary vehicle.

Now, though, a big man's honour is at stake; and more than honour, pride. It is not just the arrogant tone of Mr Portillo's letter, with not a trace of deference towards the great, lion-maned President and his vast experience of public office. You just cannot say to a man like Heseltine, talking of one of his department's few remaining spending commitments, 'I do not see why you do not move straight to abolition,' when the thought had not even occurred to him.

In attacking the European Space Agency, moreover, Mr Portillo has jabbed the central ganglion of Mr Heseltine's political being. This is a *European Consortium* (*cf*. Westland Helicopters, 1986), safeguarding European technology, providing European jobs, in which Britain's hesitant participation is already viewed on the continent as a sign of the country's generally dog-in-the-mangerish approach.

Portillo's rash, intemperate letter is likely to mean that Mr Heseltine will have no choice, if he is to retain credibility and the esteem of Cabinet colleagues, but to react in the opposite direction.

As Mr Heseltine will know, if there is one goal every French minister wants, more than preserving the role of French as the chief official language of the EC and obliterating franglais, more than an independent *force de frappe*, more than safeguarding French films from the corruption of Hollywood, it is to put a man on the moon: a Frenchman, in fact, and one propelled thither by beautiful French machines.

Now one must imagine that 'the President', tight-lipped with fury, is tempted to rebuke the pompadoured whippersnapper of the Right in the most crushing way; using British money to help gratify the French extra-terrestrial dream. In October 1995, ESA will test launch the first

Ariane V, 31 metres tall, ten times bigger than any rocket built by Europe so far.

In 1987, Kenneth Clarke laughingly declined to join in. What better put-down for Mr Portillo than to revoke that decision, and sign Britain up for the $6.6 billion Euro-rocket, which, if previous Ariane launches are anything to go by, will usher in a new cycle of detonations in the Caribbean skies, terrifying the tribes of Guyana and shrapnelling the leper colonies of Devil's Island?

For now, the DTI maintains a semblance of cynicism about the returns from space. 'We're not in the prestige projects business,' says Victoria Street. Mr Heseltine's department points out that the present limited investment in ESA observation satellites brings work for firms such as BAe Space Systems and Matra Marconi. 'We've got contracts, jobs and technology,' says the department. 'What more could you want?'

But if the President truly wishes to rub Mr Portillo's nose in it, he has only to sign a few more cheques, and soon British equipment will join Ariane V. One day, who knows, GEC and BAe will rival the French in supplying the cargo cults of Pacific Islanders with twisted, shiny objects of veneration.

Mr Heseltine might even accede to a joint attempt to revive Hermes, a sort of astronautical Concorde, aborted in 1992. All that remains of poor Hermes is a mockup in the European Space Agency's headquarters in Noordwijk, Holland: a desolate place, lashed with the spume of the North Sea, where disconsolate Dutch astronauts sit in the canteen, puffing their pipes, and awaiting the call from the heavens.

This was not intended to be a little-earther rant. Space exploration has its points, no doubt. After billions were spent on the ESA satellite Giotto, the probe exceeded the wildest dreams of scientists. It discovered, after all these years, that Halley's comet was an encrusted black rock emitting radiant gases.

I fully accept the argument that without space exploration there would be no teflon, no velcro, no potty putty. If it is necessary to spend hundreds of billions on rockets to make sure eggs do not stick to frying pans, then perhaps that is cheap at the price.

Mr Heseltine could go further. My colleague Adrian Berry quotes an idea to use special thrusters to dislodge Enceladus, a moon of Saturn, from its orbit, until it collides with Mars, so – by some process, beyond my understanding, involving 30 million cubic miles of water – turning the Red Planet into a kind of cultivable paradise. Now that would really stick it to Mr Portillo. If that is not interventionism, I do not know what is.

All Mr Portillo will be able to offer in return is babble about fundamental expenditure reviews, the concept of abuse of tax-payers' money, the notion that our children and grandchildren must pay for the budget deficits of their parents. No, in the 25th anniversary of the moonshot that put Neil Armstrong and Buzz Aldrin on the moon, the dream will not die. The romance is too strong.

The Heseltine-Portillo feud, in fact, is but a detail in the endless race for the stars; exactly like the terrible rivalry, which even today Nasa officials are ashamed to mention, between Armstrong and Aldrin: the one pair battling over who should set foot on the cold, sterile soil of the moon, the other competing as to who shall eject the Prime Minister from Downing Street. It is a tragic fact of human life that when a great prize is at stake, only one man can take it. Who is Neil, then, and who is Buzz?

The Tory turmoil was intense, and some of them seemed to be willing a Labour victory.

The Kamikaze Squad

They're revving the engines. They're putting on their goggles. The explosive has been packed into the noses of their Zeroes. Their objective is death, never mind the glory. The Kamikaze Conservatives are preparing for the final conflagration of the next General Election, and with an effort one can almost catch the words forming on their lips: Tory Tory Tory! Banzai! Die for the Empress Thatcher.

Lagging by 40 points in the polls, there are those Tories who have resigned themselves in a spirit of honest pessimism to defeat by Mr Blair and Labour. Oh, they would like to win in 1996 or 1997. It is just that they feel that the public is irreconcilable and that the tide of history is against them.

And then there is an altogether tougher, more radical breed. There is a group of Tories who have meditated profoundly on the future of Conservatism. In the cynical slogan of Lenin, they have concluded that 'the worse the better', that there is nothing for it but to adopt a stance of revolutionary defeatism.

They do not merely foresee the extinction of John Major and 17 years of Tory rule. Looking at the inseparability of Tory and Labour policy on everything from law and order to taxation, the emptiness of the last Queen's Speech, the even greater emptiness, if that were possible, of the next Queen's Speech, and above all the next manifesto, they believe the time has come to die. Most of these political suicide-bombers, for obvious reasons, are anxious not to be quoted.

If one wished to date the spiritual inception of the Tory Kamikazes, one might cite the night of the last General

Election in April 1992, when a gathering of Right-wingers, including the deposed Prime Minister, Lady Thatcher, watched the returns on television at the Westminster house of Lord McAlpine, the former Party Treasurer. When the news was flashed that the proven moderate and Party Chairman Chris Patten had lost his seat in Bath, some wag allegedly shouted 'Tory gain!'

The group hooted. It laughed because a taboo had been broken. From that joke, future historians may conclude, originated the notion that it could be desirable for Tories to lose, if that meant being rid of centrist Majorites, and realigning the Party to the Right.

This week the same Lord McAlpine, scion of construction tycoons, has publicly called for the entire Conservative Party to have a rest cure for the sake of its soul. As he told a weekly magazine, he wants it to 'go into the wildnerness, take a sabbatical. I want a clean slate. I'm looking for a charismatic leader, a sort of John the Baptist. The Party needs a good scrub with a hard brush.'

Ranged behind Lord McAlpine is a phalanx of distinguished right-wing pundits not known for their admiration of Mr Major and the present regime. Of these, my esteemed colleague Simon Heffer is perhaps the most cogent. Ranged in turn behind the pundits are, so they believe, a large band of Tory grassroots activists who have long tended to be Right of the leadership.

That, one might think, was the logical limit of the Kamikaze movement. One might think it defied reason that the Tories' Lemming tendency could extend to the ranks of the parliamentary Conservative Party.

One can see that the Right-wing pundits, driven to distraction by the indefatigable moderation of Mr Major, are praying for Götterdämmerung. But can any Tory MP logically desire his party to be cast out on to the Opposition benches? Even the most muddle-headed Conservative must see that it is a precondition of Opposition that the Tories lose many seats, perhaps including, Great Scott, his own.

The amazing fact is that there exists just such a group of revolutionary defeatist Tory MPs. Patrolling the corridors of Westminster, I have come across a number of Eurosceptics, albeit a handful, with safe seats, who fantasise about a collective act of Tory suicide – on the understanding, of course, that they, as individuals, will be spared.

Naturally they would prefer Mr Major to make way soon, of his own accord, for one of their kind. They would rather see their party undergo moral and intellectual catharsis without the inconvenience of giving Labour the keys to Downing Street. But they recognise that, if the pattern of recent years is any guide, Mr Major may escape a challenge again this autumn.

And even if there were a serious leadership contest, the Thatcherite Right knows that the likely victor would be Michael Heseltine – the matricide! And since they reckon that it would be impossible to install a man of sufficient ideological rigour now, their best bet, they reason, is to hope for the blood-letting that will follow an election defeat.

What they want thereafter is little short of revolution. Opposition would be like the period 1974 until 1979, they promise. 'It reactivated the Party in a remarkable way,' says one MP. It was the period of intellectual ferment in which the Right, Keith Joseph and Margaret Thatcher, regained the ascendancy after the Heathite corporatist government, the frittering of power in 1972 and 1974. And so it will be again, they believe. 'There will be reconsideration and discussion,' says the MP, putting it mildly.

There will be a rediscovery of Principle with a capital P, of 'True Conservatism', and to that end the Right plans to put in Mr Michael Portillo, the Employment Secretary, as leader of the Party.

The programme will be to advocate Europe as a free trade area, with no more cessions of sovereignty. Vicious cuts will be demanded in public spending. The distinction will be restored between the deserving and the undeserving poor. There will be a serious policy on law and order. As for Mr Major and what the Kamikaze Tories regard as the odious apparatus of Majorism, they will be purged. The most the Ken Clarkes of this world can hope for, we are told, is that they will not have to undergo show trials.

You and I might think such a strategy was fraught with risk. You might think it rash for Tories even to talk of taking a dive at the next election; especially when, if Labour wins, it will inherit economic circumstances far more favourable than those of 1992. You might point out that Mr Portillo, currently 41, may be pushing 60 before his party has even a chance of putting his Right-wing manifesto into practice.

You might think that if the Tory party is really to begin whittling away at the welfare state, it is in a better position to do so with Peter Lilley at the Department of Social Security than, assuming he keeps his seat, in Opposition. You might feel it odd that some Tories are so defeatist that they are plotting about Opposition, when the election could be anything up to two years away. You might think it rum, in particular, that Right-wing Tories could wish the economy to be passed into the hands of socialists, with all that means for policy on tax, spending and Europe.

You might think that. Or perhaps it is just me. Perhaps the Kamikaze Tories have answers to these questions as they narrow their eyes and stare at the rising sun of Michael Portillo. It would be reassuring, though, to hear those answers.

What made New Labour so hard to fight was that no one really knew what they stood for ...

Mr Blair has learnt a valuable lesson

Any businessman rolling the Labour Party's new improved Clause Four about his mind will instantly recognise the kind of texts that have inspired Tony Blair. Harping as the new constitution does on words like 'quality', 'service', 'endeavour', 'achieve', 'community' and 'prosper', it belongs unmistakably to a modern literary genre: the US-style corporate Mission Statement. In deciding to revamp the charter of Labour Plc, Mr Blair is mimicking the world's most successful companies.

For instance, in 1952 one 'Colonel' Sanders of Kentucky dipped a chicken drumstick into salty batter-mixture and (allegedly) pronounced: 'It's finger-lickin' good!' Ungrammatical, likely to encourage bad table manners; and yet the founder's words have been inscribed on countless boxes of Kentucky Fried Chicken. Recently, however, the strategy men in Kentucky have decided that this sentence is no longer enough, alone, to uplift the workforce and to convince an apathetic public of the moral dimension to selling fried chicken.

After what one can only assume was a full process of consultation with franchisees, Kentucky Fried Chicken has a new Mission Statement. Like the words of Sidney and Beatrice Webb, the honest exclamation of Col Sanders has been updated and blurred. KFC's goal in life is, I can reveal, 'to provide families with affordable, delicious, chicken dominant meals'. Notice the adept insertion of the hot-button word 'family'. 'Families' also appears, for the first time, in the new Clause Four.

In the development of their Mission Statements, the Labour Party and top corporations have converged from opposite directions. The 1918 Webb formulation has been junked essentially because Labour has so crushingly lost the argument about the role of commerce in society. Commerce, on the other hand, has understood that the public likes capitalism to sound caring. By 1995, both the Labour Party and Big Business have adopted identical methods of selling themselves. Both have produced Mission Statements in which the strategy is, within a few honed words, to achieve the smooth yoking-together of antithetical ambitions; or, to put it another way, to have one's cake and eat it.

Compare the 'Corporate Mission 1992–2000' of McDonald's Hamburgers, which strikingly resembles Blair's effort in language and tone. Perhaps conscious of accusations that they employ student hamburger flippers on Third World wages, McDonald's says: 'The company will be led by the needs of our customers and committed to the welfare and development of our staff.' See what taut equipoise is achieved between (a) the 'needs' of customers, chiefly for cheap food, and (b) the duty of McDonald's to its wretched staff. One might compare Labour's new balancing act, in which 'the rights we enjoy reflect the duties we owe'.

Like Blair, commerce has understood how valuable the Mission Statement can be for fudging a failure to stick to principle. One thinks of Anita Roddick's breathtaking assertion that the Body Shop's mission is 'to passionately campaign for the environment and for the protection of human and civil rights, against animal testing within the cosmetics and toiletries industry'. Brilliant, eh? On the one hand the Body Shop is (a) in favour of animals. On the other hand, it must, like Labour, deal with the world as it is, so (b) like the rest of the cosmetics and toiletries industry the Body Shop has to use products tested on animals.

78

Just such a recognition of reality lies at the heart of Tony Blair's new Labour Party constitution. The Fabian goal of public ownership is still there. But a future Labour Britain in which 'those undertakings essential to the common good are either owned by the public or accountable to them' must face up, Blair admits, to the existence of 'a thriving private sector'.

Statements of this kind give an opportunity for a delicate adjustment of stance. Remember KFC's wonderful new aspiration to provide 'chicken dominant' meals. Yes, even as the menu at KFC is no longer in thrall to chicken, so Labour is no longer dominated by the Unions. Just as a KFC Family Feast now consists of additional fries, cole-slaw, BBQ beans and Sara Lee apple pie, so New Labour will also co-operate, says the revised constitution, with 'voluntary organisations, consumer groups and other representative bodies'.

Not least, the Mission Statement is an opportunity for rhapsodising. Take the sweep of ambition of Ben and Jerry's ice-cream, which is apparently intended to 'improve the quality of life of a broad community, local, national and international'. Just so is Labour committed to working with 'international bodies to secure peace, freedom, democracy' and so on. A mission statement can say what the firm does not want. Pret A Manger, the fashionable new sandwich chain, says, 'We ruthlessly avoid preservatives, additives and obscure chemicals.' Tony Blair's new-look Labour is still hostile, we gather, to the wealthy few.

The similarity between Labour's new Clause Four and the most right-on commercial Mission Statements is uncanny. I don't know whether John Prescott is the sort of ex-sailor to make use of the Body Shop. But I could swear he has cribbed Roddick's vow 'to *courageously* ensure that *our* business is ecologically sustainable, meeting the needs of the *present* without compromising the future'. Labour's new Clause Four calls for a 'healthy environment which we protect, enhance and hold in trust for future generations'. The new Labour Party speaks of 'solidarity, tolerance and respect'. The Body Shop offers 'honesty, fairness and respect'.

It would be dangerous, though, to mock. My purpose is not necessarily to debunk Labour's new constitution. After all, these companies whose guff-filled Mission Statements Mr Blair imitates are phenomenally successful. If Anita Roddick can persuade millions of people to buy her delightful coconut oil shampoo or taramasalata facial scrub, then why should identical techniques not persuade us all to vote Labour?

Where is the Tory Mission Statement? One thing is certain: more people will buy Big Macs in 1997 than will vote Tory. The time is approaching when the Tories may have to consider following Blair's lead, sacking Mr Hanley, and putting Colonel Sanders in charge of Central Office.

And no one knew what Tony Blair really believed in.

Who was fibbing – the old Blair or new?

There is a rather good parlour game where you pick up the Bible or Shakespeare or Baedeker, or, even better, the Koran, and quote a passage until you start improvising parodically, while the listener has to guess at exactly which point you departed from the text. Well, I thought I would give you some Tony Blair. All you have to do is yell or whistle as soon as you think I am starting to send up Blair's efforts to sound like a Tory. Ready? Here goes. This is Blair in the spring of 1995:

'Duty is the cornerstone of a decent society.'

'I believe Margaret Thatcher's emphasis on enterprise was right.'

'Parents must be warned that non-attendance by children can lead to court.'

'Top-rate tax does not equal wealthy any more.'

'I am in favour of capital punishment for those who kill policemen.'

All right, I admit it, I made the last one up. But you take the point, I hope.

This is the brand of 'socialism' that is about to administer the most unholy drubbing to the Tory party in the local government elections on 4 May, and, some would have us believe, precipitate the downfall of Mr Major. As *The Spectator* went to press, Blair's chances of losing the vote on changing Clause Four dwindled to vanishing point.

The Labour leader is by any standards formidable in his public relations. Like a master organist he flits between the stacked keyboards of the press, playing us all simultaneously without hitting a bum note. His handling of the 'teachers' who frightened Blunkett's dog was assured, turning a minus for Labour into a plus.

Such is the lust for change, the desperation to trust him, that the electorate would seemingly forgive anything. Should they?

In theory, it is a measure of a statesman's fitness for power whether he is *tenax propositi*, whether he adheres to principle. So let us play another game, the one that the BBC would play, were its presenters a tiny bit tougher on what we are invited to call 'New Labour'. The game is an old, crude politician's stand-by. I only resort to the trick because it is so unfashionable and because Labour is still handled with such deference. This game is called 'But You Said, Mr Blair – And I'll Read It To You'.

We've all heard of Blair the Moderniser. Blair the Moderniser has reassured Middle England that he isn't going to tamper with the Tory trades union law which largely restored confidence in Britain overseas. But there is another character: we might call him Ur-Blair. Here is Blair the Archaiser on the subject of the 1984 Trade Union Act, an essential, democratic reform which made strike ballots compulsory: 'It is a disgrace that we should be debating today the taking away of fundamental freedoms for which British trade unionists have fought ... We shall oppose the Bill, which is a scandalous and undemocratic measure.' Young Tony was scarcely less Spartish, Hansard reveals, about the 1982 Act and the restrictions on secondary picketing.

Anyone can change his tune, especially in response to four election defeats. But it is more difficult, one would think, for a politician to change his or her instincts. The important question for us all, as voters expecting a Labour government, is, When were they telling the truth about what they really thought, then or now?

One of the pair, Ur-Blair or Blair, is lying. I am fairly sure the fibber is, or was, Ur-Blair the Archaiser. In other words, what you *now* see is what you get; he *really* is a social democrat-cum-Tory who happens, amazingly, to be leading the Labour Party. Many of the converts among us will want to see it like this. They will be inclined to be indulgent of Ur-Blair. They will know why he said things like, 'We'll negotiate a withdrawal from the EEC, which has drained our natural resources and destroyed jobs' in his 1983 election address. He said them, fingers crossed, because he was a bright young man who wanted to get on in the Labour Party, like those Tories who stoutly defended the ERM in 1991 and 1992 and then repented.

The more interesting question, perhaps, concerns the rest of them. Which set of propositions reflects the true instincts of the Shadow Cabinet, the senior figures whom Blair must heed, especially if, as seems likely, he has a small majority in Parliament? Were they faking it for all those years, and did they decide – about a year ago – to tell the truth? Or are they dissimulating now? It should not be too tiresome to repeat that the entire Shadow Cabinet was opposed to every one of the Government's privatisations, that 14 of them are known to have been members of CND, that six of them voted against Britain's membership of the EU.

I wonder if these colleagues of Mr Blair can really have lost the emotions that actuated them then, that made them want to go into politics: the deep distrust of capitalism; the hatred of the profit motive; the warines of commercial competition; the class anger; the instinctive belief that business is best organised by the state; the urge to take and redistribute money.

Which is the real Jack Straw on the subject of education? There is the Jack Straw who has beamed at Tony and Cherie Blair's decision to send their son Euan to a grant-maintained school. Or there is the Jack Straw who at a local government conference in 1992 called Tory plans for opting out, which broadly took power over children from left-wing councils and gave it to parents and governors, a 'disreputable and failing system'. In a press release of 1988, the old Jack Straw, Ur-Straw, said City Technology Colleges and opted-out schools are 'designed systematically to sabotage the central value of the comprehensive school'. As recently as 1991, he wanted to axe the 'wasteful' City Technology Colleges, thereby, he said, saving about £50 million.

I have an idea which is the real Jack Straw. Think into the mind of someone who believes that 'the monarchy is a deeply decadent and detached system for which we are all paying'. He is obviously an overgrown student socialist.

Which is the real John Prescott? Is he the man who, with Blair, turned Clause Four into a kind of fast-food mission statement, or the man who told us all in February 1994 that 'I come from the bowels of the trade union movement. I am a typical creature of the movement.' The psychologically convincing Prescott, surely, is the one who said in May 1994, 'I don't believe in ditching Clause Four because I do believe there is a role for public ownership'; the one who told *Labour and Trade Union Review 1990* what he would do with the Tories' employment reforms: 'There's nothing you can keep of this legislation. It all has to go.'

We are told by New Labour and New Blair that a minimum wage would not cost jobs. But Ur-Prescott gave the game away on Sky TV on 18 March 1992: 'I think you have to accept that there will be some shake-out of jobs in certain areas.' Again, Tony Blair has been ingeniously vague about what New Labour would do to our tax bills. He's not saying anything on tax, except that the Tories have lied and robbed.

But wait, here is Prescott, only last year: 'There's certainly going to be a higher top rate than we have . . . You can argue about what that might be, but if we want a fair tax system, you're certainly going to have that.'

And which is the real Labour policy on nationalisation? Tony Blair's office told me that suggestions that Labour might take control of some industries were 'rubbish'. But according to the master mariner and deputy leader in the *Morning Star* 30 August 1986, 'The public utilities should be returned to public ownership and there should be state intervention where capitalism fails . . .' Or take Frank Dobson, who said in the House on 2 July 1991, 'We have said all along that we will bring the National Grid Company back into public ownership. It will be a high priority, I assure Hon. Members.' Margaret Beckett, Robin Cook, Tony Blair, Ann Taylor: all have called for water to be returned to the state sector.

As for their policy on the single currency, well, the

answer is Yes. As Blair put it in the House of Commons, 'The answer is unequivocally Yes;' or, as Prescott said on the *Today Programme* on 15 June 1991, 'Yes, we're against a single currency.'

Now it will be up to Jeremy Hanley, or whoever succeeds him as party chairman, to persuade the electorate that New Labour is really Old Labour, that they are still the same under the skin. It is, he must suggest, a little like the film *Invasion of the Body Snatchers*. They have seized a plausible guise, while underneath are invisibly gibbering creatures from political outer space.

In fairness to Labour, the party is changing under Blair. Some leftish MPs report that they receive the odd letter of protest from constituents lamenting the loss of radicalism. Old-fashioned constituency associations have been deeply offended by the Blairite decision that 50 per cent of all candidates must be women; and a revolt is brewing on that score. But those 80,000 new members who have joined since he became leader are, it is said, diluting the hard-left activists.

It should be recorded, too, that some of the old-style Labour Left don't really believe that the U-turn will become an S-bend when New Labour comes to power. 'It's like Gorbachev's Communist Party in the Soviet Union,' says one sad and distinguished Labour MP. 'They just go along with whatever the leader says.' They've been lobotomised by defeat, he argues. The Shadow Cabinet are not only docile now, they would be docile in office.

'Maybe I'm too pessimistic, but I don't think John Prescott is going to kick over the traces once he gets into power. John is a good guy but he loves his Jaguar. Meacher has never really rebelled. Cook will go along with almost anything.'

Remember, though, that these are criticisms from the Labour Left. For believers in common sense, there is only one way to test whether New Labour's conversion is sincere, and that is to put the following questions to Blair and Co:

Will you reduce the burden on posterity by following the Government in encouraging private pensions? Will you discourage spongers by keeping the Jobseeker's Allowance? Will you maintain Mr Lilley's attempts to stop malingerers from claiming Disability Benefit? Will you keep compulsory competitive tendering for local authorities?

I believe the answer to all those questions, and others like them, is No. That is a fact that should be exposed. Mr Gordon Brown is apparently telling his friends that Labour has done enough allaying of middle-class fears. Soon, he says, Labour will have to spell out its positive policies.

Come on, New Labour. Now is the time to go on the offensive and tell us what you really think. It is the Tories' only hope.

Major's position became so grim that he finally turned on his critics, resigned as leader of the Conservative Party, and dared them to challenge him. John Redwood did, and lost.

So much for the pen and dagger men

Once the drumming of feet had died away last night in the committee corridor, and mobile telephones of the TV men had ceased to beep like crickets, a soft noise could just be heard, if you strained your ears, in the newspaper bureaux above the ministerial corridor. It was the gentle mastication of humble pie on the part of much of that which used to be called Fleet Street, and – for there is no point in denying it – your reporter had a mouthful himself.

It was Major One, Hacks Nil. 'Not for the first time the pundits and commentators have been absolutely routed!' said Gillian Shephard. And the Prime Minister himself was careful, in the final words of his triumphant statement on the steps of Number Ten, to plant his foot figuratively on the mounded bellies of his real adversaries; not in Westminster, he said, not in the constituencies – no, he knew where the real enemy was:

'This has been settled in Westminster, not by commentators outside Westminster with their own particular views!' he cried. Before the result was flashed through the steaming committee corridor, and before it was clear that Mr Major was at least reasonably safe, the view of Major loyalists about the behaviour of the press was barely printable.

In the lobby corridor shortly before the result, I was confronted by one normally genial minister whose face went red as he abused the stance taken by your correspondent, with a string of profanities that turned heads for 20 yards. In the run-up to this leadership election, ministers have believed that there is what Harold Wilson called 'a small group of politically motivated men', Right-wing journalists in cahoots with the parliamentary Eurosceptics, determined to bring down the Prime Minister.

For the last four years, they believe they have launched their cowardly darts against John Major, actuated either by a misplaced intellectual snobbery or resentment that he is not Mrs Thatcher.

These pinpricks, though, have been nothing to the extraordinary barrage of artillery trained on Mr Major yesterday by what was once the loyal Conservative press. *The Daily Telegraph*, *The Times*, the *Daily Mail*, and almost all the rest of Fleet Street bar the *Financial Times* and the *Daily Express*, were convinced that Mr Major was leading his party to defeat in the next general election, and that he should therefore go. Such 'disloyalty' has enraged ministers. They see journalists as grossly inflated and self-important figures, irresponsible bomb-throwers.

They would sever all relations, were it not for the reality that, as with other terrorists, politicians have no choice but to talk to them. Across much of the party in the country, there is a parallel outrage at the behaviour of the press.

'Why can't you give John Major credit for what he has done?' local Tories demand. 'Why is he never congratulated for his success in bringing about sustainable economic growth and delivering the makings of a lasting settlement in Northern Ireland?'

Why indeed? Why has he taken such a pasting? Before we discuss the objections of principle to John Major's premiership, we should not forget the iron law of Fleet Street: you build 'em up in order to knock 'em down.

When John Major was a younger MP and rising fast, he cultivated political editors. Members of the Downing Street lobby say he was charming, personable, a man who caught your Christian name first bounce and lobbed it back. He was always on everyone's reshuffle list as a man likely to make the Cabinet. And once he had attained great office, and was no longer able to cultivate journalists with the same familiarity, it was always likely that relations would decay.

As Prime Minister, his great attraction was initially his very ordinariness, his decency, expressed in his campaign for a 'classless society'. But it is the professional deformation of journalists on broadsheet newspapers to be in search of Grand Ideas for their columns, and John Major did not provide them. They were never likely to be satisfied with a Major 'vision of Britain' which seemed to revolve around the frequency with which lavatory facilities occurred on motorways. They began to say that Mr Major had no real ideological backbone; and it was his mistake to be too sensitive to these jibes.

Unlike Mrs Thatcher, who some would say was eventually toppled because she failed to listen to her critics in the press, Mr Major listened too much. He seemed to care too intimately what was written about him by men he imagined sitting in book-lined rooms, with fancy waistcoats and fancy degrees.

He was known to be wounded by impertinent pseudo-psychological profiles. The journalists smelled vulnerability, and they piled on their attacks more thickly, characterising him, without much evidence, as a man who might wear his shirt tucked into his underpants.

Mr Major's best defence – and it has proved highly effective – is to inspire feelings of sympathy. Unlike Mrs Thatcher, though, he did not inspire fear; and to that extent Mr Major must blame himself for the way some back-benchers and the press engaged in bidding each other up in their insolence.

All this though is in a sense secondary. The press can in no way be blamed for the axial moment of Mr Major's prime ministership, when the pound crashed out of the Exchange Rate Mechanism. One can blame the Bundesbank for failing to do enough to help; one can blame the speculators.

One might conceivably follow Douglas Hurd, and blame *The Sunday Telegraph* for encouraging the Danes to vote No in 1992, and so triggering the Maastricht crisis. But one cannot blame Fleet Street for the decisions of Messrs Major and Lamont to stay in the ERM long after it had ceased to be economically defensible, squandering billions and sending thousands of businesses to the wall.

It was not the press which landed some of the most damaging blows to the Prime Minister's authority. It was

Norman Lamont, his former Chancellor and campaign manager, who said in the House of Commons, that he gave the impression of 'being in office but not in power'. It was Tony Blair who said that 'I lead my party, while he follows his.' Above all, the row over Europe has not been a mere figment of the imagination of the press.

It has been obvious to a wide section of his backbenchers – not least the 89 who voted for John Redwood – that the Prime Minister's March 1 statement on the single currency was less than decisive. The press did not cause the Conservative Party to plunge to defeat in the local and European elections.

The press has the power to convey its own public dissatisfaction to the Prime Minister. But it does not have the power to break him. Last night's result proved that.

And still the middle-of-the-roaders were flocking to Blair.

Who *are* all these people?

The taxi throbs deep into the evening of darkest Dulwich, into SE22. It is a voyage of discovery. I have come in search of a new and mysterious group of people whose importance is known, but whose characteristics are, as yet, imperfectly understood by political science. 'No one knows who these people are,' one of Tony Blair's advisers confessed to me. 'We're rather curious, actually.'

As of this month, (September, 1995) the Labour Party claims to have 351,000 members, almost doubling its strength in 15 months; a figure all the more remarkable when you reflect that across Europe political party membership has been in chronic decline. Gone is the mass adherence to Christian Democracy and Social Democracy, and their counterparts in Britain, which gave the Labour Party a million members and the Tories an amazing 2.8 million in 1952. These days we devote our energies to the RSPB, to campaigning for Aids sufferers, to chaining ourselves to lorries carrying veal calves.

Only one party is bucking the trend, and most of its 100,000 new signings in the last year are attributed to one man: his flashing eyes, his floating hair, his chipped front tooth. When Tony Blair addresses the Labour Party conference next week, much will be made of the 'head and shoulders' argument: that Blair may indeed be a social democrat, but that the party as a whole has failed to move, and remains wedded to punitive redistribution and public spending. In the run-up to the next election, that must be the chief burden of Tory propaganda.

So it will be all the more vital for Blair to prove that the party *is* changing, from the grassroots up. The taxi stops at a tiny terraced house in Grove Vale. We are there: at the HQ of the Dulwich Labour Party, where they are recording 80 new members per month. Through the dusty front-room window, I can see the shadowy forms of men and women of various ages. On closer inspection, they are drinking wine and orange juice.

They are not so very different from you and me, in tidy sweaters and skirts. These are the specimens, the new members of the Labour Party, very kindly assembled for me by Tessa Jowell, MP for East Dulwich, who is not only highly energetic and intelligent but also 'close to Tony'. As Peter Snow likes to say when the general election results are coming in, this is only a first sample. The reader is warned that our methods are not, cannot be scientific. But after spending more than an hour drinking Bulgarian Merlot and eating taco crisps with about a dozen new members, it seems that Blair is right to say that the party is changing. Blair's old Labour deputy, John Prescott, were he here, would hang his head; and yet there seems no reason, *prima facie*, for Mr Major to be altogether discouraged.

On the wall is a nicotine-stained map of the constituency and a 1930s poster with the slogan 'Tomorrow – when Labour Rules', depicting the workers in various attitudes of triumph. In the past, perhaps, this was the place for cloth-capped harangues and pipe-fuelled disputations about free collective bargaining. No longer. Barbara Richardson, a JP in her mid-40s with short hair and a cerise suit, tells me she has to push on shortly, and so briefly explains why she joined new Labour. She had been a social worker in the area (as had Tessa Jowell) and a member of the Norwood Labour Party. But she had despaired.

There was 'Red' Ted Knight. There was the way the party would not let her send her children to an independent school. And there was Neil Kinnock. 'I couldn't stand Neil Kinnock,' she says, and admits she feels guilty for saying so. Her view is shared, with less intensity, by a couple of others here. 'I was driven into the arms of the SDP – and I met some very nice people in the SDP,' says Barbara. So why did she rejoin? Unprompted, she hits the coconut: 'It was mainly because of Tony Blair'; which is the reason given by a quarter of new members in an April survey by *Labour Party News*.

It is also the reason given by Tom Ward, a bearded 19-year-old Carthusian wearing a Jim Beam T-shirt, who is just going up to Pembroke College, Oxford. 'I wanted to be more of an activist, and Blair made it acceptable to someone with a public-school background,' he says. At this point Ward is interrupted by John McTernan, the man acting as my cicerone in the world of the Dulwich Labour Party.

McTernan is a sophisticated Scot who was head of the debating Union at Edinburgh University, and who is now a big wheel in the local party. He wants to make sure I have got the point. 'This,' he exclaims, with the excitement of a scientist showing a visitor the world's first cyclotron, 'is New Labour! Tony Blair is the issue,' he continues. 'He is the first political leader in Britain since Margaret Thatcher whose distinctive social values could change the way we live our lives.'

That is a bold assertion. It is true that there must be many people who would have been quite uninterested in British politics had it not been for Mrs Thatcher. Is Blair about to re-order political life in the same way? I try the proposition on one of the younger types, a grinning chap of 30 wearing a beige leather jacket. He is called John Balme and was educated 'at the same school as Mrs Thatcher's son' (Harrow) before reading classics at King's College, London. Mr McTernan put it to me, 'New Labour comes from an interesting mix of backgrounds.'

Balme, it seems, joined less out of admiration for Tony Blair than out of respect for the memory of John Smith, whom he describes as 'the greatest prime minister we never had'. Certainly, Balme is enthusiastic about Blair. But it would be an exaggeration to say he is enthused by Blair's ideology. 'I think he could nail something down,' he says, meaning, for instance, that Blair could spell out what he intends to do with the privatised industries. But other new members admit they are rather unclear as to what their leader really represents.

'I still haven't quite been able to place him,' says Ian Richardson, a 72-year-old former *Birmingham Post* journalist wearing a woolly tie and stout brown shoes. Richardson has drifted across the political map. He almost became a communist in the 1930s. He voted for the Tories twice in the 1950s and once, to his shame, for Mrs Thatcher. But he describes himself as 'temperamentally a Labour man'. Again, though, he does not appear to hunger for any specific agenda from Mr Blair.

He is actuated more by rage against the Tories. I should have mentioned rage earlier. It is almost universal here. 'I'd like to shoot them all,' says Richardson, meaning all Tory ministers. He is angry about what he sees as the running down of the NHS. 'I have a handicapped child and I am 72,' he says in his educated voice. 'If I became even more Alzheimerish I might be faced with the possibility of having to sell my house. Where's the money for the oil and gas?' he demands, and there is a terrific amen-ing.

When I feel obliged to point out, like some hapless Tory candidate, that the economy is recovering, unemployment falling, 3 per cent growth, lots of lovely cheap houses, I come under fire from Judith Fitton, a woman in a blue denim dress who used to be first flute in the English National Orchestra and who has two grown-up children. 'You're sort of all I'm all right, Jack, aren't you?' she says consideringly. 'You don't know what it's like to try and get housing.'

The white-haired and white-sweatered curator of the River and Rowing Museum at Henley on Thames is also 'angry'. Mr Chris Dodd is in a strop because the Millennium Commission has failed to stump up for his project.

'It's their incompetence and their inability to take their hands off things,' says William Millinchip, another ex-journalist.

'Homeless beggars are something you associate with the Third World,' says Jenny Wick, a sweet-faced 60-year-old who is just dashing off to her swimming class.

'What has got my goat,' says Dodd, 'is that I don't believe anything this Government says.'

'My 80-year-old aunt in Halifax hasn't got any water,' says Jenny.

What we have here is nothing more original than middle-class leftish whingeing against the Government. All these folk here tonight have probably come from the slightly swankier Ruskin ward of Dulwich, with its semi-detached Edwardian houses. According to Tessa Jowell, her association has just been joined by the former British ambassador to Bogota and the deputy women's editor of the *Sunday Express*. They are decent, caring people who have decided that they can help their fellow man, and perhaps themselves, by putting Labour in power.

That does not mean that they were ever natural Tories, or that Mr Major need utterly despair. Successful though the Labour membership drive is, the party is only now approaching the membership levels of 1983; and at least a third of all the recruits are what Mr Blair's office describes as 'SDP retreads'. What these people in Dulwich have in common, it seems to me, is that they are angry middle-grounders who have given up on the idea of a centre party and found that Labour membership is no longer socially embarrassing. Almost all of them have at one time voted either SDP or Liberal.

It is not good news for the Tories, certainly; but it is worse news, surely, for Mr Ashdown. 'That's the strength of Labour's new membership,' explains McTernan. 'We're coming back to our true home.' If Mr Blair wants to turn his party into an SDP Mark II, he will have these people's undying support.

At one stage even the Daily Telegraph editorial column seemed half to succumb.

The 'new' gospel

Anthony Charles Lynton Blair is an attractive politician, who yesterday delivered a calculating and confident speech expressed at times in the hot-gospelling language of the star of a religious rock musical. Many will have been pleased to hear a politician infuse his discourse with such moral vigour, even if they may be irritated to hear Mr Blair proclaim that socialists have a monopoly on morality. Like most of the Labour leader's speeches, this sermon was pitched squarely at the disgruntled middle classes, and most of it could have come from the lips of a One-Nation Tory.

Mr Blair pledged to swell the ranks of policemen on the beat, for instance; and he appealed to traditional conservatives by suggesting that the sexual revolution had produced insecurity and spiritual doubt. To the remaining Scargillites in the hall at Brighton, he gave a warning that 'New Labour' was the party of patriotism and national unity, not class warfare on behalf of the international proletariat. The speech owed less, though, to Disraeli and John F Kennedy, than it did to the last Labour leader to rival Mr Blair in cleverness and sleight of hand.

In the year of Lord Wilson's death, and with Mary Wilson sitting behind him, Mr Blair paid conscious homage to Harold Wilson's 1963 pledge to deliver a new Britain forged in the white heat of the technological revolution. He echoed Harold Wilson, too, in the fundamental fraudulence of his rhetoric. 'Feel New Britain come alive,' rhapsodised Mr Blair. 'Feel the vitality that can course through this country's veins and make it young again.' It was not quite clear, however, what elixir was on offer. Apart from the renationalisation of British Rail, there was one new concrete promise: that every child of five, six or seven shall be educated in a class of fewer than 30 pupils. This, said the Fettes-educated Mr Blair, would be paid for by cancelling the assisted places scheme, and the chance of thousands of children to attend independent schools.

Mr Blair's central economic proposition was that the nation would be rejuvenated by the use of the information superhighway, the fashionable system of electronic communication. Never mind the irony that British Telecom, which would supply the network's infrastructure, would never have been privatised under Labour. Important though the information superhighway may be, it hardly amounts to a credible cornerstone for an economic strategy; and yet that is where it stood in Mr Blair's 'vision'.

For the rest, the Blair prescription for recreating a 'young' Britain was at best dubious. Labour would revivify the constitution by creating new tiers of bureaucracy in the form of regional assemblies for Scotland and Wales.

Businesses already groaning beneath the weight of regulation, would face, as *The Daily Telegraph* revealed yesterday, the extra costs of Labour's 'agenda for rights at work', including the Social Chapter. On the central question of how Labour's aims would be funded without an explosion in public spending, Mr Blair was silent.

As a piece of inspirational guff, the speech rated an alpha. As a coherent economic and political call to arms, it was less than satisfying.

And so were the civil servants.

The permanent secretaries are preparing to demonstrate their permanence

So confident is Tony Blair of obtaining power in the next 18 months that he is already demanding tuition in how to run the country. In what is described as an unprecedented move, a group of ex-permanent secretaries has volunteered to give the Shadow Cabinet a series of seminars entitled 'The Hardware and Software of State: Whitehall under a Future Labour Government'. Guided by Sir Nicholas Monck, formerly Michael Portillo's permanent secretary at the Department of Employment, Blair will learn the tricks of his most wily opponents. These are not the putative Tory Opposition. Of course not.

No, Sir Nicholas will be telling Blair and Co. how to foil the mandarinate. Look down the list of the permanent secretaries, by now bristling with knighthoods bestowed by the grateful Tories. These are men who will have known nothing but a Conservative administration for 18 years. For nigh on two decades they will have been preparing and executing government policy, on everything from privatisation to opting-out of schools. By all normal laws of human nature, they should have become politically acculturated: if not Thatcherised, then at least Torified.

Imagine, purely for the sake of illustrating their state of mind, that a great national newspaper was about to undergo a parallel convulsion. Suppose that a change of corporate governance was at hand, after a decade or more in which the agenda and style have been relatively clear. For the senior executives who will be asked to implement the revolution, there is only one question that really matters. Among the Sir Humphreys of the op-ed department, the alpha minds of the leader-writers' desk, and among the purring Rolls-Royces of the features and news departments, the issue is one of survival.

What, they will be asking themselves, are my chances of hanging on to my slightly ridiculous title and my chauffeur-driven car? They hear some of their colleagues talk longingly of 'geysers of blood', and they wonder whether their faces will suit the political disposition of the new regime. And so it is in Whitehall. Some senior Labour Party figures have already promised that 'there will be no bloodbath'. There again, there are those in the Labour movement who smack their lips at the prospect of vendetta.

At Lord Wilson's funeral, Lady Falkender was seen to

grab Tony Blair, point at the Cabinet Secretary and head of the Home Civil Service, Sir Robin Butler, and say, 'That is the kind of man you have got to get rid of.' As with newspaper offices, memories in Whitehall go back with a shudder to the last change of government. For the first six months of Lady Thatcher's tenure, a kind of truce prevailed. Then it became clear to the Treasury mandarins, who had helped preside over this country's most lamentable post-war economic performance, that they had a phenomenon on their hands.

Sir Douglas Wass, the Permanent Secretary to the Treasury, was to be heard at dinner parties in 1980 saying things like, 'We're all Keynesians here, but we've done our best to follow the government line'; and, 'We're doing our best, but we don't think it will work.' For this eeyoreish talk, he was unsurprisingly punished by the promotion of an outsider, an academic economist called Terence Burns, to cut the ground from beneath him. Well, what future now under Blair for Sir Terry, the man who was at the very epicentre of Thatcherite economics?

I inquired of some very, very senior civil servants, and the view is that 'Teflon Tel' will be fine. A man, after all, who can survive the complete implosion of government economic policy on 16 September 1992, can probably survive a mere change of government. And indeed, so will all these mandarins, apparently, be fine. Andrew Turnbull, the perm sec at the Department of the Environment and vaguely thought of as a Thatcherite, recently gave a paper at the Civil Service College at Sunningdale on 'The Impact of Government Policies' in which, perhaps with a trace of cunning, he moaned about the 'Underclass'.

Hayden Phillips, the socially ubiquitous and shotgun-toting perm sec at the Department of National Heritage, is even touted as Labour's successor to Sir Robin (who is due to retire, regardless of Lady Falkender's Black Spot).

As one Labour MP close to Blair has put it, 'We're all very fond of Hayden.' Partly this prospect of survival is assisted by the immense flexibility of the species. I remember being shocked, in 1992, by the fluidity with which certain Foreign Office wallahs began to trim their analysis of Britain's position in Europe to suit their perception, supported by the polls, that Neil Kinnock was about to become the next prime minister.

Mainly, though, there will be no blood-bath in Whitehall because no great intellectual sacrifices will be demanded. It will not require a huge mental contortion to convert from Majorism to Blairism. For those at the Department of Education it will be painful to see the end of opting-out. But testing, the National Curriculum, and other advances will remain; as will privatisation and almost every other Tory improvement As for 'new' Labour's policy on 'Europe', the issue which Malcolm Rifkind last week called the new fault line in British politics, officials admit there may be some temporary embarrassment.

One week, Mr Stephen Wall, our man in Brussels, will be bashing the foreigners furiously, and refusing to accept the slightest expansion of Qualified Majority Voting in the intergovernmental conference. The next week, after the election, he will suddenly announce to his counterparts that Britain has not the slightest compunction about giving up the veto. But as one Foreign Office man puts it, 'That won't matter, as long as they understand the way we're playing it.'

That is the kind of breezy machiavellianism which has assured and will assure the success of the British bureaucrat. Indeed, in spite of these seminars being offered to Blair by turncoat ex-perm secs, it is one of the consolations for those contemplating a Labour government, that the senior civil servants will continue, at least for a while, to run the show. If only the same were true for newspapers.

It would be a shame, though, to forget John Major's solid achievements not least the reviving of the peace process in Northern Ireland (December 1995). Bill Clinton was keen to help.

Hello Mr Adams

It was about 10 minutes to midday, and an unemployed ex-barman and amateur poet was sitting in the tearoom at the back of McErlean's Bakery in the Falls Road, Belfast.

Suddenly the old biddies seated at tables around him were on their feet, clucking in amazement.

Just fancy! Of all the little eateries in the Falls Road for Gerry Adams to pick for a cup of coffee, he had lit upon the very one to be graced in an impromptu visit by the President of the United States.

The President, his wife Hillary and their 40-car motorcade had been rolling past on the way to East Belfast, and he'd suddenly conceived a desire to pop into this particular shop – and who should be there but his old acquaintance from the White House, the bearded leader of Sinn Fein! The White House coyly described the encounter as 'semi-spontaneous'.

One of the bakery's staff, Pauline Leonard, was trying afterwards half-heartedly to maintain the fiction of coincidence. 'I don't know if it was pre-arranged or not,' she said. 'We didn't know he was going to call in until about 10 or 15 minutes before, when they came and told us.'

'Oh, he was very pleasant,' said Mrs Leonard of the President. 'He shook hands with us all.' In the first visit of a sitting US president to Belfast, Mr Clinton then went out for a photo-call with Mr Adams – though there was no official video footage of the event. Yesterday's motorcade was so long, and the narrow Falls Road so crowded, that the White House 'pool' camera crew could not fight its way through in time to capture the moment. It was left to a passer-by to snap The Handshake.

The shopgirls then gave the President some potato cake, suitable either for frying or toasting, as well as wheaten bread and cakes in a paper bag. And that cleared up one of the mysteries of the President's visit.

Until he stopped his Cadillac in the Catholic Falls, no one quite understood why the most powerful man on earth had earlier spent £3 on four apples and a bunch of chrysanthemums in Violet's, a fruiterers on the Protestant Shankill.

'It was a complete shock. He paid for them himself, and he didn't take his change,' said Violet Clarke, the proprietor. She could not guess that it was all part of the White House's scrupulous attention to balance.

It was to be apples from the loyalists, and potato cake from the nationalists. If Mr Clinton was to meet the political leader of one of the world's most feared terrorist organisations in a teashop, it was a good idea to take in a loyalist grocer's first.

By the end of the day, the balancing act had paid off, as a crowd of 50,000 gathered in Donegal Square, Belfast, to give him a rock star welcome. And as the multitudes were seized by Clintomania, one suddenly realised that the President had performed an amazing political conjuring trick.

Presented for the first time with the chance of truly celebrating 15 months of peace, it was he, William Jefferson Clinton, who was reaping the plaudits, and was bathed in the warmth of their thanks: not John Major, nor John Bruton, nor Albert Reynolds, nor any of the other true protagonists of the ceasefire.

It was sheer effrontery, from a man who is mainly on the hunt for Irish-American votes. But it had a logic. In a still divided province, the American President is almost the only statesman capable of bridging the gap.

As the election grew closer, I made the best case I could.

Don't let it be mourning after the night before

It's early one Friday morning in April next year. As you come to the surface you are conscious of a sense of doom. The television is still burbling faintly. There are empty cans of beer on the floor. Cigarette ash has been ground into the carpet. You can't quite place what is troubling you. Then you remember. It was election night last night, and it has been won by ... Omigosh ... Ouch ...

It has been won by the Tories. You cradle your head in your hands. The shock. Above all, the tedium. You voted for them yourself, of course, furtively, nose held. But you never expected so many others to do the same. There is Michael Howard, Michael Heseltine, the whole lot of them, grinning like idiots on *Breakfast News*. Unpunished. Unchastened. Unbowed.

All those familiar Tory ministers, you realise, are going to hang on to their Rovers and their Red Boxes and their Zeppelin-like self-esteem. With shaking hands, you have a cup of coffee. Yes, they are going to be ruling us for another five years, complacent, convinced as ever that they are the natural party of government. All that so-called sleaze will go unpunished. The party whose members took cash for questions is back in power.

No one, in the end, rubbed the Tories' noses in it for what they allegedly did to the housing market, or the creation of negative equity. The electorate at last had the chance to cane them for their incompetence in the 1992 ERM fiasco, and they blew it. Aargh, you groan. Not five years. Not five more years.

Irrationally, you contemplate ringing up the travel agent

to book that ticket to Australia, France, whatever you can afford. Indeed, you notice blearily from the radio that the pound is holding up remarkably well, gone up a few pfennigs, in fact. You mix a pick-me-up of tomato, lemon juice, Worcester sauce and a few other things. Once you have detached your eyes from the far wall and the top of your head from the ceiling, you begin to feel a bit better. You begin to try to count your blessings.

Golly, it occurs to you: no more minimum wage. The polls had been so confidently predicting a Labour victory that you had already made provision to pay your workers at least £4.10 an hour, putting up your costs and greatly reducing your ability to re-invest. Your mood lifts a notch higher at the thought – when suddenly the *Today* programme breaks through your consciousness. Virginia Bottomley is exulting uncontrollably, her voice drowning the protests of Sue MacGregor. You feel a need to press a cold flannel to your temples.

You close your eyes, and then you remember that the Social Chapter won't be coming into force after all. Hmm. None of that mandatory four-week holiday for the staff, none of that ridiculous compulsorily paid paternity leave, none of those extra non-wage costs. That could be vital for a small business like yours, making colourful kitchen tiles with fruit in bas-relief. And then another happy thought strikes you. Your children are at a local grammar school, and you had been dreading that Labour-imposed ballot about abolishing selective admissions. At least that socialist plan is off, and St Olave's can continue to make an effort to be among the best. By this time you are starting to feel quite chipper.

But as you totter towards the bathroom, the head seems to swim and the queasiness returns. It occurs to you that there has been no vengeance on the beastly utility barons with their share options and their salary increases, such as the wretched Mr Bill Fraser of South West Water, whose salary shot up by £67,000 to £164,000 in 1994, plus £63,000 in share options and pensions contributions. And as you run the taps, you curse the Tories for their carelessness in breeding these fat cats and their extortionate water bills. When you sink back into the bath, though, a sort of optimism rises with the steam.

It has to be said, you reflect, that you have been spared Labour's windfall tax on utility profits: quite handy, in view of the fact that you have shares in the utilities yourself. What is more, you won't have to put a proportion of your income into a mandatory state pension fund to be run by Mr Frank Dobson. As you begin to get dressed, it occurs to you fleetingly that, with the Tories in power, the country has a marginally better chance of avoiding the toils of a Frankfurt-run single European currency. And then, at least in theory, the Tories will be tougher than Labour would have been in the next round of negotiations on the Maastricht Treaty. Mr Blair, after all, had vowed 'never to be isolated in Europe'.

Adjusting your tie, you find yourself tentatively whistling the first few bars of the *Chorus of the Hebrew Slaves*. Then you stop in mid-toot, when you remember that the train you are about to take to work will still be privatised in accordance with the Government's complicated rubric. And then you resume your warbling, when you consider that the railway network could scarcely have been worse, and that we have been spared a silly Labour plan to re-nationalise the service.

As you saunter along the sunlit street, it strikes you that the United Kingdom as a whole has escaped destruction at the hands of Blair, and his plan for Scottish devolution. The Tory victory has avoided months of parliamentary torture, as Labour attempted to legislate for a separate tax-raising Scottish assembly. You pause to buy a newspaper, fishing a pound coin from your pocket, and the central point strikes you like a thunderclap.

Even on a relatively modest income, you are better off than you would have been without last night's astonishing reversal of fortune. Sure, you muttered in bitter agreement when Labour accused the Tories of breaking promises on taxation and raising VAT by eight per cent. But never in your wildest dreams did you believe that Labour would be cheaper than the Tories, or would restrain the desire of the unions for pay increases, or take the knife to the soft parts of the welfare state. Now you are to be allowed to keep those Tory tax cuts of late 1996. You will be able to savour the gentle return of economic optimism in 1996; the cash windfalls from the Building Society demutualis-ations; the Tessas. You might even continue to enjoy the slow resurgence of the housing market. And all at once, as it hits you that your savings are probably safer from inflation than they would have been under Labour, you find your hangover has vanished, as when the sun scatters the morning mist.

A wild, surging optimism fills the breast. You even attract glances as you dance a little spring jig. No peerage for Melvyn Bragg! Or Nigel de Gruchy! You have over-come your initial ennui at the idea of a Tory victory, and thought about the advantages. If the Tories are to have any chance of victory, that is the mental journey that they must hope the voters will take. Except, of course, they must somehow encourage them to take it the day before the election, rather than the day after.

The party is so full of revolutionary defeatists, those who believe in the desirability of extinction at the polls, that the events of the past 10 days have come as something of a shock. Indeed, the Tory rebels are experiencing a kind of cold turkey, as they are asked to turn their fire on Labour's hypocrisy on education rather than Tory hypocrisy on Europe. No one, looking at the opinion polls, would pretend that there is a strong probability of waking up next April and finding the Tories still there. But if Labour comes to power, it will be a different kind of hangover altogether.

But the Tories seemed powerless to resist, as misfortunes rained upon them. The Scott report was not as bad as had been predicted, but it was bad.

Small earthquake in the Commons: no casualties

It was just after Robin Cook sat down at 4.15pm that the House of Commons seemed to lose it altogether. The noise boiled and burst through the galleries, as Labour MPs flailed themselves with copies of the Scott report, like Islamic fundamentalists at an ayatollah's funeral.

It was louder than the Italian chamber of deputies. The Russian parliament has seen nothing like it. It was like some demented Asian bourse. Yes, sometimes the House of Commons lives up to expectations.

As MPs learned, sentence by sentence, exactly what was in the Scott report, the reputations of senior ministers seemed to ebb and flow like gold, or commodities, or the Hang Seng index.

'Buy Waldegraves', the Tories appeared to roar, waving their order papers, as Lang mounted his defence, showing that the Chief Secretary had no intention of deceiving the House. And then, as other MPs drew attention to paragraph D4.42, and other embarrassing conclusions of Sir Richard Scott, selling fever swept the Labour benches. 'Sell Lyell! Sell, sell, sell,' screamed the Labour Nikkei.

Down, down, down sank the ministerial reputations, while faces lengthened on the Tory benches. And so it went on into the evening, as Westminster eventually realised that, after three and a quarter years, and after ministers have had the chance to make their own comments, the Scott report is positively biblical.

It is like the collected speeches of Winston Churchill. You can find a text within it to support any proposition you choose.

The report was first glimpsed by the public at 3pm through the plate glass of the Department of Trade in Queen Victoria Street, as big brown boxes were being loaded to be taken over to the Commons. It was more than the size of a telephone directory. It was five telephone directories, business and residential. 'They reckon a couple of top MPs are going to resign,' said one of the crowd outside St Stephens entrance, with an air of authority.

The House was packed to the gunwales, and no less a person than Miss Esther Rantzen was in the public gallery, perhaps with a view to a new programme called *That's Lies*.

In Prime Minister's Questions at 3.15pm, Mr Major gave the first hint of confidence. 'If either of the ministers have knowingly misled the House, then they cannot stay, and that remains my position.' It seemed unlikely that the Prime Minister would have used such a formula if Sir Richard said any such thing.

At 3.30pm the House was adjourned for 10 minutes as MPs queued in the Lobby to receive their copies. 'Phwargh', groaned one, clutching his back, and within minutes people were fanning through the Commons, toting Sir Richard's *oeuvre* like puffing coolies. As soon as Mr Lang stood up to make his statement at 3.40pm, the whole business of whether or not Mr Robin Cook had long enough to swot up was forgotten. Mr Lang was mounting a one-man blizzard of propaganda, a snow-job of Himalayan proportions.

The Opposition struggled to follow. 'What page?' Labour MPs roared, when Mr Lang told the House that Sir Richard had exonerated the Government of trying to send innocent men to prison. They rifled through the green books in search of killer quotes, raging that the Government's 'digest' failed to help them through the 2,000 pages.

As Mr Lang spoke, a fresh question formed. 'All ministers who signed Public Interest Immunity Certificates did so without any impropriety,' said Mr Lang. Aha, the Labour benches murmured. That might clear Clark, Lilley, Rifkind, Baker, Garel-Jones and Heseltine. But it still seemed to leave one Tory Attorney General on the hook.

What about Sir Nicholas Lyell? What about the man who had not only egged on a reluctant Heseltine to sign the certificates, but who had failed to communicate Hezza's reservations to the trial judge?

'There is no doubt that he acted with complete propriety and integrity,' said Mr Lang. The Tories cheered, and Mr Heseltine cheered very slightly. If Sir Nicholas was allegedly in the clear, that left Labour still trying for the real prize.

William Waldegrave sat intent, thumb on chin, index finger on cheek. This was the decisive moment. As Mr Lang turned to the question of the concealed change in the guidelines, George Galloway (Lab, Glasgow Hillhead) pretended to hang himself with his own tie. 'Guilty as charged!' the cries rang out from Labour benches. 'Guilty! Guilty!'

But Mr Lang had ready the talisman phrase that the Tories believe will save Mr Waldegrave's political life. Waldegrave, he said, citing the report, 'had no duplicitous intention'.

Mr Lang turned his fire on Robin Cook. The Tory benches had been well primed. 'Resign! Resign!' they chorused, as he accused the shadow foreign secretary of making scurrilous and unfounded accusations. The crucial point was that Sir Richard has accepted that ministers did not have what legal folk called the *mens rea*. They may have misled Parliament. But they did not intend to mislead Parliament.

At least one Tory is ready to revolt over the report, and perhaps even give up the whip.

But by late last night, it was pretty clear that Mr Waldegrave and Sir Nicholas were hanging on by more than their fingers. MPs, journalists and spin-doctors were still poring over the report's text in a state of rabbinical absorption, searching for that one lethal phrase which meant that, in the judge's opinion, Mr Waldegrave and Sir Nicholas had acted in bad faith. It was not there.

Downing Street were already calling the Wykehamist 'Lord Chief Justice Scott', exciting wild speculation that there was some plan to promote him.

But it must be wondered whether judges remain as popular with Labour as they have latterly become.

Under fire for the BSE disaster, Mr Major launched a curious jihad on Brussels. Cry havoc! and let slip the cows of war . . .

Do these little Europeans know how the EU works?

Take that. And that. And that. The siege of Brussels began in earnest yesterday (May 28 1996). Only yards from where I sit in the giant Justus Lipsius building, ministers have been firing their first salvoes in the great beef war of 1996, and the cordite lingers. Over the top they went,

Roger Freeman, Lynda Chalker and Phillip Oppenheim, with the war yodel on their lips: Eat our beef, you pasty-faced cowards!

One by one they fell beneath the British assault, the latest madcap plans of the Community. With a single how-itzer shot Freeman announced that he had 'placed a general reserve on items 3a, 4 and 7' of the meeting of industry ministers. And that was it! A Brussels directive on the health of cacti and other ornamental plants was killed.

At a stroke, Britain's new Mr Niet stymied plans to harmonise regulations on cement and bricks, while Lynda Chalker brought low a scheme to help you get an emer-gency passport in Third World countries, if you lose the other one, and then put an Aids scheme on ice. It was grand, I tell you. Gentlemen of England now abed will think themselves accursed they were not here. 'Ere we go, 'ere we go, 'ere we go. The Government have at last stood forth, clad in Union flag boxer shorts, to avenge the insult done to British beef, and all that is jingoistic in the British soul will approve.

And the greater the enthusiasm of the tabloid press and among patriotic members of the British public, the greater, of course, the disgust of the liberal elite. It is ridiculous popgunboat diplomacy, says George Walden, Tory MP for Buckingham, threatening to resign from a party which insists, he says, on waving 'little plastic Union Jacks', and so to annihilate the Government's majority.

It is just so 'embarrassing', says the *Economist*. The whole business makes the editor of this supposedly free-trading paper want to curl up and die. My dear! It's just too, too dreadful, says Hugo Young in the *Guardian*. Cactus health! So-called 'Europhile' Tory MPs warn that they will not allow the erstwhile party of Europe to slide any further towards a strident and petty nationalism. Some Government ministers signal that they are not happy with the policy, and wonder where it is heading. Whatever will they think of us? demands the *Economist*'s editorial. What will happen to Britain's reputation abroad?

The more one listens to this moaning about 'reputation' and Britain's 'international standing', the more one wonders whether these *bien-pensants* have any idea how the Community works. Yesterday I did not notice any serious antipathy towards Britain. I *did* hear warnings that the non-cooperation strategy might not work. But there were no hysterical recriminations; no recriminations whatsoever. That is for the excellent reason that our Community partners have seen it all before, though not from Britain. George Walden, I have news for you. Before you resign in disgust at the Government's petty obstructionism let me remind you of how France behaves.

France blocked a Gatt deal for three years, depriving the planet of a trillion dollars' worth of growth, because of some notional future damage the deal might do to the economic interests of her farmers. Britain's beef industry is haemorrhaging money; the beef crisis is costing the Exchequer billions, now, in real time; and because the Government temporarily blocks a directive on cactus health, it is damned as xenophobic. Nobody accused the French of xenophobia when they were seen to be standing up for their national interests.

No French politician would dream of succumbing to the mushy-minded inversion that has beset the British establishment since Gladstone, that in any dispute their country is more likely to be in the wrong. Then we are told that Britain's 'xenophobia' is worse than France's obstructionism, because the Government is now committed randomly to block every item on the Community agenda. To thwart a Gatt deal is one thing, apparently; to impede the councils of Brussels is heinous, especially if electoral considerations are suspected.

Does the editor of the *Economist* not read the dispatches of his own correspondents? The Germans delayed the negotiations on the Maastricht Treaty *for a whole year* because Chancellor Kohl was worried about his elections. Has everyone forgotten how the Spanish blocked the EU membership of the Nordic countries for so many months, until Felipe Gonzalez received a satisfactory quantity of extra fish (mainly at British expense)? Does no one remember how the Italians dragged out their gripes over milk quotas – even though they were guilty of state-sponsored fraud – and so delayed an agreement on the EU budget?

Don't talk to me about xenophobia. Before the German *land* elections on March 24, there were signs in the streets of Munich advertising a political party whose slogan is 'Germany is also for the Germans'. There are more chilling forms of xenophobia than the *Sun*'s crusade for British beef.

In any other country but Britain there would be something absurd in the spectacle of educated people holding their handkerchiefs to their noses and wishing the earth would swallow them up, just because they behold ministers trying to rectify an injustice against a great national industry. The point is that Britain is in the right.

The Government made a Horlicks of an announcement about new evidence – so far unverified – which might link BSE with a fantastically rare human brain disease. This Horlicks was turned into a full-dress disaster by an irrational EU decision to ban British beef, which compounded public anxiety and led to a precipitate fall in consumption, especially on the Continent.

If it can do anything to lift that ban, the policy of non-co-operation will be right. It is an incidental attraction of the policy, but only incidental, if it exposes Labour's bad faith on Europe; for the policy helps to tease out the hypocrisy of a natural Euro-sceptic like Robin Cook. He was yesterday tying himself in knots, trying to sound at once supportive of the Government's tough stance 'in the national interest', yet somehow disapproving of the 'damage' to Britain's 'reputation'.

Mr Cook knows well that there is only one way that the Government can damage its reputation abroad now, and that is to back down. The *Economist* and others are right to think that British politicians – not Britain, mind you – are sometimes viewed with exasperation overseas. But they have got the reasons for this upside down.

The reason for this mistrust is that so often the Government has threatened to provoke a crisis and then it has run up the white flag. They saw it happen during the Maastricht talks, where Britain eventually acceded to all the essential revisions demanded. They saw it at the Ioannina meeting of foreign ministers in 1994, where Britain swore it would block a dilution of the national veto, only for Mr Douglas Hurd to capitulate. Now they see it again.

They hear it in the voices of British ministers who say they could be satisfied without a timetable for lifting the ban, only a framework. They hear hesitation. Their impression of weakness is confirmed. Their negotiating position hardens.

We are now in a poker game in which Britain is trying to secure the fastest possible lifting of the ban on British beef, not just the by-products. The strategy can be made to work if British obduracy is such that they feel Britain might do more serious damage to Europe's agenda than that wrought yesterday by Mr Freeman.

That means the Government must mean it. And it must not listen to any bleating about reputation. In the end, the countries with a high reputation are those which do not easily allow themselves to be wronged.

And nothing seemed to arrest the rise of Blair, and this written in 1996.

Hail the New Messiah driven by a Ford Sierra

It was when the blonde sitting two away from John Mortimer started blubbing during the peroration that the uneasy feeling started. And as Tony and Cherie danced down the hall the crowd started clapping in unison like a mob of drunken Russians at a Black Sea circus, and then, as the music thudded on to the hypnotic anthem of 'Thiiings can only get beddah!', the crowd was not just clapping but dancing, bobbing in rhythm like maenads; and then it was that one gazed at the long red banners draped from the balcony, and the beaming images everywhere of the leader, and the uneasy feeling got worse.

Never in its history has the Labour Party succumbed to such Fuhrerprinzip. Never has a Labour leader indulged in such grandiosity, which, in view of Mr Blair's claim that Labour has only 'a thousand days to prepare for a thousand years', invited, however preposterously, comparisons with 1930s Germany. Seldom can any politician, let alone a Labour leader, have indulged in such bare-faced quasi-messianic effrontery as Mr Blair, eyes gleaming, his arms wide like a fullback for the high ball, or like a holy roller about to be clasped into Abraham's bosom, made his 10 vows to his country.

'This is my covenant with the British people,' he said. Maybe it will become regular for our hotgospelling New Labour to echo the language of the Eucharist, but it made me gulp. Does he really think he is some kind of messiah? Is New Labour seriously preparing for a thousand years in office?

Or is the vacuum of content causing Mr Blair to strive too hard, frankly, for oratorical effect? He weaved like a

115

drunken magpie from allusion to allusion, now plucking a phrase from Sir Cecil Spring-Rice, now the whole mawkish lyric of Baddiel and Skinner's Euro '96 song. Lyndon Johnson had his 'Great Society'. Tony Blair promised the 'Decent Society', which is presumably a cheaper version. It is a comment on the lobotomised state of the Labour Party that the hall even managed to clap when he denounced tramps, squatters and down-and-outs, saying 'Try living next door to them!' Most delegates would not have been aware that this was a pinch from Jacques Chirac, who said the same of immigrants.

Now Mr Blair put on the raiment of an Old Testament prophet; now a Spanish freedom fighter; now an 18th-century antislaver. But mostly the clothes he wore were borrowed from the Tories. Gordon Brown was the 'Iron Chancellor' – another uncomfortably Germanic metaphor – who was going to bear down on inflation. Labour was the party of small business. Labour would be tough on crime.

And suddenly it became clear to me why Mr Blair has this born-again, enthused quality. He is a man who has seen a great truth. He told us, with breathtaking candour, how the scales fell from his eyes. 'I can recall vividly the exact moment that I knew the last election was lost,' he said. 'I was canvassing in the Midlands, on an ordinary, suburban estate. I met a man polishing his Ford Sierra. He was a self-employed electrician. His dad always voted Labour, he said. He used to vote Labour, too. But he'd bought his own house now. He'd set up his own business. He was doing quite nicely. "So I've become a Tory," he said . . . In that moment he crystallised for me the basis of our failure.'

Whoever was that man polishing his Sierra – and perhaps he was an angel, an epiphany – he has changed Tony Blair and the Labour Party. In that flash, Mr Blair understood that he was wrong! That he had been talking rot for most of his adult life! That the Tories were right! That people don't want a giant state taking their money and telling them how to run their lives; they want a house and a garden and the right to polish their cars in peace. The Tories know that the one class shrinking in size is the working class, because of the simple desire of people to better themselves.

In that moment by the Sierra, Mr Blair became a Tory! Or at least the better part of him did. For there was precious little socialism in that speech. He wanted to complete the Single European Market, he said; and the crowd clapped, though they cannot possibly have realised that this means introducing competition into energy, telecommunications, posts, transport and other sectors which they, and even Mr Blair, until his awakening by the Sierra, have battled to keep owned by the state. But he wasn't entirely a Tory. He simply parroted the Tory line on the Single Currency; but he has already pledged to abolish the veto in several areas, and indeed, his pledge on the Single Market would seem to involve scrapping border controls – or perhaps he hasn't read the Single European Act.

He wanted to abandon the Tory reforms of the NHS, with consequences for the health budget which he failed to spell out. He wanted to scrap the assisted places scheme. The £100 million raised by this petty mutilation, by which the Fettesian will deprive thousands of children of the chance he had at an independent school, is to be used to take 250,000 youngsters off the dole and put them into makework schemes of moss-picking and origami. In so far as he was neither entirely Tory, nor remotely Old Labour, Mr Blair seemed to be a social authoritarian. He has pledged to ban handguns; and he has decided that children will be made to do their homework. Laggard 11-year-olds will be forced to attend a three-week intensive literacy course in the summer, which seems on the face of it to be a fresh intrusion of the state into family life. It is of a piece, I suppose, with Labour's plan to give the state new rights to crack down on noisy neighbours. This may be popular with the public. But it is not socialism, and it does not amount to a vision.

All this is not to say it was a bad speech. The hall was uplifted. Women wept. John Mortimer clapped, jaw working furiously, and rose to his feet with the rest. There were moments of fine savagery against the Tories. But it was at its heart an empty speech, with moments of pure Peter Sellers. 'As a father, as a leader, as a member of the human family, I ask this question of the future,' he whiffled. Half his sentences had no verb, but consisted of high-sounding abstractions such as 'a new age of achievement'.

It is because he has so little to offer except a watered-down, born-again Toryism mixed with authoritarianism, that Mr Blair was forced to his odd rhetorical expedients. There are two dangers for Labour if he persists with the vacuum until the election. The first is that New Labour will explode like a giant puffball, if people decide he is simply an imitation of the Tories.

A more serious risk is that his tanks will have crossed so far into Right-wing territory that he will find he has neglected his lines of supply. He lamented the fact that Aung San Suu Kyi could not be there, but in the game of political repression, the Burmese police have little to teach New Labour: that much was clear as dissident Peter Shore was brutally forbidden from disrupting the federalist rhapsody of the European debate.

Sooner or later, he will face a serious revolt from those who have not felt what he felt by that Ford Sierra. His rivals, notably Robin Cook, are waiting. Sometime they strew his way, and his sweet praises sing, to borrow his own eccentric comparison. But it would be a different matter if he were to disappoint them in power.

Blair's desert island discs

This is one challenge Tony cannot afford to muff. It's bigger than the duel in Prime Minister's Questions. In its impact on the floating voter, it will be bigger than his party conference speech.

On Friday (November, 1996), Tony records his all-time favourite tracks for *Desert Island Discs*, and the spin doctors know the price of getting it wrong. With six months until the election, Mr Blair could not *possibly* do as he did recently on the Nicky Campbell show on Radio 1.

He may possess a Fender Stratocaster and know how to play it, but he simply cannot again choose *Killer* by Seal, just when his party is cultivating public hysteria about gun control.

Get with it, Tony! As I am sure Peter Mandelson has already told him, he has got to trump John Major for patriotism, after the Prime Minister chose Elgar's *Pomp and Circumstance*. He has got to make up his relative unpopularity with women over 35. He has got to reach out to every taste in the country. If we know Tony, this is how he will do it . . .

(Noise of seagulls, music etc.)

Sue Lawley: My guest this morning is unusual among politicians in that he was once the lead singer of a rock and roll band. In the past two years he has established absolute control of his party, while losing control of his hairstyle. He is, of course, the Leader of the Opposition, Tony Blair. Mr Blair, good morning.

TB: Good morning, Sue.

SL: Mr Blair, you grew up in Scotland, the son of a prosperous solicitor. In fact, there are those who say that if you were to become Prime Minister, it would be the first time someone of your background had held that office for 30 years.

TB: Well, Sue, I'm glad you mentioned that, because things were pretty tough, you know, after my father was taken ill. My mother had to scrape to get by, and so I know what it's like to feel want. (Blair continues in this vein . . . family lived in shed . . . hole in the road . . . ate cardboard boxes etc.) That's why this first record means so much to me.

Music: Dvořák's New World Symphony, from the Hovis ads.

SL: And despite these troubles, the family managed to save enough to send you to Fettes, the famous public school, where you were a bit of a terror on the rugby pitch.

TB: Ha ha. No, but seriously, Sue, I think what I did learn on the rugger pitch, and it's a lesson that has never left me, is the importance of teamwork. (Authoritarian Blair soundbites continue . . . discipline . . . rights and responsibilities . . . elasticated garters . . . come on, Fettes . . . no slacking.)

SL: Next record, please.

TB: And, you know, actually I think it was at school that I first felt those strong patriotic feelings, singing this hymn.

Music: Blake's Jerusalem.

SL: And then Oxford, where you grew such long hair.

TB: Yes, and those days are wonderfully evoked for me by a brilliant band, a Scottish band, and pro-constitutional reform.

Music: The Bay City Rollers, Give a little love, Take a little love.

SL: You became a barrister on going down, joining a Left-wing set of chambers.

TB: Well, quite frankly, I decided to work to heal the Tories' fractured society.

Music: Hey, won't you play one of those somebody-done-somebody-wrong songs.

SL: And you fell in love and married.

TB: Yes, and I suppose you could say what attracted me about Cherie was that she was strong, she was political, she wasn't just going to be someone's little woman.

SL: Next record.

TB: And so this song is really for her.

Music: Don't Cry For Me Argentina.

SL: And then you entered politics, and in an amazingly short time, and in tragic circumstances, became leader of the Labour Party. Most political commentators would say the past two years have been a revolution, scrapping Clause IV and so on.

TB: Well, without false modesty, I do think that's true, and I do think that New Labour is finally coming home to the people. (Blairspeak continues . . . the old false division between Left and Right, etc.)

SL: And does any piece of music sum up this transformation?

TB: It does.

Music: Procol Harum, Whiter Shade of Pale.

SL: *(sigh)* Lovely. But some people are still in the dark about what you really believe in, now that you've admitted Labour was wrong about everything. Is there a final record that expresses your deepest political beliefs?

TB: Well, er . . . you know there is, of course . . .

Music: Happy Birthday To You.

Blair takes a football as his luxury, and several thousand remaindered copies of his book New Britain, My Vision of a Young Country, with which to build a wigwam.

And he was duly elected with an enormous majority.

Blair takes middle road to 'New Europe'

Like scrofulous beggars they queued for the touch of the new king. Kohl, Chirac, the big men of Europe, jostled to have their photograph taken with the winner.

Across the Noordwijk summit yesterday doors were opening, windows were going up, lights were being switched on, dawns were breaking and new eras were being ushered in. 'Blair and Cook use another language when they talk about Europe,' said Hans van Mierlo, the Dutch foreign minister, 'and I like it!'

For the anointed one himself, it wasn't just New Labour and New Britain. His very arrival had inaugurated 'a New Europe'. So how did the other leaders react, Mr Blair? he was asked in the press conference afterwards.

He grinned, the full gigawatt, and with only a passing stab at modesty. 'I am tempted to say, a bit like the British electorate!' And what a change that press conference was from the tension, the massive concentration, the formidable swotting of his predecessor.

Waving aside the convention of a Prime Ministerial statement, Mr Blair launched into questions, opened his shoulders and went for the boundary every shot.

Inevitably, he gaffed. Asked how much he had enjoyed the summit so far, what it was like to be the new boy, he said, with what seemed like unnecessary candour, 'If you were to tell me that we had to stay overnight and have another 24 hours, I'm not sure how enthralled I'd be.'

One could almost hear Dutch teeth being sucked. What? He wants to get out of Noordwijk an Zee, pearl of the North Sea? Is he saying he's had enough of our fine Dutch cooking, with the deep fried dairy patties? Mr Blair had spent the morning apologising for an earlier gaffe. Robin

Cook kicked off his tenure as Foreign Secretary by announcing a new Franco-German-British triangle would run Europe.

This dismayed Mr Prodi, the Italian Prime Minister. Sorry, said Mr Blair. For triangle, read square. But of course, said Mr Prodi, who had earlier accused Mr Cook of 'inexperience'. It was a 'misunderstanding'. And those other European leaders, who might feel Europe was a polygon, were equally disposed to be forgiving.

Naturally they were: Mr Blair abandoned that last threat issued from the bunker of the Conservative regime, to go thermonuclear over quota-hopping Spanish fishermen. Mr Blair confirmed that there was no question of holding the Amsterdam summit to ransom next month – keen followers of the Government's position will know that this is a modulation of his view before the election, but never mind – Mr Blair was joining the rest of Europe in agreeing more majority voting. He was signing up to the Social Chapter. He was even tip-toeing towards a key concession the old Government had forsworn.

In exchange for a guarantee that Britain will be allowed to continue to ask passengers at Dover and Heathrow to produce their passports, Britain will allow the European Court to have some say in justice and home affairs. That's right! Surely the federalist cup was by now running over?

But the great thing about the federalist thirst is that it is inexhaustible. 'He has a 179-seat majority. Why is he so negative?' asked one German colleague. Mr Blair was still holding out, just like his predecessor, against turning the EU into a defence pact.

In the very act of agreeing to the Social Chapter, he insisted that there should be 'no avalanche' of legislation of the kind to frighten British businessmen. Some might say that this was a curious tactic, a bit like throwing away your umbrella and shouting 'No rain, please!'

Mr Blair didn't want a 'federal superstate', and yet he wasn't prepared to rule out the single currency. The more he spoke, the more one was reminded of Mr Major's debut. Mr Major wanted to be 'at the heart of Europe'; Mr Blair wanted to be 'at the middle'. It may have been a 'New Europe', but in many respects it was the same old British position, and the same old European Union.

Watching the first Tory conference after the massacre, I felt the first stirrings of optimism. Premature optimism, as it turned out.

Disaster, I see no disaster

But where now? The sweaty baseball caps have been tossed in the air. The guilt has been expunged. The blame has been apportioned. The party gave John Major such a throbbing, stamping ovation, thankful for what he did, thankful that he was gone, that I saw one woman in green collapse with emotion, disappearing from the ranks like a soldier shot in a Napoleonic battle.

They've got up off their knees and drawn a line in the sand, presumably with the aid of a stick, and they've hailed their new leader. William Hague made a judicious and intelligent speech, not even put off by Lord Parkinson's Dada-ist introduction.

'From Oxbridge to Uxbridge,' raved the veteran party chairman. 'He's the right man for the job. There you are. You're supposed to clap!' Clap they eventually did. The Tories had a good day yesterday. The future was fresh.

It was not new – the word's been bagged by Labour – but fresh, like one of those scented wipettes that you get on airplanes; as fresh as Jane Wallace, a tribute to the resourcefulness of the Tory talent scouts. Not only is she 26, not only does she shop at Marks & Spencer, but she listens to pop music! Pop music! One could see the old dears nodding with pleasure.

The future is Munish Chopra, the 15-year-old who yelled at the top of his voice, 'Let's put the great back into Britain!' The fresh Conservative future involves the leadership's emphatic folding of minorities of all kinds to the party's ample bosom – even while Lord Tebbit rages offstage against 'multiculturalism' and sodomites.

Of course there is a trap for Tories in being too right-on, too dreadlocked. Conservatives will always want to value the two-parent family, to argue against teaching African history in inner-city schools as though it was as important as European history. But Hague has correctly understood that if the Tories slide into a gay-bashing, wog-bashing, sexist fronde, they aren't history. They are biology. They are physics.

So the fresh Tory party must be inclusive. The trouble is, Labour is inclusive, too. What else can the Tories offer? Looking at the appearance of New Labour one is at first tempted to make a biological analogy. Perhaps the Tories have accomplished their function on earth. They have reproduced; they have spawned. The phenotype of Thatcherism is preserved in the genes of Blair.

Perhaps the time has come for the Tories to be quietly eased into a retirement home, to die, full of years and honour, after 114 party conferences. Is Conservatism irrelevant, now that its free-market nostrums have been picked up by the Labour Party? It would be pretentious, in the humble crucible of this column, to try to reforge Conservatism. So here goes. Ahem. I think Conservatism is about taking an optimistic view of people's ability to take charge of their lives, if only the state can be shoved aside.

Conservatives believe society has a duty to those who

cannot help themselves, but they also accept that material inequality is inevitable, and that trouble comes from too zealous an attempt to change this. They believe vaguely, in a despairing sort of way, in institutions such as the family.

The Conservative tends to defend the imperfect arrangement against what might be immeasurably worse. He or she thinks there is often a hidden wisdom in old ways of doing things, while of course – of course! – being prepared to change. On the whole the Conservative thinks that nation states are a perfectly good way of organising humanity, and believes that no compelling case has been made for destroying them in favour of a European superstate.

Er . . . that's it. Doubtless snappier formulations exist, about choice, and freedom, and so on, but that, roughly speaking, is the credo, and it *is* different from Islington socialism. The Blairites have been reconciled to free markets not because they instinctively believe in them, but because any other approach seemed historically absurd.

They are currently restricting their urge to tax and spend, not because they see any moral case for low taxation – far from it – but because of electoral pledges they feel temporarily unable to break. 'When he was wearing his CND badge we were standing resolute against Soviet tyranny,' said Hague of Blair, and he scored a bull's-eye. Bang on. These people are turncoats, and there will come a time when fresh Tory will seem more attractive than New Labour.

The assumption has long been that Europe will provide the *casus belli*. When Tony Blair is forced to decide over monetary union, the Tories will at last be able to tap back into the mood of the nation: or at least into the mood of the conference, which is gurglingly anti-Europe. Blair might well come a cropper in a referendum on EMU. He might, just might, go to the country next year, and ask for

126

them to vote in favour of a project that has not even been launched, hoping to benefit from the warm glow of approval in which he currently bathes.

The trouble for him is not only that Labour might lose, but also that, once the referendum was over, the Tory agony would be over, one way or another. The beauty of their position is that the decision is not in their hands. This mistake is Labour's to make.

The most succinct and sensible analysis was made by young Jane Wallace. 'We must dump our baggage and travel light for the first few years of opposition,' she urged. The Tories must melt into the maquis, ready to reappear for lightning, lethal raids. This winter there will be a crisis in the NHS, people left on trolleys in corridors. What price those Labour promises? The social services budget is simply inadequate for the demands placed upon it for residential care.

Will the Iron Chancellor bend, or will he betray the hopes of those millions who thought Labour was building a New Jerusalem? Of course the Tories seem almost hilariously unfashionable this week. But by the iron law of radical chic, Toryism will be cool again. Young people will not always vote for Labour just because it is associated with Oasis, or because it has caught the taste of the moment. Even William Hague may one day be deemed cool.

As one style guru said of Hague yesterday, in a thoughtful, narrow-eyed way, 'Hair is a very 1980s thing'. One final thought: notice how bustling this conference is. I see no zombies. I see no morgue. I see bright-eyed thrusters, at the best-attended conference in recent memory, who know there are no disasters, only opportunities. They are frantically buying into a blue-chip stock that the market has recklessly undervalued.

Many believed that the real fault-line, and the best hope for the Tories, lay in the split at the top of Labour.

Tony has the smile but Gordon has the brains

It was confrontation time last night (January, 1998) in Downing Street, apparently. A livid Tony Blair flew in to have it out with the Chancellor of the Exchequer. 'Brown faces Premier's wrath' said the headlines. Blair wanted an explanation from Gordon, we were told, and it had better be good.

There he is, thousands of miles away in Japan, when he hears that the Chancellor has been stabbing him in the back: whingeing, in fact, in an 'authorised' biography, about his failure to become Labour leader and about his 'betrayal' by the Blairites.

Oh, to have been a fly on the wall last night as Blair read the riot act to Brown! This is dynamite stuff, a split between PM and Chancellor. We do not yet know in what terms Blair reproved his erstwhile friend, and yet I doubt if he was too stern. What can he possibly say?

Brown is unsackable and impregnable. Indeed, as one Labour source put it yesterday, 'Blair is the President and Brown is the Prime Minister'; or, to take a showbiz metaphor, does anyone remember a pop group called Wham? There was Andrew Ridgeley and George Michael. You *must* remember: wham/bam/I am/a man was one of their hits.

The essence was that they were a duo, blood brothers, just as Tony and Gordon were the golden young modernisers of the Labour Party. All went well with Wham until it became obvious that George, the brooding, heavy-jawed one, had all the talent – and Andrew, well, Andrew was more of a pretty face. So they split up amid much acrimony and tears; and if you doubt the analogy, look at the respective roles of Gordon and Tony and ask yourself, which is truly First Lord of the Treasury?

In today's Britain, half the national wealth is already taken by Gordon Brown and allocated to other departments for spending, which gives a sense of his natural dominance in Whitehall. Gordon has gone further. Such is his authority over Welfare to Work, his brainchild, that the Department of Social Security was not even informed of the decision to extend its scope beyond the 18- to 25-year-olds. When the Chief Whip, Nick Brown, totted up the numbers of potential rebels over single-parent premium, who saw his report first? Not Blair, nor anyone in the Prime Minister's office. No, it's got to be Gordon.

Gordon Brown and his small team took the momentous decision to give the Bank of England independence, and then sold it to Blair. Gordon reaches across Whitehall to the departments of Education and of Social Security to take control of welfare reform, the one policy on which Labour has asked us to judge its performance. It is a rule of thumb that in every important department of state, there is a minister loyal to Gordon Brown. There is Andrew Smith at Employment, Nigel Griffiths at the DTI, Doug Henderson at the Foreign Office. Gordon Brown lobbied hard to instal Harriet Harman at Social Security.

To inspire such loyalty bespeaks a certain intellectual aura, and he is by far the brightest star outside No 10. At one time, that accolade might have gone to his old enemy from Scotland, Robin Cook, the man who believes he should have been Chancellor. Poor Mr Cook has had too many appalling experiences in airport lounges. Worse, he has allowed himself to be bullied by Alastair Campbell: anyone with gumption would have paid for his mistress to travel with him from his own pocket. And while Cook writhes between the hammer of his wife and the anvil of No 10, the single biggest foreign policy dossier – EMU –

is, apparently, entirely out of the hands of the Foreign Office.

Gordon Brown is so self-confident that last year he and his officials made an attempt to bounce the Prime Minister into supporting early entry to EMU. Someone in the Treasury briefed the *Financial Times*. The market reaction was so extreme that Blair was forced to call a halt. Charlie Whelan, Gordon's trusted press man, was overheard dictating the future of the pound in the Red Lion pub over a mobile phone. Has Whelan been reprimanded? Of course not.

He spins away, independently of Downing Street, allowing the television cameras into the Treasury, and admitting that he sometimes misleads; and the reason Blair allows the Brownies to get away with it is, simply, guilt.

As Paul Routledge's new biography makes clear, Brown is still bitter about the leadership election of 1994. It had always been the understanding in the Brown-Blair duo that Brown was the one who would stand for the leadership. Peter Mandelson, in theory, would support him. Brown still feels the treachery of Mandelson, who wrote a cunning letter to the effect that he would support a Brown candidacy, but that it would gravely damage the Labour Party.

He still smarts from the smears, emanating from the Blair camp, that he was homosexual. The reality, perhaps, is that Brown was always likely to lose a race against Blair. He was too dour, too Old Labour, for the task Mandelson had in mind. But it was Gordon Brown who had the credentials. Blair just had the teeth. Brown's family were farm labourers, while Blair's father was a *Conservative*!

Brown had a first-class degree in history from Edinburgh before he was 20 and was made Student Rector. Blair achieved a second from Oxford and played in a band called Ugly Rumours. Brown has written books on obscure Scottish socialists and on the case for a Scottish assembly. Blair has hoovered up his friend's ideas; and if evidence were needed of this, ask yourself, what is the slogan for which Blair was best known before he became Prime Minister?

That's right, it was 'Tough on crime, tough on the causes of crime'. And who minted that phrase, and innocently offered it to his buddy? Gordon, outmanoeuvred by a man two years his junior. Brown is the animating intelligence of the modern Labour Party; Blair is the man who takes the policies, and puts a nice shine on them.

It is, in a way, a good fit. They complement each other. Brown is in the Treasury at 6am, dreaming up wheezes for stinging the middle classes. Blair goes on television to reassure those about to be stung. This week we hear that Labour proposes to tax the universal benefits that currently go to the middle classes. Child benefit, disability living allowance, maternity benefit could be reduced for the better-off, without any countervailing cut in tax. So Blair will tomorrow go on the stump in Birmingham to assuage public anxiety about his plans – or rather, Gordon's plans.

And yet the double-act has its strains. The two men have different priorities. Tony Blair wants to end this parliament claiming that he has kept his promises, kept faith with the ex-Tories who flocked to his banner. When one talks to Gordon Brown one feels he is actuated by a sense of social injustice; he wants redistribution of wealth.

Gordon wanted a top rate of tax of 50p. Blair said no. Gordon proposed to axe tax-exempt savings of more than £50,000. Now Downing Street is saying the policy was 'badly presented'. Gordon Brown is consciously positioning himself, in the words of one MP yesterday, as 'the soul of the Labour Party'. Blair may have nothing to fear from his friend in the short term, since their interests so largely coincide. In the longer term, though, he might remember Machiavelli's dictum that it is wise not to trust a man who knows you have done him wrong.

But if Blair was an actor, he was brilliant at it. He borrowed from everyone, even his supposed ideological foes.

He went on and on, but he's no Mrs Thatcher

Give that man a handbag! And while you're at it, tell him to wear a powder blue suit and a pineapple-coloured wig next time he wants to impersonate this century's greatest peace-time prime minister.

We have had Tony the public school prefect with his half-time pep talks. We have had the bursting-chested evangelical. Yesterday we had a shameless piece of drag artistry.

The road is long. There is no backing down. There Is No Backing Down. TINBD, said our leader and his eyes flashed with something like the Caligula gleam of our lamented Leaderene. As Mr Mandelson, a man who claims to have forsaken the arts of spin, suavely confided: 'Basically, it's Tony's equivalent of the Lady's Not For Turning Speech of 1981.'

That's right. You turn if you want to, you moaning minnies, said Tony, showing the world he had all the *cojones* of La Dama di Hierro. 'Backbone not back down,' he barked at the conference. Straighten up, you 'orrible lot!

In true Thatcherian style he flailed at vested interests, or at least a judicious selection, and it would be dishonest to pretend that the tough-guy passages did not warm the brutal cockles of my heart. Teachers would have to brace up and get used to performance-related pay, he scolded. And they clapped!

Industry! chided the Prime Minister. What a shower. Dithering bosses and idle workers; well, he attacked the bosses anyway, only murmuring something about 'lack of productivity'. Bashing the workers is still going it a bit for Tony, but one lives in hope. He was pro-car, just like Herself.

'Family life has changed for good reasons as well as bad,' he said. You mean a Labour leader actually thinks there could be *bad* reasons for family breakdown, morally bad? One could almost hear the sucking of teeth.

The welfare state was being ripped off by scroungers, said Tony Blair, and such is the lobotomised state of his party that they clapped that, too. He said he was proud of cutting corporation tax to an all-time low. This did not elicit applause. But it could, of course, have come straight from an oration by the former Tory leader. All he had to say was 'We are a grandmother' or 'No, No, No', and the act of homage, or plagiarism, would have been complete.

Blair has tried this stunt before. He saw before the election that there was a significant group of erstwhile Tory voters who warmed to Mrs Thatcher's style of leadership, and felt disappointed by the less bone-crunching style of her successor. 'Say what you like about her,' said this type of disgruntled Tory, 'at least she knew what she thought.'

That was why Blair began cunningly to put it around that he 'admired' Mrs Thatcher; he allegedly sought her advice; he sucked up to useful idiot Thatcherites in the Right-wing press, who could be relied upon to bash Mr Major. And since the election we have been repeatedly tipped the wink that the Thatcher era is programmatic of the Blair reich.

Like Thatcher, Blair wants to be seen as a leader at war with the fainthearts, the wets, the Left in his own party, calling for a U-turn as recession bites. That was why so much of yesterday's speech was about 'challenge', that fierce flaired-nostril exhortation to rise on the stepping stones of our dead selves to higher things. He even challenged the media not to wreck his moralising by unkind prying into the private lives of Labour ministers: a bit rich from a man whose party profited so grossly from the exposure of the sex lives of Tory ministers during the 'Back to Basics' fiasco.

But there is another and more important way in which Blair yearns to be compared to Thatcher. Hers has gone down in history as a time of ideological triumph, in which the ideas of the Right vanquished those of Mr Blair's party. Mrs Thatcher pioneered a revolution which was imitated in one way or another, around the world; and *that* is the analogy which Blair hopes will be drawn.

That is why he was sycophantically introduced yesterday as the model of aspirant leaders from Germany to Japan. That is why he banged on so relentlessly about the 'Third Way'. Emptying his sentences of verbs, he tried impressionistically, with blobs of vacuous uplift, to explain what this meant. 'And in this new era, a new agenda. Economies that compete on knowledge, on the creative power of the many, not the few. Societies based on inclusion, not division. Countries that are internationalist not isolationist, this is the "Third Way" . . .' If you can make head or tail of that, my friend, you ought to be a Labour spin doctor.

Mrs Thatcher never tried to define Thatcherism, in advance of the fact, with a lot of de-verbed drivel. The term was coined for her, once her achievements were so palpable. Why does Blair bother with the 'Third Way'? Because Blair's deepest fear is that there isn't really any such thing as Blairism.

In Mrs Thatcher's first term she embarked on a programme of reforming the supply side of the British economy and containing government expenditure. In a way, the problems facing the incoming Labour government have been of comparable magnitude: how to reform the welfare state, and how to reach a settlement in Britain's relations with a federalising Europe.

On both these questions, Tony Blair's approach is more striking for its continuity with Tory governments, than any revolutionary 'Third Way'. He did put in Frank Field to think the unthinkable about welfare. Mad Frankie duly unthunk it, and was kicked out for his pains, along with Harriet Harman.

The Left of the Labour Party see that as a victory, and they are probably right. As for his European policy, it is identical to that of John Major and Douglas Hurd. Make up our minds on the euro in due course, keep a seat at the table, oppose interference in the nooks and crannies of our national life.

It is not that it is a bad policy; but sorry, Tony, it lacks that Thatcherian zing. Which brings us to the final attribute of the Thatcherian epoch which Blair undoubtedly hopes to emulate: longevity.

Looking at him yesterday, and looking at the state of the Opposition, one could indeed see him going on and on and on. But if this is the 'year of challenge', as he kept saying, next year could be the year of raiding our wallets, as Labour's extravagant spending commitments coincide with the burdens of a recession.

One day, in a way we cannot foresee, this demi-god will complete his imitation of Thatcher. He will be turfed out with tears and ignominy. It is the common fate, as Enoch Powell said, of all politicians.

*There were some Labour disasters, and they were glori-
ously self-inflicted.*

He lived by Spin, he died by Spin

Weep, O ye shirt-makers of Jermyn Street, ye Cool Britannia tailors and whatever exists of human finer feeling. In
the Ministry of Sound, the tank-topped bumboys blub into
their Pils.

In the delicatessens of Elgin Crescent, the sawdust is
sodden with tears. For months, years, Carla Powell will
go into mourning, her plumage as black as night. For
Mandy is dead, dead ere his prime!

Yes, one can already hear the chokes and the sobs, even
from those Left-wing quarters that were yesterday calling
for his pomaded scalp. 'So noble', 'So honourable', 'Fell
on his own sword', 'A good end – so unlike the other lot!'

In the soft-lit Soho drinking clubs frequented by Mandy
and his pals, his deed will be likened to Captain Oates
stepping out into the blizzard to spare his comrades. We
are asked to imagine a kind of pre-Raphaelite scene, 'the
self-sacrifice of Mandy'.

On one telephone, Blair, haggard, appalled, pleading:
and on the other, Mandelson, unswerving, resolute, his
convex brow transfigured by a strange shaft of light. Blair:
'Peter, reconsider, I beg you!' Mandelson: 'My mind is
made up. I must go for the good of the party,' and so on.

That is how Mandy would like us to imagine the events
of the past 24 hours. Alas, it does not square with the
facts. This time on Tuesday, Peter Mandelson was saying,
'I have done absolutely nothing wrong' and 'I won't quit'.
He was writing complicated self-justificatory letters to
Elizabeth Filkin, the Parliamentary Standards Commissioner, all about the loan from Geoff and the absolutely-
above-board, Midland-Bank terms on which it was agreed.

136

Downing Street was announcing that this was 'not a hanging offence', and some of us were so dunderheaded as to believe the spin doctors.

We thought Blair and he would stand shoulder to shoulder, and I should like to make clear that, when I wrote yesterday that Robinson would go and Mandelson would 'survive', this was, ahem, correct in the purely biological sense, the Gloria Gaynor sense.

It is now clear that Mandelson was hanging on by his cuticles and it was Tony who was suddenly remote, down the line, watching events in Chequers. And what was he watching? He was watching this space, or spaces like it. In the end, it was the sheer volume of coverage in yesterday's papers – the multiple avenues of inquiry whose end one could not quite see – that convinced Ali Campbell that Mandy must go.

He lived by spin. He died by spin. Do not for one minute believe that this is some ingenious 'tactical' resignation, *reculer pour mieux sauter*, that will simply win sympathy and speed his comeback. Peter Mandelson will ever bear the epithet 'disgraced', as in 'disgraced Cecil Parkinson'. That is what a resignation is. It is an admission of guilt.

Mandelson has not resigned because he has caused embarrassment to the Prime Minister through the wilful misrepresentations of the press. He has been chopped because (a) there are unanswered questions over his Britannia mortgage application; (b) he would seem to have broken the letter and spirit of the Code of Conduct; and (c) he was hopelessly compromised as the chief regulator responsible for this country's business and financial probity, since one of the main targets of his department's investigations had lent him £373,000, at such advantageous rates that Mandelson had, effectively, already received a present of £10,000.

It is almost incredible folly, and the Tories must be

staring with that look of amazed joy that you see in war films, when a bomb falls miraculously down the single chimney pot into the fortified nerve centre of the enemy. Mandelson has been integral to New Labour, both to what is good – and a lot of it is good, if one takes Old Labour as the yardstick – and what is bad.

In so far as the party has moved to the Right and abandoned some of its hostility to enterprise, he must take his share of the credit. True, he has been happily festooning business with more red tape, imposing Euro-regulations on hours of work and so on; and yet there is no mistaking his popularity with the CBI, or their sense that he has made a good start.

And in so far as New Labour is flashy and meretricious, Mandelson must also take the blame. If anyone is responsible for the triumph of style over substance, he is. He is a marketing genius: and he saw that you could take a red rose, and add flashing teeth, a quivering lip, gobbledegook about the 'Third Way' and pretend that it was something new and wonderful.

The danger for Tony Blair, now that Mandy has gone, is that the lipstick, the varnish, the gloss will start to come away . . . and behind the gloss? What do we see? Just a load of politicos on the make: men and women actuated by nothing nobler – and nothing worse – than the urge to govern, to take on the trappings of power, to be wooed by media moguls and have their ears nibbled by society's loveliest hostesses: not so very different, in fact, from the last years of the Tory party.

Mandelson was the man whose inventiveness with image and message did so much to make this party seem special; and now New Labour seems less special, and the vacuities of its leader less protected. He had one further, vital function. I don't mean the Millennium Dome, though you may be wondering, parenthetically, who will speak now for that monstrous puffball (the answer is the glamorous Chris Smith).

Who will have the pzazz to con everybody into going there, as I am sure Mandelson would have done? My name is Ozymandelson, king of spin; look on my works, ye mighty and despair. No, more important than his function as chief Domocrat, he was to be the man who finally reached a settlement between the British people and the European Union.

Mandelson made no secret of his desire to emulate his grandfather, Herbert Morrison, and become Foreign Secretary. The fact that Robin Cook has had such an abysmal year can be at least partly attributed to Mandelson's hot breath on the back of his neck. Mandelson is a key player in the European Movement, a man whose judgment Blair utterly trusted on the question of when and how to take Britain into the single currency. Will he trust Mandelson's judgment now? Why should any of us trust that judgment?

This is a disaster that arose, in the classic tradition, from an earlier evil done to another. We may never know quite how this story reached the ears of Paul Routledge, the journalist and partisan of Gordon Brown: but I wonder whether it can be wholly unconnected with the sense of wrong that Gordon still feels, after Peter backed Tony, and not him, for the leadership in 1991.

In the very genesis of New Labour there was bloodletting and backstabbing: and now the miasma has claimed its first and most spectacular victim. Mandelson, we may be sure, will have his revenge. The tragic cycle of New Labour has begun.

Some things even Blair, with his enormous majority, was not brave enough to try.

Come on then Tony if you think you are hard enough

Funny, but it seems my invitation must have gone astray. I was sure there was going to be some big beano next month to launch the campaign to scrap the pound. Ever keen for a free lunch, especially if paid for by the European Commission, I rang the European Movement to find out the drill.

Yes, said a huissier stiffly, there would be an 'event', sometime in July. The location would be central London. But he couldn't tell me where or when, or who would be showing up as the guests of honour.

What? I said. Surely Tony Blair was going to look in. Surely this was the moment when he would lend his natural authority, his tooth-glistering integrity, to the great project of joining the euro. No, sniffed the fonctionnaire, Mr Blair's attendance had not been confirmed.

Well, for heaven's sake, I said, what about Ken Clarke and Michael Heseltine? Surely they would be there to give the thing some, some – cachet. Alas, said the ephebe; it seemed there was some mix-up. Ken and Michael were willing to come only if Mr Blair was there, and alas, Mr Blair seemed to be otherwise engaged, especially since they weren't yet sure of the date.

So I put down the telephone, thinking the whole thing sounded like a bit of a frost, and that these scrap-the-pound merchants couldn't organise a profiterole in the EU canteen. Anyone would think this 'Britain in Europe' campaign was jinxed. Their first 'launch' last November was overshadowed by the former German finance minister Oskar Lafontaine's call for tax harmonisation and an economic government of Europe.

Then they had a 'launch' on the day the entire Brussels commission decided to resign, having been accused of systemic corruption. In April, they had another crack, with squads of federalists fanning across Birmingham to distribute leaflets on the joys of monetary union. These at first went down quite well, until the punters noticed the message beneath the Union flag cover and drove the poor euro-enthusiasts back to their hotel in disarray.

Now they seem to have ordered the vol-au-vents for a mystery party about which we know nothing except that no one much is coming. And today, to sap their confidence further, they will see the Business for Sterling conference swarming with lovely young women and eggheaded economists. Giants of our day, like Lord Owen, and Martin Taylor, formerly of Barclays Bank, will extol the pound, and every brochure and fly-sheet will be lustrous with the sheen of money. The millions of private donations slosh over the gunwales of Business for Sterling, while the European Movement is financially dependent on the propaganda directorate of the Commission. The disparity is all the more extraordinary when one considers how the forces seemed to be shaping up a couple of years ago.

When the battle began, the anti-Emu forces were a dismal rag-tag-and-bobtail collection of mutually antagonistic fronde groups, united only in their loathing for each other. It was the pro-Emu bunch that looked formidable, on paper. There was the City, the big multinational corporations, the more sortable elements of the Tory party. Above all, there was the Labour leadership.

Even in February, when Tony launched the 'National Change-over Plan', the Prime Minister seemed to be a man with a mission, an evangelist for Europe. There was a 'change of gear', he announced, while Alastair Campbell said that we were witnessing 'a big moment' in our island story. Back in February it was arum-arum-arum-araaagh

141

and into fifth; and now it's screech, clunk, down into neutral, and the wretched European Movement can't even persuade Blair to attend an innocent thrash to launch its campaign.

In fact, the whole pro-Emu enterprise has become blighted by a circularity. Everybody is waiting for everybody else to give a lead, to show some conviction and guts. Blair seems to want pro-euro businessmen and Tories to go over the top first, to take the flak and heroically change public opinion.

Oh no, say Hezza, Clarke and everyone else. You're the man with the stonking majority, the personality cult, and the laurels of Kosovo on your brow. You jolly well show you are officer material, expend some of your vast political capital, and charge out of the trench first.

So why is Blair so yellow? Why is the man who defeated Milosevic so rabbit-like in the face of a few anti-euro newspapers? It's quite simple. The focus groups said repeatedly that the war against Slobo was a popular cause; and they say exactly the opposite about the plan to scrap the pound. And in case he was in any doubt, he now has the Euro-election results to prove it.

Blair is now becoming increasingly 'conflicted', as we pop psychologists put it, about what he wants. With one half of his mind, he yearns to take Britain in. Only then, he knows, can he achieve the leadership of Europe he craves, the continental adulation, the Kohl-esque authority, and the Foreign Office grail of maximum 'influence' in Brussels. Full integration would complete the New Labour project, the 'modernising' of British institutions. It would gratify his woolly internationalism and demonstrate his disdain for outdated notions of national sovereignty.

But with the other half of his mind – the half that listens to Alastair Campbell and his economics guru Derek Scott – he has noted some interesting results of the euro's birth.

142

Britain has not imploded. The City has not been destroyed; in fact, London has gained market share in forex dealing since January, and Liffe's share of short-term interest rate contracts in euro has risen to 90 per cent.

It is the euro that has slumped, not the pound; and with the Italians busting out of Maastricht's corsets, and Romano Prodi warning that his country may have to leave the euro altogether, the whole project looks dodgier by the day. Blair's strategy, of course, is to wait, and hope that the position will change, and that public interest and enthusiasm will suddenly take off.

He intends to rope-a-dope the Tories, dancing round the ring and refusing to show his chin. The trouble with this approach is that we have seen it before.

Suddenly Blair is in the position of John Major, one day petrified lest he offend the naturally sceptical majority in the country; the next day keen to reassure his chancellor that he is still fundamentally committed to going in, and his every word seized on with alternate rage and joy by either faction.

It might work for a while. It cannot work for long. If, as I believe, Blair wants with the dominant lobe of his brain to go in, then sooner or later, before the next election, he will have to clear his throat and say so. And then, united after nine years of indecision, the Tories will have a target. Blair's chin will finally be visible, and a glass chin at that.

If the euro problem was intractable, the same was true of Ulster. John Major had brought to bear his considerable powers of conciliation. Blair added charm, guile and a gift for moral uplift.

Don't take pith out of the Orange

They don't hold out much hope for the peace process here in the most important Portakabin of Portadown. Trimble has no room for manoeuvre, says Harold Gracey, the be-ringed district master of the Portadown Orange Lodge. Yes, says his comrade, Alec Hyde, who served in the British Army in Malta.

'Do you want to see civil war in this country? Kosovo won't be in it,' he says. The walls of their temporary dwelling are covered with the insignia of the Orange. There are Orange Lodge key rings for sale at £2 and Orange T-shirts, and the image of King Billy. But you don't get anywhere by mocking Loyal Orange Lodge No 1. You don't take the pith out of the Orange.

'If the Protestant people rise from their bunkers, it'll be a sad thing for this country,' says Mr Gracey, a former employee of Northern Ireland Electricity. No, they haven't succumbed to any limp-wristed desire to enjoy the benefits of peace. 'What peace? I don't know where you get the word from,' says Alec Hyde, the World War Two veteran. 'Kneecappings and beatings daily. It's worse here than it was in Kosovo,' he says with what is perhaps forgiveable hyperbole.

Here in Drumcree the battlefield is being prepared, rather as groundsmen attend to the turf before a big match. Outside in the field you can see the ditches that the water authority proposes to flood, to stop the bowler-hatted Bashi-bazouks from attaining their objective: that dull strip of Tarmac which it is their ancestral human right, as the

Queen's loyal subjects, to tramp. You can see where the Army will station its armoured personnel carriers.

You can see the green and orange fluttering limply over the Garvaghy Road, where the nationalist residents have once again won the first round. The Orangemen will start mustering for Sunday, seething that the Parades Commission has blocked their march; and then, truly to give the Orange the pip, the officers of the Lodge could find they are deceived in Trimble as well.

'All the parties have told the Prime Minister that what needs to be done will be done,' said Alastair Campbell confidently. To judge by the air of expectancy among the Stormont *galère*, the lycanthropic Gerry Adams, the assorted flat-visaged thugs in jeans and tattoos who roll shiftily around and represent the loyalist paramilitaries, something is cooking. Tony Blair's artificial 'deadline' could yet be met, if not tonight, then soon.

The word is that the Unionist leader will accept a declaration by Adams and Martin McGuinness that the war is over, coupled with assurances that they will, fingers crossed and hope to die, hand over the IRA's arsenal, down to the last seven SAM missiles, by May 2000. The argument last night was about the 'safety mechanism'. What sanctions can the poor, morally compromised Unionists exert over the terrorists if they rat? If this thing works, then the 10-strong Northern Ireland executive will spring into being, complete with Martin McGuinness as a minister.

That's right, the former IRA brigade commander in Londonderry will have his Rover and driver paid for by you and me, though one imagines he will eschew the red box. What if he and Adams continue to cheat and lie about decommissioning? In those circumstances, Trimble will need a means of kicking them out, or bringing the whole thing to a halt, which does not leave the Unionists taking the blame; and that is the issue, or one of them, they were masticating last night.

You can see why Trimble has tried so long, and so hard, and has been so willing to swallow so much more than his enemies like. This deal could still be good for him, for the Unionists, and perhaps even for the Union. Yes, of course the whole exercise has been disreputable, in the sense that merely to talk to Sinn Fein/IRA has been a capitulation to violence. Yet for all the punishment beatings and the kneecappings, there has been a change here. There has been a big falling-off in the bombings and the destruction, not just in mainland Britain, but in Northern Ireland.

Unemployment has fallen in some Protestant areas to around two to three per cent, from 20 per cent in the 1980s; and that must be good for the Unionists, who still control large chunks of the economy. David Trimble has the chance not just to lead Ulster, but to create a political culture, an establishment, a career path, for some of those brainy young Ulster men and women who continue to flee the province. That is why he has taken so many risks, and why he will take another one, the biggest yet.

There are many possible nightmares. McGuinness the schools minister could propound some mandatory teaching of the Irish tongue, which is then forced on teachers in Unionist schools by the overt or covert threat of the gun. More likely, the continuing possession of the guns and the bombs will be used as an immoral adjunct to negotiation. As I wandered down the Garvaghy Road in a totally non-confrontational untriumphalist way, I came across Mr Brendan Mac Cionnaith (pronounced McKenna), the 'independent' councillor who speaks for the nationalist residents.

Our conversation went well at first. He didn't mind me asking whether he was a member of the IRA, saying that he had only been convicted of hijacking a car in 1981. Hijacking, eh? A mere trifle (though he omitted to mention that this was said to be for the purpose of blowing up the British Legion hall). But when we turned to the future, and the question of decommissioning, his mood changed. The IRA should hand over its weapons, he said, only if that meant that 'the gun was being taken out of politics'.

He wanted the British Army out, and he wanted the RUC disbanded. Hang on, I said, surely he didn't see a moral equivalence between IRA weapons and those of the security forces? He did. In the warped logic of Sinn Fein, there is no difference in intention between the men who laid the Birmingham or Omagh bombs and the Paras. This man genuinely believes, or so he claims, that the calculated murder of random civilians is no different from the shooting, in the line of duty, in the heat of the moment, of people who seem to be shooting you.

The risk of allowing Sinn Fein/IRA to keep their weapons is that it will play up this bogus symmetry. They will try to engage in mutual 'build-down', like the strategic arms limitation talks. They have bargained with bombs for too long; and if this deal is to mean anything, it must make clear that they cannot do so again.

Still struggling to define the meaning of New Labour, those close to Gordon Brown were starting to talk about imitating America. But were they prepared to do what it took?

American revolution

A curious consequence of the end of the Cold War is a change in left-wing attitudes to America. Now that we no longer depend on the United States to protect us, or to uphold freedom against tyranny in Eastern Europe, left-wingers seem to have dropped their loathing of Uncle Sam. If reports are to be believed, both Gordon Brown and Tony Blair are in thrall to a book by Jonathan Freedland, a *Guardian* columnist, called *Bring Home the Revolution*. Many of Mr Freedland's sentiments were echoed in Mr Blair's egregious attack, last month, on the forces of conservatism.

The Freedland thesis, broadly, is that America is a very wonderful place, for two reasons. The American people are bursting with enterprise and a spirit of get-up-and-go; and they have a real sense that they, The People, are in charge of their own democracy, in that they tug their forelocks to no man, and regard the very President of the United States as their servant, not their master. How marvellous it would be, says Freedland, if we in Britain could import that spirit of classlessness and gumption. The answer, he suggests, is to remember that British thinkers inspired the American revolution, and the end of the rule of George III over the North American colonies. Let us bring the revolution home, he urges, and step number one is, of course, to get rid of the monarchy.

Abolish the Queen, he says, and suddenly a huge symbolic weight will be lifted from the shoulders of the British people. The great invisible apparatus of class will be magicked away, and a new nation will be born: unstuffy, undeferential, dynamic and exploding with new ideas for Internet startups. Though Mr Blair and Mr Brown have been careful not to echo the Freedland line on the monarchy itself, they are avid supporters of the underlying thesis: that we need a new idea of 'Britishness', in which the oppression of ancestral symbols is cast off, in favour of a 'new nation' of equal citizens, each thrusting vigorously in the best American way.

Now it would be possible to do battle with the Freedland

argument, and reply that the Queen is held in harmless affection by the majority: that any replacement – as the Australians have just shown – would almost certainly be worse, in the sense that he or she would be the product of party politics; and that, in any case, the existence or otherwise of the institution of monarchy (or, indeed, the hereditary peerage) has no bearing for good or ill on the spirit of enterprise, or democracy, in this country. But that, in a way, would be too kind to Mr Freedland, Mr Brown, Mr Blair and their hilarious mistake.

You don't have to be the new de Tocqueville to see that America's stunning economic success has little or nothing to do with getting rid of the King in 1776, and everything to do with the American approach to business; with their cult of success, and their ability to bounce back from failure. Why has American business prospered so mightily, and why has America found it so easy to create jobs? Because, for one thing, total taxation in America is about 32 per cent of GDP, while it is slightly over 40 per cent in this country; and because employment regulations are nothing like as onerous as those in Britain. By all means let us bring home the revolution, if that means cutting taxes by 20 per cent, and creating the true, American conditions for enterprise. If Gordon Brown means what he says, he will presumably halt the astonishing rise in taxation under Labour, now the fastest increase in any European country. And, as for importing the American love of democracy, we say yippee, and it couldn't come a moment too soon.

By all means let there be elections for the municipal dog-catcher, as Mr Freedland suggests, and let the British recover their sense that We The People really run our country. It is a striking feature of American democracy that the Americans will not tolerate the subjugation of their sovereign will to international bodies. The United

States habitually ignores the rulings of World Trade Organisation panels. Which country is against the establishment of a supranational Court of Human Rights in The Hague? Not China, not Indonesia, but the United States. One need not go as far as some American politicians, who think the UN represents an unacceptable intrusion. But perhaps there is something in the American love of national self-government; perhaps that is one reason why their democracy feels so healthy to Mr Freedland: the Americans still believe that the politicians they elect are running their country and having an impact on their lives.

So come on Freedland, come on Brown and Blair. Let's bring home the revolution; let us do honour to the Anglo-Saxon principles of democracy still alive in America, and end the cession of sovereignty to Europe. If Mr Freedland and his Labour supporters had the slightest intellectual honesty, they would recognise that the American revolution was based on one founding principle, which is wholly incompatible with the euro, and the growing economic government of Europe. It was called No Taxation Without Representation.

Groundhog Day. Blair succeeded in losing his chum Mandy twice from the cabinet and the Tories were still not making any progress.

A refusal to mourn the death of Mandy

Just as some people can remember exactly where they were when they heard that John F Kennedy was shot, so I expect it will ever be engraved in my mind that I was at my desk in Doughty Street, three quarters of an hour from *The*

Spectator's 2.30pm production deadline, when the news broke that Mandy had gone – again. 'Not again!' I yelped into the telephone. 'Not again,' said everyone else, and for the next 45 minutes all was pandemonium, until two peerless pieces had been produced. Anyone who knows it will agree that this is one of the joys of journalism, when something big happens, on deadline, and the adrenaline rushes.

It was only then, after the magazine had gone to press, that a strange post-coital mood descended on us all. Where was the exhilaration? Where was the dancing on his grave? 'Aahh', cooed my secretary, as she stared at Mr Mandelson's waxy face in the *Evening Standard*, 'I think it's really sad.' Even *The Spectator*'s political correspondent, who had just composed a dithyramb of vengeance, seemed prey to a kind of melancholy. 'I just do feel sorry for poor old Mandy,' he announced, and rolled out into the afternoon like a druidical rocking-stone.

Across London, one imagines, there was a dabbing of eyes in the trendy shirt-makers, and in the coffee bars of Notting Hill the crowds fell silent and stared at the tragedy of Prime Minister's Questions on the TV, as Mandy sat, pale and shattered, by the side of the man who had just sacked him – again. As for Blair, how skilfully he squeezed the pathos from the moment. The fiercer the Tory attack, the more disdainful Blair seemed. Didn't William Hague understand, said Blair in his best public-school prefect way, that it was just not on to bait a chap who had already taken his punishment? Gosh, sighed Blair, as the Tories demanded to know (perfectly reasonably) quite why Mr Mandelson had resigned. Honestly! he clucked, as they asked exactly what was the sequence of events at the Home Office between Peter Mandelson's 'non-intervention' with Mike O'Brien, the arrival of £1 million of Hinduja money for the Dome and the granting of a passport to Hinduja ma. As far as one could understand the Prime Minister, his line was that Mandelson had suffered enough and any more monstering of the poor lamb was in bad taste.

The ex-Northern Ireland Secretary should be an object of pity, not censure, we understood. And as I watched them together on the Treasury Bench I suddenly had an insight into the relationship between Blair and Mandy, and why Blair took the amazing decision to bring him back, after a mere 10 months in the wilderness. It is part of Tony's general Jesus complex that he likes to walk with sinners, and always to look for goodness in Mandy, when everyone else is tapping their skulls and saying he'll regret it. Of course Blair knew Mandy was a colossal fibber, and pretty serpentine in his dealings; but then it was a mark of Blair's holiness, surely, that he should be able to forgive these failings. And when Mandy proceeded to let him down, in almost identical circumstances, by lying and then spending the next 24 hours on radio and TV in a bizarre and convoluted effort to save his own skin, what is Blair's reaction? An elaborate display of sadness, like a hypocritical Victorian preacher who discovers that the verger is back on the bottle.

Sadness is the appropriate reaction, Blair seemed to tell the Commons; and all this Tory anger, and derision, and petty questioning – well, he sighed, what else do you expect from the Tories? And how many others, I wonder, felt a little twinge of compassion as they beheld the corpse? Did you? Did Srichand Hinduja, who was reported to be bathing in the holy Ganges yesterday at the giant Hindu Woodstock? Did he say a little prayer for Mandy, that his next political incarnation should be more fortunate than his last two? Well, to all those who for one second felt sorry for Mandy, I say: fight it; forget it. Don't be sad. Be happy. He had it coming.

In the words of the *Guardian* headline at the conclusion

of Jonathan Aitken's trial, he lied and lied and lied. He lied on his mortgage application form to the Britannia Building society, when he failed to disclose the £373,000 he had been loaned by Geoffrey Robinson, a minister whose financial affairs his department later had to investigate. He lied to the *Observer*, by pretending, absurdly, that he had not intervened in support of the passport application by the Hindujas, who were promising to fund the inanities of the Faith Zone. He lied because he knew it would look bad, and that it was bad; what he failed to see was that the lying would make it worse. Now he is gone, and this time it seems unlikely that he will be having dinner tonight, with Reinaldo da Silva, in a foursome with Tony and Cherie.

Peter Mandelson was a good thing for the Labour Party, in that he made it electable. He made them repudiate everything they believed in; and that is why, for all Blair's preachy sighings, there will be no grief for Mandy on the Labour backbenches. He is not the only minister to be caught up in Hindujagate; my old mate Keith Vaz seems to have snuck through it all unscathed. But Mandy is the one they have been obsessed with; because in his persona he incarnates the deception they have been obliged to practise on themselves and on the electorate.

Now Gordon Brown will take control of the election campaign, finally avenging the insult that Mandy did him by backing Tony in 1994, and for Mandelson it is finito. Curtains. La musica. There is no way back – though, if I look back, I see that I made the same prophecy last time.

As the election day approached, and the Tories braced themselves for another thrashing, I was driven to make a rash prediction.

What it feels like to eat my hat

Mmmmble mmmble. Pass the ketchup, someone. All right, all right, that's enough for the time being. I have just removed from my jaws a slightly sodden *Bonhomme de Neige* blue woollen bobble hat, and I beg readers to allow me to explain why I have been trying to eat it. You may remember (though I think it unlikely) that this was the first signed political column to urge Blair to do the decent thing. Oi Blair, it said, on March 1: why are we having a general election when the country is in the grip of a terrible plague? But the trouble with this political commentary game is that you never know whether your depth charges have hit the mark.

Will the Government continue to cruise invisible and untroubled, with your bombs detonating in the inky deep around them? Or will ministers suddenly break surface, gasping for air and spilling out of the conning tower with their hands upraised? Day after day the foot and mouth crisis grew worse, and yet the Government and its acolytes continued to trumpet that May 3 was the only possible date. The farmers called for delay. The Leader of the Opposition called for delay. Oh come on, replied Blair in the Commons, the last time we had a foot and mouth crisis, it went on for eight months.

Finally, by last Wednesday, when he had allowed the uncertainty to drag on for five weeks, and when all his ministers were still chirruping that it would be a grievous blow to Britain if local elections were not held on May 3, I decided that he was really going to do it. By the cocky way he baited the Tories, it seemed evident that he was

154

going to stick to Millbank's timetable, and I said: 'If that man is not in Windsor by early next week kissing hands and asking for a dissolution, then I will eat my hat, garnished with bacon from Heddon-on-the-wall.'

And that is why I sit here taking (chomp, gag, retch) my ineffectual bites from this hat, and pondering where I went wrong. It would be nice to imagine that my prediction suffered from Heisenberg's uncertainty principle: that in the very act of making the observation about the Prime Minister's intentions, I affected those intentions. Perhaps that column radiated such scorn, such derision for his motives, that Mr Blair couldn't take it, and produced a last-minute swerve.

Hmmm? Well, it's the best I can come up with to salve my columnar ego, and I think you'll agree that it's pretty thin. No, the reason Blair changed his mind was nothing to do with me, or the bishops, or the farmers, or the state of the countryside. It was all about himself, his desire to be loved. He no doubt calculates that he will get marks for statesmanship; that he will appear to the goggling populace as a *pater patriae*, a reverse Cincinnatus who left his desk in Whitehall to sort out the crisis on the farm.

In point of fact, the delay by one month may make no great difference to the Government's shambolic handling of the crisis. The pestilence may not abate, and the objections to an election, the diversion of government time and effort, may be just as strong in June as they are now. But Blair won't care about that. He won't mind the absence of logic. It's about gesture, and seeming, and above all it's about seeming to care. He made his U-turn because he finally couldn't ignore the weight of evidence from Philip Gould's focus groups, which said that people did not want an election now. The only question is why he dithered for nearly a month.

And the answer is that they were hooked on May 3 not

just for reasons of timetabling, and not just because they had bought the advertising space. For weeks Blair has known that any attempt to abandon May 3 would be a major problem of news management. They were rattled by the calls for delay, but they were determined to keep May 3 alive, and to that end they incited their supporters in the media to set up a great yammering chorus in favour of the sacred date. Postponement would be a heavy blow to Britain's image abroad, we were told. Blair would be right to go ahead, the Blairite papers yapped loyally, and the *Sun* was loudest of them all. At one stage the newspaper devoted its entire front page to a picture of Britain as a kind of padlocked, plague-ridden prison. That was how the country would appear to the world, said the *Sun*, if Blair accepted the arguments of the rural interest, and delayed beyond May 3. Any postponement, the paper added last week, would be a 'massive blow to Britain'.

Well, here we are. He's delayed by a month, and where is the evidence of this 'massive blow'? There was certainly nothing about it in the *Sun* yesterday. There was a free hamburger offer, and more news of national cleavage week, but no sign, as yet, of the massive blow. But then the *Sun* is generally admired for its brazen effrontery, and its readers can tolerate a sinuousness in its editorial line. What is less forgivable is the abject behaviour of Downing Street.

In order to appease the *Sun* which has been made to look ridiculous, it was necessary for Blair to give the paper news of his U-turn before he even told ministers. The result has been that poor Chris Smith was left prattling on the *Today* programme in defence of May 3, while Trevor Kavanagh of the *Sun* had already told the world it was June 7.

Much as I admire Trevor, is it right that he should know the date of the election before the Queen? And is it right that Blair should be able to move the local elections by a month – an arbitrary and possibly irrelevant interval – because he wants them to coincide with the general election, and so to maximise Labour's turnout? I don't think it is. But he thinks it looks better that way. And that, with him, is what counts.

As I have chronicled elsewhere, the Tories were given another stuffing, and William Hague, who will one day be Chancellor of the Exchequer, at the very least, threw in the towel.

This is no fight for the Tory Soul

Right, I can't take it any more. If one more well-meaning person begs me to consider that the Tory party is on the verge of extinction, I think I will jump in the Thames. You never heard such needless pessimism, much of it from the readers of this newspaper. Oh, there will be a plague of boils if so and so becomes leader, says one group of correspondents. Plague of boils? says the other group. We'll be lucky. Why, if the other chap becomes leader, there will be a plague of boils and a blood-red moon, a murrain on our cattle and our children will all get nits.

Nits! says the first group. That's nothing. If so-and-so becomes leader they will be mutant shampoo-resistant nits . . . and so on and so forth. Come on, folks. Let's get a grip here. It is true that, under the curious algorithm used to produce a new leader, the Tories have just left a brilliant candidate by the wayside.

You could at this point compose an enormous sermon about why he lost, the hidden agenda of the newspapers, the slightly fascistic tone of some of the articles about 'fatherhood'. You could prose on about his inner torment, complex personality, artistic temperament, proud Spanish origins and blah blah fishcakes. But since Michael Portillo lost by only one vote to the man everybody said was the front-runner, I think you will agree that any such article would be an inverted pyramid of piffle.

So we are left with two candidates, and already this is being portrayed as a Manichean struggle between light and dark, yin and yang, *Tom and Jerry* and all the rest of it. On the one hand, according to one group of gloomster letter-writers, there is the man who wants to scrap the pound and turn Westminster into a branch of the Brussels Bundeskanzleramt. Oh yes, they go on, he wants to drive the Euro-sceptics into priestholes, and force all our children to learn the choral part of Beethoven's ninth, and tattoo the hideous 12-star Euroemblem on to the very bellies of our once-proud football hooligans.

Ha! say my other group of correspondents. But if we go off with the other chap, he'll lead us into some Right-wing cul-de-sac redolent of the 1950s, full of authoritarian morality and secret sock drawers with leopardskin accessories. The air will resound to the thwack of the sjambok against the riding boot, and the men will look like Terry-Thomas, and the public will think the Tories are more irrelevant than ever. Those are the symmetrical doomsday scenarios, and they are both, of course, utter nonsense.

Everybody now agrees with Michael Portillo's analysis: that the party failed in some sense to 'connect', seemed to cherry-pick a few relatively minor issues, and didn't seem to have anything to say about public services. If you read the manifestos of Clarke and Duncan Smith, they are saying almost exactly the same thing about the way back.

So let's stop this pretence that either of the two remaining candidates would cause the end of civilisation as we know it. Call me a blithering optimist, but it is time we looked at this question from the other end: not at the damage either man could do, but at the great virtues of both of them.

Here is Iain Duncan Smith, a young man, affable, amiable, able, who was identified by this column in 1994 as the future of Conservatism. He has oodles of children (though I hasten to say that this is not remotely important). He has lived and worked in what politicians and journalists touchingly call 'the real world', and in his straightness he would provide a splendid contrast to Tony Blair.

Then there is Ken Clarke, who also has bags of hinterland, jazz, cricket, Angevin kings and whatnot. He also has children (not that ... etc) and a brilliant wife who does tapestry. He is massively experienced in government, and with his boisterous, biffing, bonhomous temperament and his great spinnaker of a belly he would provide a splendid contrast to the actorishness of Tony Blair.

It is true that they do not agree about Europe. Duncan Smith would be able to lead the Tory party during a referendum campaign, in full-throated defiance of the single currency. Clarke would not, though he would allow full-throated defiance from the rest of his party.

The question is whether this would make any difference (a) to the fate of the pound and (b) to the fate of the Tory party. My hunch is that the referendum result would be completely unaffected. The experience of other countries' euro-referendums is that the best way to achieve a 'No' is to ensure that the political establishment is in favour of a 'Yes', in which case the public has the exquisite pleasure of telling them all to go to hell.

If Blair were so foolish as to call a referendum, he would almost certainly get the bum's rush whether Clarke were the leader or not, and a pretty delirious experience that would be. As for whether or not it would be a disadvantage to the Tories to have this split at the top during a referendum campaign, I wonder. We had a more or less united position during the last election (though it was too weak for many of us), and we didn't exactly storm to victory. Among the acute observations that Michael Portillo made during his campaign was that Europe would not have the same salience during the next election.

Let us see which of the two comes up with the most interesting stuff, over the next few weeks, on public services, but also on the issues that are starting to interest affluent Britain: the environment, globalisation, even the Third World. Whatever happens, let no one say that this is a struggle for the Tory party's soul. There is no such thing. The Tory party is a vast organism animated by a few vague common principles such as tradition and love of country, and above all by the pursuit and retention of power.

In spite of their colossal majority, Labour ministers showed their splendid gift of self-destruction.

Now can Blair make Mandy Chancellor?

Drat. Double drat. I had just come up with a brilliant campaign for the Tories. It was the Keep Stephen Byers campaign. By the sixth month of his epic resistance, as tenacious and demented, in its way, as the German survival under the Soviet shelling at Stalingrad, it had become clear that there was no longer any advantage in removing him from office. The Tories should have recognised that he had achieved landmark status in our national culture, and slapped a preservation order on him. His place on the Labour front bench should have been blue-plaqued, in tribute to his personal evolutionary breakthrough: the prehensile buttock.

The Byers seat in the Cabinet should have been designated a Site of Special Scientific Interest – a unique habitat for a new and remarkable form of human limpet. English Heritage, English Nature, the Council for the Protection of Hopeless Politicians, every quango in the book could have been mobilised to protect Mr Byers from the bulldozer; because after months of ludicrous falsehoods and incompetence, he had become a Grade I listed monument to Labour mendacity. Byers incarnated all the vacuity, the spin-driven vanilla-flavoured candyfloss nothingness of this Government. It was surely the duty of all good conservatives to conserve him, and keep him before the public as a constant reminder of what Blair and co are really all about. It was of course about 24 hours after this inspiration had hit me that Mr Byers was accorded the bizarre privilege of resigning from Downing Street, which shows, perhaps, that Labour minds were working on lines similar to my own.

By giving him the Downing Street send-off, Tony is sending a signal that Stephen is still a much-loved disciple, but one who has been cruelly martyred. Like the eponymous saint, Stephen has been pelted to death – only this time it's by the missiles of Fleet Street, says Labour. He has been hounded out, silenced by the cacophonous yapping of the press; or at least that is the Downing Street spin, and it seems to be working. I was pretty shocked on Tuesday afternoon to witness the response of some of the female staff at *The Spectator*, when Byers was saying bye-bye. There were oohs and aahs, and there may even have been a brushing away of a tear by Kimberly Fortier, our generally tough-minded American publisher.

What's the matter? I yelled at them. How could they fall for the fellow, just because he looks all suave and neat and sorrowful? He hasn't been the victim of a concerted media campaign, I reminded them. He's been the victim of his own intergalactic bungling and ineptitude, which he has repeatedly covered up with lies. If there is one man to be singled out for causing the current chaos in the railways, that man is Stephen Byers. No one knows when Railtrack will come out of administration, where it is being cryogenically preserved by lawyers and accountants. It may be November. It may be longer.

No one knows when someone will get a grip on the company, restore morale, and sort out the delays caused by infrastructure faults, which rose by 45 per cent in the two months after Byers's Mugabe-style expropriation of October 2001.

What we do know for sure is this: that with the bill from Ernst and Young and everyone else running at £1 million per day, and with the cost of compensation to shareholders already standing at £500 million and climbing, Byers has pulled off a stunning feat. The taxpayer is already paying more, for administration, than Railtrack was asking for to keep going last year.

Byers dispossessed the Railtrack shareholders, and stunned the City, not so much, as some have suggested, because he used to be a Trot. It is true that 'Take back the track' used to be an old Trot slogan; but it is probably fair to say that Byers has self-lobotomised away his ideology. No, he did it because he thought it would be popular with the Labour back benches. In order to accomplish his aim, his conduct was far more serious in its implications than misleading the House over the non-sacking of Martin Sixsmith.

Before he could renationalise the company back in October, he had to make a case to the courts that Railtrack had no alternative source of income. That was not the case. Railtrack was not insolvent, at least in the sense that it was always open to Tom Winsor, the Rail regulator, to put more money into Railtrack by raising the rate charged to the train operating companies. The bill paid by the 25 TOCs would then be picked up by the taxpayer – so that, in a way, Winsor controlled the cash spigot from the tax-payer to Railtrack. Byers was aware of this; and to prevent Tom Winsor from saving Railtrack, he had recourse to threats. If Winsor exercised that power to bail out Rail-track, Byers warned him, he would simply force through legislation to countermand him. In other words, Byers was prepared to make an utter nonsense of the idea of an inde-pendent rail regulator.

Taxed on this question of whether he ever threatened the rail regulator, Byers has repeatedly denied it. No one – especially in the City – believes him. Had he not resigned, he would never be trusted again in any dealings with the private sector, because he might arbitrarily decide to change the regulatory framework.

Byers was a liar, trimmer, bungler, who made the final mistake of blurting the truth about the euro referendum. He had to go. Pity. I wonder whether there is anyone who wants to join the Protect Prescott campaign? Or since Mandy has said that he believes that he was 'put on earth to be a minister' (by what alien life forms he did not say), perhaps we should urge Blair to make him chancellor.

And I started to feel optimistic again.

We gave Blair a gong – and then the bubble burst

Sell. Get out now. Are you trying to offload some property? Flog it now, because this thing is going down the pan, and I can tell you now, with complete confidence, that the game is virtually up.

You don't need a canary in the mineshaft to foretell the coming collapse. You don't need to watch the flight of the birds, read the entrails of an ox or even to look at the numbers in the estate agents' windows.

I have found the key economic indicator, the one that tells you which way your house price is about to go. It is, I am afraid, the political fortunes of Tony and Cherie Blair.

Look back at the history of the British property market over the past 10 years: compare the trajectory of New Labour, and shudder. Let us imagine that this couple, the Blairs, were an Islington town house, being brought to the market, as they figuratively were in 1994.

Handling the sale – initially to the Labour Party – are the thrusting firm of Campbell Millar, consisting of Alastair Campbell and his partner, Fiona Millar, among the most go-getting of all the go-getters in the world of Islington estate agents, which is saying something.

'We are delighted to offer this highly desirable conversion,' gushed Campbell Millar in their first particulars, 'which has the benefit of extensive modernisation throughout. The accommodation is deceptively spacious,' they said, which is of course estate agent speak for deceptive.

But never mind. The buyers, the Labour Party, were enraptured, and their investment proved fruitful. The housing market powered ahead between 1994 and 1997, and, symmetrically, the Blairs prospered mightily, the hottest political property Britain had seen for some years.

Tony axed Clause Four. He created New Labour. He won the 1997 election by a landslide – and then his market value really took off. He was Supertone; he seemed invincible.

He wobbled his chin emetically when Diana, Princess of Wales was killed, and everyone loved him. He bombed the Serbs, and was hailed the saviour of Kosovo. His poll ratings climbed to unprecedented heights for a sitting Prime Minister – and, in a quite eerie way, the housing market tracked his performance.

Tony and Cherie's initial popularity had been founded on genuine achievement. It was, on the whole, a good thing to kill off socialism and to destroy Old Labour. But after 1997, the attachment to Blair – and lust to invest in bricks and mortar – seemed to acquire an element of irrationality.

Nothing could quite deter the punters from buying houses. Manufacturing industry began one of the longest recessions since the war. Gordon Brown brutally raided the nation's pensions. Britain slid slowly down the list of the world's most productive economies; and still the housing market was going gangbusters, with only the odd fit and start on the upward progression. And the story with the Blairs was much the same.

The Ecclestone scandal, the Hinduja passport business, the shameful and ludicrous Dome – affairs that would have chipped a good deal of paint off almost any other leader – left him unscathed.

By 2001, his poll ratings were so robust that he stormed through his second general election – and then, quite frankly, the housing market seemed to take leave of its senses. In 2001, it grew by some 30 per cent. Garages in Islington were going for a quarter of a million; gentlemen's conveniences in Chelsea were changing hands for the kind of money that, a mere three years earlier, might have bought you a house in Fulham or a chateau in the Loire.

The stock market was now a sea of red, and had been for ages, and still everyone poured into property with a gadarene mania. And so it was, alas, with the Blairs. Everyone could see that the economy was heading for the rocks, that Brown's borrowing figures were bound to go through the roof, that taxes were likely to go up with no tangible improvement in public services – and still people were ready to take a punt on Tony. In Europe, people started to wonder, in all seriousness, whether or not he might deign to accept a newly created post of president.

In a fit of madness, a group error for which I principally blame Frank Johnson, the jurors of *The Spectator* parliamentarian awards gave him not the wooden spoon, not the booby prize, but the Top Gong.

That moment, that award, will be seen by future historians as the occasion when the needle of approval teetered to its zenith. That was the instant before the value of Blair, as a property, began its rapid and inexorable decline. That was the sell indicator.

That told you everything you needed to know about the market in the Blairs: that they were grossly oversold. And then, as if to bear out my analysis exactly, the Blairs did something that precisely expressed how ludicrously inflated the housing market had become. They took £500,000, and blew it on two flats in Bristol, one for family purposes, and one as an investment. You only had to study the flats, with the funny wavy lines on the façades, to be reminded of all those exorbitantly over-priced Docklands flats that went into negative equity in 1992.

I don't know exactly in which respects Cherie lied. One feels rather sorry for her, in a way, being monstered by the *Daily Mail* for her friendship with a topless his 'n' hers massage-offering female Rasputin and her conman lover.

It is a bit off for the *Mail* to complain that she is interested in New Age crystals, when every day that paper invites its readers to believe that ancient fishgods built the pyramids, or that sunspots cure cellulite, or whatever.

Never mind. She lied. The Home Office is being forced to investigate any skulduggery surrounding the extradition of the slim-kit conman, and Tony has been forced into the ludicrous extreme of claiming that his wife spent the family fortune, on two flats, without telling him a word. Sell! Sell! Sell Blairs!

We end fifteen years of British politics with the Tories still stuck on about thirty per cent in the polls. Blair may be the victor in Iraq – but welfare is unreformed; the public services are not better; the European issue is unresolved – and his constitutional reforms are a mess.

Kylie's bottom shows the way ahead for the Lords

Like finding a sixpence in a pudding, like watching a crouton float from the depths of some baffling minestrone, the world yesterday discovered a concrete policy in the primordial verbal soup that passes for the political discourse of Tony Blair. He took a stand.

After sitting on the fence for so long that some of us feared he would need to be surgically removed, he told us what he thought. While Robin Cook's brows bulged indignantly beside him, Blair gave his opinion about the future of the Upper House. Now before I tell you what he said, I am conscious that this subject, reform of the House of Lords, is not regarded as box office stuff. Some readers may wish that I could think of linking it, like so many other important articles in this paper, to Kylie Minogue's bottom.

All I can say is that I will do my best, over the next 900 words, to get her into the article. I know what the features editors want these days. I merely ask them to accept, before we come to the bit about Kylie Minogue's bottom, that this, too, is an issue of vital significance. There are many depressing ways in which this government has mucked about with people's legitimate expectations, and for which, frankly, they deserve to be sacked. One thinks of Railtrack, A-levels, and pensions. But there is something especially sickening and casual about the way they have decided to take the shears to our very constitution, hacking away like a drunken topiarist, and without the foggiest idea of what ultimate shape they want Parliament to have.

Next Tuesday, MPs will be asked to vote on a series of seven options on the future of the Lords. They are all bad, but it should go without saying that the one Tony plumped for yesterday is the most objectionable of the lot. He wants to expel the remaining hereditaries, and have a fully appointed Upper House. As soon as one imagines the Appointments Committee that will create this chamber, one sees how rank the whole operation will be.

Think of the lunches; the hackery; the behind-the-scenes schmoozing and fixing; the quiet words from the Government Chief Whip; the winking, the nose-tapping, the soft belching in the Savoy Grill Room, or Glyndebourne, or Ascot. It is a disgusting way to choose the revising chamber of a great and ancient legislature. That is why it attracts a machine politician and power freak like Blair, and that is why it repels Robin Cook, who still has something of the democrat about him. Like some thoughtful people on the Tory benches, Cookie wants a wholly elected second chamber.

The advantage of this is that it would protect the Upper House from jobbery, and the Prime Minister's desire to stuff it with his cronies. The disadvantages of popular election, alas, are almost as great as those of the appointive system. It would mean creating yet another cadre of busybodies calling on the electorate for their support, at a time when voters can barely be bothered to turn out for the general election, and when we have more elected politicians, per head, than at any time in our history. It would mean paying for these people – their salaries, their pensions, their housing allowances, their fuel discounts. But worst of all, it would mean that they could claim a democratic mandate. It is in the nature of things that the two Houses should disagree; but under Robin Cook's proposals there is no very obvious reason why the elected members of the House of Commons should prevail over the elected members of the Upper House. It is a recipe for gridlock and disaster.

That is why a great many Labour and Tory MPs reject this solution, and their arguments have force. So what does that leave?

On one point Blair was right yesterday: any hybrid system – part elected, part appointed – combines the vices of both, and has this extra disadvantage: that members would not be there on the same basis, and with the same authority. Some would swank around and claim popular support; some would always have the embarrassment of being a crony. Whatever we come up with, members of the reformed Upper House must have parity of legitimacy. We need something that combines the advantages of both – a dash of election, but no popular mandate – and I think I may have it. This is not one of the seven options for consideration on Tuesday, but it should be urgently taken up.

This solution is that the Lords themselves, almost 700 of them, should form the electoral college; and when any one of them dies or gives up, they should elect someone – whomever they choose from across the country – to fill his or her place.

One beauty of this idea is that, quite unlike the appointive system, it would confer great distinction and prestige on those elected to serve. It would be a fine thing to be judged worthy by your peers. It would be much harder to fix, much less open to governmental bullying and Buggins' turnery, than the appointive system; and yet it would not involve a new species of elected politician claiming a popular mandate.

It might perhaps be necessary to stipulate 10-year terms of office, and to draw up candidate lists to ensure the widest possible representation from groups and interests across the country. But that, frankly, would probably not be necessary.

Their lordships are already famed for their independence of mind; Labour and Tories are now almost level pegging, with the cross-benchers holding the balance of power, and they are the kind of people who would delight in bringing in everyone from all walks of life.

The two halves of Parliament would then be properly matched to allow the body politic to proceed, each House flawless in its own way, but each readily distinguishable from the other. It is a solution as beautiful, in fact, as the two halves, symmetrical but wholly anatomically distinct, of the rear end of Kylie Minogue.

WHO ARE THE
BRITISH?

Never have the British felt more under threat. Scarcely a month goes by without some new elegy by Roger Scruton or Peter Hitchens, called something like 'The Death of Britain', and mourning the vanishing of our ancient nation. Whence this menace? There is the EU, with its insatiable love to harmonise national differences. There are Labour's constitutional reforms, which have split the country up and provoked English nationalism. There are the moves to do away with things most redolent of Britain: foxhunting, the hereditary peerage, corporal punishment. And then there is the general rise of political correctness and touchy-feely American sitcom values, most sensationally displayed after the death of the Princess of Wales. The country has changed, become more diverse and more tolerant. Which can't be altogether a bad thing.

A good example of the clash between tradition, and the logic of Euro-harmonisation.

Delors is no shepherd to Chaplains

As flies to wanton boys are we to the Brussels commission. In London this week, Jacques Delors back-slapped and glad-handed as the precise equal in protocol of the great ones of G7, pouted presidentially at a podium adorned with the 12 stars of Europe, and came and went amid the wails of his motorcycle outriders.

Fifty miles up-river, another ancient English tradition was being removed with all the random senselessness of a poppy felled by a passing scythe.

For under EC directive 76.207 the chaplain tutor is doomed. No longer will the much-loved figure shamble, gown billowing behind him, from pastoral care in chapel to biblical exegesis in his rooms. No more will he look up from his illegible lecture notes to hear, with a tired smile, the appalling confessions of an undergraduate.

The EC commission has given the heirs of the Rev Drs Spooner and Jowett a brutal ultimatum: preach *or* teach, not both.

New Brussels law on sexual equality demands that the academic post they hold within the college – normally fellow and tutor in theology – must be open to both men and women. However, the job as chaplain is open only to the clergy of the Church of England – who are men.

Oxford has decided it can no longer risk funding the hybrid species, half chaplain, half tutor, and all male. It fears the wrath of Brussels, and embarrassing cases before the European Court in Luxembourg between the theology faculty and disappointed female applicants. As a spokes-woman for the Equal Opportunities Commission explained: 'They might be challenged in court for using a back door way of getting teaching that was open only to men.'

Now, as the hoary-headed, dwindling band of chaplain tutors face retirement or renewal, some of them recognise that their colleges will not have the wherewithal to replace them.

They don't want to make a fuss, they say. They don't want to launch an – er – a big anti-Brussels crusade. But they say plaintively that this may be the end of a tradition which, until the 1870s, meant that every Oxford don had to be unmarried, if not actually a man of the cloth.

The Rev Trevor Williams, chaplain and tutor of Trinity College, Oxford, is already taking informal soundings among his ex-pupils in theology – many of them now busily serving mammon in the City or making a fortune in fitted kitchens – about a special rescue fund.

'We [the dons] had a discussion recently about the implications of the EC law for Oxford, and perhaps making a special case, but – ah – no-one thought the grounds were strong enough,' he said with heroic restraint. In a discreet round-robin letter, he has appealed to his worldly former charges for help through 'trusts and other contacts'.

It seems the Oxford colleges, unlike Cambridge, receive vital public university cash for their chaplain tutors. Now they will be forced either to pay for the chaplain tutors entirely out of overstretched college funds, or to find money for both a college chaplain and a separate theology tutor, or, worst of all, just abandon the teaching of scripture.

Mr Williams, as befits a man of his calling, is determined to look on the bright side. He said the development would have the benefit of 'opening the academic field to women'. He pointed out that Oriel had recently appointed a female tutor in theology as well as the male college chaplain.

'It is just the end of one tradition. It is not a vacuum and total disaster,' he said earnestly. But come, come,

Mr Williams. Is this the spirit of Cranmer, Latimer and Ridley?

For the smaller and poorer Oxford colleges, he accepts, it will mean the end of the most economical and simple arrangement for both teaching and providing undergraduates with pastoral care. Since all colleges are obliged by statute to have a chaplain, the measure will hit the theology school, already groggy, in the solar plexus.

There is only one answer – to supplicate Mr Delors himself. He is a religious man, praying so often before commission meetings that his officials say 'Delors is my shepherd'. More to the point, if he wants to remain in power in Europe, as he seems determined to do, he must have the support of the Christian Democrats.

Mind you, the most ludicrous laws often turn out to be British.

Congratulations! It's a Belgian

Mr Howard, Home Secretary, you have a reputation as a Euro-sceptic, justified or not. Allow me to suggest to you another reason why it is nonsense to suppose Britain is now at the 'heart of Europe'. We British can live here on the continent. Under basic EEC principles, we can work here. But if we are so foolish as to have our children here, in the continent's broadly excellent maternity hospitals we run the risk of forfeiting, by your laws, what is most precious in their inheritance. When I look into the faded-denim-blue eyes of my seven-week-old daughter, Lara Lettice, the injustice almost chokes me up. Home Secretary, my daughter is a Belgian.

When this shattering truth emerged at the British

Embassy's swish, new velour-and-pine quarters on Rue d'Arlon, Brussels the edge was, at first, taken off my indignation by the charm of my informant. 'I'm very sorry,' said Mme Michelle Roelly, a largish Belgian with octagonal reading glasses and plenty of jewels. Had it been one of those chalky British officials, breaking off from his crossword to tell me my girl was not British, I think I might have started yammering at the attack-proof glass like a drunk in a benefit office.

At the next window, a Hong Kong Chinese called Mr Tang and his two small pudding-basin-haired sons were in similar perplexity. 'Wha-ha-happened?' Mr Tang asked the embassy official, also a Belgian, fanning out three apparently identical maroon British passports against the glass. How could it be that one of his sons was fully British and one was not? 'Wha-ha-we-gotta-do?' he demanded, politely, hopelessly.

Further down the line, a runaway Tamil was trying to get a message to his folks in Streatham that he was OK. At once, it was as if one was on Ellis Island. Is this what they feel like, those poor, huddled masses that we read about, longing to burst into Europe from the Mediterranean littoral or eastern Europe in a tidal wave?

It had come to this. After four years of plugging away in Brussels, reporting on British interests in the European Community, for a largely British readership, had I *gone native*? Were we *foreign*, then, Marina, my wife, and I?

Call me an idiot if you like – and some of my relatives have – but it did not occur to me, *ante partum*, that the issue of two freeborn British citizens could be foreign. 'Oh, but he or she can,' said Michelle. 'The child may not be British,' she added finally, surveying our various birth certificates. The reason is Willie Whitelaw's 1981 British Nationality Act, which came into effect in January 1983.

A Home Office man was quite candid about its target.

The Tories were determined to slam the last bolt against immigrants from the Caribbean and the Indian subcontinent. 'Your sin,' he said jovially, meaning Marina's and my sin, 'is that you were both born abroad.' True, we were. But had our fathers in 1964 been working in what the Home Secretary has been pleased to define in Note K as 'Crown Service' within the meaning of the Act, for instance, the War Graves Commission or the European Patent Office, all would be well.

As it was, they were merely employed by the BBC and the World Bank. In consequence, we suffer the shaming sheep-and-goats separation of Willie Whitelaw's 1981 Act. No matter how British our antecedents, the fact of our nativity in Berlin and New York means that we are merely 'British by descent'; while all you blessed readers who were born in the UK to British parents are, in the prissy, topsyturvy locution of Whitehall, 'British otherwise than by descent'; for which read, True Brit, Jolly British, No Question About It.

And the essence of belonging to this second-class category, 'British by descent', is that you cannot, while abroad, transmit your nationality to your children. The object, says the Home Office, is to prevent large families in, say, Calcutta disseminating British citizenship down the generations, without setting foot in the UK, and then arriving in one of those aforementioned tidal waves.

By default then, as the Belgian Interior Ministry glumly admitted, we have a bonny Belgian baby. She does not even get dual nationality, unless you count Walloon and Fleming.

Never mind the worrying practical disadvantages: her dubious eligibility for British local authority education grants, the cancelled right to play cricket for England, to join the Foreign Office, to stand for parliament, to become head of MI5. What concerns me now is the *principle*. She is just *not* Belgian. It is no consolation to say, as the chirpy Home Office man said, that she would have 'the same colour passport' as a Briton.

So, Mr Howard, let me put it to you straight. Do you really wish Lara Lettice to be loyal to Baudouin and Fabiola, rather than Her Majesty? Do you wish to see her claimed by a nation which refused to sell us ammunition in the Gulf war? Shall she scamper, her face gleaming with chips and mayonnaise, as thousands of Bruxellois did the other day, to watch the National Day firework display, her heart beating at the sight of the black-red-yellow flags?

Remedies exist. We could apply to you, Mr Howard, enclosing a non-refundable £85, asking you to review her case. But, as Michelle points out, no one has been successful in this for at least two years. Myself, I am tempted by the Zola Budd option. Even at seven weeks, it is possible to discern how she could do an adoptive country some service in the track and field events. Why not waive the rules, Home Secretary, with an eye to the 2012 Olympics?

But the best course, Marina, an EEC lawyer, tells me, is to go to Luxembourg, to the European Court of Justice. Of course, it goes against the grain to invoke this slayer of British national sovereignty. Yet the British Nationality Act seems in conflict with EEC law, restricting workers' rights to move freely and settle in another member state, by depriving them of the right to pass on nationality to their children. 'Looking at jurisprudence such as the Choquet ruling in 1974, you would have a 50 per cent chance of success,' says an EEC legal expert. We can go with that.

You may say that there is an element of the Rees-Mogg about such a court case. But, as he has discovered, in the face of government stupidity on this scale litigation is the only answer.

A theory about our schizoid approach to Europe.

Revelation on the road from Hastings to Maastricht

If you have not seen it before, you walk in a sort of stupor down the darkened corridor in Normandy, listening to the narrative on the headphones and taking in the blue, ochre and rust-coloured wool that is scarcely faded for being more than 900 years old. You perceive the little jokes, the cooking techniques, the dainty hands and the etiolated early medieval bodies swaying at the hips and neck. In this 70 metre strip cartoon you see also a morality tale justifying the Norman invasion.

The Bayeux tapestry ranks with the Pyramids and the Parthenon as one of the wonders of the world. Perhaps it was the magic of this work of art. Perhaps it was the effect of a flagon of Norman cider. But the experience prompted in me a sort of revelation, an interruption of my almost incessant meditations on Britain's place in Europe.

It is regularly said that Britain is special in Europe, in that she was never conquered in modern times; and that this makes her reluctant to hand over sovereignty to Brussels. All the other European countries, the argument runs, were subjugated. Their political classes were discredited during the Second World War, their institutions destroyed. By contrast, it is observed, Britain has not been invaded, or at least, people will add, not since 1066.

I have always felt this analysis left something unsaid. What of the Norman invasion itself? What was the effect of the conquest? I will lay my cards on the table. I have long been troubled by the political significance of the Battle of Hastings.

Et fuga verterunt Angli, says the last line of the Latin commentary, as the Norman knights charge on their heavy steeds. And the English turned in flight, the weeds. England was captured by the people the tapestry calls 'Franci', the French. Oh, the shame of those words. Perhaps it is important to Britain that it has not been invaded since. But it is also important, surely, that in 1066 it *was* invaded, and how.

You could argue that the conquest was a good thing, good for the construction industry, for instance. And it would be an exaggeration to say that patriotic Englishmen hang their heads today if you mention the Battle of Hastings. A silence does not fall in pubs if you say 'Pevensey' or 'Tostig'. But for the English who were then alive, Hastings was a disaster.

It was more than just one in the eye for Harold. It was our battle of Sedan, our Aegospotami; and worse. It was not just a defeat, followed by proconsular rule by an occupying power. The events of 1066 were, in the words of the historian John Gillingham, 'a catastrophe for the English. No other conquest has been followed by so total an elimination of the Ancien Regime.' What became of them, these house-carls of Harold, those whose corpses are not shown nude and dismembered at the bottom of the tapestry? The entire aristocracy was dispossessed or expelled. Their language was adulterated. They fled to Scotland, Denmark, Russia. Some turned up in the imperial guard of Byzantium. As William of Malmesbury wrote in 1125, 'England today is the home of foreigners and the domain or aliens'. The country became *Outremer*, the term the French government now uses for Guadeloupe or Martinique, an overseas dominion.

Almost everything was pillaged from a country that was regarded as a northern Eldorado. The Normans were robbers, says Orderic Vitalis, the Anglo-Saxon chronicler. The Norman monk Guitmund told William the Conqueror to his face that 'the whole of England was like the hugest robbery'. Sir Richard Southern summed up the conquest:

'No country in Europe, between the rise of the barbarian kingdoms and the twentieth century, has undergone so radical a change in so short a time as England experienced after 1066.'

And the insight I had, whether fuelled by cider or not, was that it might be politically important that we were conquered. Come off it, I hear you say. Talk about an old story. And what do you mean 'we' lost the battle? Are the English not now a happy melange of the combatants?

Well, remember that by 1075, when all the Normans had crossed, they were a tiny minority: perhaps 10–20,000, of a population of 1.5 million. Therefore the genetic inheritance of the modern Englishman is overwhelmingly non-Norman. Ask your friends: Who won the Battle of Hastings, them or us? and I'll wager the answer is 'them'. What interests me is the consequent national myth, and national consciousness.

My suggestion is that the memory of the conquest is one of those many things that puts us in two minds, about whether to rejoice in our links with the continent, or whether to be dismayed. The dispute over the conquest was alive in the 17th century, and it flared up for the Victorians, in their search for national identity. Some popular historians, such as Edward Freeman, emphasised England's splendid isolation and thought the conquest an assault by foreigners. 'We Englishmen,' he wrote, 'live in an island and have always moved in a world of our own'.

Thomas Carlyle, on the other hand, was thoroughly in favour of the takeover, on the ground that Britain was inhabited by a 'gluttonous race of Jutes and Angles, capable of no great combinations; lumbering about in pot-bellied equanimity'. Carlyle's point is debatable. Most modern historians would say that in music, dance, literature, embroidery and other artwork, pre-conquest England was at least as civilised as Normandy. The tapestry itself is of Anglo-Saxon work, and probably survived only because, unusually, it was not made of gold or silver thread.

The central point, though, is that the controversy lives, at all levels. The schism is in the essence of the country. Everything is a compromise between two inheritances. Our language is the confluence of two mighty streams (which is why it is so uniquely rich in puns). It is not stretching things too much to note that Mr Major compromises between the Little-Englanders in the Tory Party, and those who have no hangups about integration with a continental system of Government. I do not say that all pro-Europeans are of Norman stock, and vice versa, though I note that Budgen, Marlow, Shepherd sound fairly convincing Anglo-Saxon names.

Now the two tendencies in the national psyche are preparing to do battle in the next Treaty-changing conferences, the preparations for which will start in June. Last week the European Commission proposed plans for more qualified majority voting, ending Britain's right of veto.

If you want a first clue as to how the political classes will react, think of the most famous date in English history. When the Tory party splits over the 'Son of Maastricht' reforms and the single currency, think of Hastings. We never got over it.

Thoughts on the death of Diana.

Where is this – Argentina?

Many of us who were shocked and upset by the death of Diana, Princess of Wales are still asking a question. Why was the mother of the future King being driven through a Parisian tunnel, at enormous speed, by a drunken driver in the employment of a man once condemned as unfit to run a public company?

It strikes me that whoever on the staff of the Ritz sent poor, inebriated M Henri Paul to drive the Princess was *at least* as culpable of her death as the paparazzi vultures who were yesterday charged with manslaughter. But the story of the drunken chauffeur tells us something more important than whom to blame. The miserable fact tells us everything about her status. Diana was an outcast. This emblem of Britain was so cut adrift from the Royal Family, partly by choice, that she lacked the elementary protection of her own driver; that insider-outsider status lay at the heart of her attraction, and partly explains why this supposedly buttoned-up country is undergoing a Latin American carnival of grief.

There are elements in her troubled story that explain the queues to sign the condolence books, the mounds of Cellophane at the gates; and our responses say more about us than they say about her. For the ideologically correct, the rebel princess was potent. Left-wingers saw how – like Mohamed Fayed, with his store of unsavoury revelations – she might be a battering ram. She could be deployed against the weevilled edifice of the 'establishment'.

'She won't go quietly,' she warned in that *Panorama* interview, adding that she doubted the Prince of Wales wanted to be King. Even in death, Left-wing commentators have been speculating breathlessly that her image, soon to be blazoned on millions of T-shirts, posters, and the rest, will become the standard of a republican New Britain. The haloed smile will live on, such a bitter reproach to the husband who avowedly never loved her, that it may yet terminate the House of Windsor – not her objective at all: she just wanted William to succeed instead of Charles. Then this republicanism, sometimes mild, sometimes virulent, shades into feminism.

The Princess is a symbol for every woman who has ever felt wronged by a man. She means something to every woman who has worried about her weight, every woman who has felt she was struggling in a stuffy, male-dominated society. Add them together, and you have a lot of women. Then there are the downtrodden, the halt, the lame. Like Evita, whom she is coming in death to resemble, she appeals to Britain's equivalent of the *decamisados*, the shirtless ones. Like Evita, she was partly vulgar, with democratic tastes in rollerskating and baseball caps. Like Evita (who once said 'I want to be queen in your hearts'), she has become an icon for homosexuals, drawn as they are to strong women with a wide emotional range. Then there are ethnic minorities, perhaps inspired by the way this preeminent English woman embraced the poor and wounded around the world. Did she not take an Egyptian as her lover?

Then there are people who just want to believe in the fairy tale, a princess who was *like us*: not academically successful, not always lucky in love, with the same marital problems, even if her engagement ring cost £28,000. It is a huge sweep of humanity she reaches. Of course, politicians have noticed (the smart ones, that is): she has been virtually expropriated by the Labour Party.

In what has surely been an odd breach of protocol, news about the funeral has been emanating from Downing Street. We are to have a People's funeral, to go with the People's Wimbledon, the People's Opera, the People's Question Time, and all the other innovations of the People's party. 'She was the people's Princess. And that is how she will stay, how she will remain in our hearts and memories – for ever.' So spoke Tony Blair on Sunday morning; by the following day the label was everywhere. It is, according to your taste, an amazing piece of effrontery, or brilliant branding by Mr Blair.

It is like the ingenious party conference speech that echoed the song of the football terraces, 'Labour's coming home', another example of Alastair Campbell's gift for second-guessing the simple emotion of the tabloids. William Hague was fine in his tribute. Mr Blair was better.

Many Tories were privately appalled at his lip-trembling display. Many people – including many intelligent women – are infuriated by the Argentinian peasant hagiography of the Princess. We all know there was another side to the story. This was a woman who invited journalists into her car, who planted stories about herself. The reality is they may be partly right, those courtiers and constitutionalists who felt she was hysterical and selfish, a destructive force. There are plenty of cynics, and plenty of people will be thoroughly irritated that the shops are shut on Saturday. Wherever there are icons there will be iconoclasts.

But all this is to miss a brute political fact. As Mr Blair has seen, the big numbers are with her. We live in an age where feminism is a fact, where giving vent to emotion in public wins votes. Those who have been tempted to criticise the Princess, especially Tory males, are just as much in danger of revealing their weaknesses, of telling us more about themselves than about her, as those who sanctify her. If the Tories are ever to be re-elected, they must study the ruthless populism of the People's party; otherwise, the public will begin to think nothing remains of the intellectual irreverence of early Thatcherism but a pompous collection of stuffed shirts.

As for the supposed risk the dead Princess now poses to her former husband, and to the Succession, those who fear this should follow the feline strategy Douglas Hurd hinted at yesterday. Forget the image of the renegade princess. Why should she now become, in death, an appurtenance of the Labour Party, and all those who would secretly or openly like to destroy the monarchy? Those who believe

184

in continuity are also free to praise and magnify her achievements, as they deserve to be praised.

No one can have watched the coffin being unloaded from the BAe 146 on Sunday evening without a lump in the throat; and what made it doubly poignant, at least for me, was that the outcast Princess returned to England shrouded in the Royal Standard. There is every reason why the extraordinary national feeling her death has unleashed should strengthen, not weaken, the Royal Family; which seems only fair, since her achievements would not have been possible had she not been royal.

You may have forgotten Cool Britannia. Apologies for bringing it up again.

Britain: so cool it's baaad

Man alive, I've just seen the hippest, most jiving place on earth. I've been mingling with the baddest dudes and the grooviest chicks in suits and spectacles and shoes with buckles and all kinds of crazy gear ... and guess where they were? Right here in my office in Canary Wharf!

I've just been out to buy my trendy Prêt à Manger sandwich 'with no obscure chemicals' – only famous ones – and, having greeted the editor, 'Chuck' Moore, with the usual high five, I sat down to write in the blissful certainty that I am where it's seriously at: in the funkiest office, in the funkiest town on the planet.

It says so, here in *Time* magazine; and it's all thanks to Tony Blair. It even has a picture of our office, on the contents page of *Time*: 'Tower Power: Canary Wharf reflects the new Britain'.

'Renewed Britannia', says the cover of the international

185

news magazine. 'With a fresh government, a sturdy economy and a confident mood, Britain bounces back.' Zowee. Inside, Blair explains to *Time*'s Atlantic editor, deputy Atlantic editor and London bureau chief how he proposes to 'rebrand' the country.

'When I see pageantry in Britain, I think that's great, but it does not define what Britain is today,' says the PM. This Friday in Edinburgh, while 2,000 delegates assemble for the Commonwealth Conference, the redefining begins, a new identity for us all. A video called *Britain: The Young Country* will be shown, made by Spectrum Communications.

No bagpipes, no brass bands, none of that *traditional* old codswallop. This video shows stunning images of the best of British: brash young designers, advertising whizkids, hot young chefs from Sir Terence Conran's Mezzo restaurant, cool young Liam and Noel in their Kangol finery, and, of course, the Dear Leader himself.

Yes, Britain is undergoing nothing less than a product relaunch, says 10 Downing Street, and not before time. According the think-tank Demos, which has had a big influence on Blair through his adviser Geoff Mulgan, we have a serious image problem abroad. We're fusty, crusty, and musty. 'Britain is seen as a backward-looking country with bad weather, poor food and arrogant, unfriendly people,' says Demos. The very word British is so embarrassing that companies such as British Telecom and British Home Stores now prefer acronyms. Blushing British Airways has axed the Union flag from the tailfin. And can you blame them? Seventy-two per cent of the world's largest companies see national identity as crucial to buying products, and the very word Britain connotes strikes, drafty houses, dreams of empire, snobbery – or so says Demos.

Now Blair can hardly abolish the word Britain – not yet. But he can change the associations of the name. Hence

Operation Rebrand, which *Time* calls *Britannia redempta*. Hence the Young Country video, the celebration of new sunrise talent.

You will have spotted at once the staggering hypocrisy. After decades of raging at the Conservatives, for allegedly promoting useless service industries at the expense of good old heavy manufacturing, Labour now hails these luvvies as a great British triumph. It was the Tories who produced the conditions that allowed this flowering. These restaurants and outrageously expensive artists with their pickled animals are indirectly funded by the Tory financial boom, the reforms which meant that London-based firms manage 60 per cent of the turnover in internationally traded equities. It was just that the poor old Conservatives couldn't articulate the mood. When Saatchi and Saatchi said 'Britain is booming' during the last election campaign, everyone tittered. When Michael Heseltine made speeches about 'Cool Britannia', no one listened. John Major's idea of a popular hero was Colin Cowdrey.

Barely six months later, everyone seems to attribute the British revival to Tony Blair. It's an affront to the intellect, but never mind. Let us pass on, grinding our teeth, and consider what on earth Labour means by a Young Country. Mr Blair cannot mean it literally. Britain's population is the sixth oldest in the World, with 15 per cent over 65. If Tony Blair wants to rule a really young country, he should go to Côte d'Ivoire, where 50 per cent of the population is under 15.

The phrase must be metaphorical and, for some Blairites, one suspects that the rebranding of Britannia is really a smokescreen for destruction. As Mark Leonard says in his ground-breaking Demos pamphlet, *Britain TM*, it is time to review 'stamps, letter-heads and official documents'. That's right: it's off with the Queen's head, off the stamps, anyway. Young Country means abolishing the Old

Country: the House of Lords, foxhunting, weevilled old notions such as parliamentary sovereignty and the union of 1707. It means tilting at windmills like 'the culture of deference' – which hardly exists any more – and pulling down Oxbridge from its eminence.

In so far as it has substance, the move to create a 'Young Country' is likely to be damaging. As a PR stunt, it seems unlikely to work. People don't invest in Britain because Tony Blair has glamorous parties for footballers at Number 10 or can play a Fender Stratocaster. They invest here because Britain still has a flexible highly educated labour force, now likely to become less flexible through Labour's decision to sign the Social Chapter and inflict a minimum wage.

Whenever British prime ministers try to capture the genius of the nation, they always seem to be groping and missing. Stanley Baldwin spoke in 1924 of 'The sounds of England, the tinkle of the hammer on the anvil in the country smithy, the corncrake on a dewy morning, the sound of the scythe against the whetstone, the sight of a plough team coming over a hill, the sight that has been in England since England was a land, and may be seen in England long after the Empire has perished and every works in England has ceased to function, for centuries the one eternal sight of England'.

Well, when did you last see a plough team coming over the brow of a hill, let alone hear the tinkle of hammer on anvil? Baldwin's vision was irrelevant within 30 years. John Major's vision, from Orwell, of 'long shadows on county grounds, warm beer, invincible green suburbs and old maids cycling to holy communion through the morning mist', was laughed to scorn by Blair's assistants.

Will Tony Blair's vision of 'The Young Country' fare any better? Lots of young designers specialising in buttock exposure, a few loutish and derivative Britpop stars, multi-millionaire restaurateurs who charge you £5 for a bun? It catches the taste of the moment, all right. After a few years of this boosterism, though, I wager we will all be crying out for the old Majoresque understated, tongue-tied self-effacement.

And in my experience, that is the feature of the British that foreigners prize the highest.

Blair's devolution 'project' begins to irritate.

Cry grows for England and St George

You see it on taxis. It flutters from the roofs of pubs, the flag that only 10 years ago seemed to be of purely anti-quarian interest. Yes, amid the crashing chords of *Jerusalem*, and the baying of the red and white warpainted terraces, and with a faint aroma of beef, Bisto, custard and socks, the new nationalism is at hand.

Dared and goaded by the prospect of Scottish autonomy, wound-up by Welsh whingeing, recoiling from regionalism, baulking at Brussels, and sensing that the end of 'Britain' may be inevitable, a forgotten sentiment is occurring to the one people in this island who, says Alan Ford, never get a fair suck of the sauce bottle.

And the murmur grows to a chant, and the chant to a roar, and, to the horror of the politically correct and to the joy of some romantic Right-wingers, the cry is England! Eng-er-land! Cry God for England and St George, whose day falls at the end of this week.

Simon Heffer has written their manifesto, *Nor Shall My Sword*, just published by Weidenfeld, and now the BBC has found Alan Ford, whose *Counterblast* programme is broadcast tomorrow. 'I want my country back, and that is the bottom line, and I am not on my own,' says Ford, a Lincolnshire father of two.

Mr Ford was raging in comparative obscurity until an article by Sir Peregrine Worsthorne sent him utterly ballistic. Sir Perry was saying that Scottish and Welsh nationalisms were perfectly lovely, he said, but that 'the English mustn't have it because it turns us into football hooligans and fascists. I took exception to that and I whacked down a letter to *The Spectator*.'

Mr Ford, a sales manager for a publishing firm, says he received overwhelming support, including a very handsome offer from the BBC to give him a platform. You can see him denounce the PC jobsworths who refused to give an Essex landlady a special licence for St George's Day, while St Patrick's Day was nodded through.

He has uncovered the absurdity of the ban on *Land of Hope and Glory* from Gillingham football club; and the monstrous intrusion of the Leicester police, who confiscated a woman's collection of porcelain pigs, breaking some of them, because their position in her front window gave offence to Muslims.

The media, says Mr Ford, are skewed against those of Anglo-Saxon origin. 'The news presenters are not English. They're Irish, Scots, Indian or African. When they go out into the supermarkets to interview the public, they interview anyone but the English.'

He thinks our schools are failing to teach English history, while Welsh, Scottish and other cultural identities are sedulously encouraged. 'If we can't teach them history, they'll have no respect, and if they don't have any respect, they won't care. If you can't give these kids some sense of the history of their country, you can't expect any loyalty; and you can't live here, and be protected by the state here, and say, "My loyalty is to Bangalore" or wherever.'

But Mr Ford, I say, aren't you being a little bit paranoid

about this threat to English 'culture'? English is the language of global commerce, the Internet, air traffic control. Whence this insecurity?

'As a nation which represents 84 per cent of the people on these islands, we are being marginalised, because a third of the Cabinet are Scottish, and our institutions are paralysed about offending minorities.

'I have no guilt complex about the Empire, but I find the history of my country is being undermined so that six per cent are not offended.

'The overall *modus operandi* is that the English must be controlled. We are demeaned,' he says, citing an ad for Ikea that has the slogan: 'Don't be so English.'

Yes, but what do you mean by English? 'Fundamentally, our culture is Anglo-Saxon white European. It is ethically Protestant, even if most of them don't go to church. We are pagan more than anything else. The thing that has made me English is several thousand years of accumulated culture. If you take a group of white Anglo-Saxon Englishmen, we can trace our roots back 6,000 years.'

You can't be black and English, says Mr Ford. You can't be Indian. Can you be Jewish and English? He hesitates. 'Quite possibly, because of the eastern European background, and as my wife's partly it, yes. They've suffered enough. Cromwell, who was a hero of mine, let them back in.'

So there we are. That's the point. 'Englishness' is about race, or 'culture', whichever you prefer.

Mr Ford wants to stop all nonwhite immigration. There is no doubt that the English pay through the nose for Scotland, and if the Scots are so foolish as to break away, the English taxpayer can expect to do well. But if we then experience English nationalism like that of Mr Ford's, and we lose the term 'British', we may be throwing away a protective catch-all identity.

Mr Ford will doubtless think me a wet, but wouldn't it be better for people to think themselves 'British', than to think themselves either English or foreign?

'We're told we're a nation of racists. My retort to people who say that is, "If that's what you think, why don't you leave?"'

Ancient ways under threat in the new era.

Yes, I did feel lucky

'OK, punk,' I breathed to the bird, sighting that sucker down the polished barrel of the Beretta 12 bore as it flew fast and dark and hard, and the heart knocked in the ribs.

'Are you going to get lucky?' I hissed like Clint as the creature attained its maximum speed, of maybe 40 knots, high and clear against the stark silhouettes of the trees, and I covered the thing with the barrels, comme il faut.

Blam. Yup. It was going to get lucky. But hey, punk, did I fire one or did I fire two? And blam I fired two; and the pheasant lolloped on, untroubled by the vast penumbra of lead we were pumping into the sky.

And I turned to look at Bill Mitchell, and he looked at me sorrowfully from under his tweed cap adorned with badges of game and sport, and he said the inevitable words which I still found somehow unbelievable.

'You were well behind there sorr.' Behind! Teufel! Unless one of these punks went right ahead and made my day, we were in for humiliation here. There I was, dressed like a mixture between Lord Emsworth and Otto von Bismarck, equipped with the finest ordnance, schooled, cajoled and instantly reloaded by the most thoughtful shooting tutor in Scotland – and wasting pounds of pellets on the desert air.

In spite of the cold, so cold that I was wearing pyjamas underneath, a flush was mantling the back of the neck. There seemed to be some misapprehension about us Telegraph folk, perhaps because of the reputation of editors past and present who like to hold leader conference by mobile phone from the moors, while churning the ether with lead.

'I can't believe you've never been shooting before,' said Cazzy, aka the Countess of Derby, at dinner in Dalmeny Castle the night before. Well, ahem, I sort of never got round to it, having aged 13 failed something called the Empire Test, which involved safely cleaning, loading and firing one of the Lee Enfield 303s used at the battle of Mons.

In fact, the closest we ever came to field sports was when my brother shot me with an airgun, I explained to the astounded Countess, who will be familiar to many as the girl who used to go out with Prince Andrew. That was it, until the previous afternoon, when Bill and Harry Dalmeny gave me a session with the clay pigeons.

Intended to buck up morale, the result was ambiguous. To put it mildly. One by one the orange clays floated in a dreamy autumnal arc from the machine through my field of fire, until they landed virgin, intact, in a growing mound on the turf. After watching me blaze away for a while, Nicky the nice German count, who was staying at Dalmeny in exchange for maintaining some of the furniture, said: 'I'll go and move the cars a bit further away.'

Finally, when they had lugged the machine up a hill so that it was whanging them directly at us, one of the clays virtually alighted on the end of the gun like an exhausted snowflake, and I gave it what for. Pow. But as Bill pointed out, in the first paradox of shooting, you don't go for the ones like that. 'You only shoot the sporrrting birds,' he said.

Before daybreak, as I stared through the curtains at the darkling lawn, and the shapes of the slumbering pheasants, the brain fizzed with whisky-induced paranoia. Was that bird fated to die by my incompetent hand? What if it embodied, on the Hoddle doctrine, the soul of one of my more sinful ancestors?

Worse, what if I failed to hit a thing? Harry, aka Lord Dalmeny, 31, had issued me with one of the favourite sets of tweeds of the sixth earl. As I came into the breakfast room, the most extraordinary sight seemed to me to be the panoramic view over the golf course of the Firth of Forth. Oh no, said everyone else, sniggering, the best thing was the sixth earl's plus fours.

You could have fitted a pheasant or two down the seat, apparently. 'The Sixth Earl must have been a bit of a lardarse,' said someone, and they all rocked over their bacon and mushroom. 'What fun,' said someone else, looking at my purple and white games socks. Then we were off.

We stood outside the castle, a seriously crenellated grey coadestone affair built in 1815 by the fourth earl on an estate occupied by the Rosebery bunch since the days of Charles I. Harry Dalmeny, son and heir of the Earl of Rosebery, gave us our instructions, including the numbers of the pegs we were to stand at on the first drive.

'We're moving off in five seconds, shooting pheasant, pigeons and woodcock if you see them' . . . Or if you have the faintest idea what they look like. Then it dawned that the chicks were coming too; not only was this humiliation time, I was to be outgunned by the gorgeous Tamsin Lennox-Boyd, and Harry's wife, the divine Caroline, aka Lady Dalmeny, the one-time Portillo policy wonk whose 30th birthday we would celebrate that night. 'Tamsin only shoots to kill,' said Ted Lennox-Boyd, as we got into the 4 × 4s.

And now we were standing at our pegs, straining our eyes at the trees like GIs looking for Vietcong. From somewhere over the horizon Joe Oliver, the head keeper who has been here since 1974, blew an old British Rail platform horn to announce the start.

Nothing happened. Then there was a vague racket in the wood on the top of the hill and you could see the dogs and men rootling around. 'They'll be coming fast and furious, sorr,' said Bill. Still nothing happened, and the moment of judgment drew closer, and the words of Harry Dalmeny from yesterday tea-time echoed in the soul.

'It's all about *cojones*,' he said. Deep down it's a primal act that expresses your virility; and when you contract the fever it can become a necessary part of you. The sixth earl, Harry's grandfather, whose glutei so magnificently filled the rear compartments of this suit, used to be wheeled out in advanced old age, mounted upright and a gun fixed diagonally in his grip: and still he hit them.

That is the hormone, the jaegerlust, which drives these heroic toffs to keep the thing going, in spite of the financial haemorrhage and the oppressions of the modern age. Lord Rosebery, who does not shoot, but who entertains the corporate visitors to Dalmeny with spotlit mini-tattoos from the battlements, explained that Labour had done some dastardly thing with tax.

This means, as I understand it, that it is no longer possible to offset losses from shooting against profits from the estate as a whole. Then, as Harry Dalmeny put it, 'public acceptance of shooting is on more of a knife-edge.' The Scotsman won't even let them advertise, he said. And the butchers won't buy the birds in case someone breaks a tooth on the shot, and they are sued.

If things don't look up, they said, the Dalmeny shoot,

where birds have been blasted from the heavens since the first fowling-piece was invented, will close. Never! I vowed, and had some more tea.

'Are you a crumpet person, Basil?' asked Lady Rosebery. And suddenly this reverie was interrupted. Just as I was pondering the cojones question, there was a flapping to my left and Woah! a bird whizzed past at shoulder height.

'No,' said Bill as the hands scrabbled feebly with the safety catch. 'You don't shoot those ones.' Of course. The Dalmeny pheasant is not as other pheasants, being a dynamic breed called the Scandinavian or blueback.

Since it is the slow, fat ones, which, by refusing to become airborne, have the higher life expectancy, your British pheasant is evolving towards slowness and fatness. But these Scandinavian or bluebacks, whether through athleticism or stupidity, are still determined to fly and – and here they were coming now: one, two over to the right, and the palpitations resumed . . .

But no, curses, they kept swinging away the wrong side of the beech tree, suicidally aiming for Harry and pow pow, the lovely streamlined missiles were transformed into moulting cartwheeling feather dusters, and Harry's dog Ben ran in, like Lord Cranborne. And then another dark shape appeared against the grey sky. OK, baby, you're mine. Time for Operation Cojones. The gun was lined up. Blam, blam. We stared. The bird sailed on. And – blam blam – it happened again. 'You need to follow through more,' said Bill. 'You need to aim eight or 10 feet ahead,' and the prickling fear began.

The topography of Dalmeny is ideal to assist the bird escape the gun. There are woods on steep hills, so that they are quite high overhead by the time they reach you. This is thought by shooters to be a good thing. Then huge efforts are made to ensure that they are as frisky and elusive as possible.

196

This batch of kamikaze bluebacks had come from Shrewsbury at the age of seven weeks, and then had a lovely early autumn in the woods, with drinkers and managers and wire to keep the foxes out. 'The art of pheasant shooting is to breed them in one wood, feed them in another wood, and shoot them in a third,' said Harry, obscurely.

Whatever the secret was, the pheasants seemed to regard my 45 degree sector as a kind of safe haven, beating their wings between 12 and 20 times, as pheasants do, and then just gliding insolently as the triple A burst around them.

OK, so this wasn't going to be a pheasant hitting day. But there was the pageantry to enjoy, the sheer ritual. Soon, after the second or third drive, it would be time for the consomme with chili sherry and the vast Thermos full of sausages with marmalade. There was the sight of the 18 beaters, stops and picker-uppers, one aged only three, like something out of Tolkien or Hardy with their amazing green tweed kit, all with purposeful flaps and pockets and double lapels.

There were the dogs, the romantic language, the walking across fields of winter barley and always the expectant adrenalin-filled standing and staring at the trees. 'Yes, Bruno,' said Lady Rosebery, my hostess, who used to work in the theatre. 'I've set the stage and I've designed the setting, and everyone comes and does their own little turn. It's the thrill of school plays. There's a light in the eyes of the people taking part.' And she was right, of course, even if that part was to be the buffoon who couldn't hit a barn door.

Such were my reflections when, hey, another one, high, fast – and it was a miracle. It was like the feeling when you catch a cricket ball right over the top of your head, and you can hardly see it. I looked at Bill and his eyes were wide with delight, and I realised he was mirroring my own expression. 'That was a sporrrting bird!' he cried.

Yes, I gave that bird the gift of death, as Hemingway puts it: one of those things, to judge by the bird's response, which it is more blessed to give than to receive. Then Bill was unscrewing a flask full of something he called 'hare's blood', a mixture of whisky, Drambuie and cherry brandy, and a feeling of elation flooded through.

Hey, what was going on now? He was approaching with the pheasant and daubing blood on my forehead. 'It's bad luck to take it off,' he said. So the day was saved from ignominy, and after the first drive we went to look at the bag, tied up in rows on a trailer pulled by an ancient Massey-Ferguson 35X.

The pathos of those closed eyes, the invisible wounds, the shimmering blue ruff, the red, the green, the black. Thou wast not born for death immortal bird, said Keats. But in your case, alas, I am forced to make an exception.

The day went on, up hill and down dale, and as my tally mounted to four, my cockiness rose, like an Osaka shipping tycoon on the moors for the first time. Enough of Blitish way! What this job needed was a bigger and more powerful gun. Give me bazooka!

Ah, what did I understand? When Teddy Derby said 'the birds were flying very nicely', he didn't mean they were easy to hit. He meant they were high, difficult, *sporting*. We were told of a man called Cunningham Reid, who is such a dead-eye dick that he uses some kind of rusty old popgun. Lunch came: chicken pie followed by blackberry and apple crumble, with bits of Kit-kat thoughtfully broken up and added to the fruit bowl; and after lunch the wine and the confidence took their toll.

'Och, how can you miss that?' asked Bill sadly as yet another bird taunted our muzzle. 'Well,' said Harry at the end, 'you definitely killed five birds.' Hang on . . . Bill and I had put the tally at the eight. Eight going on nine. Still, the awful truth was that Harry had put me in the best possible stands, and I'd expended huge boxes of cartridges.

Harry had himself shot 35 of a total of 106. Both the girls had left me for dead. Lennox-Boyd, my next door neighbour, had overhauled me after a slow start. As he put it, 'I couldn't hit a sausage all day, and then I could hit – a sausage!'

It seemed there was a Czech cosmetics tycoon who had been at Dalmeny the other day who had shot worse. He had a wooden leg and glass eye and various other infirmities. At the end I went down to the sounding sea, in a state of apres-shoot euphoria, and reflected like Fotherington-Thomas on the dead birds.

Their last sight, before death folded them in his wings, was of Dalbougle castle and the Firth of Forth. A great way to go. Did I feel guilt? No, though I had felt no particular blood-lust either. These pheasants had done nothing to me.

It was pure competition. That night was wassail and celebration and bagpipes on the stairs, and, as the eyes closed, I could see the birds coming fast from the skeletal woods, one and then another: high, free and above all safe from harm.

An attempted rallying cry against Labour's majoritarian tyranny.

We few, we happy few

We were having a tough time of it at the Oxford Union the other night. The place was stifling, jammed with well over 1,000 students – some said 1,400 – flouting the fire regulations and goggling from the gallery: freshers intoxicated by their first debate and the chance to hear, for the first time in this chamber for 20 years, a Labour Cabinet minister.

My partner was Ann Widdecombe, at least in the sense that we were trying to persuade the young ones not to have confidence in Her Majesty's government, and it wasn't as easy as you might suppose. Every time Chris Smith, Secretary of State for Culture, Media and Sport, gave vent to some Labour party banality, like 'the future not the past', a girl in the gallery would go wild.

She would remove her lollipop from her mouth and ululate, like a woman wailing for her demon lover. 'The many not the few,' Chris Smith would say, and she would throw back her head, shake her liquorice locks and assent in Bacchic fashion. Our student opponents were frighteningly able and well briefed. Every time I stuttered some defence of the Tory years, the benches opposite would writhe and coil like vipers, and a young man of Indian extraction would hiss to his feet and spout statistics.

So relentless was his psychological warfare that another student (plainly public-school educated) was driven to cross the floor and physically shut his tormentor's lips. Uh-oh, I thought, as I felt our support draining away. This is going to be bad, I thought. What have we Tory-types to say to these 18- to 20-year-old thrusters?

Their ethos is aspirational, post-Thatcherite. They are just as rapacious as our lot were in the mid-Eighties; still the same load of gizzajob Oxbridge CV-packers; and yet they are different and – I blush – in some ways better. They seemed to understand the forms of the House better than we did. They observed the difference between Points of Order and Points of Information; they spoke fluently, without notes. And, worst of all, they seemed, to some extent, nicer.

Political correctness has done its work, so that when

Chris Smith made a pawky little joke about not being the 'Secretary of Straight', they laughed respectfully, politely. I tell you, back in our day, the mediaeval Thatcherite mid-Eighties, that would have been met with incredulous silence. But that is the change that Blair understands and expresses. To the undergraduates, I realised, he offers a Britain in which you can get rich quick, become a virtual billionaire with www.hotcroissantforbreakfast.co.uk, and still feel gooood about yourself.

As the genetically-modified cash washes over your gunwales, you can still hug yourself and think of your values, like those creeps who make Ben and Jerry's ice cream. What rival rhetoric can we offer, we throwbacks from the era of kick-ass, redbraced yuppiedom?

'The many not the few,' chirruped Chris Smith for the umpteenth time, and then it hit me. Just as a girl at my feet was yodelling her delight, I saw a way of turning this ghastly slogan to our advantage. How could the decent, compassionate undergraduates miss the brutality of the phrase? We know whom the Labour leaders mean to pick out by the 'Few'. They mean the collection of overlapping minorities which Tony deems it prudent to revile: the fox-hunters, the hereditary peers, those who have two homes or three cars, the entire Conservative party. These are the Few who are excluded from the Blairite Kingdom of Heaven. Those who send their children to private school, or who use private medicine (so alleviating the state of a considerable burden): these are the groups for whom the government is avowedly not working.

That, especially after Blair's speech, is the only construction one can put on the phrase. Labour does not say, 'the many, not *just* the few'. The Blairites say that the Few are shut out, not wanted on voyage; and as soon as people understand the divisiveness involved, the bullying majoritarian tyranny of Blairism, they will take fright.

Who are the Few? Which minority is really safe? Single mothers have had their benefits cut. Old people living in rural areas find petrol prohibitively expensive. Sheep farmers are driven to shooting their flocks. Children who were counting on the assisted-places scheme have found their education truncated. Each of these groups, of course, represents an electorally insignificant handful. They are not part of the great metropolitan mass that New Labour is so desperate to woo and keep.

But add those 'Fews' up and you have the makings of a coalition. 'Weird, weird, weird,' said Blair of Ann Widdecombe. Well, Tony, old bean, we are all a little bit weird in our own way, each in our minority of one, and if you are going to be weirdist you condemn a sizeable chunk of the British people. From Henry V to Churchill, after all, the Few, not to speak of the Weird, have had an honoured place in British literature and history; and that is why the Tories should turn the slogan on its head.

Forget the exclusiveness of New Labour, the sneering at those who don't belong to the shiny-toothed Islington elite. Let the Tories be the party of the many AND the Few. 'That's it!' I cried, bouncing on the bench with Archimedean excitement. That's the stuff to give the troops. The Many AND the Few. That's the phrase for Hague.

That's the way to counter Blair and his appeal to these post-Moonshot, nicey-nicey, Generation-X students. By all means let us assist the many. But let us not oppress the Few! The Tories spent 18 years finding various minorities – miners, dockers, nurses, teachers, taxpayers – and roughing them up. The Tories paid for it in the end.

Perhaps Blair, obsessed as he is with imitation of the Thatcher imperium, is determined to find his own set of enemies. All the signs from his recent speech are that he wants to radicalise society, turn neighbour against neighbour, and hound out those whose lives and opinions are not acceptable to him and Cherie. Well, let him be careful; because we who are Few are also Many, and the Many are nothing but the agglomeration of the Few.

It was too late for me, since my speech was over, but perhaps these thoughts somehow communicated themselves to Ann Widdecombe as she strutted the Floor and harangued us about health; because the students decided we Tories weren't entirely objectionable and voted by 449 to 409 to carry the motion. So there, Blair. The ranks of the Few are swelling.

I bet they voted New Labour.

Huh, I thought. Double Income, No Kids. That's what we have here. Bastards.

The plane was full of middle-class Brits, tanned by the alpine sun, fit, in so far as the chalet diet allows it, and the charter company had made the usual balls-up. Every time you turn up with a load of children, they decide for some reason that you are to be dispersed as widely as possible throughout the flight.

So when my wife, baby and one child had installed themselves in row one, seats A and B, and I had installed myself and two other children in row 20, I turned to my neighbours. Usually one might ask a stewardess to help out, but I decided to trust my own powers of charm. The plane was still stationary. The flight was still at the gate and would be for about ten more minutes. 'I wonder,' I began in the most cordial and winning way to the husband-and-wife team seated on my right, 'I wonder whether I could persuade you. . . .' What I was about to ask was whether they might be able to see their way round to swapping seats with my wife and her section of the children.

As far as I could see, this was a win-win situation for the lucky couple. They would extricate themselves from the company of myself and my two children and find themselves in the front row: the coveted position from which they would be the first out of the plane. As for us, the manoeuvre would enable us all to be together, and share the joys and sorrows that go with taking four children on an aeroplane. As I say, it is a piece of trivial diplomacy which I have comfortably pulled off several times.

So you can imagine that I was astonished when the man, sitting furthest from me, by the window, did not allow me to complete the sentence. 'No,' he snarled. 'For Christ's sake, the flight only lasts an hour and a quarter. What are you staring at?' I realised that I must have been gazing dumbly at him, and muttered something about not meaning to stare. 'What are you staring at?' he repeated, more belligerently. 'You asked me a question and I've given you an answer; now what are you staring at?' I must have appealed mutely to his wife (she had a wedding and engagement ring), but she rolled her eyes, looked away and said that 'it had been a bad day'.

Well, I dare say it had been a bad day. We had all been struggling back from the slushy passes, looking for gloves under beds, waiting in our coaches in interminable traffic-jams in Bourg St Maurice and all the rest of it. But nothing, or so it seemed to me, could conceivably justify this sheer downright nastiness. As my wife pointed out later, she would have given the couple what for. She would have said something snappy, like 'I'm staring because I've never come across anyone so rude and unpleasant in all my life.'

Alas, I didn't have the nerve. I quivered, like a puppy unexpectedly kicked. I had one brief, feeble moment of retaliation, when one child said he wanted very badly to be sick, so I said in a voice loud enough to be heard for several rows, 'Why don't you come and be sick on this chap here?' But mainly I sat there, seething and brooding. And my thoughts turned to a fragment of the newspaper that I had come across, soggy and sat-upon in the chalet, about some bishop who had been laying into those who elect, for one reason or another, not to have children.

Yeah, I sneered to myself, as I sneaked a good look at them both. They were in their early thirties, plainly married and pretty well-off. He had a watch by Tag Heuer, designer spectacles and – though his face was buried in the window in an effort to avoid meeting my eye, and though my memory may be contaminated by loathing – it seemed to me that he looked very much like a priggish, puffy, pathetic squashed tomato. She was reading *Tatler*. In fact, to compound my distress, she was buried in an article by our own Toby Young, one of his ones about dressing up as a girl or going to bed with supermodels or something. Huh, I thought. Double Income, No Kids. That's what we have here. Bastards.

As if sensing my gaze, the couple started huddling away from me and twining their hands together, and he was rubbing her hair with his hands as if to say it's all going to be all right, darling. Yuk, I thought, and stoked my rage with half-remembered fragments of the bishop's remarks. It was 'selfish' not to have children, the bishop said. Yoh! Marriage was all about having children, and those who opted out were frauds, he said. Right on, bro. Only people who didn't understand what it was all about could behave like that, I told myself, and sat fizzing and popping until, for such is our training, my intellectual faculties demanded a change, and I began to argue in the adversative.

Hang on a mo, I thought. Why the hell should the childless couple always be expected to defer to other people's snotty little kids, the product of nothing but their selfish desire to replicate their genes? Wasn't it grim enough already for the childless mother – and Heaven knows why she might be childless – without being forced to abase herself before the noisy, smelly, inconsiderate fecundity of other people? Why did I think I had a divine right to shove people about an aeroplane, just because we'd gone to the trouble to have a 'family'? Family schmamily.

Good for old Tag Heuer, I started to think; perhaps, after all, he was evincing nothing but that old-fashioned Anglo-Saxon bolshiness so admired by Rudyard Kipling. Perhaps, in refusing to budge from row 20 to row one, he was showing the same mulishness which defeated Hitler . . .

I think I must have been lost in meditation because at that point one of the children spilt his water and it was necessary to mop it up, and the other one wanted to go to the lavatory, and I knocked my coffee over; and I thought how much handier and jollier it would have been if we were all together, and my incontinent rage returned, against Tag Heuer and his wife.

Remember this, Mr and Mrs Tag Heuer, if you are sensible enough to have jacked *Tatler* in favour of *The Spectator*: you may be paying for the absurd child benefit that mounts up in our children's bank accounts, but when you are old and frail, and in need of state-subsidised nursing and medicine, it will be our children who are paying, out of their earnings, to keep you alive.

So next time you face a bashful, sheepish request to swap places for the sake of the kiddies, I suggest you leap to attention; or else it won't be long before some smart political party pledges, as part of its pro-family crusade, that it will be illegal for indolent charter companies to separate children and parents on planes, and anyone making any trouble will be put off at Geneva airport.

Jack Straw suggests a feeble means of putting the tooth-paste back in the tube.

One Nation

The world of football was rocked the other day when Jack Straw had an idea. I know, he said, let's have a British football team. England, Scotland, Wales, Northern Ireland, all united to produce a band of superstars. His proposal was not greeted with joy on the terraces, and there was much snickering by men in sheepskin coats. The wretched Straw was forced to go on television and issue a retraction; and yet there was a logic in his thinking with which many of us will sympathise. The Home Secretary has to deal with the lawlessness of our inner-city estates, instantiated in the feral murder of Damilola Taylor, a ten-year old Nigerian immigrant.

Thoughtful Labour figures have for some years been brooding on why Peckham, and other such areas, are so much nastier than, say, the Nigerian suburb from which Damilola originated. The answer, they think, is to do with the anomie of the inhabitants, a sense that they have no stake in their society. They take their benefits from the state, but feel no particular loyalty in return. In areas where primary immigration is still taking place on a large scale, there is only the vaguest sense of belonging. To what do they belong? The Afro-Caribbean community? The Vietnamese community? The answer is often unclear, and this has psychological consequences. There seems no reason to behave respectfully towards that little old woman coming out of the Post Office if you feel that she belongs to a culture that is alien from your own. That feeling of alienation will be all the stronger if you suspect that she, for her part, looks down on you. Why not piss against the wall if you feel that it is not really your wall, but part of a foreign country?

One response to this problem is just to call, in Enochian fashion, for a hauling-up of the drawbridge. That is unattractive, not least because there is a strong moral and economic case for allowing limited immigration for those who want to work, and who will not just be a burden on the state. Jack Straw's solution is different, and involves borrowing (yet again) an old Tory idea. Labour ministers hope to create that vital sense of belonging by building up 'Britishness', and asserting the virtues of Britain as a country with which all its inhabitants can identify. Gordon Brown and other ministers have studied America, and the strong civic sense that is inculcated in immigrants. American children are all made to pledge allegiance to the flag. It is still necessary, for all citizens, to have some basic knowledge of the constitution. When people immigrate to America, it is because they want to be American, and they puff with pride when they succeed. Can anyone honestly say, surveying the arrivals in our inner cities, that they have come here because they want to glory in the name of Briton?

Labour ministers have been groping desperately for the symbols of Britishness that will create this sense of belonging, which will in turn produce responsibility. The irony, of course, is that while Mr Straw babbles about British football teams, there are plenty of institutions which have served to unite a disparate people for hundreds of years. To enumerate them would make a sensitive New Labour soul wince, so here goes: the crown; the flag; the rule of law; the British army; and parliamentary democracy, the image of Big Ben with which Britain is still identified across the planet. How weird, how whacky, that Mr Straw should call for loyalty to a British football team, when Labour has done more than any other government to break Britain up. It is utterly absurd that Labour should be calling on us all to remember the value of that inclusive word

'British', when it is the government's own devolution programme which has fomented the rising sense of Scot-
tishness, and Englishness.

As for the other symbols of Britishness, one can see why
the government finds it difficult to appeal to them. The
crown, the flag, the army – they're all victims, one way or
another, of Cool Britannia. It is hard, finally, for Labour
to ask the people to rally round our national heritage of
parliamentary democracy, when this week the government
is busy undermining Parliament at Nice, and slowly turning self-government into a nonsense. If they want us all to
feel loyal to British institutions, they could start by not
destroying them.

*The Tories used to have a good slogan. 'Labour says he's
black. We say he's British.' It's possible to be anti-racist,
and against the race relations industry.*

'Am I guilty of racial prejudice? We all are'

Am I a racist? I jolly well shouldn't be. Look at my life.
House in some Islington media gulch. Kiddies romping
around in the minimalist basement. A couple of snowball-
head Aryans and then one with fairly olive skin and one
in between. They are the produce, within the space of four
generations, of India, Turkey, France, Germany, Russia,
international Jewry, Wales and England.

In fact, I like to think my instincts, in this respect, are
as blameless as those of the average Guardian reader; and
the thing is, I am guilty none the less. Not of racism, I
hope, but of spasms of incorrectitude, soon over, soon
regretted. When I shamble round the park in my running
gear late at night, and I come across that bunch of black

kids, shrieking in the spooky corner by the disused gents, I would love to pretend that I don't turn a hair.

Now you might tell me not to be such a wuss. You might say that I am at no more risk than if I had come across a bunch of winos. But somehow or other a little beeper goes off in my brain. I'm not sure what triggers it (the sayings of Sir Paul Condon? The *Evening Standard*?), but I put on a pathetic turn of speed. You might tell me that when they shout their cheery catcalls, I should smile and wave. And, you know, maybe a big girl's blouse like me would break into an equally rapid lollop if it were a gang of white kids.

Quite possibly. The trouble is, I'm not sure. I cannot rule out that I have suffered from a tiny fit of prejudice. I have prejudged this group on the basis of press reports, possibly in right-wing newspapers, about the greater likelihood of being mugged by young black males than by any other group. And if that is racial prejudice, then I am guilty.

And so are you, baby. So are we all. If there is anyone reading this who has never experienced the same disgraceful reflex, then – well, I just don't believe you. It is common ground among both right-wingers and left-wingers that racism is 'natural', in that it seems to arise organically, in all civilisations. It is as natural as sewage. We all agree that it is disgusting, a byproduct of humanity's imperfect evolution. The question is, what to do with the effluent? It seems to me that today's solutions are almost as wrong as those of Enoch Powell 30 years ago.

One of the features of conservative cant is the assertion that 'Enoch did not have a racist bone in his body'. Oh no, say my friends the Powellites. He was simply pointing out that other people – the benighted folk of Wolverhampton – could not be expected to show the same restraint. It is all very well for the Hampstead liberals to be tolerant;

but what of the urban poor, those at the sharp end? Powell himself was not a racist, say the Powellites, but he spoke for those whose baser feelings were too sorely taxed by their neighbours. He was not a racist; he was merely the prophet of racism. Well, even if you accept the distinction, you have to admit that, as a prophet, Powell got it crashingly wrong.

Where is the foaming river of blood? Call me a media milquetoast, but I don't see a race war; I see innumerable examples of colour-blind cooperation. On questions of race, the man to listen to is not Enoch Powell, but WF Deedes, who served in the same Tory cabinet, and who thinks our record in this country is as good as anywhere in the world. Powell got it wrong, by underestimating the tolerance of the British, and by conjuring up a racist genie that proved not nearly as vile as imagined. And the same mistake, of course, is being made by the race relations industry today.

Heaven knows why Macpherson made his weird recommendation, that the law might be changed so as to allow prosecution for racist language or behaviour 'other than in a public place'. I can't understand how this sober old buzzard was prevailed upon to say that a racist incident might be so defined in the view of the victim 'or any other person'. This is Orwellian stuff.

Not even under the law of Ceausescu's Romania, could you be prosecuted for what you said in your own kitchen. No wonder the police are already whingeing that they cannot make any arrests in London. No wonder the CPS groans with anti-discrimination units, while making a balls-up of so many cases.

Suppose a racist phrase or incident were really defined entirely according to the perception of some third party. Here's the Guardian's own Gary Younge, on the subject of Ali G. 'Imagine the tables were turned, and a black comedian created a white Jewish character, who made jokes about being a tight-fisted, highly ambitious mummy's boy.'

Of course Mr Younge was using this ugly stereotype to show that some people could take offence at the comic's portrayal of black men as 'stupid, sexist, drug-taking lay-abouts', but isn't it possible that someone might have taken offence at Gary's own words?

If the Macpherson report had been implemented in full, you might not get away with that, Gary. And that would be crazy, wouldn't it? Where the left, the Guardian, Macpherson and the whole PC brigade are just as wrong as Powell, is in thinking that we should endlessly hunt for evidence of one of humanity's worst features, tease it out, legislate for it, bang on about it, create thousands of jobs financially dependent on discovering it.

In reality, provided we have a reasonable legal framework for minimising the problem – like the infrastructure used to remove sewage – we could probably achieve the same results, if not better, if we axed large chunks of the anti-racism industry, stopped taxing so many people with the threat of legal action, and left a bit more of the struggle against racism to tolerance and good manners.

Didn't the old boy have a point after all?

Interview with William Macpherson

Ladies and gentlemen of the jury, this is not just an appeal for clemency. It is an appeal for us all to lay aside our prejudices. The accused is well known. Indeed, I would say that his name has become a byword of our culture.

Wherever right-wingers wish to rail against 'the race relations industry', or 'political correctness gone mad', they reach for a copy of his two-volume £26 report, and use it to belabour their opponents. In the panda cars and the famously barbaric canteens, wherever policemen and women gather together, one imagines that they utter his name softly, sibilantly and perhaps not always smilingly.

Consider him well, members of the jury. He is 74, and a retired high court judge of great distinction. He was the commander of a territorial regiment of the SAS. He is not only Sir William Macpherson of Cluny. He is, technically, Cluny Macpherson, the clan chief of the 3,000 paid-up clan members and of the 20,000 Macphersons, including the Jamaica Macphersons and the Macphersons that are doubtless to be found in the ghettoes of Harlem.

Until he produced his report no one would have said he was a softie. Before he was commissioned to investigate matters arising from the death of Stephen Lawrence, the left-wing media were alarmed by his record in cheerfully bunging illegal immigrants back on the plane. The first time I saw him in court, I watched a keen old buzzard who vigorously ejected an animal welfare case. That is why the ice rattles in the gin-and-tonics of the Bromley saloon bar when they discuss him. How could he? they cry. How could he have succumbed, this canny product of Wellington and Trinity, Oxford?

He was brainwashed, they say. He's Macpherson of Loony. He should have foreseen that his words would be picked up and used, unscrupulously, to persecute the police. I ask you to consider that this is painful to Sir William, who is not, as I say, a man of the Left. It is painful because he finds himself duffed up by newspapers and journalists with whom he normally agrees.

It is also painful because he believes his report has been misconstrued, and after several enjoyable conversations with him, I felt there was no option. For much of the holidays I have sat re-reading the great *œuvre*, all 335 pages plus maps of the crime scene and the scrunched-up tip-offs that were followed up too late. I have had savage arguments with my nearest and dearest, and, slowly, I have begun to see things his way. I now think that on the fundamental question posed by the death of Stephen Lawrence, he may very well have a point; and even on the peripheral stuff, the stuff that sends us ballistic in the clubhouse, he has made a case that is at least worth hearing.

Sir William Macpherson is a fascinating study in how a sceptical mind, a conservative mind, can gradually come to accept that there is an underestimated problem, and that this problem might require solutions which appear, on the face of it, strikingly illiberal. As I put the report down, I realised that he had found no evidence of overt police racism; and indeed, he says so. What he did find, and what earned him the wrath of the *Daily Telegraph*, was 'institutional racism'; and this is what his critics find so wicked. With one breath he seems to exculpate individual police officers; but with the next he damns them all. How did it work, institutional racism? I asked him.

Macpherson wants us to grasp that the phrase was not his, and that he hesitated before using it, and that he expressly denied that every Metropolitan police officer was racist. But it was the only way he could see to sum up what was clearly a systemic failure of policing, in which unconsciously racist assumptions had played a part at several stages. 'It was a collective failure, little groups of people. Not just one person, not the rotten apple in the barrel, but each infecting the other.' He sees this vice, for instance, in the decision of one officer to go off to a pub in search of culprits, rather than question the agitated Duwayne Brooks about where they went; in the delays; in the general slovenliness; and it is hard to disagree.

There are places in the report where he goes out of his way to praise the police. He throws out the charge of the

214

Lawrence family, that the police would not tend the dying boy, because they were reluctant to touch his blood. He rubbishes efforts by Michael Mansfield QC to prove that there was some corrupt link between police officers and the father of one of the accused. He warns that those black activists who keep bashing the police are guilty of their own brand of racism.

He never wanted the police to abandon stop and search. 'We said two or three times that it was an important weapon in the armoury of the police, and must not be discontinued, but must not be done in a discriminatory way.' As for the five suspects, who have been judged guilty in the court of public opinion, a close reading of the report makes it pretty clear that Macpherson himself is far from convinced. He makes much of the 'blond' attacker with frizzy hair, and the unreliability of Duwayne Brooks's evidence. The most he will say is that the five are 'leading suspects'. It is an article of faith on the Left that those five, seen on video engaging in racist rants, were guilty, and that only police incompetence failed to nab them. I am not sure how far Macpherson shares that assumption.

But at no stage does he exonerate the police of his central charge. 'If they are losing their morale, still, if they are still being shot away by it, that's because they ought to be rightly ashamed of what happened during the case. It was primarily inefficiency and lack of proper control, but also infected by racism. That is what is at the root of it all. I could have bottled out. I could have decided not to mention racism at all, and stuck to the policing questions. But as this procession of coppers came in, our mouths sort of fell open, and we thought, we are bloody well going to have the courage to say it all publicly.

'I get awful letters from people who say they are going to come and murder me, and that Enoch Powell was right, and that I ought to have said they all ought to be sent back. But what saddens me is the newspapers, because I hoped and believed they would be on the same side in getting the police to get it right for the future.'

It is very important to Macpherson that his report was accepted by the police, and by all political parties, and he finds policemen up and down the country who approve. He has no quarrel with William Hague's recent speech on policing, except that there might have been more of an effort to distinguish between those who distort the report, and the report itself. What grieves him most is the hostility of the *Daily Mail* and the *Daily Telegraph*, otherwise his ideological kinsmen. He singles out a particularly ferocious demolition job of March 2 1999. 'I can't understand why I am assailed. What they have done may be counter-productive. They have a go at what we have done, and that protects the police.'

Yes, but some of these recommendations were pretty controversial, weren't they? I ask him. Well, says Macpherson, the suggestion that the double jeopardy law might be changed has been picked up by the Law Commission, and by William Hague. 'Hague's speech was pretty good stuff, really, and most of it was from the report. I don't think he was playing the race card.'

Not all of us are convinced of the wisdom of abandoning the principle that the state should not try a person twice in the same cause; but let us leave that on one side, and accept that his suggestion has become mainstream. What about the Ceaucescu-ish recommendation that it should be possible to legislate against racism even in a private place? Macpherson explains that this was simply an attempt – a wholly tentative suggestion – to deal with the hideous, videoed spectacle of the five youths waving knives and vowing to chop off the legs of niggers. If there is no way of making such restrictions work, he says, 'if there is no way private racism could be dealt with, because it

216

would spill over into dinner parties, then of course we would abandon it.'

As for his suggestions that there should be more race awareness sessions for the police, and possible adjustments to the national curriculum to stamp out racist attitudes, he is vehement that this should not be exaggerated. No. he doesn't want to build up the race relations industry. It is just that we must understand that there is such a thing as the unconscious racism he identified in the police. 'And it's more dangerous, in a way, than out-and-out racism, because it just sort of happens, and it fouls up the atmosphere between those who are misunderstood by the police when the police won't react properly to them and so on.'

In the end, the Lawrence case boils down to this: did the family of the murdered Stephen Lawrence receive exactly the same treatment from the police that the family of a white victim would have received? After sitting interminably in Hannibal House in the Elephant and Castle, and listening to these coppers, and noting the cut of their jib, this judge decided that the answer was no. I am inclined to give him the benefit of the doubt. We weren't there. He was.

Even the most bizarre recommendation of the report, that 'colour-blind policing must be outlawed', turns out to have a kind of sense when you listen to Macpherson. All he means is that police cannot approach all families, of all races, as though they had the same culture. 'It's a lack of respect or discernment,' he says, and adds that the police would not use the same manner going into a 'Glasgow tenement where they are all supping meths, as they would in a semi-detached in Surbiton.'

Macpherson's *itineratio mentis* has been from the sceptical, conservative position on racism, which is that the least said the better, to the standard modern view: that it is an evil that must be actively confronted.

Why *are* we racist? 'How difficult to answer. I suppose in the end we started in this country by being a totally white insular population, and there is a resistance to the gradual arrival, and the spread of immigration.' I ask him, finally, whether there are any legitimate grounds for worry about the changing racial mix of Britain. 'I don't think there are. I think it's something we've got to face, and it's going to happen more and more. Asylum-seekers are one thing, but there are a tremendous number of people who come in legitimately, and so lots more places are going to become like Leicester, because they tend to settle in the same area. It's something that's got to be not confronted, but accepted, because you can't do anything about it.'

LITERARY HEROES

In so far as I have learned how to produce half-readable English, it is thanks to the sub-editors of the Daily Telegraph. Whenever I slipped in an adjective, they cut it out. Whenever I tried a joke, they carefully edited it so as to remove the punchline. They always improved things. Here are some of my other heroes, though for balance we should have had articles about Homer, Shakespeare, Milton, Evelyn Waugh and the rest of the usual suspects. I still quite enjoy reading PG Wodehouse, though these days it's a bit like listening to Van Morrison: more than half an hour and you overdose.

An interview with the cat in the hat

This was no time for play.
This was no time for fun.
This was no time for games.
There was work to be done.
There was deep,
Deep, deep gloom.
There was gloom in my room.

All week I was hunting
By phone and by fax.
I used all the tricks
That are known to us hacks.
I rang the PR girls.
I looked low, I looked high.
I was hunting a cat
And shall I say why?

This cat is a weird cat.
This cat has a HAT.
This cat is a winner.
He's the champ, he's the best.
His books have sold more
Than all of the rest.

Take a two and two zeroes.
Add three zeroes more,
Then three zeroes again.
Watch them go out the door!
His sales are so big
They would go round the planet.
He is much, much, much bigger
Than *Peter* or *Janet*!

And he's 40 today,
40 years of success.
I needed to talk to him.
I could not. What a mess!
Did he answer my calls?
Did he phone? Did he heck!
I just sat in my office
And I felt like a wreck.

So there I was
Moping like that
When who should come in
But the CAT IN THE HAT!
'Relax,' said the Cat.
'I like hax to relax.
I don't like to see
Some poor hack get the sack.'
Yikes, Cat! I said
And I sank back in my chair.
Cat seems an odd name
For what we have here.
To be blunt your old face
Looks more like an ape
And as for your nose –
It could be a grape!

'Well the kids seem to like it,'
Laughed the Cat as he sat.
'They like me like this,'
said the Cat in the Hat.
My name is Ted Geisel
But I'm called Dr Seuss
(You can say it like "juice",
Though I say it like "voice").'

Why, Cat! You great thing,
You taught me to read!
How can I thank you
For such a good deed?
'Good deed?' laughed the Cat
'My my my, what a hoot!
I'm a tinseltown adman.
I did it for loot.
From *Green Eggs And Ham*

And other such bosh
The money rolled in
With a great slosh of dosh!'
But why did it work, Cat?
What tricks did you do?
To make us kids like
A Hat Cat like you?
'Do tricks?' laughed the Cat,
'I should say I did lots.
I drew funny pictures.
I wrote funny plots.
I ate cake in the bath.
I turned the house pink.
A big long pink cat ring!
It looked like pink ink!

'And did the kids like it?
Well, what do you think?
I like kids to have fun
When their mother is out.
The mess they can make!
The things they can shout!
I took off in the 60s,'
said the Cat. 'It was cool.
If the rule was a bother
You just broke the rule.'

And then I went VOOM
Inside of my head.
I was struck with a thought.
Hey, Cat, I said,
That hat on your head,
I have seen it before
On the head of the guy
Who says, 'Go to war!'

That hat is a spoof!
It's like Uncle Sam!
Say, Cat, was your theme
Against Vietnam?
'Hey, hey, hey,' laughed the Cat,
'don't think me rude,
But you kind of sound
Like a bit of a pseud.
My work is not art!
That stuff is for the birds.
I just keep my vocab
To 225 words.
Here's a tip,' said the Cat.
'I've read some of your stuff.
You use lots of Latin!
Get rid of that guff!
Keep your words short.
One vowel sound will do.
Then people might read you
All the way through!'

Gee, thanks, Cat, I said,
I'll scrap that old junk!
I'll axe that long tosh!
. . . but that Cat did a bunk!

The case for Hornblower

Oh, the paeans of praise for Patrick O'Brian. Never was
an author so showered with fashionable testimonials. Max
Hastings throws banquets for him. William Waldegrave
writes scholarly monographs on the fascinating coincidence between the life of Captain Jack Aubrey and his
great-great grandfather aboard HMS Thetis.

And how snooty everyone is about the hero of my own childhood. Wooden, lifeless: that's what *le tout Londres* says about Horatio Hornblower. Not a patch on O'Brian, they say; and, for those of us who spent their nights with a torch under the bedclothes reading of the salt-spumed scourge of the French fleet, it is all dimly insulting.

That is why, after an interval of some years, I have risen early and read 100 pages of each, C.S. Forester and O'Brian; and I say now to the Hornblower-knockers: belay there, splice your futtocks lads, and stand by to go about.

Patrick O'Brian's Post Captain gets under way on page seven, and one is grateful for this head start. Come on, one feels like muttering at Aubrey and Maturin, as they play endless games of piquet and talk about their love lives: Engage the Enemy More Closely!

I will grant that O'Brian is a man of delightful erudition, subtly playing on Jane Austen, who never mentions the Napoleonic Wars, by plonking his characters in the middle of an Austen-style set-up, complete with bustling mother, and daughters darting glances at black-curled officers.

OK, so he is chock-full of gags about 18th-century medicine and diet. He has a wonderful ear for dialogue. But, as our heroes fritter their time in inconclusive boudoir assignations, one longs for the crack of the timbers beneath the roaring carronade, the raking of focsles with red-hot grape. Look at Hornblower's amazing 100-pages of derring-do.

We've hardly left Spithead before he's beaten off Simpson, the awful bully, and scandalised the navy with a duel. By page 21, Mr Midshipman Hornblower has been promoted to an exciting frigate, called the Indefatigable, prowling the Channel in search of Frenchies to duff up.

By page 40, it's ahoy, top-gallants athwart and let go the halliards, a ship in view. 'I don't like the cut of her jib, Sir. It's a Frenchie.' In next to no time, Hornblower, a mere 17, is in charge of the prize, the Marie Galante.

A few pages later, to his shame, his prize sinks beneath him, as a hole beneath the waterline causes the cargo of rice to expand; and I remember, as a child, meditating on the weight of that dreadful risotto. Next, he's captured by a French privateer. Then he sets fire to the ship, and the French are captured. Then they capture another French ship because Hornblower masters the icy pit of fear in his stomach and runs along the yard, 100 feet up, without any foot-rope.

Soon after, Hornblower breaks up a hideous game in which a man called Styles kills rats with his teeth. Then he helps French counter-revolutionaries blow up a bridge, witnesses a guillotine in action, and, at the bit I've got up to, things are obviously about to turn nasty . . .

Talk about action, eh? At a comparable stage in O'Brian's narrative, Aubrey and Maturin are still saying things such as 'By God, I wish I were in Bath' and 'You do look miserably hipped', and taking about two pages to walk up a hill and notice a rabbit.

They say Hornblower has no character; and it is true that he is described in nothing like the ornate detail of Aubrey, the hard-living Tory rake, and Maturin, the saturnine spy and man of medicine. But Hornblower has always seemed so economically limned by Forester.

Seasick and yet a burgeoning naval wizard; skinny, pale, froglike, youthful and yet authoritative: an Octavian figure. We are told he reads Gibbon, and that this inclines him to atheism. He has a keen sense of honour. He says things 'icily'. He is tone deaf. If that isn't characterisation, I don't know what is.

The more you set O'Brian side by side with Forester, the more obvious it is who is the true master of the genre. Forester saw first the dramatic potential of the wooden universe which was a ship of the line; and O'Brian has simply lifted motifs, such as the interesting dodges for getting a ship out of trouble. Which is not to detract from O'Brian's literary achievement, only to say that it is an evolution, not a revolution.

In defence of Wodehouse

If anyone thinks P.G. Wodehouse was a Nazi collaborator or, as the *Independent* described him last Friday, 'a sinister character with extreme right-wing views and even Nazi sympathies', then that is a comment on the catastrophic illiteracy of the age. There can scarcely have been a more devastating portrait of a fascist than in Wodehouse's *Code of the Woosters*. You will recall the figure of Spode, the would-be dictator, whose eye could open an oyster at 50 paces, and whose followers went around in black shorts ('You mean footer bags?' cried Bertie. 'How perfectly foul').

In the magnificent climax of this work, Bertie rounds on Spode, who has been behaving in an overweening fashion in the matter of the silver cow-creamer. Yes, for once in his career of masterly inactivity, Bertie Wooster lets another man have a piece of his mind. 'The trouble with you, Spode,' he says, 'is that because you have succeeded in inducing a handful of halfwits to disfigure the London scene by going about in black shorts, you think you're someone.

'You hear them shouting "*Heil Spode*!", and you imagine it is the Voice of the People. That is where you make your bloomer. What the Voice of the People is saying is: "Look at that frightful ass Spode swanking about in footer bags! Did you ever in your puff see such a perfect perisher?"'

It is to Wodehouse's eternal credit that this satire of Mosley and fascism, and all their hysterical pomposity, appeared in 1938; which was the year of Appeasement, and the Oxford by-election. In that election there appeared on the pro-Appeasement ticket one Quintin Hogg, who in 1941 was to disgrace his family name by accusing Wodehouse of 'treason'.

The charges against Wodehouse are so feeble, so deformed by spite, that they are worth repeating only for the light they cast not on Wodehouse, but on his enemies. In a nutshell, Wodehouse was at Le Touquet in 1940, trying to finish a Jeeves novel called *Joy in the Morning*. He had four chapters to go, and it seemed inconceivable to him – as it did to the British High Command – that the Germans would reach him before he had reached his lovingly plotted conclusion. As it was, and here, perhaps, are the real culprits in the whole business, the French folded in record time. Wodehouse was captured, and imprisoned in Loos, Liège, and later in a place called Tost, about which he made some jokes. He spent the war in captivity, and that was why he had to chase up royalties from neutral countries such as Sweden and Spain. This money was paid through the German foreign office; and, we now learn from the Public Record Office, this wholly innocent procedure put MI5, and now the *Independent*, in something of a state.

On being transported to Berlin, he was prevailed upon to give some light-hearted talks on German radio about camp life: how they made a cricket ball out of a nut with string round it, and what it was like to be given a shower by a French warder ('You come out of it a finer, deeper, graver man') – that kind of thing. 'Of course,' he wrote in a letter to a friend on 11 May 1942, from Berlin, 'I ought to have had the sense to see that it was a loony thing to do to use the German radio for even the most harmless stuff, but I didn't. I suppose prison life saps the intellect.'

If anyone's moral compass was scrambled by the episode, though, it was that of Hogg and everyone else in Britain who was moved to persecute him. As George Orwell pointed out in his essay 'In Defence of P.G. Wodehouse', the Left saw it as a 'chance to expose a wealthy parasite'; which, as anyone who has studied his modest life and indefatigable working methods – he produced five novels in prison, and ten short stories – will know is about as far from the truth as the *Independent*'s cretinous assertion that he was 'extremely right-wing' or had 'Nazi sympathies'.

Some of his assailants were authors, like A.A. Milne. For some of us, the doings of Christopher Robin become yet more emetic, when we remember how his creator behaved. Worst of all, the government started to take a hand. Duff Cooper, the Minister of Information, incited the BBC to do Wodehouse down, to sneer at his name, and to call him a 'playboy'. Soon the letters column of the *Daily Telegraph* was full of bile, and Quintin Hogg compared him to Lord Haw-Haw.

There used to be on my reading-list at school a book by one Wolf-Trotter, called *The Herd Instinct in Peace and War*, which explained how the Athenians were incited to turn against Socrates during the Peloponnesian war. Nothing is uglier than the whipping-up of prejudice, by demagogues, against those who are for some reason believed not to share the correct spirit of the age. It is a skill, of course, in which this government excels.

We caught a taste of it during the Kosovo crisis, during which the impartial reporting of John Simpson from Belgrade was denigrated by Alastair Campbell, and the patriotism of other reporters impugned; or one might mention the way the Prime Minister joined the mob in baying for the blood of Glenn Hoddle, who has some curious but harmless views on reincarnation. Wodehouse, in his own way, was as innocent as both. It was not as if he was some holy fool, who failed to understand the moral dimension of his predicament. As others who listened to his broadcasts appreciated, he saw the Nazis for what they were. His broadcasts were used throughout the war, at the American intelligence school at Camp Ritchie, as models of anti-Nazi propaganda.

He made fun of his captors, as he gently and lethally satirised Spode, who 'looked as if Nature had intended to make a gorilla, and had changed its mind at the last moment'. His only failure was in not seeing how, as the mood of the country changed in 1941, his actions could be seized upon by the bullies and creeps who still, unfortunately, have so large a role in public life. Like Spode, whose dark secret it was to be the proprietor of 'Eulalie', a lingerie store, they will get their comeuppance. They have their dark secrets, too. Campbell has his Eulalie.

Iron Tongue

Lines Not By Ted Hughes, Poet Laureate, on the Occasion of the Piercing of Zara Phillips's Tongue with a Metal Stud and the 98th Birthday of Her Majesty The Queen Mother.

I sit in the cavern where
Jaws eat and are finished
Shut wombed in a dark shed of mouth.

A big trout muscle I dart
And writhe through oceans of speech
or tirelessly piranha

The gulleyed chinks between the
Skull-rooted tombstones in search of
Spinach, cornflakes, spaghetti

Al Vongole, anything else that gets
Stuck . . . The light breaks from
the gibbet-hung tattoo parlour.

They see me. I try to get up
And run. 'It's him. It's him.'
A freezing hand catches me by the

Blind root and comes the drilling
Pain and flesh twirled like
Dry bark bits and blood in

The loud tunnel. In goes old stud,
Deep in otter gaffed by welding cold
Fish fur fang fowl fox ow ow ow.

It'th frankly jolly unthightly
and maketh it hard to thpeak.
Happy 98th Birthday, Your Majesty.

Virgil's message for the Middle East

It was the custom for many centuries, and in some places
it still is the custom, to mark any great crisis by consulting
Virgil. You flip open the collected works of the greatest
Roman poet, close your eyes and jab; so that, for instance,
if your finger lights on *equo ne credite, Teucri* (trust not
the horse, Trojans, *Aen.* II 47), you don't bet on the 4.15
at Doncaster. The habit seems to date from early Christian

times, because the Fourth Eclogue, published in about 40 BC, was found to contain some stunning stuff about the birth of a saviour-child, not to mention a virgin. 'This chap Virgil,' said the early Christians, 'he must have been a prophet.'

King Charles tried the *sortes Virgilianae* on the eve of the battle of Naseby and, if you read Virgil, you can dimly see why. Perhaps it is the elevated diction, the poetic compression. It may be that his words, which, as he said, he licked into shape like bear-cubs, can bear a multiplicity of meanings. Or it might be that he truly was a marvel, that he understood human nature in some deep and universal way.

I have never been so amazed by his gifts for prophecy as I was one summer, while languishing on a kibbutz in Israel. The invasion of Lebanon had recently taken place, and the massacres of Sabra and Chatilla. The name of Ariel Sharon, who is now Prime Minister, was already the object of international vilification. I was trying in my undergraduate way to apportion right and wrong, while mugging up on the *Aeneid*, when suddenly the words seemed to swim. I saw the hidden meaning of the text. And the vatic truth of Virgil is all the more useful now when the Middle Eastern conflict seems so bitter, and uncontrolled, and has spilled on to the letters pages of this magazine.

What is the second half of the *Aeneid*, which tells of the foundation of Rome, but an extraordinary allegory, 2,000 years in advance, of the postwar foundation of Israel and the cruel struggle with the indigenous Palestinians? Do you remember it? Do you hear your Latin O-level tolling from the depths, like the church bell of some sea-drowned village? You don't? Then let me remind you.

At the end of the Trojan war the city is in ruins, the population massacred. There is a small band of survivors, led by Aeneas, and they have no choice but to flee overseas in search of a new homeland. Throughout the voyage they are persecuted by Juno, queen of the gods, with a bias and vengefulness that border on the irrational. Finally, they come to their destined land in Italy. Now when I say it is destined, I mean just that. Throughout the poem, we are told that Italy is the location marked out by fate, a special place, reserved by the gods, for the survivors of the Trojan massacre. Virgil goes to some lengths to contrive a link between Troy and the site of the future Rome. We are informed that a very long time ago a shadowy hero called Dardanus had left Italy and made his way to Troy.

In other words, it is important to Virgil that we should think of the Trojans as having some right of return to this land, some link with it sanctioned by myth (though you will agree that the Trojans had a much less impressive territorial claim to Italy than the Jews had to Palestine). And, of course, when Aeneas and co. arrive there are people already there, indigenous people, and they view the newcomers with fear.

Aeneas and the Trojans find themselves sucked into war with Turnus and the Italians, the Latins. Ostensibly it is a struggle for the hand of the beautiful Lavinia, but her name also connotes the geographical area around Lavinium. This is a struggle for land and for mastery. The Latins live in Latium. The Trojans want to live there. One or other will have to give ground. Latium, incidentally, is on the West Bank of the Tiber. For the last six books of the poem, this means *bella, horrida bella*: war, bristling war.

Who is in the right? With whom should we expect Virgil to side? For a lesser poet, that question might have been easy. The *Aeneid* is a political poem, written to please the emperor Augustus. It is an epic that glorifies the foundation of Rome. Virgil was a Roman. He could have demonised all those who stood in the way of Rome's greatness. He could have blackened Turnus, so that Aeneas might shine the more brightly. And what does he do instead?

Respectfully, I say to all those who have strong feelings on the Arab-Israeli question that they could do worse than read the climax of the poem, in Book XII, to see how Rome's best poet dealt with the tragic dilemma.

Here is Turnus, fleeing for his life before the wrathful Aeneas. He has no weapon but a stone and, as he tries to throw it, his blood freezes and his limbs fail, and he falters in fear. And there is Aeneas, infinitely better armed, his spear and sword newly forged by Vulcan. Does he stay his hand? Does he show mercy to the underdog? He does not.

He hurls that spear like a black hurricane, and it passes through the outer circle of the sevenfold shield, and through the cuirass, and into Turnus's thigh. Then, as Aeneas stands over him, the stricken Latin holds up his hands in the universal, eternal gesture of surrender. For a second or two, as we enter the last 20 lines of the epic, the Trojan hesitates. He lets fall his sword arm, until his eye is caught by a trophy on Turnus's shoulder, the baldric of Pallas, another Trojan whom Turnus has killed.

Then, on fire with fury, and terrible in his rage, Aeneas gives way to vengeance, and he butchers Turnus. Boiling with anger, he buries his sword in the chest of his adversary, and, as the poet tells us, 'his limbs relaxed and chilled, and his life fled moaning and resentful to the Shades'. And that's it. That's the end.

You put down the *Aeneid*, as they used to say on the back of blockbusters, breathless and stunned. No one can read it without being aghast at the sudden brutality of Aeneas. No one can fail to feel pity for Turnus. That is what makes the poem, and the greatness of Virgil. He has been venerated down the ages because he has the moral depth and poetic sensibility to see tragedy on both sides.

It wasn't the fault of Aeneas that he was to found a new homeland in Italy. It was an act preordained by the gods. And, in any event, where else were the Trojans to live, harried as they were over land and sea by the hatred of Juno? And it wasn't the fault of the poor Latins that they should be living in the exact spot which fate had marked out for the new nation.

I remember munching my felafel back in the kibbutz, and preparing for another 12-hour session of washing-up, and thinking, by gum, yes, Virgil is right. That is how to look at Israel and the displaced Palestinian peoples. It is possible to support Israel's right to exist, and to believe in the destiny of Israel as passionately as Virgil believed in the destiny of Rome, and still to feel moved by the sufferings of those who were forced to make way.

With Virgil in your hand, you begin, too, to see the enemies of Israel with new eyes. There is a trace of Juno, surely, in the blistering fury, the implacability, of some of the recent correspondents to *The Spectator*. I think of Juno's raging speech in Book X, where she denounces the Trojans and their illegal settlements. 'They take up the pitchy firebrand and violently assault the Latins, they lay a heavy yoke on farmlands not their own and drive off their plunder,' she froths, furious with Jupiter for letting it happen. And there, I think, speak Ian Gilmour and his kind, as they call attention to the breaches of UN declarations, the shootings, the disproportionate Arab casualties.

They have a point; they have a view. But it is a partial view and one wonders whether deep down they accept the hard, fated necessity of Israel to exist. Lord Gilmour has elsewhere analogised between the Israeli occupation of the West Bank and the Nazi occupation of France, as well as the Soviet occupations of Hungary or Afghanistan. These do not strike me as happy or accurate comparisons. For all its faults, Israel is the only democracy in the region;

and it seems to me that critics of Israel pay insufficient attention to another aspect of the Palestinian tragedy: the mad way in which young Arabs are manipulated into violence by their leaders.

But then you will find all that in Virgil, too, if you look. You will find how the virus of madness, *furor*, infects the Latins, when a peace might have been attained. You will also find a prophecy that one day, after Turnus is dead, '*paribus se legibus ambae invictae gentes aeterna in foedera mittant*' (both peoples, unconquered, will join with equal laws in an everlasting pact). In the days when MPs could quote Latin they used to say this about Ireland with such blissful persistence that O'Connell had to beg them to stop.

I know it sounds optimistic to talk now about a pact between Arabs and Israelis. You may also say that they haven't much call for Virgil these days, the suffering peoples of Nablus and Hebron and Jerusalem. To which I would say that nothing much else seems to have worked. Virgil the prophet has not always been wrong, and he understood the tragic symmetry of a war between predestined settlers and displaced natives. Read him, Gilmour, and see the position of Juno for what it is.

WHAT HOUSE?
WHAT CAR?
WHAT THE HELL?

It was the end of the Cold War, and the consequent universal spread of free market capitalism, which, as I say, was the pivotal moment of the last fifteen years. Here we consider just some of the glories which our consumerist society has been spreading across the planet: fast cars, porn, post-ironic game-shows, expensive children's toys, luxury bodyguards, house market speculation and, joy of joys, a privatised railway system.

London house prices

There used to be an iron law of economics, I think, that when the crocuses were out, or possibly the daffodils, then, first in ones and twos and then in joyous, colourful clumps, the 'For Sale' signs would sprout in the streets of London. Clearly, this has not been true these last few years. As one in search of a house, who has pushed buzzers and admired rockeries across the nation's capital for two months, my guess is that this year the choice and availability will be little better.

'It'll pick up,' say the estate agents, the hounds of spring, snuffling and chivvying. At this stage, surely, any such optimism will make matters worse. It sows hope, the hope that, if owners will just wait, it is only a matter of time before prices once again take off. For the English owner-occupier, the hope is more dangerous than the despair. My guess is that he or she could have further shocks in store.

Let me at once say that these are merely the observations of a provincial oaf, a bumpkin, stuck away in Brussels for five years, without the benefit of countless dinner-party symposia on the housing market, the immense learning on the subject shared by most *Spectator* readers.

But I can say with authority that the mind-set of the London vendor is to be found nowhere else in western Europe. Speaking as a would-be buyer (buyor, I almost said), the assumptions seem as demented as ever.

Despite the punishment of the last four years, the middle classes cling to the superstition that the natural trajectory of their houses' value is vertiginously upwards. So strong is this belief that, as far as I can see, instead of dropping their sights, they would rather sit in a dim, cold property, progressively selling off the furniture and eating Kit-e-Kat, waiting, waiting for the market to turn and for the mass mania to begin again.

In consequence, very little habitable property seems to be for sale, and almost nothing central and affordable. I know that some of the potential sellers, in fact, 2 million across the country, are in the negative equity trap, the mortgage being worth more than the value of the property.

One feels the pathos of these debt desperadoes, the DIY fiends who have spent tens of thousands wrecking a perfectly good house with peach-coloured fitted wardrobes and walk-in mirrored bathrooms, all half-built because they ran out of money.

Then there are the other, equally frantic reasons why

some want to sell: the young couple in an intensifying hell of noise and perfumed nappy bags; the wife of the musician suddenly stricken by a disabling illness. Take your time, they say, as one tears one's eyes away from the fascinating self-analytical jottings on the bedside table; as one speculates, how unfairly, about their lives; the pitiful testimony of the built-in chopping board, scored with 20 years of devotion to Mrs Beeton, now to be abandoned; the cats, that sure index of unsatisfied human cravings – the flaps, the scratching-posts, the multi-storey cat-baskets.

One almost flinches at how obviously the owner, usually the wife, has made an effort with her appearance, doubtless on the advice of some hectoring property supplement – lipstick, haircut, necklace – and how she has laid out photographs of the minuscule yorkstone patio in the summer when the creepers are in full leaf.

And then, after they have been anxiously watching from the corner of their eye, one hears the painful gush, almost of relief, when they detect that one is not likely to be a taker for the place where they have occasionally been so happy. 'Oh, I think it will be far too small for you, with your baby' etc. One feels so intrusive, so callous.

And yet, however much the heart bleeds for them, these people are fundamentally deluded. The asking prices are still crazy.

I had always thought Notting Hill was meant to be a vaguely bohemian area. Marina and I would be very happy in this house here near Ladbroke Grove, for example, amid the ulcerated stucco of what appears to be a disused international ganja exchange. But Mr Faron Sutaria is asking us to pay £395,000 for the privilege.

Laugh, if you like, at my naïvety; but is it not frightening that my generation is expected to go into debt to the tune of hundreds of thousands of pounds to live within a long cricket ball's throw of the west end of the Portobello Road?

Am I alone in finding it strange that one's parents, not, *mutatis mutandis*, appreciably better off than ourselves at comparable moments in their lives, were able to buy great schlosses in central London?

As for the present meagre market, some of the more reasonably priced items are acquiring landmark status. Almost every estate agent in London seems to be offering 'this rare opportunity to purchase' a house in Sebastian Street, EC1, which appears to be freshly mortar-bombed. Just pour in another couple of hundred thousand grand, the implication is, just add a roof and, hey presto, a bargain!

We did make an offer on what seemed to be a pricy but just manageable terraced house off Highbury Fields, and the vendors said snap at once. It was only later that a rival agent told us that the Channel Tunnel's underground rail link to St Pancras would require a ventilation shaft and escape hatch somewhere near the kitchen.

The rest of the offerings are dominated by people pitching the price at what they fondly imagine their home should 'achieve' in two years' time. If anybody is interested I could show him a small house in Brook Green, darkest Hammersmith. All right, so it has polished stripped-pine floors and a sunken bath; but it costs £350,000! *Donnez-moi un break*, as we say in Brussels. On the day we saw it, Michael Frayn, the prognathous farceur, was in the kitchen. Maybe that's it. Maybe it's an extra £30,000, just for being the kind of house in which Michael Frayn might have his hands wrapped around a mug of tea, polishing his epigrams on a Saturday afternoon.

And if, in the next couple of years, people did come to think nothing of paying that kind of money, the price rise would be treated as the most tremendous piece of good news, front-page in all the papers, pure Martyn Lewis; whereas, as the Bundesbank president, Herr Hans Tietmeyer, once pointed out, in Germany and elsewhere it would be a bad sign. It has suddenly struck me, coming from Brussels, why the British middle classes will never wear a single European currency, whatever Sir Leon Brittan may say in his new book. It would be like the ERM, only worse. It would be the end of house-price inflation.

We simply could not run our railways on these lines

I can pinpoint the moment when I thought I knew the answer to British Rail's problems. It came in a sort of blinding flash somewhere near Dalston Kingsland on the North London Line, about a month ago (December, 1994), in a train that had inexplicably stopped.

The insight was building slowly as we all sat in our overheated prison for first 10, then 20, then 30, then 35 minutes, as our appointments came and went and our mornings were wrecked and we shifted and coughed and reread the Obituary columns in an effort to internalise our feelings until finally, and, I might say, with the encouragement of my fellow passengers, I knocked gently on the door of the driver's cabin.

Yeees, said a youth in a donkey jacket; no, he had no idea what the matter might be, and no, he would not care to say when the train might move again. It depended, apparently, on five other trains with unguessable problems of their own. And no, he said, he would not allow us to mount a kind of Von Ryan's Express break-out through the brambles and into the wilds of Dalston, where one could presumably find a taxi.

And it was then, as we watched him climb slowly down from his cab and pick up an ancient black telephone on a telegraph post, presumably to find out why the signals were red, that the idea swelled into a conviction of Thatcherian proportions. Enough, I thought, is enough. Sell it. Flog it off.

Let us take the whole boiling thing out of the hands of these lackadaisical jobsworths with feudal command structures, their hopeless, statist mentality as ingrained as the bubblegum on the balding cushions, their apathetic approach to their passengers, their Spanish practices and their Swahili station announcements and their deficient signalling.

Yes, let us privatise British Rail, I thought, and be done with it. Anything that might restore an ethos of competition and service. Look at the transformation that was wrought with British Telecom. Who cares, I thought, if they close the North London Line: better than gulling people aboard on the pretence that it will take them from A to B. Nothing could be worse, I thought. Could it . . . ?

Oh, I have since realised, when passion subsided, but it could. The most extraordinary aspect of railway privatisation is that, in spite of our willingness to be persuaded, the Transport Secretary, Dr Brian Mawhinney, has done nothing to persuade me, and the many who have suffered worse at the hands of BR, that our service will be any better. Far from it.

Admirers of the railways say, and I do not dispute it, that the North London Line is untypically bad. The electorate is more interested in what will happen to the other 15,000 daily services, some of which keep to the timetable. And the more one contemplates the manner of railway privatisation, if not the generally excellent principle of selling state assets, the more one suspects that the Government is determined to slash its own wrists.

What have passengers learnt in the last 10 days alone? That they may have to travel for up to an hour by car to

242

buy a ticket, as the number of stations selling through tickets is cut from 2,500 to 294; that the 25 new train operating companies will have to haggle, like the UN Security Council, to decide the new timetable; that privatisation has already caused British Rail to spend £90 million, which could have built two tram networks, on rejigging its bureaucracy; and that the Government is now demanding further cuts of £400 million which can fall nowhere except on services.

No wonder Labour yesterday promised to unscramble much of the enterprise. And yet the form of the privatisation means that the Government is pronged on a dilemma. If it goes ahead – and there seems to be little 'if' about it – Dr Mawhinney must choose between offending a crucial swath of the electorate, and a privatisation fiasco.

In order to make the job of running the 25 putative train operating companies commercially attractive, the Government has decided that Mr John Swift, the Regulator, shall do his job 'with a light touch'. It is the prospect of his minimal interference, though, which is the cause of the uncertainty, and the scares sweeping the commuting public. It is simply not clear, for instance, whether people's special discounted fares will be preserved: the supersavers, apexes, season tickets; nor where they will be able to buy them.

If it deprives the commuter of these essentials of life, the Government will face a new foe at the barricades in Trafalgar Square, far more dangerous than the rentamobs of the poll tax or the Criminal Justice Bill: it will face an insurrection, of one kind or another, of chaps with furled umbrellas and half-completed crosswords.

And if, on the other hand, Mr Swift adds all the riders and prescriptions that will comfort the travelling public, then the Government is equally dammed. For if he fails to give the new private companies the freedom to make economies on late trains and Sunday services, the City will take fright and the sell-off will founder. Already Mr Richard Branson and the bus companies have lost interest, and we may see nothing more than a handful of management buy-outs on the more profitable routes.

For what do they stand to own, these brave few who may be prevailed upon to take over the running of our trains? Not the trains themselves (which will be leased from separate companies); not the track (rented out by Railtrack); nothing, in fact, except the uniforms of their personnel, and the Cornish pasties in the unspecified interval between their baking and their consumption. Worst of all, they will be dependent on Mr Bob Horton and Railtrack, who will charge them at an unknown rate for using the track.

It is said that herein lay the cardinal mistake of the privatisation: that the Government should have followed Mr Major's original notion and sold off BR in regional units. At least, that way, the companies operating the trains would have had the financial advantage of Railtrack's assets. With 90,000 railway arches, so we are told, BR's infrastructure offers serious scope for wine bars. The Government is accused of asset-stripping, in selling off Railtrack separately, with a view to a judiciously timed and sizeable cut in income tax from the £6 billion proceeds.

That may be true. And yet even if Railtrack's assets had been there to help the companies, they would not have been enough. Under any circumstances, the train companies will be dependent on Government subsidy. If the Government sees this complicated pseudo-privatisation as an excuse to spend less on the railways, then it has gravely misjudged the public mood. And however it juggles rail ownership, the Government, quite properly, will be judged by whether passengers can conveniently buy tickets, and whether trains run on time.

Road testing the bodyguards

In Lasne, the richest suburb of Brussels, is one of the few serious European bodyguard schools outside Switzerland; at least, so says its proprietor. As I looked through the windscreen-wipers at the perimeter fence and the high brass plaque saying 'Ecole de Gardes du Corps Roger Grolet', the place certainly seemed authentic. Three alsatians circled in the dark within, whining and wagging their tails. I tooted the horn. Cold rain dripped off the pines.

My chronic doubts about bodyguards had surfaced again recently in a Brussels press conference. Yasser Arafat was only about five feet away, and his fuzz-covered jowls, his pendulous lips leered so close that, frankly, I wondered about his security.

The question, you see, was whether Arafat's five perspiring heavies – or any professional bodyguards – were useful, or pointless trappings of power. How quick are those tarantula hands, those roving eyes? Would they be quick enough to stop an assassin standing where I was? Perhaps it could be checked, I mused. Yes: it was laborious, but it could be done.

Out came Grolet, tweed-jacketed, beaming, walrus-moustached, a man such as only Belgium could produce, balancing an umbrella and chiding the dogs. Inside his office, he unholstered a Colt hand-gun, weighing, I later established, 1.5 kilos and with an eight-inch silencer.

In case I was a villain, he explained, savouring my reaction, an agent of the kind that had tried to liquidate him more than once before. He had an even bigger one, he said, a .44 magnum, but, alas, it was illegal. 'The law, Monsieur Johnson, the law is made for the *crapule*.'

I made a mental note for Lockwood, my colleague in Brussels, who had agreed to pose as my assassin and test the mettle of Belgium's leading bodyguards: no loaded guns, not on their side anyway.

Torrentially, Grolet explained his ideas about life and death. With 'hwuk' and 'hwok' noises, and startling agility for a big-bellied man of 62, he showed the quick-draw technique he pioneered for the Belgian gendarmerie. For 35 years, he told me, he has been training young men to be bodyguards, often scions of the country's nobility, with their inchoate right-wing impulses.

Like one of those veteran soldiers, perhaps, from the military societies of Thebes or Sparta, who took novices for training in their caves, Grolet has moulded them according to his principles. He has taught them to 'decouple a fantastic energy from the cosmos'; they have heard, maybe even witnessed, how the KGB, the US marines, Arab terrorists, have all sought out his advice.

Time was passing, and I was anxious to see some training. Grolet was charming, and no doubt superbly well-acquainted with the world's hit-men, but would his defence system stand up to Lockwood?

From behind the door, throughout the interview, had issued thuds and oriental gong noises. Grolet led the way to the training room, past blow-up photographs, eye-catchingly arranged over mantelpieces, of a long-legged 40-ish blonde wearing no clothes; his wife, he explained: 'There are no taboos here.'

Four sweaty men in their late 20s, kitted out in blue judo suits, sprang to attention. Everything they did spoke deference to Grolet. At one of his Fu Manchu barks, they started to lay into tall sandbags suspended from the rafters with a great hue and cry, thwacking them with wooden staves and prowling backwards and sideways on the balls of their feet.

'Hwargh,' said Grolet, and they stopped. 'No one has this technique,' he said, waving one of the staves beneath my nose. 'We call this the Roger Grolet – the RG' (*airjay*). 'You scarcely have to touch a *crapule* and he will collapse.'

To the untutored eye, it looked like three feet of sawn-off broomstick. 'You can stop his heart,' he went on. 'Stroke the *crapule* in the right place and his brain will vibrate for five minutes. Here,' he said, 'it's just a caress.'

Before I could assent, Grolet hit me lightly on the side of the neck, near what I imagine is the carotid artery, and for several moments, I must report, the brain-pan quivered. '*Voilà*,' said the sage, adding that my 'centre of command was neutralised'. Memo to self re Lockwood, I thought: no sticks.

For our plan was to create, so far as possible, an encounter between would-be killer and victim which would test the deepest, most buried instincts of the bodyguards. There was no doubting the ideals Grolet instilled. As Bertrand Massenges de Collombes, 28, a former loss adjuster, said of his decision to sign up with the school at a cost of £11,000 for a six-month session, 'I wanted to change my life. I wanted to have stronger values and defend people who need it.'

All very well, I thought, but would he or his colleagues perform the ultimate act of protection? Clint Eastwood did it, as the title suggests, in his latest film *In the Line of Fire*. Poor brain-damaged James Brady, whose US gun-control law now seems set for success, did it for Ronald Reagan. Archduchess Sophie did it, vainly, pathetically, for Franz Ferdinand at Sarajevo in 1914.

But would Bertrand, Benoit, Werner or Eric stop a bullet? Would they take one for me?

After a couple of visits to the school, Grolet agreed genially, though with a certain mystification, to lend two bodyguards. On the appointed morning, half an hour early, they were outside my office in one of his two hulking 6.2 litre Chevrolet transit vans bearing the school's name and in several places the legend 'New Techniques in Shooting and Defence'.

Out stepped Eric Delvallee, 30, former social sciences student and Benoit, 31, Grolet's son and co-instructor. They were contending – though they did not know it – against Christopher Lockwood, 30, possessor of a good first in PPE from Oxford in 1984.

As we shook hands by the lovely ornamental pond in Marie-Louise Square, near the statue of Artemis, a man bustled along the cobbled pavement, too fast for comfort. Eric manhandled him into the street; rather roughly, I thought.

In the EC Commission's noon briefing, which I attend daily as a Brussels reporter, rumour flew about my sudden need for bodyguards. No, I explained, Euro-federalists had not put out a contract, this was just an experiment. Spaniards, Italians and others gazed as Eric, a light-haired scrum-half, moved six or seven paces in front to the left, with Benoit, tall and heavy, behind to the right. One colleague, drawing a plastic sugar-stirrer too jerkily from his overcoat pocket, had the misfortune to provoke Eric's suspicions. Fright crossed his face as the bodyguard marked him, and hands, muscled by squeezing squash balls, closed in on the elbow.

The climax of the experiment was almost too thrilling to narrate. Despite a leading alpha in philosophical logic, Lockwood had been out-generalled on the way to the Commission. After checking my car thoroughly for bombs, Benoit drove us there, leaving him in ambush behind a petrol pump.

But when we came back from lunch, as Eric walked six paces ahead into the office lobby, I was already thinking. Under the stairs – the stairs!

With a yell, Lockwood was upon us, gun waving. The heart stopped. Eric was there. Events moved in a flurry.

Eric said 'pow', making his hand into an imaginary gun, and Lockwood skidded, subsiding with windmilling arms. Moments later he rose, unhurt, breathing heavily, but clearly no longer a threat. His wallet was found days later. Perhaps, looking back, it was his refusal to wear the expensive PLO terrorist mask I had bought, which he claimed scratched his nose; perhaps his water-pistol malfunctioned. Perhaps, somehow, his finer feelings rebelled against eliminating the bureau chief, even symbolically.

But the agreement was that a substantial jet of water had to hit my suit, and, though he came within five feet, not a drop attained the mark. Eric was too quick. As Lockwood said with typical good grace, 'You always know when you have been got.' A complicated experiment, granted, and we would not claim to have settled the question decisively. But if you think your life is in danger, go to Grolet.

Early Learning Centre climbing frame

Something jabbed me as I sat down the other day, and as I pulled the lost steel nut from the back pocket, the feeling came flooding back. Like those heroes of American movies who experience harrowing ''Nam flashbacks' at the sight of a helicopter, I was there again in the drizzling garden with the Early Learning Centre Giant Frame, a test of the human spirit on a par with Hempleman-Adams and his plod to the North Pole.

It was Good Friday, and though the weather was not propitious, we began cheerfully. 'I expect we'll get it all wrong and have to begin again,' I said to my co-assembler, looking at the gaily coloured instructions. After perhaps an hour, we were vaguely aware how much force was required. Our arms were beginning to ache.

Samson-like, one of us would strain at the blue vertical bars to align them with the red horizontal ones, and then in the millisecond when the green one was also flush, the other would try to jam in the screw, with two washers and a nut; and the bigger it grew, the more difficult it became.

We were both reasonably strong. How on earth was a single mum supposed to cope with this, we asked. The hours passed, and from time to time, people would come out from the house with cups of coffee. Lunch came. Tea went. The weather turned yet colder.

I had been in the middle of reading Anthony Beevor's shattering account of the battle of Stalingrad and, in my imagination, we became like those German soldiers trying to start their tanks in 30 degrees of frost, losing the skin of their hands the minute they touched the metal, morale sinking, the veneer of civilisation peeling away.

'It doesn't need a washer,' we would say as the washers fell from our fingers into the churned grass. Sometimes, we tried using a 6in nail to keep the holes in alignment. The nails bent. We devised a kind of rope tourniquet with which we tried, futilely, to pull the bars together. As the darkness began to close in, we tried to hammer the screws in place. We laid the contraption on its side and leant on it, groaning and whimpering. At one stage, we used an ancient hand-powered auger to enlarge the holes. We only scratched the paint.

Each of us had moments when he wanted to jack it in, but couldn't face the womenfolk inside; and every time it seemed impossible, every time a joint had defied us for an hour or more, the bolt would suddenly shoot home, obeying some unknown law of physics, and we would scrabble the nut in place.

Just as supper was announced, it was done. In the twilight, our frame looked quite plausible, if you squinted a bit. The thing was certainly rigid. In fact, it was like a giant steel spring, humming with suppressed kinetic energy. We slept proud and exhausted. As my eyes closed, it was like the end of a day's skiing, when the trees and the snow seem still to be hurtling towards you, except that I could see the bars – blue bars, red bars, green bars . . .

The morning brought doubt. In the daylight, last night's triumph of the will looked like a trod-on shuttlecock. 'That's not right,' said my wife, picking up the instructions and instantly seeing where we had goofed. It was no use arguing.

In a stupor of defeat, we rang the Early Learning Centre Giant Frame Suicide Helpline, whose number we found printed – a giveaway, surely – on the back of the instructions. With the help of a mobile phone and a nice man called Terry in Swindon, we spent another day in toil. Terry's secret was keeping the joints loose until the end. 'It's got to be falling apart as you build it,' he said. We had no trouble there.

For the record, and for those who think we were just saps, it was easier after our tuition, but not much. It still needed surprising strength. At the end of the second day, it was finished – well, except for the slide, which didn't seem to have the full complement of nuts.

The children climbed apathetically on a couple of rungs, before running off to play with something else. It hardly matters. To build the Early Learning Centre Giant Frame is an end in itself. One does it because it is there.

Going on *Have I Got News For You*

Walking down the Holloway Road the other night. Feeling a bit low. On my way to buy some beer from the corner shop. Man goes by on a bike. 'Oi, you,' he cries, 'you chinless tosser.' For some reason this enrages me and I make to pursue him, but he has the advantage of wheels. I don't mind being called a tosser, but I draw the line at chinless, since I have a fine selection of chins.

As I wander disconsolately on, I wonder what has inspired his wrath, and conclude that it must be this TV gameshow I keep going on. A lot of people say an MP should not go on a show like that. They say it is not commensurate with the dignity of the office.

Think of the great statesmen of the past, they say. Would Winston Churchill have gone on *Have I Got News For You*? Would Pericles? Look here, they say. If you go on a show like that, it is like going into a ring with Mike Tyson, pointing your chin at him, folding your hands behind your back and saying, come on then you big gold-toothed wuss. Of course you are going to be decked. You are there to be made a fool of, a prat, a berk, a buffoon.

You must be utterly mad, say my many critics, to try to match the dice-n-slice wits of Merton, Hislop, Deayton. One man told me, a few years ago, that I was barely more articulate than the tub of lard they once put in the place of Roy Hattersley. Another compared my performance unfavourably with that of the late Paula Yates, who called Ian Hislop the spawn of the devil before bursting into tears.

The very nice woman who runs the *Telegraph* executive dining room once told me, as if to cheer me up, that I came across as being marginally less shifty than Neil and Christine Hamilton. If you remember, they were handed brown paper envelopes at the end of the show.

In fact, there has been so much criticism, over the years, for my three appearances, that I feel obliged to defend my motives in going on. Because I know that there will be some who read this page – high, sacerdotal intellects – who feel that the hot seat of *Have I Got News For You* is not the place for an *homme serieux*. Is that what you feel? If you do, I must respectfully disagree.

As one of the many doe-eyed producer girls told me, an invitation to appear on the programme – now in its 11th year – is by no means a rare or exclusive thing. I happen to know that they have recently invited Max Hastings, one of my journalistic heroes. And why did he turn them down? Was it because he thought the whole thing was beneath him? Possibly.

But might it not also have been that he was afflicted by an unwonted spasm of self-doubt? I do not know whether the Liberator of Port Stanley went all yellow-bellied as he contemplated an hour of tart rejoinders from Ian Hislop. I do not know whether his knees knock. Only the great war reporter can tell us if he secretly trembles at the idea of coming off second best to Paul Merton. But does he not owe it to us to prove our suspicions unfounded, pick up the phone, and accept the gameshow's challenge?

The first and best reason for going on, is that it is rank cowardice not to. And I could go further, and elaborate some political reasons, as well.

They say that the House of Commons is not what it was. They say that MPs are losing out in the Darwinian struggle for power. They are being constitutionally eclipsed by the media, by Brussels, by inventive judges. Well, is that not all the more reason for us to lever ourselves off the green benches and take the fight into the enemy camp? Why should the tribunes of the people not pop up on the big vernacular TV shows, and not just the thing after midnight with Andrew Neil?

If I understood the producer girl rightly, the last Tory MP they had on the show was my fellow Euro-sceptic Teddy Taylor, and that was five years ago. It is not for want of invitations.

And then there is a final and by no means unimportant consideration. They give you a thousand pounds. That means you can take approximately two children skiing. That's worth quite a lot of TV humiliation, in my view. And if you are still not convinced, if you still think it's all infra dig, then I give up. But I have only one question. What are you doing, at 9pm on Friday, and 10pm at the weekend, watching the thing in the first place? That is the real scandal of *Have I Got News For You* – that so many people watch it.

I am stunned by how many intelligent and educated people seem to have nothing better to do than watch this programme. They could be taking their loved ones out to dinner, or to a play, or flying by Easyjet to Nice, or taking some other measures to boost the British economy and stop us all sliding into recession. They could be reading a book – a rip-roaring account of the last election campaign, for instance, modestly priced at £14.99, published by Harper-Collins. They could be learning the piano. They could be knocking out a play. Instead, they sit like the prisoners in Plato's cave, watching the flickering images before them and mistaking them for reality. That is the shocker: not that people are so foolish as to appear on TV, but that people are so idle as to watch it.

And that, of course, is the best way to protect yourself from shame, if you do go on it. Don't watch it. I haven't . . . yet.

Arthur interrupts me in Boobtropolis

Oh flip. The door was open. The door to my office was open and Arthur the caretaker was still there, whistling as he came up the stairs. Oh jeepers, I thought. This gave me several options. I could either leap up and shut the door, which Arthur would find puzzling and possibly rude. Or else I could try to butch it out, or try to turn the hellish gizmo off. Alternatively, I could try to cover up the incriminating evidence on my screen.

Have you ever been in this position? Has any other human being ever known this predicament? Just look at the statistics. According to the newspaper, the Internet boffins say that 70 per cent of the world's surfers at any given moment are looking at pornography. Yup. That's right. It's the engine of Onan. It's a glorified intercontinental wankerama, and any second now Arthur the cigar-smoking cleaner was going to catch me with my screen frozen and up to my eyeballs in ahem . . . Cough.

Perhaps I should explain. About six years ago I suggested a column for the *Daily Telegraph* on this sensational new wheeze, which Tory ministers at the time were calling the 'electronic superhighway'. The piece we were looking for was a spooky, shivers-up-your spine effort on the lines of 'The Vile Images Which Abound In Cyberspace'. So, in the company of Kate the *Telegraph* librarian, we footled around for a while. And I am ashamed to say we drew a more or less total blank. Everything seemed to take for ever. We finally came across something that sounded faintly saucy, but it turned out to be a Chinese takeaway in San Diego.

As a result, the article was perhaps not as bloodcurdling as it ought to have been; I'll never forget the scorn on the lovely lips of the features editor as I was treated to the kind of reception that the *Mail* might give a star reporter who returns to the office with the news that the widow didn't want to talk. And so I hope you will accept it when I say that it was partly through a desire to avenge that searing episode that I was in my current fix: and partly, of course, through sheer what do you call it? Curiosity.

That's right. It was an honest journalistic desire to get to grips with a modern phenomenon. No. Wait.

We can do better than that; it wasn't a desire. It was a duty. It was my duty as an editor to evaluate – there's a good word – the type of material that was, um, corrupting, er, polluting . . . Oh, you know what I mean. There I was, innocently looking at skiing holidays, in my first go on the Internet, when I thought I'd just tap in the word 'girls' on the search engine, just to *see*, for heaven's sake.

And pow. Before you could say 'Double you double you double you dot com' I was being welcomed to something called 'Boobtropolis'. In fact, I was being given an exceedingly frank and cordial welcome by a girl with no clothes on whose name I am ashamed to admit I can't remember. Oh boy. I think the charms of Boobtropolis must have absorbed me for a minute or so, after which two things occurred to me more or less at once. The first was that Arthur was approaching and the second was that Boobtropolis was not an easy place to escape from.

Every time I clicked the little cross in the top left-hand corner, in the hope of getting back to the fresh, clean world of skiing holidays, some new gorgeous creature would appear, with yet greater enticements to get out my credit card and. . . .

'You still here then?' said a friendly voice at the door, rustling his bin-liner and, for a split-second, it was a toss-up between hurling myself at the screen, or perhaps pulling all the plugs out. Oh cripes, I thought. What were the rules? Was there not some recent case of people being fired for 'downloading' images? On the other hand, what was downloading? Had I accidentally downloaded the entire red-light district of Boobtropolis, or had I merely 'called it up'? Was there any difference?

The girls of the Internet stared back, their eyes locked on mine. They jolly well were locked, frozen, in fact; and any second now Arthur was going to come in and clear out the waste-paper basket, and the damn cursor had picked a fine time to leave me. For another couple of nanoseconds I rehearsed the possibility of just switching it off, shutting it down. But what if someone else turned it on and found all these fantastic nude chicks still there, a-pouting and a-begging? It wouldn't look good. No, it wouldn't look plausible to blame the Millennium bug, or sunspots, or someone else in the office. Arthur must have coughed outside the door, because I leapt like a gaffed salmon and jabbed again at the mouse.

For no reason that I could see, the machine suddenly started to play thudding, stripper-type music. Shut up, I hissed, trying to calculate how far the noise was carrying and then, to my amazement, it bellowed in an American accent. 'You are in Boobtropolis! Welcome to Titty City!' and then proceeded to list some of the attractions of the town, whose *centro storico* could be reached by feeding your credit-card details into the ravening maw of Cyberspace.

After a long, stunned interval, the cursor unfroze, and so did I; and was rewarded by the blissful sound of the vacuum-cleaner starting up downstairs. Somehow I made my escape from Titty City, like Odysseus escaping from Circe, and staggered through the high alpine passes of the online ski brochures to freedom. Phew-ee. And I conclude with the happy thought that the Internet will not be an unparalleled corrupter of morals – a charge that has been laid against every big advance in information technology since Adam ate the fruit of the Tree of Knowledge – for the following reason.

Not only is there the risk that your screen will freeze at the wrong moment. I am also told, by a friend who specialises in the Internet for a major newspaper, that your every foray into Boobtropolis is recorded somewhere in the

257

innards of the beastly machine. In fact, the only way of covering it up is to take an axe to the gizmo, extract something called the 'hard drive', and melt it down, like the climax of *Terminator 2*. And therefore it seems likely that society will be protected from degeneration by the eternal guardian of our species, namely sheer funk at the thought of being caught.

The iron-on lady

'OK', I said. 'Groovy', I said. Every so often the style gurus and stunt merchants of the *GQ* car department come up with a real snorter of an idea, and the only course is to snap to attention.

'It's gonna be brilliant,' said Tim Lewis, the automobile supremo. 'We get this new Mini Cooper S, a fantastic car, a real monster car, and we superimpose a picture on the roof!'

'Tremendous, Tim', I exclaimed, because it is important to humour one's bosses, 'and whose image are you proposing? Saddam Hussein?'

'Close,' said Lewis, 'but no cigar. You're going down to the Tory party conference, aren't you? Well, you are about to be the most popular MP there. You will find blue-rinse matrons blubbing and patting your flanks. Acnoid Tory boys with sterling-silver "Keep The Pound" badges are going to be licking your hubcaps, Boris. Because we are going to decorate your car in glorious, pouting Technicolor with a six-foot, two-and-a-half times life-size rotogravure photo-image of . . . Margaret Thatcher!'

'Tim,' I said weakly, closing my eyes to steady my nerves, 'that is one hell of a wheeze.' And over the next few days, as I waited for the car to arrive, I tried to persuade myself that it would, indeed, be a cinch to carry it off.

'Yeah, well?' I would say, if anyone asked me what the hell I thought I was doing with a picture of Maggie on the roof. Why shouldn't a British car pay homage to the woman who revived our motor industry, by the wise expedient of flogging it off to the Japanese and the Germans? Maybe Tim was right. Maybe it was about time we Tories started sticking up for Maggie and her legacy, and stopped leaving Blair to lay claim to all that was best in her inheritance.

I had just about persuaded myself that it was a runner, when She arrived. 'Fantastic!' I stammered, as Tim unveiled the Mini Thatcher.

She was in her *Gloriana Imperatrix* mode, in a deep-indigo dress, hands folded royally in her lap and covered with bling-bling. Her hair was immaculately bouffed, not its normal pineapple chunks colour, but more marmalade-ish, like bronze-lacquered strands of shredded wheat.

She looked terrific. In terms of motor car iconography, she was a major statement. But could she really be risked in public? If you went on *Question Time*, and said Maggie Thatcher had done a lot of good for the country, the audience would howl and curse, scratching and hooting like flea-ridden gibbons. Oh, Maggie, baby, I thought once Tim had left, how can I do this to you? They'll scratch you with key rings. They'll shake their fists.

Across Britain, sour-faced, taxpayer-funded politics lecturers are teaching the young that Thatcher was a vile shrew, who encouraged selfishness and greed, who destroyed our manufacturing industry, who denied the very existence of society. Of course it is all lies, but what do they know, the youth of today? Overcome by funk, I decided to do something I had never done before. I disobeyed Tim.

I hid the Maggiemobile in an underground car park in London's Russell Square, and went to Bournemouth by train. That night, though, something spooky happened. As I lay in my hotel, I thought I heard a voice calling in the dark, a low, breathy contralto. 'It's a funny old world,' said the Maggiemobile from the dark of the garage. 'They all betrayed me. Heseltine, Hurd, Patten – and now you, too, Boris. Why won't you drive me? Are you frightened? Are you frit?' It went on for hours, and after two nights, I could take it no longer.

I returned to London and rushed to the garage. She was all right. No one had touched her or scraped her. I caressed her shiny hindquarters, as cerulean blue as a Tory conference platform. And was it my imagination, or did her smile look especially regal tonight? I turned her on, and she barked her approval, with that splendid, full-throated noise that so embarrassed and frightened Howe, Gilmour, Pym and the Wets. Soon we were heading to Bournemouth, with all the British-made vigour and confidence of the Task Force heading for the Falklands.

My date was a black-tie awards dinner for 600 tax-collectors (I get some pretty hot gigs, you have to admit), and I was seriously late. But, boy, can that Maggiemobile shift. It seemed incredible, as she whanged and weaved through the rush-hour traffic, that she had only a 1.6-litre engine. I discovered that she had six forward gears, and at one point I was doing 70 in second, not entirely by mistake.

Heaven knows how fast we were going, when, somewhere along the M25, we hurtled round a corner into a wall of cars. There were red tail lights everywhere. It was brake or die. And the Maggiemachine showed the gift for self-preservation that kept her in power for an amazing 11 years. We halted. We waited. Soon I was beginning to get worried. I was meant to be the keynote speaker, and I had a sermon all ready about the joy of tax-collecting, or something of that kind.

Should I jink off at the next turning, and try to find another way to Bournemouth? And then the voice came on again in my head, as the mighty car spoke. 'You turn if you want to', said the car, feminine and yet brimming with conviction, 'the Lady's not for turning until the junction after next!' As so often, she was right. Soon the traffic cleared: we reached the M23, turned right, and hummed down to the coast.

It was interesting, as we cruised the streets, swarming with students, to see how the world reacted to the re-emergence of Margaret Hilda Thatcher. They craned their necks to make out the picture, and then they broke out in broad grins. 'Bring back Maggie!' someone shouted and he seemed neither old nor insane.

The following morning, having discharged my oration, I was back in London to return the car. A cowled-up black kid, not much older than eight or nine, came by on his way to school. Who's that? we asked him, pointing to the roof.

'That's the Queen,' he said, and beamed.

FOREIGN AFFAIRS

Soon after arriving in Brussels, in 1989 I went down to watch the Euro-parliament in Strasbourg. The highlight of the week was a demented attack on America, and especially Coca-Cola, by a virtually mummified French film director called Claude Autant-Lara. It is in a way reassuring to find that fourteen years later, the language of French abuse of America is unaltered. In the meantime, Europe has lamentably failed to get its act together on the first Gulf War, the Yugoslav crisis, and the second Gulf War. Everyone admits that the Common Foreign and Security Policy is a joke. By contrast, the 'special relationship' between Britain and America would seem to be in robust good health. But whatever you think of the French, they deserve admiration for one huge geo-political coup. They have created a European currency which is at least potentially a rival to the dollar.

Euro MP
in a tizz over fizz

For an institution steadily gaining in political importance, the European parliament is certainly shy about being taken seriously.

The first hour of the inaugural session of the new parliament saw a sit-in, a walkout and a torrential keynote oration by an 88-year-old French neo-Fascist ending in a rousing exhortation to European youth not to drink Coca-Cola.

Just as 12 British Greens filed into the auditorium to protest at the electoral system which had deprived them of a dozen seats at Strasbourg, the 180 Socialists walked out en masse.

As the oldest MEP, M Claude Autant-Lara had the traditional honour of making the opening address. He regaled the newly-elected 518 with assorted reflections on global culture after a long career as a Fascist and distinguished film director.

But he managed to lose 85 per cent of his audience within the first few minutes of a bizarre racist harangue, which included the complaint that tennis players at the recent Paris Open had all been interviewed in English.

For the remaining 32 Tory Euro-MPs, with their commitment to free speech, the boycott presented a tricky problem of diplomacy. They solved it for much of the speech by ostentatiously reading newspapers.

But when M Autant-Lara blamed European cultural decline on American imperialism, and said that 'nothing, nothing, nothing and no-one could do anything for a young person who continued to drink Coca-Cola', it was too much. Even the Tories left.

They were outdone in symbolism by the Socialists, who each left a solitary red rose in their microphones.

But Strasbourg politics is cutthroat. The Tory group had soon circulated the information that the Socialists had spent £10,583 on flowers in 1988 compared to their own £156.

In an increasingly Dada-ist speech, the closest M Autant-Lara came to politics, or real life, was when he pointed out that M Jacques Delors, the EEC President, bore an uncanny resemblance to one of his former stars, Buster Keaton.

It made one wonder whether M Delors could be serious when he referred to the parliament as 'the keystone of the construction of Europe', when he congratulated Señor Enrique Baron Crespo, a Spanish Socialist, on being elected President to replace Lord Plumb.

The parliament will frankly not be the keystone of anything, but it is not to be derided. The virtually unopposed election of Señor Baron, with an overall majority of 301 votes, was the first sign of the combined political muscle of the two largest groups, the Socialists and Christian Democrats, working as one.

In the coming months the effect of that pact will be seen again as the parliament exploits its ability to amend legislation. If it uses its full powers on social and environmental legislation it is to be taken seriously, not least in Downing Street.

I include this story because the Daily Telegraph was the first UK paper to record the shooting of Gerald Bull, almost certainly bumped off by the Israelis for attempting to supply a supergun to Saddam (March 24, 1990).

Weapons dealer found murdered

A leading international arms dealer has been found shot dead outside his flat in a Brussels suburb. Mr Gerald Bull, 62, an American, was president of the Space Research Corporation, a multinational which sells rockets and other military hardware.

Belgian police have ruled out robbery as the motive because $20,000 (£12,500) in cash was found on the body.

Sounds familiar? Faced with the challenge of Saddam, a British foreign secretary desperately tries to get some action from the Europeans.

Hurd warns EC of US anger at Gulf response

Mr Hurd, Foreign Secretary, gave warning last night (December 4, 1990) of an anti-European backlash in the United States over the EC's disunited and patchy response to the military challenge of the Gulf crisis. He said: 'There's a feeling in the US, as they look at the Gulf, of the disparity of effort between the US and its European allies.'

Speaking after a meeting of foreign ministers in Brussels, he said there were now compelling arguments for much closer EC co-operation over defence and security.

The subjects will be high on the agenda at the inter-governmental conference on EC political union next week.

Mr James Baker, US Secretary of State, has already protested to the EC Commission at the slow pace of aid to the front-line states of Egypt, Jordan and Turkey.

Senior British sources made clear that Washington was even more concerned about the number of soldiers Europe was prepared to commit.

Mr Hurd will be drawing up plans in the next 10 days, for presentation at the Rome summit, outlining new British ideas for closer EC co-operation on security.

The Government insists that any moves in this area must not diminish Nato's role. Mr Hurd has also rejected French proposals that detailed matters of foreign policy co-ordination, such as sanctions, could be taken by majority vote.

He envisages a 'triangle' of the EC, Nato, and the Western European Union, a nine-strong defence co-ordination body, although last night he gave few details about the exact relationship between them.

Foreign ministers agreed yesterday that Italy, current holder of the EC's rotating presidency, could hold talks with Iraq if meetings proposed by President Bush between the US and Iraq take place.

Mr Hurd told a news conference that the question of Western hostages in Iraq and occupied Kuwait would top the agenda in any such talks.

As in 2003, the Europeans stubbornly fail to coalesce.

MEPs squabble on the sidelines

'I am afraid we are on the margins of history,' sighed an ardent federalist close to M Jacques Delors, President of the European Commission, at the outset of the European Parliament's 'emergency' debate on the war.

Some emergency debate: it was due to take place last Thursday as the war began. But French members protested because the short notice meant it had to take place in Brussels instead of Strasbourg.

No matter that the Gulf was in flames, the leader of the Socialist group of Euro-MPs, M Jean-Pierre Cot, rallied the French to defend the rights of the restaurant-rich Alsatian city.

The feud between France and Belgium over where to house the European Parliament resulted in the Brussels meeting being cancelled with two hours to spare.

Finally, on Monday evening, the debate began in Strasbourg. Amid the tasteful brown furnishings of the parliament lobby, Socialist MEPs were canvassing each other assiduously over a detail which had assumed major significance in their minds.

Should they support the German Socialist, Herr Gerd Walter, in declaring that the coalition should cease its bombardment forthwith? Or should they insist that President Saddam Hussein must first withdraw from Kuwait?

For those EC officials of a cynical turn of mind, it is hard to imagine anything less important than whether the Socialist MEPs contrive to send the 'wrong signal' to Saddam.

The MEPs and the EC Commission are kicking against the pricks of a cruel and sudden marginalisation. Only a month ago, when EC leaders met for the second Rome summit, there was launched a grand inter-governmental conference on 'political union', in which a common EC foreign and security policy seemed to be adventurous, and promising avenues for discussion.

Yesterday, the most confident supporters of European union were admitting that the Gulf War had changed that utterly. 'Political union is not destroyed, but it has been gravely damaged,' was the consensus of official sources.

M Delors, Commission president, is a shrewd enough politician to know when the slogans of EC union would sound hollow. He has said virtually nothing.

His staff recognise that the Gulf War has blown away too much of the rhetorical cloud-cover that was so essential for 'building Europe'.

It has revealed a German public psychologically allergic to war, a French government still addicted to the possibilities of its independent diplomacy, and, across the rest of the Community, a variegated landscape of military and political attitudes.

M Delors recognises that it will get worse before it gets better. When the allied body bags are flown home, they will disproportionately contain Britons and Americans – no European solidarity there.

The inter-governmental conference will climax in the aftermath of a war in which a united Europe – at least in the eyes of the United States – has acquitted itself feebly.

At the end of the flurry of diplomacy that preceded the outbreak of hostilities, the efforts of the EC to intercede with Saddam looked like vainglory. The EC agonised over whether to call Mr Tariq Aziz, Iraqi Foreign Minister, to parley. Saddam was simply not interested.

Many speakers in this week's debate, which is due to conclude today, have sworn that the 518 Euro-MPs represent the 'will of the people of Europe'. The concept seems empty.

Some are still hoping that the inter-governmental conference will produce a collection of far-reaching changes to the management of the Common Market. But most recognise that the project of a thorough-going 'political union' has been incinerated in the crucible of the Gulf.

Despairing of the French, British diplomats try another tack.

After You, Helmut

When John Major flew in his BAe 146 to Bonn on 11 March 1991, prime minister for just three months, on his first bilateral trip to another EEC country, he turned, says the Foreign Office, a new page in our island story. With his 'Heart of Europe' speech to the Konrad Adenauer Foundation, he won the tentative sympathy of Helmut Kohl; on that day he forged the first link of an 'Anglo-German alliance' – at once revolutionary and logical – which, nine months on, rescued Britain from isolation at Maastricht and changed the balance of power in Europe. That, at least, is the Foreign Office line.

From that day on, while Paris choked with jealousy, our Prime Minister became 'Chohnny Major' to the powers in Bonn; and Herr Kohl was awarded the stock epithet 'avuncular' in the British press.

Above all, as John Major told the House of Commons much later, the new entente was based on trust. Helmut came through with the goods at Maastricht on 11 December 1991, saving us from the Social Chapter and compulsory abolition of the pound. He plucked our chestnuts from the fire, says the Foreign Office. This Anglo-German understanding, so valuable, so delicately poised, is the pre-eminent reason, we are told, why it would be unthinkable not to ratify the Maastricht Treaty on monetary and political union. As the Prime Minister warned his backbenchers, it would destroy our reputation for fair dealing.

'You should have seen him [Kohl] at Maastricht,' the Foreign Office line goes on: it was midnight in that pill-box on the river Maas, the last table round, the last topic. Like some paternal pachyderm, Kohl had protected the British opt-outs and options against the federalist darts. Mitterrand was exhausted and mutinous. Twice, finally, 11 countries asked Mr Major if he would abandon the use of the national veto in the EEC's new competence for 'research and technology', and twice he chirpily refused; and, British officials reminisce, just as the French President turned to him to point out, poisonously, that this was a *community* – do you know what? Helmut just roared with laughter.

It was a mixture of admiration at his cheek, say the British, and, dare one speculate, a sort of *avuncular* pride; at any rate, they say, Helmut snorted and howled until the chairman, the Dutch prime minister, Ruud Lubbers, gave up, and that was the end of the Maastricht Summit.

Of course, the mandarins aver, it was not just John Major's charm that did the trick. Six months before that flight to Bonn, amid the suspicions of Prime Minister Thatcher, the seeds were being quietly prodded in. Chris Patten, Tory party chairman, had been out to Bonn to see his opposite number in the German Christian Democrats, Herr Volker Ruhe, with a view to some kind of inter-party pact in the European parliament. Ruhe spoke, unobtrusively, at the Conservative Party Conference in October 1990; by the time Mr Major replied in Bonn, after the Tory putsch in November, German CDs and British Tories had become ideological kinsmen – if, again, you believe the rhetoric.

A big role, too, is credited to Sir Christopher Mallaby, the sepulchral, Charles Addams cartoon figure who has been Our Man in Bonn for the last five years, the man who bore the brunt of the Thatcher-Ridley plain-speaking on Germany. It was more than just an ambassadorial coup to secure the first prime ministerial visit to an EEC ally; it was a chance to suture the rents in the bilateral relationship.

271

But, you know, say the British diplomats, even so we just weren't prepared for the *personal* feeling, the *chemistry* – a joy intensified by memories of the cordial loathing between Kohl and Thatcher. Now, the two leaders greet each other, apparently, with little whoops. Kohl calls Major '*Du*', not '*Sie*' – a familiarity he would never attempt with Mitterrand. To hear the FO rhapsodise, one would think there was something almost physical in the Kohl-Major relationship. 'The great object [Kohl] sort of quivers when Major speaks: It makes small noises of pleasure,' says a senior figure who has witnessed meetings between the two men. To cap it all, Kohl has a framed picture of 'Chohnny' on his desk in the Kanzleramt.

Well, well, perhaps there really is some spark of mutual regard here, between the self-effacing Tory fixer from Brixton and the chortling tripe-eater from the Rhineland (who can communicate with each other only through interpreters). If there is, it is being adroitly utilised by Herr Kohl. After 18 months, most diplomats in Brussels would agree that the Anglo-German entente is either a failure or a sham; it has delivered little or nothing to Britain, and much to Germany. The warm embrace of March 1991 has turned into a bear-hug, and the Government is being squeezed.

In the higher reaches of the Foreign Office, they still refuse to blame Kohl. It is not him, they say, so much as the abiding pro-French culture of the Chancellor's officials. 'With Bitterlich whispering in his ear, it's different,' sighs one senior negotiator.

Joachim Bitterlich, who runs the European Affairs department in the Bundeskanzleramt, epitomises all that Our Men are up against in Bonn. His introverted, blondish mien is compared, predictably but accurately, to that of an SS colonel, but one who loves France. He has a French wife. He went to the Ecole Nationale d'Administration in

Paris. Not only did he befriend Pascal Lamy, Jacques Delors' brilliant, barking, bullying, bullet-headed French chef de cabinet, who runs the Commission like a Saharan penitentiary; the young Bitterlich actually received instruction from M. Delors when the Commission president was a don at ENA.

No wonder, then, Bitterlich and his kind continue to throw Germany's weight behind the Franco-German 'army', the 4,200 listless soldiers near Stuttgart who are supposed, one day, to guarantee peace for the continent. With its multilingual parade drill, incompatible ordnance and unspecified field of deployment, this body still belongs, clearly, to the wilder shores of French Euro-ideology. But it is an irritant, a growing one.

Why should the Germans continue to support it? Have they really become, as the Foreign Office says, 'so close to us on defence', such strong supporters of Nato? Or is German European policy shaped to this day, as it always has been, by the moral blackmail of France?

The truth is that the francophile faction in Bonn is strong, perhaps stronger than ever. But even the Bitterlich clique cannot quite account for the way, since the new 'Anglo-German entente' began, key planks of British policy have been warped by Germany out of recognition. Let me give half a dozen examples, in chronological order.

Britain 'had no choice', the Prime Minister said at Lisbon on 27 June, but to reappoint M. Delors as Commission president for an unprecedented extra two years. Since there were 'no other candidates', the British veto was worthless. Of course there were other candidates, some of magnificent dullness, such as the former Dutch finance minister, Mr Onno Ruding. What in fact happened, as one British diplomat confessed, was that 'Helmut wanted him'. Delors, remember, was the first French politician of any standing to speak out in 1989 in favour of German unification. Shortly before the summit, Helmut gave him the Charlemagne prize, the highest German civilian award. He only had to say the word, and the job was his for another two years.

That same evening, over dinner, Mr Major was set upon in the kind of summit ambush that, one might have supposed, had been reserved for Mrs Thatcher. Did someone say London would be the site of the future European Central Bank? Ha. Nine countries, quite unexpectedly, voted at Lisbon for 'Germany' (either Frankfurt or Bonn). And why? Because they accepted Helmut Kohl's protestations that his people would never give up the deutschmark in a monetary union unless the Euro-bank was at least on German soil.

Only Mr Major prevented a deal being rammed through over the port, with the help of Belgium and Luxembourg; it is not an awesome alliance. By the Edinburgh summit in December, some in Brussels predict, Mr Major will be on his own, and Tory backbenchers can look forward to the day when Britain's monetary policy is run from Germany not just *de facto*, but *de jure*.

To judge by events only three days later, even British fiscal policy of the most basic kind depends on Germany. Trapped amid the fake marble and formica of the lobby in the Luxembourg Kirschberg, having conceded for the first time that the EEC could set a minimum VAT rate of 15 per cent, Mr Lamont could not have been more explicit: he had surrendered the principle – that the House of Commons should guard its sovereign revenue-raising powers – out of deference to German domestic politics.

This is how it happened. Chancellor Kohl was near desperate to raise VAT from 13 to 15 per cent, to help pay for unification. Alas, in 1989 he had lied to the German public, saying this would not be necessary. Here, praise be, was a binding EEC directive, 'forcing' him to raise taxes. The only difficulty, a trifling one as it turned out, was that Britain objected on fundamental ideological grounds to the directive. Said Mr Lamont in his candid way, after throwing in the towel, 'I understand that they [the Germans] need a Community reason for doing this.' That is what Mr Lamont said in June to an informal gathering of European journalists. But by this week, when the deal was formally agreed to, Mr Lamont was understandably much more reticent about pointing the finger at the Germans. He told BBC Radio 4 that it was a great victory for Britain.

And where, in the week after the VAT concession was actually made, was the alliance between Tories and Christian Democrats, between Chris Patten and Volker Ruhe, when it came to the European Fighter Aircraft and the saving of 40,000 British jobs? Was this defence minister the same Volker Ruhe who spoke of Conservative-Christian Democrat brotherhood to the Conservative Party Conference? He reneged on a deal (because of German public opinion) in a manner which would have been unimaginable if France had been one of the contracting parties.

The week after that, the Bundesbank acted to raise the price of Europe's lynchpin currency. He is credulous who imagines that Herren Schlesinger and Tietmeyer, president and vice-president of the Bundesbank, fix the Lombard rate, the discount rate, or any other instrument of monetary policy – no matter how devastating their decisions for British industry and mortgages – with anything else in mind than German domestic economic considerations (though, of course, it is a convenience of the ERM that, by forcing up the value of other EEC currencies, it prevents German goods from being priced out of the European market). Much has been said lately on this, and there is no need to expand.

And, finally, at the risk of repetition, it was for German domestic political reasons that the EEC was dragooned into recognising Croatia, now perceived in Whitehall as the most catastrophic error of the last year. That laid what Lord Carrington has called the 'powder trail' directly to the present detonations in Bosnia. Douglas Hurd has never seemed so upset – not just miffed, or out of sorts – as when, in the early hours of last 16 December in Brussels, Hans-Dietrich Genscher threatened independent recognition, and effectively held a gun to the head of the rest of the Community.

Before acceding to German wishes for a joint action, Mr Hurd – on the rack of conscience – stressed, uncharacteristically, that he had telephoned Mr Major (who was at Jeffrey Archer's cocktail party) for advice. He knew it was a dreadful, misconceived policy. But Kohl wanted it, for his Croatian minority, but mainly because of public opinion and German theories of self-determination. Major approved, it was acknowledged, because it went with the 'deal' at Maastricht.

Even if they accept, or partly accept, the strength of this handful of points, government officials retort snappily, 'Well, at least we've got a *big power* ally in Europe, which we never had under Thatcher.' Germany stands four-square with us, they say, on the crunch issues of the British presidency – opening the Community to more members, pruning the excesses of the Delors budget. Others say Germany has yielded little to Britain, since that famous Major mission to Bonn, which it would not have given anyway. It is fairly predictable that Bonn should favour, as Britain does, the early accession to the EEC of Austria. Thereby it will achieve, at last, the effective economic *anschluss* which France always forbade the Teutonic tribes. As for the budget, is it really any surprise that Germany, paying both £6 billion net to the EEC and the price of unification, should admire financial rigour?

Of course it is good to have allies in Europe. There is

no alternative. But we are entitled to expect some balance in a relationship, and here there is none. Perhaps, some would say, it is time for Mr Major to reflect on whether his friendship with the Chancellor is one of those political fealties he wishes to honour, in his own phrase, 'through thick and thin'.

Kohl won a British signature on Maastricht. It seems odd, when one examines the fruits of the 'Anglo-German entente' in the succeeding seven months, that the preservation of that relationship should be given as one of the key reasons for ratifying the Treaty.

Europe is meant to be sorting out the Balkans, and it is a bloody shambles. Douglas Hurd has been meditating on his role in the disaster

The public conscience of Douglas Hurd

In a building once intended to be a suburban Brussels maternity hospital, the biggest ever deployment of Nato troops is being planned. At Nato HQ, Evere, they envisage 75,000 troops for Bosnia, with about two thirds to be committed by America, Britain and France. The peace-keeping force for the former Yugoslavia would be the grandest thing, some would say the only thing, Nato has ever done. The troops have not gone yet. Indeed, the longer the West dithers, the longer Serbs mock western impotence, the less likely it is that they will. But if they were to go – and the martial hubbub is rising – it would be an extraordinary reversal of British foreign policy. Some would say it was absurd that Britain should even think about sending fighting troops to Bosnia; and not just because of the risk to British life.

Eighteen months ago (November 1991), it was Britain which, seemingly single-handedly, blocked military intervention in the former Yugoslavia. Then, arguably, deployment was feasible. Ceasefires were evanescent, but existed. Then, the battle-ground was Croatia. Then, thousands, tens of thousands, of Bosnians now dead were still alive. Only now, when the dangers are so much greater, is intervention again being seriously contemplated. That is an irony which one would expect to surface.

And it does, not in Foreign Office briefs but in the extra-curricular writings of Douglas Hurd. In the last year, since Bosnia became a battle-ground, the Foreign Secretary has given us two vivid, workmanlike short stories (and a fascinating Oxford speech, reproving the 'critics', or journalists, for their constant carping at 'achievers', viz. D. Hurd). They reveal an honourable mind ill at ease with what he has done.

These are not ordinary short stories. This is the British Foreign Secretary publicly meditating on the issues that underpinned his decisions – which were crucial – about the worst European war for 50 years, and, oh yes, justifying himself. For the student of Hurd, Europe and Yugoslavia, these texts read like a palimpsest of confessions and clues.

On 18 September last year, the *Daily Telegraph* published *The Last Day of Summer*, a 3,000-word tale by Hurd of how war spread to Bosnia, through the eyes of Borisav the Bosnian Serb. It is well-crafted, gripping stuff, with flashes of real humanity. Briefly: Borisav, a lowly forestry official, and his friend Tomic the Croat have together built a summer house. It is later symbolically mortared, with Tomic inside it. Borisav flees.

Hurd begins the tale one year before that tragedy, as Borisav stands gloomily by the local cemetery, pondering the still remote war in Croatia. Would it spread? The location of time is precise – 'The gnarled apple tree was heavy with unripe fruit.' This is the late summer of 1991. At exactly the time that Borisav was brooding, Hurd was in The Hague, arguing against European military intervention in Croatia.

On 19 September 1991, after the failure of sundry EEC ceasefires and the EEC monitoring mission, there took place the meeting of the Western European Union in The Hague, called by Herr Hans-Dietrich Genscher of Germany, at the urging of Mr Hans van den Broek, the Dutch foreign minister. Van den Broek wanted to send 50,000 men under the Western European Union, to enforce the stuttering ceasefire. The Germans were favourable, but – *Teufel!* – the constitution said they could not take part *themselves*. The Italians were favourable, but said they were ineligible because they were Yugoslavia's neighbours. The only countries that mattered that day were Britain and France, and possibly Holland.

'It was only the Brits that didn't want it,' says one Dutchman, who attended the meeting. 'It was Douglas Hurd who killed that idea off. We still think we should have done it.' According to French officials at the time – and they may well have been lying – the French foreign minister, M. Roland Dumas, strongly supported van den Broek, making it two out of three. With 20–20 hindsight, military experts now say that this was one of the last few moments, when the Serbs were still travelling in convoys of tanks, when the style of battle was favourable to intervention.

Importantly, the WEU meeting took place just after the coup in the Soviet Union: the Serbs could no longer count on their great Slavic supporters to stymie western initiatives. It was a window of opportunity – and Hurd, so it seems, closed it.

Memories and reports of that meeting are perhaps unfair on Hurd; quite likely there was no appetite, in any country, for military intervention while there was the slightest whiff of a firefight. Maybe the continentals knew they had to make a gesture; and they also knew, cynically, that they could count on the intellectual honesty of Hurd to bat their suggestions aside.

And yet there will always be that element of historical doubt: not just whether the WEU option was really feasible, but whether it was right, in view of what was to come (which was hardly unpredicted), to close it off.

How could I have known? Hurd asks us in his short story. Back in September 1991, he could see the future no more clearly than Borisav the Bosnian Serb. As Borisav contemplates a circle of first world war graves, with their split and illegible stones, all was perplexity in his mind. Would war really return to Sarajevo? 'Was history coming back?' asks Borisav-Hurd. It was.

By the end of January this year, the horrors had multiplied on television to the point where they were prompting renewed public calls for action. In 'Ten Minutes to Turn the Devil', published in the *Observer* on 31 January, Hurd's conscience drives him back to the theme of the European intervention force that never was. This time the hero is Richard Smethwick, the British defence secretary, who must convince a mutinous Brighton Tory party conference of the wisdom of having sent British troops to 'Caucasia'.

This time, Hurd asks us to imagine that he had gone ahead with the WEU force. (It is quite clear, incidentally, that he means the WEU, the putative defence arm of the EEC, so beloved of the federalists, which figured so largely in the Maastricht talks; the 'European Safe Haven Force' in the story comes from France, Germany, Britain, Spain and the Benelux; this is not Nato – no Americans here, no Canadians or Norwegians.)

Already, amid the alien guerrillas, British troops have sustained 96 casualties. Britain has been swept by a movement called 'TON' – Troops Out Now, whose supporters drape Brighton with banners showing a huge weight crashing down on the defence secretary.

Smethwick is the thinnest of masks for Hurd himself, from the stiffeners in his shirt collars to his knowledge of Ovid and even his political CV: 'He had served in Northern Ireland . . .' Like Hurd, he must face down the bloody-minded blue-rinsed Little Englanders (shades of Hurd's conference roastings over Maastricht, or capital punishment?), and, as he rises to speak, he is suddenly 'angry with the Party for the crude anti-foreign mood in the hall' – pure Douglas Hurd, at his prefectorial finest.

Mastering his doubts, waving aside the autocue, he shames the Little Englanders with statesmanship and an old-fashioned appeal to internationalism into support of the British presence.

Eighteen months after he blocked intervention in Croatia, Hurd, on this evidence, is still tormented by the dilemma of August and September 1991; increasingly tormented, in fact, as the chorus begins again for western military action, in far more perilous circumstances. In 'Ten Minutes to Turn the Devil', that dilemma is melodramatically pointed up in the last sentence, when Smethwick-Hurd learns, after receiving his standing ovation and the thanks of the prime minister, that his brother-in-law has been killed by a sniper while commanding British troops in the mud of Caucasia.

Mr Hurd lays it before us. You judge, he says: did I do the right thing? Far from finding his story self-serving, we are moved to admire him; for his candour, and for his doubt. We should also examine his motives.

That day in The Hague, 19 September 1991, a fierce scrap, however histrionic, appeared to have taken place. Against the WEU intervention proposal, seriously meant or not, the Foreign Secretary was forced to deploy the utmost vehemence. He appeared to the press in the evening in the basement of the bunker-like Dutch foreign ministry, tired and with the grimness of a pyrrhic victor. He had won the argument, but allowed himself to be painted as the spoiler.

His officials immediately circulated verbatim accounts of what he had said, a trenchant opposition to engagement, based on his own experience of Northern Ireland; that it was madness to send western troops to keep apart blood-thirsty bandits; that escalation was inevitable; that once committed, the troops could be there for decades.

Those are good reasons, ones that will satisfy most Tory MPs. But, in view of subsequent catastrophes which might have been averted, do they still satisfy Douglas Hurd? I believe there was a further reason for the British veto, one that preys on his conscience and may explain the literary searching of the soul.

When the Yugoslav crisis ignited in the summer of 1991, western Europe was half-way through the Maastricht negotiations, and at once there was a bizarre ideological contamination between Maastricht and Croatia. From the start, Jacques Delors and other EEC generalissimos saw not so much the threat to the lives of Yugoslav civilians as the threat to 'federalism' itself.

Pathetic inducements were offered to keep the Croats and Slovenes from splitting away – presumably to prove what Joe Brandt, in a paper for the Woodrow Wilson Centre in Washington, has called the 'federalist fiction', that monetary and political unions make intrinsically better sense; new EEC-Yugoslavia trade and co-operation agreements, new EEC-Yugoslavia financial protocols, studies showing the costs of 'non-Yugoslavia', all were dandled before the heedless separatists.

All they achieved, of course, was to convince Milosevic and the Serbs (the 'federal' government) that Brussels was somehow on their side in their murderous campaigns.

In fact, only one thing was more misconceived than the EEC's attempts to promote federalism in Yugoslavia. It was the miserable effort to use Yugoslavia to promote federalism in the EEC.

Jacques Poos, Luxembourg's bouncy-quiffed foreign minister, has earned immortal ridicule for his remark in June 1991, made in my hearing as we flew on a publicity-stunt mission to Belgrade: 'This is the hour of Europe!' Time and again, we were told that Yugoslavia was the 'laboratory', the 'melting-pot', the 'crucible', in which the new Maastricht Common Foreign and Security Policy was to be tested with fire. It was not just Jacques Poos.

Those were the high old days, remember, when Britain was 'at the heart of Europe', loyally playing along with the various fancies. Douglas Hurd himself said Yugoslavia was 'a European problem which had to be faced by Europe alone'.

As we know, the Community flunked it, tragically. It is a story riddled with flaccidity and lack of nerve. One could point to the fateful July 1991 decision of Jo ven den Valk, the EEC's chief 'ice-cream man', or monitor, to deploy his men only in Slovenia, leaving the Serbs to do what they would in Croatia. One could point to the complete inability to speak with a single voice over recognition, until 15 December 1991.

But mainly, one must point to the EEC's chronic failure, despite several lulls, several 'windows', to provide a credible military deterrent to Serb – or anyone's – aggression. As Warren Christopher, US Secretary of State, said to Hurd and others at Nato on 26 February this year, 'The West missed too many opportunities to contain the suffering, bloodshed and destruction when the conflict was in its infancy.

'The lesson to be learned from this tragedy is the

importance of early and decisive engagement against ethnic persecution and aggressive nationalism.' *Touché*.

So the question is put again: Why did Hurd, who had *accepted* that Yugoslavia was a 'European' problem, block off Europe's only decisive means of intervention? Was it simply the risk of loss of British life?

Or were his calculations, like those of everyone else, contaminated by Maastricht? You have to remember that the body in question, the nine-strong Western European Union, was perhaps the biggest political football in the Maastricht talks. France and others were determined to build it up as an EEC-sponsored defence pact, independent of America, to rival and in time supplant Nato.

Britain, naturally, wanted to reinforce Nato, embracing as it does the advantages of American leadership, British lieutenantship, and a US presence in Europe; the WEU, in Britain's view, should be kept as a glorified talking-shop.

Now, as long as Yugoslavia was a 'European problem which had to be faced by Europe alone' (perhaps the root delusion of the whole disaster), a Nato force was out of the question. But to have sent a WEU force to Croatia in September 1991, or in the ceasefire in the New Year, would have suddenly incarnated the French dream; it would have been an irreversible victory for the federalist side.

My contention, therefore, is that Hurd had to say no, not merely because of the risk to British lives (had they not just been risked in the Gulf?), but because his veto was, apart from anything else, a move in the Maastricht negotiations.

Today, the Nato *vs*. WEU battle has ended decisively in Hurd's favour. Out there at the Nato HQ, the Americans are back in the saddle and the French, far from setting up their own Euro-defence pact, are virtually back in Nato's integrated military command, which they left in 1966. Whoever heard of the WEU, these days?

In the meantime, it has become convenient for the Foreign Office to blame the Bosnian conflagration, behind their hands, on Germany: apparently they should not have 'bullied' us into recognition of Croatia at the end of 1991. But the reality, surely, is that at several junctures before and after that date Europe failed to show either side, especially Belgrade, that aggression would not pay.

The war now having become so bad and so vicious, the West as a whole will almost certainly fail again – perhaps over Macedonia – whatever the preparations at Nato.

It is admirable that Mr Hurd's conscience should be so troubled; he emerges as the greater statesman for it, head and shoulders above his glib and insouciant colleagues. As he says of Hurd-Smethwick in his dark night of the soul, 'It was not as if in these small hours, he was sure that the policy was right.'

None of us can be sure. Nobody can know whether prompt and well-armed intervention to enforce a ceasefire in Croatia would have worked, or merely brought fresh catastrophe. But the truly tormenting possibility is that thousands of Bosnians may have died, thousands of lives been ruined, for the sake of a negotiating gambit in a largely defunct treaty.

The eternal verities of French European policy.

After Mitterrand nothing much will change

We stood in the Salle des Fêtes of Napoleon's Elysée Palace as the old man gave out the Legion d'Honneur. Above us hung chandeliers the size of small cars, from a gilded ceiling writhing with putti and mermaids. The honorands stepped forward: a man who had consecrated his life to the study of the circumflex accent; Sylvie Guillem, the ballerina; a stout old man who once escaped the Nazis. Each received the thanks of the President of the Republic, with a perfectly turned speech; and each then kissed François Mitterrand on either cheek, somewhere in the region of the ear, with the mixture of devotion and egalitarianism that marks the French presidency.

The ceremony was made all the more moving – and it *was* moving – for the small audience of family, loyal Mitterrandist politicians, and the odd interloping journalist from London, by the fact that we all knew, looking at his waxy skin and hair thinned by chemotherapy, that it might be the last. By May, at the latest, Mitterrand must leave this palace, his allotted span of two seven-year terms fulfilled.

One wondered what eulogy Mitterrand would himself deserve. He would like to go down, no doubt, as one of the progenitors of a more united Europe. But the Mitterrand legacy is under threat. He has failed even to nominate his successor. The Socialist Party he created is in ruins. The blood of Michel Rocard, his one-time prime minister, is on his hands, and Delors has bowed out. With four months to the presidential election, French politics is in a kind of frenzy, the bright young men in a delirium of doubt about which Right-wing horse to back.

Will it be Jacques Chirac, the snarling, brilliantined leader of the Gaullists? Or will it be Edouard Balladur, the Jeevesian wearer of cardinal's mauve socks whom Chirac mistakenly allowed to be prime minister? The betting is heavily on Balladur, though Chirac has the advantage of the party machine. Whoever wins, something has changed with the passing of Mitterrand. In the Elysée, the feeling is elegiac. Europe, they say, will founder without his florentine skills. 'It is a question of élan,' said an aide, 'the difference between a static and a dynamic vision.'

The inevitable triumph of the Gaullists has been hailed in London. If we are to believe the Foreign Office, we shall see a return of the Gaullism which places the sovereign state foremost and deprecates Brussels. If it is true that we are about to witness the obliteration of all M Mitterrand's efforts to construct a Franco-centric Euro-polity, that would be of momentous importance, for Britain and Europe. Such an assumption would, however, be premature.

Let us state, as powerfully as we can, reasons why Downing Street might be cheerful about a Gaullist French president. Agreed, the fall of the Berlin Wall fundamentally shifted the European balance of power. The old equilibrium between France and Germany has gone. Britain, so long despised and rejected of nations, is also to be clasped to the gallic bosom. 'It is simple good sense that France, Britain and Germany should be the directing countries of the EU,' M Maurice Couve de Murville told me. Yes: the self-same Couve de Murville who, as prime minister, blocked Britain's entry to the EC in 1963.

France and Britain have been brought closer by the experience of Bosnia. More effective than 100 Francophile speeches by Douglas Hurd has been the sight on French television of General Sir Michael Rose commanding French troops and speaking a kind of French. France's politicians have finally followed Britain's too, in spotting that there are votes in bashing Brussels. M Pasqua, the Corsican who aspires to be prime minister under President Balladur, has more or less scrapped the Schengen plan to abolish frontier checks, which once threatened embarrassment for Britain.

If anything, the French view of the Euro-parliament is more caustic than Britain's. London's excitement at the imminent Gaullist administration will be intensified, moreover, by signs that it will mean further Thatcherian privatisation, of Radio Monte Carlo, and who knows, even

Air France, as well as an attack on the enormous employer contributions to the welfare state.

There is a difference, though, between a Gaullist modulation of rhetoric and a political earthquake. One should not exaggerate, first, the desire of the French Right to follow Britain's economic lead. In France, where growth is poised to overtake Britain's, and where the Bank of France last week predicted that the criteria for monetary union would be achieved by 1996, the attitude towards Britain's economy remains irritatingly compassionate. A Chirac victory is assumed by Tory Right-wingers to be the best outcome; yet in some ways he is more Left-wing than Mitterrand. His Gaullist concept of the nation would mean a France even more bloody in defence of its farmers; even more prone to flout EU competition law; even more protectionist of its workers.

Granted, federalism is now as bad a word in the French political lexicon as it is in Britain's. M Balladur's officials say they want to chastise the Brussels Commission, which appalled the French establishment by using its prerogatives to negotiate for freer world markets. And yet the solution of the Gaullists is a million miles from what might be acceptable in London. I heard a group of Gaullist senators outline their plans for the 1996 Inter Governmental Conference. They want to squash the Commission with a permanent Council of Ministers in Brussels, and a second chamber for the European Parliament: in other words, two more centralised EU institutions.

Whether the next president is Chirac or Balladur, the French remain committed to creating a European '*pouvoir politique*', said one political scientist. One politician fanatically opposed to the single currency warned: 'I would say to Mr Major, do not think the French are going to abandon their strategic goals'. Too much, perhaps, has been made of Delors's decision not to run. The reality is that it might not have made much difference. When Delors was finance minister in Paris, he was hardly Monsieur Europe. He restored exchange controls and devalued four times against the Deutschmark. It was Jacques Chirac who signed the single European Act and who last week wrote a dizzy article in *Le Monde* lauding the Franco-German axis.

Mitterrand is now an old man in a hurry, desperate to plot a future he will not see. If you ask, has France's European programme lost its quasi-religious urgency with his departure, the answer must be yes. But if British politicians believe that the French have abandoned their policy, that European institutions, based in Brussels, offer the best means of protecting the French language and culture, projecting French influence, and controlling the Germans, then they are guilty of fantastic self-deception.

The triumph of Delors, Kohl and Mitterrand.

The birth of the euro

Snow had fallen in Madrid yesterday (December 1995), snow on snow. In the bleak midwinter, wise men came, mainly from the East, to behold a wondrous thing.

They came to bear witness to the nativity of the single European currency, and they came to give it a name.

From this day forward, the apostles of Euro-money will be able to spread the glad tidings in a vast Brussels propaganda campaign.

'Euro, Euro, Euro' the bumf will chorus, as it drops through the letterbox of a yet unknowing continent.

'As Peter was the rock on which the church was built, so the Euro is the rock on which the European Union will be built,' raved Antonio Guterres, the Portuguese prime minister. Babes unborn will lisp the name.

If the commission plan succeeds, Euro will litter the daily conversations of millions; and our grandchildren will ask themselves how on earth Britain could agree to this neologism, in half-an-hour before lunch on a freezing December day in Madrid's equivalent of Canary Wharf.

Did the Government not have a view? Did the sentiment of the ordinary people of these islands count for nothing? If ever a coin was the lowest common denomination, this is it.

This is a name which can be pronounced no less than four ways in Denmark – Ayooro, Aeaeooro, Yuro and Oiro – and all of them translate roughly as 'Yuck'.

And when the little ones turn to us and ask with big round eyes, 'Grandma, Grandpa, why is our money called the Euro?', we will blush and say: 'Well, darling, nice Mr Major didn't have much of a choice.

'He had these people called the Tory Euro-sceptics waiting for him to come back from Madrid.

'They were cruel, blinkered men who often plotted to get rid of Mr Major. If he had really pushed for a better name, like Florin or Crown, they would have been very cross. They would have said he was preparing to give up the pound.'

And the little ones will pause and look thoughtful, and then say: 'So John Major sort of said nothing?'

'That's right, darling.'

'And so he agreed to Euro because he didn't dare say anything much on the subject at all.'

'That's right, darling.'

It will be especially difficult to explain events if, as seems likely, the Germans cheat. It was Herr Waigel, the German finance minister, who yesterday proposed 'Euro', and who pronounced himself thrilled with the result.

That is because it remains Germany's intention to win round their public to monetary union by calling the currency the 'Euro-mark' abroad, and, slyly, the mark at home. Britain, true to form, will stick to the rules it apathetically agreed. If Britain ever joins the single currency, Euro it will be.

Ah well, you may say, there's the rub: surely the Government believes that monetary union will never happen?

Far from it. Yesterday's most astonishing development was Mr Clarke's admission that he believed there was a 60–40 per cent chance that European monetary union would actually take place. Hitherto, no doubt to reassure those Westminster sceptics, the Government has taken a different view.

Mr Major has famously compared the foreigners' deliberations about a single currency to a 'raindance'. And his Chancellor has said that EMU had 'less chance than a snowball in Hades'.

Well, it would seem the Government has good news for the primitive tribes of America: your average raindance has a 60–40 per cent chance of generating rain.

And Mr Clarke evidently believes – as indeed did the ancient Greeks – that Hades could be rather chilly, a place where a snowball could easily have a 60–40 per cent chance of survival.

As they looked out at Madrid's wintry landscape yesterday, plenty of officials could be found who put the odds on the Euro even higher. As for the survival chances of a snowball, they were better still.

In Brussels, things are going from bad to worse. Delors has gone, and the whole commission, for reasons that now escape me, has been forced to resign.

A bacillus at the heart of Brussels – the end of the Commission

So, it has come to this. After 42 years of unstoppable integration, of directives on everything from lawnmower noise to maximum permissible odours in farmyard compounds, the European commissioners have finally met their match.

They have routed the Tory Euro-sceptics. They have defied the Great American Banana Peril. The pharaohs of Brussels have raised up the pyramids of butter and beef.

With a few strokes of their Mont Blanc pens the *hauts fonctionnaires* have abolished newspaper delivery boys and rebaptised English chocolate and called into being oceans of surplus Valpolicella: and yesterday – *kerprang*.

The Santer commission has been destroyed by its own sheer, exuberant incompetence. Like peasants queuing to pass the catafalque of a dead king, journalists swarmed outside the press room in the belly of the Breydel building. Some of the real veterans had been there at Messina in 1955.

They had seen some pretty cataclysmic cock-ups in their time, but nothing like the exit of the Santer gang. There he sat, the heir of Monnet and Schuman and Delors, the man who had driven the gravy train slap bang into the buffers at *Très Grande Vitesse*.

For two long minutes, while his spokesman pleaded with them to have mercy, the camera popguns blazed at this portrait of bureaucratic bungling as he silently shuffled his papers and grinned his hanging grin.

You would have to be a pretty stony sort of soul not to feel sympathy for Jacques Santer yesterday.

The colour was fled the cheeks of the man who is known as *Le Digestif* after his liking for a *petit pousse-café*. You could see he was angry.

He raged at press 'harassment'. He claimed that his 'honour' was at stake. In a curious piece of logic, he said that he rejected the conclusions of the report, but that he and the rest of the commissioners felt obliged to 'take their responsibilities' and resign.

He was glad that he was himself *blanchi*, or whiter than white. He took comfort from the existence of the euro, which would 'go down in history' – and, as if to prove his point, the euro was already going down yesterday morning.

But for all his Bourbon insouciance, you could tell that deep down Jacques Santer knows he has crashed and burned and that the propeller is six feet under the tarmac.

Poor chap. There he was in 1994, quietly luxuriating in the office of prime minister of Luxembourg (pop 375,000) when John Major decided that a pointless gesture was needed to appease the foaming Euro-sceptics.

Jean-Luc Dehaene, the corpulent Belgian prime minister, felt the full force of the British veto and Jacques was co-opted.

'I remember,' said an official yesterday, bitterly, 'Mr Major said he didn't want someone with an idea every minute. Well, he certainly succeeded there.'

Mr Santer's watchword on taking office was to 'do less but do it better'.

He has now perfected this principle by causing the entire commission to be fired, so that they are now, legally speaking, not allowed to generate any new legislation at all.

Yes, the more one studies yesterday's events the more it looks like a fantastic piece of generalship by Mr Major.

No Tory Euro-sceptic will dare attack his record on Europe again after he planted Santer – this time-bomb, this bacillus, this agent of deep penetration – in the heart of the Brussels machine.

And as the journalists fled to the telephones, we tried to understand the scale of the disaster for the great Brussels machine and its many-splendoured budget.

Does this mean a freeze on EU spending? Will the lobster picks rust in the restaurants of the Rue Stevin? Will the *poules de luxe* spend nights alone and tapping their heels on the Avenue Louise?

Mais non! It turned out that Santer and Co have not actually resigned and gone ... Under article 159 they remain until new commissioners can be found.

They will be paid, in homage to the system they created themselves, to do nothing. That's right: it is bureaucratic set-aside.

Clinton puts his finger on a major intellectual difficulty facing the Euro-federalists.

Bill Clinton is right

Bravo, Clinton. Well said. After eight embarrassing years, in which we have had to endure his ego-sexo-psycho-drama, the President of the United States has made a major foreign policy pronouncement, which is at once exciting, profound and far-sighted. What bliss it would have been to have sat among the corpulent Euro-worthies last week and watched with them as Bill received the Charlemagne Prize for 'contribution to European unity', which is, these days, the highest honour the Continent can confer. The day before, the *Financial Times* had published an oleaginous leader, congratulating Mr Clinton for supporting EU inte-gration. Yet, when he spoke after accepting the gong, he made a suggestion so stunning, so alarming to the tender federastic sensibilities of the *FT* that the newspaper hissed that he was 'not entitled to make such an offer'.

He spoke with the simplicity of the child who spied that the emperor was naked. He recommended that Russia should be admitted not just to Nato, but to the EU as well; and one can only imagine the girning he evoked among the Continent's elite. Mr Clinton's point is unanswerable, which is why they fear it. If you say that Mr Clinton is wrong and that Russia is not a European country, and is therefore not admissible under the terms of the Treaty of Rome, then you have to say what Europe is. So what is it?

In their efforts to exclude the Turks it has been customary for German Christian Democrats, and the likes of Jacques Delors, to hint that the EU is the successor to Charlemagne's empire, in that it is coterminous with Christendom. This will obviously not do. If 'Europe' means Christendom, then you might as well include America, North and South, where there are far more Christians per head than in most European countries, and you certainly couldn't exclude the Russians. More furtively, some in Brussels will hint to you that Europe really means chaps like us: you know, white men on the end of the Eurasian landmass.

Let us leave aside the racism this implies towards the Turks, the Israelis and other inhabitants of the Mediterranean littoral, though it is worth noting, in passing, that all those who accuse Eurosceptics of being 'xenophobes' are in reality defending a political construction whose avowed intent is to keep out the Muslims. Even if this, deep down, is the rationale of the builders of Little Europe, they still have no answer to the question posed by Bill Clinton. Let us suppose that Ken Clarke, Michael Heseltine and Tony Blair are really so ugly in their prejudices that they want to build a Europe to keep out the 'towelheads'; they still have no reply to the claims of the Slavs and the Balts and the endless vista of Christian white folk stretching to Vladivostok.

What Mr Clinton, or whoever wrote his speech, has realised is that in the last ten years Little Europe has lost its geo-political logic. European integration was a noble idea, born of the desire that France and Germany should not go to war again. As the 1950s and 1960s wore on, the Americans strongly supported an integrated EU as a valuable bulwark against the Soviet threat. In 2000, more than ten years after the fall of the Berlin Wall, both those considerations look absurd. There will be no war between France and Germany, and the Soviet threat is a busted flush. That leaves no urgent necessity to create a tightly unified Little Europe, except in the hearts of those who are so anti-American that they would abandon national independence in the chimerical hope of creating a rival superstate. To that end, they continue to pour out federalising legislation (this week, abandoning its pretence of defiance, Labour accepted a new EU law to change the burden of proof in race discrimination cases) and militate for Britain to join the euro.

Everything is intended not just to complicate the lives of businessmen, but to frustrate would-be applicant countries. What is the point of this preposterous new Charter of Fundamental Rights, which is to be bestowed upon us by the EU? Why do we need Brussels to give us 'the right to reconcile family and professional life'? What the hell has this to do with the free movement of goods, people, services and capital? The objective is to pull up the drawbridge against those nations, especially, perhaps, the Turks, who cannot subject their national traditions to such a detailed and intimate destruction. Tony Blair has indicated that he will veto the Charter when it comes before the Nice summit at the end of the year. Let us hope he does so, though his record of resistance is not convincing.

Before then, the Prime Minister might tell us whether he agrees with Bill Clinton, his political mentor. Is Russia part of Europe? Is there any reason why Russia should not ultimately be admitted to membership? If not, why not? If the Prime Minister or one of his gnomes in Downing Street would like to write us an article, our columns are open. Come on, Mr Blair: is Chekhov a European author? Is St Petersburg a European city? Yes or no?

Chirac is assured of victory.

Blunkett and Le Pen: what's the difference

It may be that *The Spectator* will be burnt across Britain this morning by a public which feels that this time we have gone too far. We carry the first English-language post-election interview with Jean-Marie Le Pen, who seems to be the most hated politician on the planet. His success in winning 17.5 per cent of the popular vote in France has been denounced, so far, and in no particular order, by the Russian Chief Rabbi, Herr Gerhard Schröder, Mr Blair, Mr Duncan Smith, Mr Kennedy, the Spanish foreign minister, the President of the European Parliament, the Prime Minister of Sweden, the Catholic Bishop of St Denis, Commissioner Kinnock, and the entire British media, in quite hysterical terms.

The Vatican does not seem to have a view on the matter, and the White House is keeping schtumm, although Tom Daschle, the Democrat leader in the Senate, has said he is 'worried'. The only two politicians I can find who seem pleased by M Le Pen's success are Vladimir Zhirinovsky, who believes Russia should hurry up and bomb America, and Filip de Winter of the Flemish Vlaams Blok, whose campaign symbol is a pair of pendulous pink boxing gloves. Otherwise Le Pen has earned a more or less universal chorus of boos – and quite right, too, of course. He is a moderately disgusting thug and demagogue, who used to strut around the European Parliament, when I was a reporter there, guffawing, swigging champagne with leathery blondes, and occasionally indulging in fisticuffs with rival French politicians. As John Laughland's masterly interview reveals, he is also something of a nutcase. He expatiates on his seven years at sea, staring at the billions of stars, which, he says, gave him an insight into the importance of the family; he believes that Germany is fated to take over the rest of Europe; and he derives an apocalyptic significance from the fact that, before its fall, Babylon had a *périphérique* rather like the one surrounding Paris. That this man should come second, in the first round of the presidential elections, is not, perhaps, the earthquake that has been widely suggested in London.

It just means that Chirac the *énarque* will now beam effulgently for another five years in office. Nor does the success of the National Front show that the French are incipient fascists. It does perhaps validate Lady Thatcher's suggestion, a few weeks ago, that extremist politicians sometimes do alarmingly well on the Continent; and perhaps all those who vilified her for making that point might now like to apologise.

The election does not even tell us very much about the popularity of Le Pen. As Laughland points out, he polled only slightly more than he did in 1995 and 1997. The real event in the first round, the really stunning fact, was the total and abject humiliation of the Socialist party of Lionel Jospin, which, in theory has been governing the country.

He took 16 per cent of the vote, which is less than half of what the Tories have been attracting in some recent polls. It was a quite amazing thrashing.

Part of the problem was that Jospin, a former teacher and communist, is a pretty bloodless and desiccated fellow; and the French decided that for all his faults they would rather have the ageing Chirac, with his Johnny Hallyday gift for maudlin self-dramatisation. But if you really want to understand why Jospin fizzled, you should lay your hands on a sensational new volume which has just been published by something called the 'Policy Network'. This timely offering boasts the name of the author in huge letters on the cover, showing that the publishers clearly thought he was a coming man. 'LIONEL JOSPIN', it says, 'My vision of Europe and Globalisation'. There is even an introduction to this indispensable manifesto by – you guessed it – Peter Mandelson. 'Lionel Jospin is a modern thinker of the Left,' gushes Mandy, who, you will remember, is now Blair's all-purpose Euro-bore. 'His record shows his ability to translate confident analysis into practical policy,' Mandy goes on, plainly weighing his words.

You might say that M Jospin's record shows his ability to translate a viable political party into a disaster zone, but that is another matter. You only have to skim a few of his book's narcoleptic pages to see why the French told Lionel to *ficher le camp*. There is the customary Euro-federalism of the French socialists: Europe must have its own television channel, there must be a proper Euro-police force, a common law area for Europe, harmonised taxes, says Lionel (with, we must take it, the approval of dear Mandy), but above all, he says, 'Europe must help devise the regulation which the world needs'. There you go; that was the platform of the French socialist prime minister – a clarion call for more Euro-regulation.

You may think harshly of the French electorate, but they

weren't particularly keen on this. Rather like the British electorate, they wanted something done about crime, and what they saw as the uncontrollable behaviour of illegal immigrants. That is why Le Pen did well; and it is a lesson that has plainly not escaped the Labour Party. Jospin – their nominal counterpart in Paris – whiffles about the need for more regulation, and crashes to defeat – but what do we get from British New Labour? We are treated to the kind of rhetoric about immigrants which, from the mouth of Jean-Marie Le Pen, would be attacked across the civilised world.

Mr Blunkett, the Home Secretary, yesterday talked about asylum seekers 'swamping' certain schools. He has not withdrawn the word, which – as he well knew – was once used by Mrs Thatcher, and which earned her the eternal obloquy of the Left. He has announced segregated education for immigrants; and he does so because he is responding to the same set of public concerns that boosted Le Pen. Mr Blunkett is no fascist, merely an authoritarian. You may think he is quite right in his policies. But be in no doubt: he succeeds by playing to essentially the same gallery as Jean-Marie Le Pen.

Our man in Washington on why we should stick with America.

Droll diplomat finds his place in history

It was the end of greatness. Forty years ago this week, on 31 Oct 1956, Britain launched its mission with France to reverse Nasser's nationalisation of the Suez Canal.

Upon which the Americans kicked the British political establishment so hard between the legs that in some ways it never recovered. The pound fell, and the Americans did not prop it up. A Prime Minister fell, virtually on America's say-so. A humiliated nation knew we had lost the ability to use force independently overseas. Britain's idea of itself had changed, and it was a climacteric in the country's relations with America.

That is the view of Sir Robin Renwick, Our Man in Washington under Bush and Clinton, and author of *Fighting With Allies*, a new history of the Special Relationship. Renwick is one of those products in which Britain excels, the Rolls-Royce-brained ambassador with the feel for history and the puckish aside.

As he says now of the protagonists of Suez: 'I really didn't know how deeply Dulles had been offended by Eden calling him My Dear.'

That is the kind of drollery one can imagine Renwick using after dinner in Washington, and today, in Fleming's Bank. But the anecdote also glances at a deep truth which we have almost forgotten: the amazingly durable chippiness of the Americans, in spite of everything, towards the Brits.

One sees this chippiness most nakedly in the support of some Americans for the IRA. I suppose, in a way, it goes back to 1776. But Renwick starts us off with the British General Sir George Cockburn, sitting uninvited down to dinner at the White House on Aug 24 1814, after President Madison and his family had fled, making obscene jokes about Dolley Madison's cushions, and then torching the place, along with the Library of Congress.

We forget how high-handed we could be, even when we craved American help. In 1941, Our (then) Man in Washington, Lord Halifax, who cheesed off the American press by going foxhunting, observed that the Americans were 'a mass of nice children, a little crude, very warm-hearted, and mainly governed by emotion'. One can imagine how this stoked the chippiness of his counterpart in London, the loathsome Joe Kennedy. Mr Kennedy caused Chamberlain's adam's apple to bob by calling him Neville in public.

Worse, he continually predicted, with apparent relish, that Britain would be destroyed. 'Britain is fighting for her place in the sun,' he reported to Washington in 1939, 'just as she has in the past. Democracy as we conceive it in the US will not survive in Britain or France after the war.' By the time America entered the war, Britain was sucking up desperately. Renwick well evokes Churchill's wooing of Roosevelt, to the point of allowing the President to see him naked, pink and steaming from his bath.

The Americans responded magnificently, if belatedly. But then Renwick describes how Roosevelt tried to get in with Stalin at Teheran by baiting Churchill, and Churchill going red and growling, and Stalin guffawing; and then Roosevelt's final betrayal at Yalta, overruling Churchill and consigning several European countries to half a century of Soviet tyranny.

All the while America was motivated by an instinctual desire to repress British ambition. As the former US ambassador to London, Harry Hopkins, said: 'The American people simply do not like the British colonial policy.' There was more than a whiff of this at Suez.

A year after Suez the European Community was formed. Britain was eventually admitted, and since then, as Britain continued its relative decline, different resentments have grown up. Now the British political classes mourn vanishing sovereignty.

Renwick is himself a Eurosceptic of sorts. 'My own view is that it would be the height of folly for Britain to go in with the first wave into the single currency,' he says, though he negotiated the Single European Act. He takes the slightly politically correct Foreign Office view that Britain is of greatest value to America if it is inside the EU, but acting as a brake.

Renwick says the Special Relationship still exists, and is tradeable. He cites the Rhodes Scholars in the White House, the deal with the Tomahawk cruise missiles, 'an offer made to no other ally.' Above all, he cites Bosnia.

All the months and years in which Bosnia was deemed to be a 'European problem requiring a European solution', Western policy was catastrophic. 'After the fall of Srebrenica I saw Clinton and I said, if we let the same happen to Sarajevo, the reputation of no Western leader will survive.' Then the Americans brought their might to bear.

'As long as we disagreed, it was impossible to do anything. By the end it was a vindication of the relationship.' The rule is the same as with Suez: even after 40 years of European integration, we can't project military power abroad without American help.

Clinton is having girl trouble, and Blair shows what the special relationship is all about.

Scandal in the wind as Elton strikes a chord

Like Butch Cassidy and the Sundance Kid, they came out firing against the worst their enemies could throw at them.

Bill Clinton and Tony Blair stood forth as the two buddies. They were Achilles and Patroclus. They were Castor and Pollux. They were Wallace and Gromit.

United even in their blue suits, blue ties and white shirts – in fact, they only lacked the dark glasses – the brothers brushed off the collective might of the White House press corps and Fleet Street's desperadoes.

Swivelling his clenched chin, eyes bright in search of

anyone who might attack his chum, Mr Blair dared the world to fault his faith in President Clinton.

Of course, he defended him at the gala dinner last night! Too right he jolly well did. And he would do so again. 'I said it because I believed it,' he said, his voice taking on that special husky tone.

'And I said it because I think it is the right thing to do. President Clinton is someone I am proud to call not just a colleague but also a friend.'

His voice dropping, as though choked with feeling, President Clinton glared at the cameras. People like the British Prime Minister were rare in politics, he said. 'People who stand up and say things they believe in when it would be just as easy to walk away.'

He wagged his finger, that famous crooked finger, and prophesied: 'It will strengthen his ability as a world leader.'

While Wolf Blitzer, of CNN, and other titans of American journalism furiously raged together and tempted the leader of the free world to speak his mind to Monica Lewinsky, their questions broke as waves on twin granite rocks. As we flooded from the East Wing, you might for a moment have believed that Blair's heroics had done the trick.

Had he done what none of these men and women with fawn macs and curly tubes in their ears could do? Had he stopped a bullet for the Prez?

Of course not. Operation Fresh Blair was never going to work. Yesterday Washington remained awash with rumour, new allegations about the President's attempts to silence Betty Currie, his secretary.

The depth of the trouble was obvious at 11.30pm on Thursday. The Clintons, Blairs and their 240 guests were on little gilt chairs in the white marquee on the West Wing. So far, it had been a sensational party.

The White House was awash with red-tunicked marine

bands and men from silicon valley with silicone valley wives.

Here were social X-rays, women starved to perfection. Here was Tom Hanks, Barbra Streisand and the portly figure of Teddy Kennedy. For the millions of fans of Harrison Ford, I regret to report he was wearing an earring and a punk haircut.

The champagne had washed down the pudding of chocolate Big Bens. The glutinous toasts had been offered. Blair paid tribute to Mr Clinton's 'determination, statesmanship and courage' and thanked Hillary for her 'dignity and grace' at the funeral of Diana, Princess of Wales.

Then it was time for the 'ennertainment'. 'Tonight we proudly present two musical icons who have built a bond of love and compassion and laughter with their music and built a bridge across the Atlantic,' said the master of ceremonies.

The audience whooped at the arrival of Sir Elton John, whose work for Aids awareness was trumpeted in his biographical note, and for Stevie Wonder, who invented Martin Luther King Day.

As Sir Elton prepared to hit the keys, he said it was like playing at a wedding reception, which gives you the flavour.

Yet every song they offered had some ludicrous double entendre. We snickered at *I just called to say I love you* since Clinton is alleged to have been keen on ringing Monica to roughly the same purpose. 'The fund-raising song!' chortled the roped-off reptiles at the back when the duet struck up *Give me money*.

After an increasingly sultry hour in which Stevie Wonder had been beaming and yowling for the audience to 'snap your fingers! Do anything', it was clear that the audience's hearts and minds were elsewhere.

The singing was listless and the clapping sporadic. Were

they thinking of the Third Way and Welfare to Work? Or were they thinking of the sensational new whisper about the lipsticked tissues and the Filipino cleaner?

Steven Spielberg was making a none-too-subtle bid for the exit. The cannonball head of James Carville, Clinton's intemperate spin doctor, was rotating.

Then it was that someone scurried in to give news to Peter Jennings, the ABC anchorman, that the first edition of the *New York Times* had just dropped. Never mind Elton, there was scandal in the wind.

Slowly, the rumour spread through the tuxedoed crowd. You could see people leaning over and cupping their hands to ears and, by the morning's news, the bushfire was crackling again. No, the visit has not plucked Mr Clinton's chestnuts from that fire but it has done Mr Blair no harm.

Once again, the Prime Minister has had the chance delicately to echo another politician he admires: Mrs Thatcher. At the outset of the Gulf crisis in 1990, she went to Aspen to stand firm with George Bush and here was Blair, standing shoulder to shoulder with Clinton; the former CND member pledging to commit British troops to battle.

Mr Blair's toast consisted mainly of a long anecdote about Winston Churchill, one of the few Englishmen on whose greatness the Americans are agreed. It said something about Mr Blair's versatility that he felt happy to pay such tribute to a Tory Prime Minister.

True, the Winnie the Pooh row gave rise to some Brit-bashing. 'Blimey, these blasted blokes can be unbearable!' wrote Andrea Peyser of the *New York Post*.

Mr Blair's vowels were being cruelly parodied. 'Helloo Tony Bleeah heeah,' one cameraman kept saying to the amusement of his colleagues.

But the Labour Government has successfully raised its profile in America. At one point, the presenter of C-Span looked his viewers squarely in the eye and demanded: 'Who

Is Robin Cook?' A triumph, surely, that he should even ask.

Mr Blair was seen on several early morning chat shows and, by the time he leaves, he will be viewed with a vague apathetic benignity in a few million households that otherwise would not have heard of him.

No one on either side of the Atlantic will think any the less of him for standing by the man he claims as his friend. Any other behaviour would have been frankly creepy.

And here is the man who was to prove Saddam's nemesis, interviewed in February, 1999.

George Dubya Bush

'Good to see ya,' said George Walker Bush, and without any preliminaries, even as we shook hands and his blue eyes zeroed in with seasoned intensity, I blurted the obvious question. The question that *le tout* Washington wants to answer as they prepare to wash that man Clinton right out of their hair.

'Are you going to run?' I asked; and you didn't have to be Sherlock Holmes to work out what he was thinking. The polls say the 52-year-old should run. His daddy, to whom he bears an eerie resemblance, says he should run; not to mention the 30,000 remaining financial backers from his father's machine.

More and more pundits believe this is the man who will defeat Al Gore in 2000 and recapture the White House for the Republicans after the Babylonian follies of the last seven years. He cantered through the formulae of indecision.

'It's a big sacrifice,' he said, adding swiftly that 'it would be for you, too; it would be for anyone. If I do this I will never be a private person again'. And he knew of what he spoke, having seen at close quarters what it meant to be the most powerful man in the world. 'It's a decision of the head and the heart.'

The head was getting near to deciding, he intimated, but the heart was lagging behind. 'I've got two children going through college right now. That's a pretty interesting time. It's a time you want to spread your wings,' he said – and not have secret agents follow you around the 'frat' parties.

And he has only just been re-elected as Governor of Texas which, by convention, he must extol as the 'best job any Texan could have', especially since G W Bush Jnr is really an 'uberpreppy' from Kennebunkport, Maine, who, like his father and grandfather, went to Yale before making a fortune in property and buying a Texan basketball team.

Look at the magnificent pink granite capitol building in which we were standing in Austin. Why should he swap that for the White House?

He was wearing some black ostrich skin cowboy boots marked Governor and emblazoned with the Lone Star. What need of the President's seal, the bands playing *Hail to the Chief*, when his wife Laura is already called 'The First Lady' and has her own recipe for hot chocolate on the Internet?

He has huge powers under the federal system, powers of life and death. Indeed, he cannot leave Texas before June, so heavy is the legislative programme, and under a far-sighted restriction the Texan legislature cannot meet for more than 132 days per year.

As for his lead in the polls, he said: 'The polls said George H W Bush was ahead of Clinton 11 months before the '92 election. I don't take polls.'

But for all the Hamlet stuff, it was pretty clear which way his mind was moving. His father's Cabinet colleagues, former Secretary of State George Shultz and former Defence Secretary Dick Cheney, have been coaching him in world affairs.

Do they want him to go for it? 'They do. They all do,' he said. That very evening he was off to Louisiana to confer with the Governor. Aha. What about?

'We're gon' talk about crawfish ay-touff-ay [étouffé], haw haw,' said Mr Bush, and everyone guffawed with him, since he is as popular with the media here as he is with the voters. 'We're gonna talk some politics,' he conceded.

Whatever it was old Ma Bush used to feed her sons – Jeb, the younger brother, is Governor of Florida – they have the Right Stuff coming out of their ears. Like 'Poppie' Bush, George Jnr was a navy flier, and he exudes a sense of clean-cut, square-jawed, straight-backed, hot-dang all-American values.

If we see a second Bush presidency, it will be marked by his patented 'Compassionate Conservatism' which entails, among other things, long recitation of literacy statistics among minorities.

And no, said Bush Jnr, Compassionate Conservatism was more than Blairism or Clintonism.

'Our philosophy heralds the individual, and trusts the individual,' he said, while Democrats and New Labour still prefer to trust to the ministry of the state. 'There's tremendous scope to go with the grain of human nature.'

Not that there's anything soggy about this compassionate business, or even libertarian. He's in favour of parental notification for abortion, tighter drink-driving laws, and has authorised the judicial bumping-off of 40 murderers.

His eye alighted on my garish watch. 'I'm not sure about the wristband,' he said. On learning that the face bore the picture of Che Guevara (I blush), he said: 'Now that's an interesting statement. We're kind of tough on people like that down here, so be careful.'

I tried pathetically to explain that it was my wife's, just a joke watch, the other one having bust under six Gs in an F15E; but he was off to Louisiana and stuffed crawfish.

'What you bo's gon' do now? You should head down to 6th Street to the bars,' he said, flinging out an arm.

Should we mention his name? 'If you do and you go to jail, you ain't never gon' get out.'

These are just some of the machines that make America the most powerful nation on earth.

Flying a Scudbuster

The dratted toggle for the oxygen mask still won't fit when Matt Moeller, my US Air Force pilot, makes a pumping motion with his hands and the men on the runway go 'yessir' in lollipop language; and help, we start to move.

The helmet is still not sorted as we taxi past the other Strike Eagles, 92 of them arrayed on either side like a guard of honour on their high, spindly legs, £4 billion worth of testosterone wrapped in steel and titanium.

It is a January day of abnormal beauty here in North Carolina. Prowling behind us in plane number two are the British exchange pilots, and in a few minutes I'll have the answers to several key questions. Can these things really do what the military claims: post a bomb through Saddam's letter-box and hit the Serb's bottle of slivovitz just as he is raising it to his lips?

And how on earth do you fit the oxygen mask? And will I be very ill, or just slightly ill? You've no idea of the strings that were pulled to get us this 'facility' at Seymour Johnson Air Force base, home of the F15E Strike Eagle – Scudbuster to you and me. A four-star general in the Pentagon had to give final clearance, and even then I wasn't allowed to fly with one of the British pilots in case we kidnapped the plane and headed for Bermuda.

On the Tarmac, almost weeping with envy, is MoD press man, Squadron Leader Tom Rounds, who says he would 'bite his arm off' to be in my G-suit now; and as we come to the end of the two-mile runway, we turn. Matt Moeller, 34, aka Moleman, call-sign 'Sludge', says, 'OK Boris?' Air traffic control come over the headset saying Sludge 31 has clearance for vertical take-off . . .

And thank heavens, the oxygen mask doodah slips home. The two engines make a kind of yip-yip noise as the jet nozzles tighten like sphincters to maximise the thrust, and we are on our way. After about three seconds Matt sings out '100 knots' and the nose is starting to rise. As the afterburners kick in you can feel the pressure on your back, and at 200 knots we are airborne, the base, the cars, the trees flashing by like a past life. Then it dawns that we are essentially strapped on top of two rockets in the process of sucking in 23,000 lb of fuel and in a couple of ticks, when we hit 450 knots, Matt has promised to 'pull the stick back.'

Then we will ascend vertically into the blue heavens in a $60 million taxpayer-funded firework. As everyone has been saying for the past two days, there is a small risk of death, and a rather great risk of being sick.

At the egress – ejector training – session Captain Erin Pickel jovially recounted the fate of the Australian photographer who was forced to bale out at 20,000ft. Then there was the guy who forgot to unclick his parachute when he landed and was dragged to the bottom of a lake; and the guy who, ahem, unclicked his parachute 200ft up. There was the pilot who took a 6ft turkey vulture in an air intake and listened while it destroyed the engine. They lost a plane last year and two years ago they lost a pilot, too, though the ground staff suggest they 'don't want to say a whole lot about it'.

But, hey, everyone has been saying, you'll be fine. If Matt makes the triple arm-pump, which means let's get out of here, I have strapped to my rump the following items: a five-inch hunting knife; a mosquito net, diarrhoea tablets, emergency drinking water, a 16-in saw for firewood, aspirin, Band-aids, soap, razor blades, antiseptic gauze pads, a tourniquet, malaria tablets, a silver combat casualty blanket, green dye to mark the sea as in the Apollo splash-downs, a six-foot inflatable life-raft with a CO_2 canister and two olive drab sponges for bailing out water.

More useful, perhaps, are three sickbags stowed in the knee pocket of the flying suit; and I should explain that some machismo is attached to the vomiting issue. The only other British journalist to be allowed in one of these machines, Jeremy Clarkson, tossed his cookies 11 times. They have not forgotten it.

'These screens are very expensive,' said Lt Col Del Grego, the squadron's second-in-command, in the mess-room beforehand. 'We'll have to charge the UK Government.' He guffawed, and so did everyone else. So I'm braced for the challenge now as the joystick is pulled right back, and you suddenly feel the pressure on the chest.

You stare straight up at the sky; and the thing ascends with a shivering roar and if you hold your breath and swivel your encumbered neck in the canopy, you can see the ground shrinking beneath you and then, at least if you are me, you let out a groan because the ground now appears to be where the sky used to be, and you are turning backwards upside down . . .

And aaaargh: my abiding impression of the first 30 seconds in the F15E Strike Eagle is not of its technical capacities, astounding though these doubtless are. In the view of Rich Walton, one of the British exchange officers now taking off behind us, 'It is the best fighter aircraft in the world', while Graeme Davis, his fellow British pilot, advises me to think of this outing as 'the Grand Prix of flying'. And although each of its engines is now developing 32,000 lb of thrust, and though its pods and missile emplacements are almost infinitely adaptable to new software, what strikes me is how close this machine is, spiritually and mechanically, to – well – a Sopwith Camel.

It has the same stick, the same pedals for the flaps. It's the same war between a pilot's audacity and caution, except that it's not made of wood and glue and goes at two-and-a-half times the speed of sound; though now, since we've swooped down until we're sliding only 500ft above farms, Matt is going easy on the big throttle lever.

The yowling pain in the ears is fading. The G-forces which everyone warns about have been, so far, barely noticeable; and the exhilaration begins. Oh, you can say, it is just a PR stunt. But as Graeme Davis and Rich Walton come wing-tip to wing-tip, two British fliers in an American machine, you could argue that our little sortie is a symbol of something important.

In a neat piece of historical symmetry it turns out that these very American squadrons, the 334th, 335th and 336th, originated in the bosom of the RAF. It was in 1940 that a gang of American preppies went to plucky little Britain and formed 71 Eagle Squadron. For the two years until America entered the Second World War, they flew Spitfires, and still these clean-cut Kevin Costner characters wear RAF wings at the squadron's Friday night pizza and chicken beer busts.

It is a relationship still proved weekly in the attacks by America and Britain – and no one else – on Iraq. And it is a tribute to the intimacy of this relationship that two foreign pilots are allowed not just to fly this machine, but to teach Americans to fly it. Graeme, 31, a clench-jawed

Biggles who 11 years ago transformed himself from bank clerk to Top Gun, has been here for two-and-a-half years and is clearly a star. He and his wife give Battle of Britain theme parties. He has 16 USAF personnel under him.

'He is the first exchange officer I know of to become an instructors' instructor,' says Don Seiler, his squadron leader. 'I've taken one of my billets and given it to an exchange officer.' Rich, also 31 with a young child, is a graduate of City University. He hasn't been here so long, but he loves everything except the American habit of spitting chewing tobacco into Coke cans; and I don't think the base commander, General Randy Bigum, is being mawkish when he says he'd like to have both of them under his full-time command.

So in formation the Anglo-American strike force heads east, picking up speed and height. Somewhere 80 miles away on the marshy coast in a deserted bombed-out wasteland is a big white container propped on its end – let us call it Saddam's bunker – and our mission is, as they say, to 'shack that baby'!

As we turn at high speed, we start pulling serious Gs, and it is time to prepare your mental state. The point of the G-suit, which consists of all kinds of embarrassing bondage in the groin area, is to stop the blood from your brain draining into your feet; and as the turn begins, your internal organs are squeezed, and your feet feel as if you have been queuing for Monet but far, far worse, and your lips are going blib blib blib.

You grunt as you have been told to grunt, and then suddenly it stops again. That was – phew – six Gs. They say it gets really tough at more than six, but I'm feeling perky enough. Now Rich and Graeme are circling over and over us, our metal skins only feet apart, and you have a sense of the planes shaping the air like a pair of hands. You can see why they call it an Eagle, with its massive hunched shoulders around the air intake and the soaring arrogant nose. You never saw a machine more expressive of speed and aggression. We pass a flock of swans far below on a sunlit lake. This thin Perspex canopy can take a 4lb bird full on at 480 knots. We haven't discussed what happens to the canopy at 490 knots except that if you pull this toggle with yellow and black stripes, two rockets will go off – one to push your seat slightly forward and the other to send it smashing out through the canopy, and all in four-tenths of a second.

At least I think it's that toggle. Or what about this button that says 'Select Nuclear Option'? There's one button I'm not meant to discuss because it might give the Iraqis ideas. I'm toying with the little red blip that releases the precision-guided munitions, the AIM-9 mike sidewinders and the AIM-20 alpha slammer, and I'm reflecting on the words of Graeme: 'I wake up. It's a nice day. I fill up the car for virtually no bucks and then I go and fly F15Es.'

What a life, if you have the Right Stuff . . . but do I? Matt reminds me of the little button that stops the noise from my Wizzo (Weapons System Operator) seat coming through to his part of the cockpit. 'Just a courtesy thing,' he says because the next bit 'will be a little more violent'; he doesn't want to hear any distressing noises as, oooof, we pull another six Gs, and the earth and the sky swap round again.

Now is the test. General Bigum has told me, 'The more our leadership wants a bomb to put through a window 100 per cent of the time, the more they are going to call on this plane.' Do these machines have the accuracy that democracy demands?

As I feebly try to keep my fluttering eyes on the instruments we begin the bombing run, just as they do them in Iraq: a series of hideous lunges and jack-knife turns and then, ceeee-ripes, we're pulling up again to avoid the triple A. 'That was the most perfect pass I ever made,' says Matt afterwards. Saddam's bunker was truly shacked, he says, though whether the bomb went through the letter-box I cannot testify. Because although I was the weapons systems operator, they wisely decided not to prime the weapons.

Frankly, my mind is by now on other things, like the cold sweat of nausea. Which Matt astutely alleviates by taking us through the sound barrier as we cross out over the Atlantic and then – I feel a sort of melancholy to recall, because there may never be another thrill like it – he gives me the plane to fly.

'Push it hard to the left,' he says, and we turn over and over like a tumble-dryer in an aileron roll, and then I push it to the right; and I will never forget the sea rushing up not far from Kitty Hawk, where the first plane ever flew, and the beauty of that mad corkscrew downwards, so fast that we leave the noise of the engine behind.

'Uh, I'll take the plane back now, Boris,' says Matt and then it is home into the sunset, feeling very lucky indeed, very proud not to have been sick, and that Jeremy Clarkson is a big girl's blouse.

Why are the liberal London media so beastly to Bush, when they just lurved Clinton? They are both Bible-bashing death-penalty fiends from southern states, and seem to pursue the same global agenda. Is it cos Bush is Republican?

Good on you, Bush baby: you go ahead and tell 'em

You know, whenever George Dubya Bush appears on television, with his buzzard squint and his Ronald Reagan side-nod, I find a cheer rising irresistibly in my throat.

Yo, Bush baby, I find myself saying, squashing my beer can like some crazed redneck; you tell 'em boy. Just you tell all those pointy-headed liberals where to get off. Even if you felt that he was jammy to attain the White House; even if you are troubled by his syntax and his habit of turning the lights out at 9pm, you will surely agree that there is something magnificent in the way he has taken on the great transatlantic Left-liberal consensus-loving Third Way-ers and turned them into a state of stark, staring, bug-eyed, heaving-bosomed apoplexy.

He's a monster, shrieks Polly Toynbee in the *Guardian*, adding that America has become a 'rogue state' in the two months since Clinton left office. In the *New York Times* and the *Washington Post*, the old Lefties are beside themselves with rage and grief, accusing Bush of cynically pretending to be a compassionate conservative in order to win the White House – not that he won it, they snarl; stole it, more like.

He's a nutter, they say; he's a reformed alcoholic basketball freak who got the job only because of daddy, and he doesn't understand that, if he carries on like this, it's going to be early lights out for everyone. And the more they scream, of course, the more I find myself secretly admiring the guy's style.

He sticks it to North Korea, which is still, after all, a barbaric Stalinist regime. He refuses to apologise to the Chinese for the downing of the EP-3 spy plane; and why should he? It was their fat fault that one of their fighters bumped into the American plane, in international air space, and consequently crashed into the sea. He's going ahead with his promised tax cuts of $1.6 trillion over the next 10 years; and that seems wholly reasonable, given that he said he would do so before the election, and that the American economy is badly in need of a stimulus.

He's decided to scrap the 1972 Anti-Ballistic Missile

Treaty, which also seems sensible, since that document is now about as meaningful as the Treaty of Versailles. You may doubt that it is possible to build an umbrella against nuclear attack, whether by Russia or anyone else. But I have never quite understood why, on those defeatist grounds, we should stop the Americans from even trying to defend themselves, not to mention the rest of humanity.

But of all the tough-guy acts that Bush has performed in his first few months, of all the pieces of exuberant Reaganism, nothing has so intoxicated the world with hate as his decision to scrumple up the Kyoto protocol and use it for putting practice in the Oval Office.

Malcolm Bruce, a Liberal Democrat MP, has already accused Mr Bush of being a mass murderer; not for his record in executing felons in Texas, but for consigning future generations to a dust-bowl planet. Yesterday in the Commons, a Labour MP with a beard asked Tony Blair how America could be so incredibly selfish, given that the earth belonged not to Bush, but to every soul who walks it.

Polly Toynbee, my old friend, tells her readers that America is 'morphing into an evil empire of its own'. A special EU delegation went to Washington on Tuesday, consisting of Kjell Larsson, the Swedish environment minister, and Margot Wallstrom, the EU environment commissioner. It is not clear whether Bush had time to see these great ones personally, what with his heavily charged agenda of jogging, golf and watching movies, but, according to the *Financial Times*, they received 'short shrift'.

You can see where all this is leading. It will not be long before we are told that America is so selfish, so isolationist, so obsessed with its sovereign right to put its broad-bottomed people in gas-guzzling Chevy Suburbans, that she can no longer be trusted with global leadership.

We will be told – we are already being told – that Britain

318

must make a choice, between America and Europe. We can either go for the rampant commercialism, the casino capitalism of George Bush's America, where petrol costs a dollar a barrel, and where Dubya has just scrapped some Democrat laws against arsenic in the water supply; or we can go for Europe, a softer, gentler, landscape of earnest Swedish commissioners and worker participation, and higher taxes, and tighter regulation.

If Bush is going to be so frighteningly tough on China and Korea, people will say in their fat-headed way, then perhaps we had better build up this Euro-army. And they will be guilty of a stupendous error.

Because we still need a rich, confident America; not just to provide the cash for the global military leadership that the United States has given from the Gulf to Kosovo, but also to keep the world economy moving. The hypocrisy of the Europeans over Kyoto is staggering. They attack America in hysterical terms, and yet the 15 EU countries have never come close to meeting their own eight per cent target for cuts in carbon dioxide emissions. They have not even agreed which countries should cut the most. If America were to meet its Kyoto targets now, it would require a cut of 30 per cent in emissions, and how, exactly, is that supposed to work in the current economic downturn?

There will come a time when the market, and, inevitably, US technology, will deliver a greener planet, when cars run on water, or photo-voltaic cells. But it is plain ridiculous to ask America to make such cuts in emissions now, as Clinton recognised when Congress voted against Kyoto by 95 to one.

It would exacerbate the recession, and when Bush says no, he is doing what is right not just for America but for the world. And by the way, we Europeans already allow 50 microlitres of arsenic per litre in our water.

Bianca denounces European feebleness in Bosnia. She demands action against Milosevic. Curious, some might say, that she should campaign so vigorously against American action in Iraq.

Bianca Jagger

Bianca is weeping, and I don't think she's faking. Here on the sofa in Claridges, the eyes of the world's most famous Nicaraguan are molten as she recalls her visits to Bosnia and the duplicity of the Western powers.

Yes, you can certainly be cynical about the ex-rock wife and grandmother, jetting off in her black Donna Karan pyjamas and Manolo Blahnik sandals to rescue heart-op orphans, the hot-lipped disco queen from Managua sharing her agony with the readers of *Hello!* as she leads a procession of Muslim widows to their husbands' graves.

Nor do her mercy dashes always succeed, as in the case of Guinevere Garcia, a woman on death row in Illinois, who appealed to Bianca to stop trying to save her life. But sometimes there are causes where there is no room for cynicism, and where frankly it is immaterial how much she is driven by moral outrage and how much by the desire to burnish her halo. She is on the trail of an infamy that is in danger of being forgotten.

It is two years since what appears to have been the worst massacre on European soil since the Third Reich. After many trips to Bosnia since 1993, as a representative for Amnesty International, Bianca, ex-student of the Paris Political Studies Institute, has written a long and meticulous essay in which the facts are so clear that one is left angry and depressed. It is called *J'accuse: the Betrayal of Srebrenica.*

In April 1993 UN Security Council Resolution 819 guar-

anteed protection for the Bosnian Muslim enclave of Srebrenica 'by all necessary means, including the use of force';
and the West then honoured this promise by a mixture of
dithering and appeasement, culminating in the sack of the
town by Ratko Mladic.

According to Judge Riad of the UN War Crimes Tribunal in The Hague, 'a truly terrible massacre of the
Muslim population appears to have taken place. The evidence tendered to the prosecutor describes scenes of
unimaginable savagery, thousands of men executed and
buried in mass graves, hundreds of men buried alive ...
children killed before their mothers' eyes, a grandfather
forced to eat the liver of his own grandson ...'

And what did they do, the Dutch battalion that was
meant to be 'protecting' these people? They gave Mladic
petrol from their own jerrycans. Does she think the Dutch
were cowards? 'Let me put it this way. Is it cowardly for
people who have been assigned to protect 40,000 civilians
to assist in the separation of men and women? Is it cowardly to have drafted a list of 242 people to be handed
over? They were cowards, but this was not just a question
of cowardice. This was collaboration.'

The weak men include Gen Bernard Janvier, the French
UN commander in Bosnia, whom she blames for doing a
deal to spring some French hostages in exchange for a
promise not to intervene, and Yasushi Akashi, the UN
special envoy, constantly on the line to Milosevic, when
the Serb president was supposed by the West to have no
say in the matter.

'That is why the West is frightened to arrest Mladic and
Karadjic – because they will point their fingers at those
who were accomplices. They know where the skeletons
are in both senses.'

But what could the West really have done? Fought hand
to hand with the glass-eating hordes of Serbia? This wasn't

our war, I suggest. Like all Bosnia hawks she believes it could have been done from the air.

'Air strikes. Absolutely, absolutely. You would have cut the communications of the Bosnian Serbs. It was the perfect excuse to say it was not possible. Janvier said to Mladic, "If you release those French soldiers, there will be no air strikes".

'Just think about it, Boris, the planes were flying above without striking, but they needed that order to strike. They were called back.' But air strikes would have meant civilian casualties. I bet you were against American bombing in Vietnam, I say.

'Yes I was,' she says. 'But I objected to intervention because it was a different thing . . . If you want to deter atrocities, then bravo.'

All right, I say, the fate of Srebrenica was appalling, a shameful page in the history of the post-war Western alliance. But they weren't exactly angels, these Muslims. 'I am sure everyone has blood on their hands,' she says, but avers that the majority of corpses are still to be exhumed in Republika Srpska, victims of the Serbs.

And that is when the tears begin. 'Why do I care about it? Because I am not prepared to forget and become a silent accomplice of what I have seen. We have a moral responsibility to act in the face of an atrocity such as Srebrenica . . . If I didn't speak out, I would be part of those sending a message to posterity that it is right to perpetuate massacres and genocide.'

You can attach what value you like to her tears. You may think, as I do, that the disaster of the Muslim enclaves was caused not so much by the cowardice and collaboration of the UN forces (though these may have been contributory) but by the decision of Western politicians to use the troops as a bluff without ever having the will, or the means, to make good their threats.

That does not make her wrong to draw attention, by her celebrity, to the hypocrisy and bankruptcy of the policy; before, as she puts it, 'the grass grows over the graves'.

Without any UN backing at all, Bill and Tony decide to bomb Milosevic.

Blair and Clinton – will Bill let Tony down?

It was so beautiful. They were Achilles and Patroclus. They were the two young leaders of a new generation, fighting the first 'progressive' war.

'President Clinton is someone I am proud to call not just a colleague but a friend,' said Tony Blair huskily at the White House in February last year, at the height of Bill's difficulties over Monica Lewinsky; and Bill has reciprocated wherever the pair have met.

Now Blair must be wondering whether he is about to join the long line of people who have been disappointed in President Clinton, from Monica to Mike McCurry, the spokesman, George Stephanopoulos, the aide, and countless others who have worked with the brilliant and manipulative President.

As soon as the war began, there was a division of labour between the two leaders. The United States has supplied well over 80 per cent of the military effort. Those B2 bombers which have been attacking, among other things, the Chinese embassy, have not even been touching down in Europe in their round trips from Missouri.

And yet Clinton scarcely bothered to prepare the American people for what was coming, save for a weird and rambling press conference on the night of the bombing, in which he urged his listeners to consult their atlases. Ever since, it has appeared that the rhetoric of the war has been contracted out to Blair and Labour, as though it was the kind of theatrical service industry at which New Britain excels.

It was Alastair Campbell, not an American, who went to Brussels to sort out the Nato PR machine. Young thrusters like Julian Braithwaite from the Foreign Office have been sent to allied headquarters at Mons to help Gen Wes Clarke sharpen his act. All the while Tony Blair has supplied a crescendo of bellicose rhetoric, which yesterday showed no sign of diminishing.

'No compromise, no fudge, no half-baked deals,' he warned the tyrant of Belgrade, though Britain's military contribution, in terms of sorties flown and bombs dropped, is estimated at 5.6 per cent of the Nato effort.

At what is being seen as the turning-point of the crisis, the Nato summit on April 23–25, it was Blair who was the hawk. The air war was not going well. Civilians were being killed. Milosevic was acquiring an almost Churchillian persona in the eyes of the Serbs. Blair was said to be urging the consideration of ground forces; and if he was, he was not successful.

We are now seven weeks into the war and plans for a ground invasion – the only means of speedily restoring the Kosovars to their ruined homes – appear to be dead. And who suffers, politically, if Nato fails? In a way it ought to be President Clinton who takes the rap. He made the mistake of believing Madeleine Albright and thinking Milosevic would soon buckle under a spot of bombing. Blair was merely the number one cheerleader for what was an American-inspired policy.

And yet the paradox is that because he was so zealous in his propaganda, so unbending in his Gladstonian wrath against the Serbs, it is Blair, somehow, who seems the more politically exposed. When Bill Clinton speaks to the American people these days, he speaks as much of gun control and classroom morality as of the war in Kosovo. When Blair speaks, he seems engaged in a way that Clinton is not. 'We are not talking here of some faraway place of which we know little. We are talking about the doorstep of the European Union, our own backyard,' he said yesterday in Aachen. The trouble is that for the American electorate, that is just what Kosovo is; a faraway place of which they know little. No American lives are being lost: that is the whole objective.

Somehow it is Blair, not Clinton, who has contrived to intertwine his fortunes with those of Slobodan Milosevic. Several times the Prime Minister has said there can be no future for Serbia or Kosovo with Milosevic at the helm. Clinton has been careful to say no such thing, and seems to envisage a settlement in which Milosevic retains sovereignty not just of Serbia, but of Kosovo, too.

The United States started the Kosovo operation. Only America can bring it to a successful end.

Without the determination and resolve of his friend in the White House, Blair's warlike words will amount to nothing more than a forlorn and embarrassing parp of the trumpet.

Needing someone to fill my interview slot, I chance on the famous thug and mass killer. In retrospect, I feel embarrassed about the tone. He was a monster, and he doesn't deserve to be treated as if he were some buffoonish backbench rebel.

Arkan

You instantly recognise the baby face across the Hyatt tea room, the face that is in a sealed war crimes indictment in

The Hague. He's the owner of Yugoslavia's No 1 football team, proprietor of the 'Serb Crown' bakery chain, husband of Serbia's No 1 folk singer and the man singled out by the Defence Secretary as the incarnation of Serb mayhem.

He's called Zeljko Raznatovic, aka Arkan, and he has a message for us. No, he wasn't in Kosovo when George Robertson said that he was at the outset of the conflict. But his 'tiger' paramilitaries are in training all over Yugoslavia and Arkan is waiting . . .

'If you are coming with ground troops, I will be going to Kosovo. I was brought up in Pristina, the capital,' says Arkan, so that we know how personally he takes it. The paramilitary-cum-entrepreneur is surrounded by some very smart women, including his wife in a blue satin trouser suit, and some very tough-looking eggs.

One of these is called 'Colonel Igor Igorov', a flat-eyed Russian in a dark suit. Igor sits in on our conversation while another pair of Arkan helpmeets sits behind me. So tell us, Arkan, what about your Bosnian war crimes?

'I kill many people in a fair fight because I go first and my army is going behind me. All the time I can't live without danger. There were no atrocities in Bijeljina [a town in eastern Bosnia where his men drove the bulk of its Muslim residents from their homes]. There were 40,000 Muslims and 20,000 Serbs. Those Muslims started shooting and, after that, we came in the town and we killed those bastards. Muslim people and Serb people they welcomed me and I made a speech and I address the people and they start screaming "Thank you Arkan, thank you Arkan" because I saved them from the Muslims.

'I respect Muslims. I don't eat, for instance, pork meat but I'm not a Muslim. I simply don't like pork,' says the 47-year-old father of nine.

That's a jolly fine ring there, not a knuckleduster is it,

I say, pointing to a diamond the size of a Smartie. No, he says. 'My wife gave me that present. She made a seventh record and she gave me that for my birthday,' says Arkan, who used to live in London and speaks French fluently.

And what about current Serb atrocities in Kosovo? 'It's possible that some Serbs got angry and they acted as they shouldn't,' he says. 'In this country, we have law and order. In this country, we don't have a president who is a war criminal.' And the rapes? 'It never happened. I will be the first to shoot a Serbian soldier who does this immediately. He will never live two seconds. We are not savages. We are not Nazis. We don't kill people.'

Do you think there will be a ground war? 'Of course. Why do you think I've cut my hair? Not to look tough but, when I put my cap on, it helps if the hair is short.'

Are you sure you will win? 'I don't doubt for any second that we are the winners. After that, we will be singing *We are the champions*.'

On a more peaceable sort of note, has he any business wheezes up his sleeves? 'I will sell the plastic bags, because you will need a lot of plastic bags for your soldiers. That will be good business.'

Expressively, Colonel Igor goes to turn the hotel tea room music off. Er, nice suit, I say. It is white with a thin black pinstripe. 'An Italian friend of mine brought it from Italy. I would like to be like Martin Bell. I consider him a friend of mine.'

Won't it be a shame if he can't travel around Europe now, what with this indictment for war crimes in The Hague? 'I don't give a damn. I really don't recognise that court.

'We are warriors in our blood. My grandfather fought the Austro-Hungarians and the Germans. My father was a partisan. I will tell you the truth: we don't care. We are defending our country. We are defending our children.

Anyone who is outside, we will kill. You have to understand that we are better fighters than the Vietnamese and
we will make you a new Vietnam in the heart of Europe.
The moral is on our side and we are ready to die. We will
raise an army of two million. My wife will shoot you. My
boys of 15 will shoot you.'

Aha, Colonel Igor and the others, are they, you know,
armed? Igor shifts. 'Er, well of course they carry something,' says Arkan. 'But not in the hotel.

'Personally, I will be after the Brit troops because they
killed a friend of mine and they said he was a war criminal.'

'From the back,' says Igor tonelessly.

'He was not even armed and they killed him: the SAS,'
says Arkan. 'You could see from Blair, from Robin Cook,
the British are mostly raising this war up and anger against
the Serbs.'

He touches his ear and mutters to Igor. 'They are bombing right now,' he says to me. 'I hear it. You do not have
a good ear.

'That rugby captain. They destroy him for nothing, for
fun. And that topless thing; you want to kill her as you
killed Diana. You British have something cruel in your
mentality and that is why you conquer.'

Four angry despatches from Belgrade.

Incompetent swatting from above the clouds

It may not be today. It may not be this week. But I have
a hunch that some time in the near future this demented
war will end. Amid a crashing Beethovian finale of bombs
from the American air force, Chernomyrdin will fly in for
one last time to Belgrade.

Slobodan Milosevic will sign something involving Nato principles, G8 principles and UN declarations, and everyone will leap to the rostrum to proclaim a triumph. 'Slobba caves in', the *Sun* will say under instruction from Alastair Campbell.

A proud Prime Minister will address a grateful but secretly apathetic nation, while much the same happens in Washington, though with more accent on the apathy; and in most of Serbia, where the population relies mainly on RTS Serbian television for their news, since newspapers are expensive, there will be jubilation.

For the first time since the bombing began, Milosevic will address his people directly, instead of being endlessly filmed at a green baize table, surrounded by his nodding ministers, or greeting delegations from Moscow or Athens. He will claim victory for the Serbs, in the sense that they have survived a 70-day rain of death from the most advanced and terrifying military power in the world, fending off an alliance whose collective GDP is several thousand times greater than their own.

Who will be right, in this coming cacophony of propaganda? Let us look at what they call the facts on the ground. According to its own boasts, Nato has given Yugoslavia – which was already a poor country before March 24 – a thorough pasting indeed. I've seen the bridges, the electricity plants, the government buildings, the 'fuel reservoirs', aka petrol stations, which have been turned into blackened enigmatic lumps; not forgetting the schools, hospitals, old people's homes and homes in general which have been blasted to kingdom come.

Almost every day journalists leave Belgrade in a kind of corpse convoy to see the latest enormity; and I wish I could say our eyes were deceiving us. In the past 48 hours, the bombs have been feeling especially dumb, hitting a bridge packed with shoppers and a sanatorium full of old people.

While Jamie Shea at Nato pretends that he will rootle around and investigate this or that alleged blunder, adroitly delaying confirmation in order to take the heat out of the story, the tally mounts up, to around 1,200 civilian deaths so far.

And as for poor Kosovo, the mountainous Yugoslav province of Kosovo for whose sake we are waging war, what do we see there? We don't really know, since one of the consequences of the unsupported air strikes was to make it very difficult for aid agencies and media to work in the war zone. Nato says that 340 Albanians have been executed by Serb forces, which seems a low estimate. We have no idea what kind of carnage will be exposed when the fog lifts.

We do know that there are around 1.3 million Albanian refugees waiting to go home, and we also know, from the experience of Bosnia and Croatia, that a great many of them will refuse to go. Who can blame them? Many of their homes will have been destroyed.

Under any forthcoming deal, Milosevic will be allowed to keep at least some Serb forces in the province. Remember those slippery conditions the Prime Minister keeps setting out: 'His troops out, our troops in, and the refugees back home.' We lack the crucial quantifier 'all'. Above all, as President Clinton has accepted, neither the G8 principles nor the Nato principles impugn Yugoslav sovereignty over Kosovo.

The Belgrade rumour mill is now humming with the notion that Slobba will shortly accept Nato soldiers as part of the peacekeeping force, including some kind of American and British presence in Kosovo, or in enough of Kosovo for Tony and Bill to claim that their conditions for victory have been satisfied.

If he does, Milosevic can expect something in return. Perhaps the Western powers will go easy on that war crimes indictment, as they have gone easy on Ratko Mladic and Radovan Karadjic. Perhaps they will lift the trade embargo. Whatever happens, poor Yugoslavia will stagger on, groaning under its crony-infested socialist system, and Slobodan Milosevic will remain in power.

War is stupid. War is hell. But never has there been a war so stupendously incompetent in matching methods to aims. There are plenty of theories here about why civilians have been killed in such numbers, and you can see why the Serbian population thinks the aim is to terrorise them. Nato succeeded in decapitating a priest as he crossed a bridge in broad daylight on the feast of the Holy Trinity. They killed a toddler as she sat on her potty.

Of course this was not intentional, in the sense that some brasshat at Mons did not target this priest or that toddler. But you could say it was intentional in that Nato dropped bombs from 15,000 feet in the sure-fire knowledge that civilians would be killed. One of the truly amazing things about reporting from Belgrade, where the bombs go off night and day, is that you never see the planes.

Nato is flying nigh on 1,000 sorties a day, and they are so high that you can't see them. No wonder they hit hospitals by mistake. The reason they fly so high, of course, is that this war is being conducted on the basis of a moral calculus which says that the lives of Yugoslav or Albanian civilians are worth very little next to the lives of allied soldiers and airmen. That moral calculus explains why the planes have not gone low enough either to risk the flak or to be sure of their targets, and why Mr Clinton and Mr Blair are reluctant to launch a ground war.

You might defend the air war if it was somehow stopping Serb forces from launching brutal purges in Kosovo. But that is just what it is not doing. Quite the reverse.

Yes, there was a case for intervention to protect the Kosovo Albanians. Yes, I and many others might have

331

supported an immediate, massive ground operation. But there was no case for starting a war, if the reality of American domestic politics meant it was fought in this cowardly way, incompetently swatting from above the clouds and then trotting out these phrases borrowed from the IRA about regretting civilian casualties.

If and when there is a Nato 'victory', and Blair and Clinton are paraded in triumph, then I hope there is a man behind them on the chariot to whisper in their ears, not only of their own mortality, but also of the mortality of the people they claimed to be protecting.

Milosevic under fire for accepting American terms

Slobodan Milosevic last night caved in to Nato's demands, accepting a peace plan agreed by Nato and Russia that could end the Kosovo conflict within days.

But Nato insisted that its bombing would go on until there was clear evidence that Milosevic's troops were on their way out of the province they attempted to purge of all its ethnic Albanians.

Only then would the war be over and much could still go wrong.

President Clinton said: 'Until Serb forces begin a verifiable withdrawal from Kosovo, we will continue to pursue diplomacy, but we will also continue the military effort that has brought us to this point.'

Tony Blair counselled caution 'because everything has to be tied down, everything has to be implemented . . .'

He insisted that the West had done no deals with the Serb leadership.

'These terms were on offer right from the very beginning

332

and there has been no negotiating away of the essential demands.'

He gave an absolute assurance that a 'de facto partition' of Kosovo was unacceptable.

Leading diplomats were working on the timetable for Serbia's withdrawal from Kosovo and an end to the bombing. One source said that Nato could start moving into Kosovo as early as this weekend.

Milosevic signalled his approval of the plan after being deserted by Russia, his only ally.

It calls for the withdrawal of all his forces from the province and its occupation by an international force that will contain Nato and Russian troops.

The million and more refugees driven from their homes are to be allowed to return home and Kosovo will be placed under international administration.

Belgrade was rife with speculation about why Milosevic had chosen this moment to accept so many of Nato's demands.

One theory is that he has come under increasing pressure from important business interests, which believe that the damage inflicted by the bombing is becoming unsustainable. Others attribute his change of heart to his wife, Mira Markovic.

More likely, the Serb leader judged that he could present himself as the man saving his countrymen from a callous and barbarous alliance – and save Kosovo for Serbia into the bargain.

Milosevic's move followed a 136–74 vote by the Serb parliament calling on the government to accept Nato's terms.

'Yugoslavia accepts the document for peace brought by the highest representatives of the European Union and Russia,' the official statement said.

Milosevic's Socialist Party said that it backed the plan

because 'it brings establishment of peace and a halt to the criminal bombing'.

As the news broke, Vuk Draskovic, a former deputy prime minister and an opponent of Milosevic, said: 'This is a great day for the Serbian nation, for all citizens of Yugoslavia, for the future of the peace and stability in this country.'

He described how Milosevic had called a meeting of party leaders at 8pm on Wednesday: 'He explained that this document had to be accepted.'

Official sources in Belgrade said it was crucial for Milosevic to secure the approval of parliament so that he could be seen to be acting in accordance with the will of the people. But there was also anger at what some saw as a surrender. Vojisav Seselj, the leader of the hardline Radical Party, said: 'This means capitulation. We are going to continue with our fight.'

Even as the Russian and Finnish envoys were meeting Milosevic at his presidential residence, the roar of Nato jets could be heard.

No bombs were dropped on the Belgrade area, but the sound of sonic booms served as a constant reminder of Nato's determination to prevail.

The day's events, which followed two days of intense negotiation between the Americans and Russians, unfolded rapidly.

Early in the morning the Russian envoy, Viktor Chernomyrdin, and the EU's representative, Martti Ahtisaari, briefly called on Milosevic to discuss again the plan handed to him late on Wednesday.

By mid-morning, after an often stormy debate, the Serb parliament had approved the text. Mr Chernomyrdin and Mr Ahtisaari then saw Milosevic again and received his approval.

Within minutes, news that an end to the conflict, in its

73rd day, was genuinely in sight was flashing around the world.

Last night Mr Ahtisaari was in Cologne, briefing the leaders of the EU.

Gerhard Schröder, the German chancellor, appeared at a press conference with the Finn and said: 'We have reached a political break-through. Peace is within reach and we are not going to let it slip through our fingers.'

Mr Ahtisaari said that implementing the agreement would be difficult.

He apologised for not being more sanguine. 'The English have a very good saying: the proof of the pudding is in the eating. The same goes for the peace process.'

One fear was that, despite Mr Blair's assurance that there would be no partition, Russia would be called on to police an entire sector of Kosovo, which would make it a no-go zone for Albanians.

The precise details of how Russia's presence would be structured were still being debated.

Kosovo will be placed under international administration for a transitional period of up to three years. During that time it will be given full autonomy from Serbia proper and democratic institutions will need to be developed to take over the government of Kosovo step by step.

Independence is not envisaged at this point, although it has always been accepted that this question will have to be addressed at the end of the three years.

The most difficult part of the agreement to implement may not involve Milosevic, despite his reputation for unreliability.

The accord calls for the Kosovo Liberation Army to be disarmed, and this may prove extremely hard to do.

After the atrocities against Kosovo Albanians, the KLA is likely to want to hold on to its weapons, even though its leaders have in principle accepted that they will disarm.

The Serbs will blame us and they will have a point

So we won. We blitzed the Serbs so thoroughly and with such abandon that today I walk the streets of Belgrade the bashful citizen of a victor nation.

While the talks were going on at the Macedonian border, we gave the Pancevo oil plant another going-over, killing a father and his two-year-old son. Last night, I was watching an awesomely violent film starring John Travolta on the hotel television, while the ack-ack was erupting in orange flashes outside and the petroleum was going up like white sheet lightning, and, after going to the window a few times, I just gave up and watched John Travolta blowing up planes, and boats, on the ground that it was somehow more plausible.

Yes, as this column has predicted from the very outset, Tony Blair ends up covered with glory, the laurels on his brow, his feet dripping with the slobber of his media admirers. It cannot be long before we have some carefully choreographed visit by the Prime Minister to Kosovo to escort a weeping Albanian family back to their homestead – and the Serbs will fight and lose their last great battle of the media war.

Appalling things will be found to have taken place in Kosovo. And the Serbs will have no defence. If their troops and police carried out a fraction of the killings, burnings and rapes of which they are accused, then Nato's war, even its barmy conduct of the war, will seem to be justified a hundredfold.

The crackpot raids on sanatoriums and old folks' homes, the bombing of trains and bridges, all will be eclipsed, forgotten. The public will be queasily grateful to have ended up so crushingly in the right, and will turn their thoughts to the excitement of the Royal wedding.

Some of us might say that the pogroms would not have taken place if Nato (and, in particular, Madeleine Albright) had not been so foolish as to launch unsupported air strikes, which meant first clearing Kosovo of media and monitors. But we who enter such protests will be accused of casuistry, and, in any case, it won't get the Serbs off the hook.

It will be no use them saying that they individually had no part in it, or that it was all the fault of Vojislav Seselj, the glass-chewing ultranationalist who urged Serbs to kick out the Kosovars as soon as the bombing started; and no doubt plenty of Albanians will be produced in the next few weeks, who will testify that it was Nato bombing that drove them from their homes.

That won't wash, either. Belgrade will ask us to lament the fate of the 190,000 Serbs in Kosovo, who will shortly be purged in reciprocal violence from the Kosovo Liberation Army, the extremely nasty terrorists supported by Nato.

If there was any justice, we *should* care about these Serbs in Kosovo, as passionately as we have cared about the ethnic Albanians. Many of them will be utterly innocent of crimes against their Albanian neighbours. But in so far as we give them a thought, we in the West will stretch, yawn and say they had it coming.

The very word Serb has become a kind synonym for violence or racist intolerance. You say Serb, close your eyes, and you see a tattooed, close-cropped figure in combat fatigues and dark glasses, swigging slivovitz and waving his AK47. We all know that the stereotype is unfair, that the Serbs can be gentle, peace-loving, donnish types of the kind you see in Belgrade's squares, tugging their beards over chess. Having been here for two weeks, and having endlessly consulted Vokspopovic, the Serb in the street, I can testify to his great natural politeness. Only one man has shouted about the bombing, and that was immediately after his roof was blown off. Call me a dupe, but I seem to like most of the Serbs I have met, and feel sorry for them.

To explain how things have gone so badly for this people, so that they are not only losers, but also villains, you have to look at a toxic confluence of factors. There is a natural tendency to racism all over the Balkans, where people are instantly categorised according to their grouping. In Serbia, that hidden poison has been potentiated by the manipulation of Slobodan Milosevic.

As soon as Yugoslavia began to break up – an event he had himself precipitated – he began to whip up fear that they would lose out. They did. They lost in Slovenia, in Croatia and in Bosnia, they lost Sarajevo to the Muslims and, as they indefatigably point out, more than a quarter of a million of them were 'ethnically cleansed'.

They also did terrible things. They massacred Muslims and Croats. But the beauty of Milosevic's state-controlled media was that these atrocities could be minimised along with the sense of guilt, and Serb paranoia could be fed by the rich sequence of defeats.

The more they lose, the more nationalist they become. The Democratic party, no doubt one of those Serbian opposition parties that Robin Cook fondly hopes will one day force Slobba from power, has described its policy towards Muslims as 'castration' and even Vuk Draskovic, on his day, can spout the rhetoric of nationalism.

Now Milosevic has completed the programme of defeat. He has almost certainly lost Kosovo, in the sense that there seems little he can now do to protect the Kosovo Serbs; and instead of blaming Milosevic, the Serbs will blame Nato.

Instead of blaming their leader for their country's ruin, they will blame the West; and since Nato blundered into the air war, without thinking it through – how long it would take and the suffering it would involve – they have a point.

It would be nice to think that Nato will be rewarded by pushing Milosevic from power. In reality, we may all have played a part in his elaborate game of bolstering resentment, paranoia and nationalism. In five, 10 years, Kosovo and its holy places could be the sundered homeland, the instant claptrap of anyone seeking to arouse irredentist fervour.

The Nato bombing may have been in some instances a disguised blessing, in the cruel sense that antiquated factories such as Zastava can now be rebuilt from scratch. But what will your average Serb see in that? Nothing but a Western plot to seize the best of their economy. And who will profit from the forthcoming deals to rebuild the place? Milosevic, of course, and his Socialist cronies.

Nato's problem in Yugoslavia has been fighting not just nationalism, but a manipulative brand of socialist quasi-tyranny; and you can't get rid of the one without first getting rid of the other.

If anyone should hang their heads, it is those in the West who, for the past 10 years, have connived at keeping Slobba in power.

How the Serbs were turned into a nation of victims

You see, if you were a Serb, you might observe nothing here except a charming rural cemetery in the south of Kosovo. The blue sky, the tumbling hills, the babbling birds. You would point triumphantly at the hollyhocks that have been put by the mounds of earth.

And you would shut your mind to the fly-buzzing evil of the place. Okay, so a lot of people would seem to have died at once, you might say. Perhaps there was a nasty dose of Spanish flu in the village, heh, heh. Fair enough, it seems odd that no one has bothered to write the names of the deceased on the little wooden stakes. Odd that they should use only numbers.

You would shrug, knowingly, and perhaps make a little joke about literacy rates. But if some hysterical Westerner tried to tell you that this was a mass grave, a war crime, and that beneath this earth were in all probability the mangled bodies of 89 Albanians who had been put in a road tunnel, grenaded and then shot, your mind would immediately go into autolock.

You would freeze, and whatever the evidence before you, no matter how overwhelming, the facts would immediately become part of the great anti-Serb conspiracy. They would be relegated to that tainted corner reserved for things you just don't want to know. If you are a Serb and you see a blazing block of flats on the outskirts of Pristina, you will turn logic on its head. You will defy probability, to prove to yourself and to others that this was the work of the KLA.

Yes, you will say furiously, it was the Albanian terrorists who did it. This was a Serb flat, you will say, brazenly: and when it is later revealed that it was an unoccupied Albanian property, unquestionably put on fire by Serb militiamen who had moved in to use it as a command post, you dismiss the suggestion as the propaganda of those who would make Serbs the new Jews of Europe. Even as you drive out of Kosovo, as I did last night, and you see the Albanian bars burning with freshly laid fires, and you see the very hayricks alight in the farms, so that the returning Muslims have nothing for the winter, you will perform stunning mental gymnastics.

Somehow you will want to convince any Westerner in your company that it is perfectly probable that the fleeing Serbs have done this themselves. They have burnt their farms rather than see them taken by the KLA murderers, you will insist. The mere fact that this might be true in a couple of cases begins to mean, to you, that it is true in every case; and in your topsy-turvy Balkan mind you will start to blot out the hideous destruction of innumerable Albanian homes in the past two months.

The reason you think like this, of course, is largely, though not entirely, the work of one man. You think like a victim, because every day you are told you are a victim. Unable to slough off communism, with its cosy comfort blanket of oppression, you and your media conspire with Slobodan Milosevic in his terrible game. Why does he pick these stupid wars, which he invariably loses? Because, in a way, he wants the Serbs to lose.

The more wounded, and fearful, and wronged they feel, the more they turn to the racist and nationalist politics that sustain him. Like all racism, the Serb variant comes from fear: fear of being belittled, of losing old privileges, of losing in the race to populate; and the fear produces the nationalist anger on which Milosevic depends. You could see both on the faces of my Serb friends as we pulled out through KLA country.

Their knuckles were white on the steering wheel as we drove at about 80 mph round winding defiles, and they later revealed that they had been wearing bulletproof vests (though not, of course, seat-belts; that would be sissy). Looking at their obvious terror, I suddenly understood what drives an otherwise companionable man to say, gesturing at a group of Albanians returning to their village after two months in hiding: 'They are some kind of stinky monkeys.'

He feels that about the Albanians partly because he feels

worsted by them; and for that he has to thank Milosevic. He picked the fight with Nato. He lost it. And as usual when the Serbs lose, state television shows the same awful images: the Serbs being turfed out of their houses, in their thousands, like the slow, flapping columns of Serbs who were yesterday leaving Suva Reka in the patent Balkan method of flight: red TS 133 tractor, plus family arranged in attitudes of despair on the trailer, like the Raft of the Medusa. And if we in the West cough politely, and remind them that terrible massacres of Muslims are alleged to have taken place in Suva Reka, and will probably be proved in the coming grisly disinterments, we are accused of bias. See how the West is against us, Milosevic will say.

The Serbs have fallen for it in Slovenia, in Croatia, and in Bosnia. Can Slobbo pull it off again, and dupe them into victimhood? It is possible.

At the end of the conflict, Milosevic is still in power in Belgrade, and the Tanjug news agency can talk of nothing but the injustice done to the Serb refugees. The British Army is doing a magnificent job in Pristina, bringing life back to the streets and generally displaying the kind of fairness that fills one with bursting, Soamesian pride. If, however, they begin to fall foul of the KLA, then that is all grist to Slobbo's mill. See, he will say: stupid British, poking their noses into our business. We told them they were terrorists.

As for the poor Albanians, Serb propaganda holds, in a fine piece of post hoc ergo propter hoc-ery, that the Nato bombing caused them to flee. That is certainly right in the sense that Nato's inept strategy allowed the butchery and expulsion to happen. Those mass graves were filled by Serb killers while Nato was bombing from 15,000ft. But can the Serbs conceivably exculpate themselves this time? Can they shut their eyes again?

This time, surely, Milosevic has pushed his luck too far.

As one Serb woman put it to me yesterday: 'You know, with 19 nations against us, it is time to accept that something is wrong.' This has been in many ways a miserable war. But something tells me that it will not be long before the Serbs finally rise up and chuck out the man who has for so long perverted their patriotism, allowing their country to be destroyed to prolong his rule.

And what about other evil tyrants?

Zimbabwe – we won't do anything for them

Get me the atlas, darling, before I have a seizure. Let's send a gunboat to Matabeleland, via the Limpopo. No: here we are. Let's canoe the marines through Lake Kariba and simultaneously deploy the SAS to guard the homesteads in Mashonaland. How long can we sit idly by while our kith and kin – our flesh and blood – are brutally turfed out of their farms by Mugabe and his bunch of panga-wielding thugs?

I don't want to sound hysterical, or frivolous, but does anyone agree that it is about time we did something to help these people? Every day we see fresh pictures of innocent white settlers, farmers who have toiled to make a living out of the African earth, with blood pouring down their faces. More than 1,000 farms have so far been invaded by armed 'squatters', egged on by Robert Gabriel Mugabe, the country's Marxist leader. Mobs are storming houses, firing automatic weapons and kicking out the occupants.

A race war seems to be afoot in southern Africa, and for once everyone in this country – from Right to Left – is against the Zimbabwean leader. In the higher reaches of the Government, and in the *Guardian* editorial conference, he has fatally lost sympathy ever since he said that New Labour was composed of 'gay gangsters' (though, ahem, you could say there was a grit of truth in that observation). Peter Hain, the Foreign Office minister, a man whose formative years were spent campaigning for the end of white rule and the installation of Mugabe, has denounced him. Robin Cook has denounced him. In the Commons, Francis Maude, the Tory spokesman, has accused the Government, not without some justice, of vacillation and drift and dither. The Right-wing columnists bellow for their sundered kinsmen on the veld, like the bellow of a stricken wildebeest as she sees her young being seized by the jackals.

It is time, we are told, to avenge the betrayal of Lancaster House, when slippery Carrington sold the British settlers down the Zambezi. It is time to get out the solar topees and blanco the spats and take up the white man's burden ... Except, of course, that we won't do any such thing. If we were going to do anything about Zimbabwe, we might have done it long ago; but instead we acquiesced in the handover, 20 years ago, to a Marxist who had already warned that 'none of the white exploiters will be allowed to keep an acre of land'.

Of course, some were intellectually soggier than others, as they saw the new man arrive with his curious hairy-caterpillar moustache. As Tony Benn recorded in his diary on March 4, 1980: 'Robert Mugabe has won the Rhodesian elections outright. It is a fantastic victory, and I can't think of anything that has given me such pleasure for a long time. When I think of the systematic distortion of the British press, it's an absolute disgrace. The Tories must be furious.' But, as Stephen Glover points out in this week's *Spectator*, Benn was not alone: the Thatcher government (though not Thatcher herself) emitted its own squeaks of optimism about Mugabe, if not in such lunatic terms.

The Tories didn't do anything in 1982, when Mugabe launched his war in Matabeleland and the North Korean-trained Fifth Brigade of the National Army killed between 20,000 and 30,000 black civilians; and we won't do anything now, when the country has been brought to its knees by the corruption of one-party rule, and when Mugabe is finally turning the mob on the white farmers who remain, and who have so far been sensible enough to keep out of politics. What can we do? The terrible truth – or so the Labour Government will whisper – is that Mugabe's actions have a weird sort of logic. Yes, these expropriations are hideous and indefensible; but in his imagination, they are historically symmetrical with the actions of the white settlers, who were driving blacks off the land until the 1950s.

Under the Lancaster House accords, it was agreed that Britain would pay to help resettle thousands of poor black farmers; and though Britain has contributed a few million, the operation would cost billions if it were done properly. Will we pay for that? Of course not, and neither should we, since all the evidence is that the exodus of white farmers leads to agricultural disaster: the eating of the dairy cows for beef and the smashing up of the irrigation system to make pots and pans. If there was ever a case for British help, that case has been destroyed by Mugabe's actions in dishing out the land to his cronies. And even if we had done as he wanted and coughed up for the resettlement programme, is there any guarantee that he would not now be fomenting the same kind of unrest against the remaining whites?

Some will say that Hain and Cook were always Mugabe-backers in their hearts; that they are overgrown student union politicians, remnants from anti-apartheid rallies, and that, when they look at dispossessed white settlers, they see a colonial order getting its comeuppance. Perhaps there is a trace of that instinct in their performance, which may explain their curious oscillation, from softly-softly tactics to pseudo-hardball. But that is not the determining factor in Britain's relations with Zimbabwe. That is not why we are doing nothing.

The reason we are doing nothing is that we *can* do nothing. We have neither the will nor the means to protect our kith and kin. The Americans are not in the least interested in the fate of a few British farmers in a landlocked part of Africa. The Pentagon will not be sending over the stealth bombers. This is not Kosovo, fulcrum of the Balkans. There will be no ethical foreign policy here, because it is not convenient for Washington to impose one.

We have precious little to console us, in fact, except this: that Zimbabwe has not yet collapsed; that, as I write, no settler has yet been killed (though a black policeman has, an event not widely reported in the British press); and that there is still a chance that Mugabe will not only hold but also lose the elections next month. It is not trivial that he is holding elections, or that there is an independent judiciary, or that there is still a free press, which is continually interviewing Ian Smith. Indeed, the whole set-up is a tribute to the British empire.

If Mugabe goes, it may be that sense will return to Zimbabwe, and that the white farmers will be allowed to carry on; and if he carries on with the pogroms . . . well, we will do such things, what they are yet I know not, but they shall be the terrors of the earth. Like seeking Zimbabwe's expulsion from the Commonwealth, perhaps.

Scratching the surface of the horror in Zimbabwe. The old couple died shortly afterwards; Trish was killed in a car crash and Tommy was badly hurt. Their land was stolen.

The cowardly whites who help Mugabe

Frankly, I am a bit nervous. Someone has said I'll get killed, looking all white and foolish out here in Mashonaland, and I am beginning to see why. We're only a couple of hundred yards away from the thugs wielding pipes, swords and guns who have been persecuting the local farmers. Three weeks ago, they bludgeoned one of the workers to death. Then they attacked Tommy Bayley, a farmer, and tried to throw him on to a fire. And now the idea is that we will go up to their picket line and see if they will let us through to the next house, where they are imprisoning an elderly white couple. These are Tommy's parents, and they have been besieged for 30 days.

Tommy doesn't think that we should go on foot, and, alas, if he were to come with us, they would hit him. 'I think you should go by car,' he says, and I am very much in agreement. But Peta Thornycroft, the *Daily Telegraph*'s Zimbabwe-born correspondent, is made of sterner stuff. She has just been released after four days' detention at Robert Mugabe's pleasure. 'We'll walk,' she says, and we do. We walk through the acacia and the macasa trees. The birds are twittering, and I pretend to look around at the blue rolling hills of the 5,000-acre Bayley farm.

When sauntering towards a feral band of black Zanu-PF gangsters, do you keep your hands in your pockets to show confidence, or do you take them out, to show that you mean business? In, out; in, out: I don't decide until we reach the end of the garden, where there is a poster of Comrade Mugabe and a makeshift barrier on the road, and the steel-mesh gates to the elder Bayleys' homestead.

The gates are locked, illegally, and behind them, illegally, are the thugs. They are generically called 'War Veterans', though most of them are far too young to remember Mugabe's 1970s guerrilla war. They have opaque, staring eyes, and they smell.

'You are not getting the right idea by coming here,' shouts one, with a blue forage cap and a bumfluff chin. Behind them is a smouldering log fire, surrounded by husks of the seedcorn that they have looted from this once-prosperous farm. These people, and the thousands like them across rural Zimbabwe, are wrecking the economy. They are meant to be farmers, the designated inheritors of white cultivation. Their idea of animal husbandry is to hack steaks from the haunches of living cattle, and leave them to die. For two years they have prevented the farm from functioning; and when Zimbabwe finds itself in the absurd position of importing mealie-maize and cooking oil, and when inflation is running at 117 per cent, Mugabe has the cheek to blame a 'drought'.

The terror began in March 2000, here at Danbury Park farm, and it is reaching its climax. Mugabe has stolen the election by brutality and cheating, and there is nothing now to stop him. As it happens, he is in Libya today, bartering Zimbabwean beef for Gaddafi's oil. There seems no obvious reason why he should not survive for his statutory six more years in office.

Trish Bayley, Tommy's wife, is sure that their house has been reserved for a minister or other bigshot in Mugabe's party. Technically, they can't be evicted yet, since Mugabe's expropriation order has to be approved by the courts. The idea, therefore, is to drive them out: to play drums all night, to hurl sexual taunts at Trish, to tyrannise them and their workers until they can take no more. 'They want to poke us like chickens in a cage,' says Tommy. The police have told them that they can no longer plant crops.

Tommy can't inspect his herd, so that the cattle are now infested with ticks and have developed terrible head-sores. This farm used to produce 90 tons of edible beef a year; not this year. Most worryingly of all, Tommy is not allowed to visit his parents over the way. His mother Bobs has Parkinson's, and his father Tom has had a hip replacement and can hardly move.

That is why Peta Thornycroft is so determined that we should get through to relieve them, and she works wonders of persuasion now, as we stand at the gateway.

'I have come to see my old friend who is very ill,' she says, miming the palsy, and eventually, with the help of a grinning police officer, we are admitted. 'You have 20 minutes only,' says bumfluff-chin. 'No,' snarls one in a Zanu-PF yellow visor, who looks a bit like Spike Lee, 'you have 15.' The cannonball-headed policeman guffaws. 'You must be nice,' he tells us. 'This is their land.' That is a lie, of course. Even under Mugabe's programme of theft, the land belongs to the Bayleys until the procedure is complete, but any such suggestion is greeted with a repellent giggle from the officer of the law.

As we reach the little cottage, I am reminded of visiting my grandparents in Somerset. There are Jack Russells and potted flowers, and at length a trembling hand unlocks the steel shutters of the front door. It is Bobs, and she twigs immediately that we must pretend to be related. 'How lovely to see you again,' she says to Peta, and lets us in. She tells us we are the first white people she has seen for 30 days, and she is plainly in a highly emotional state. All the curtains are drawn, she says, because the thugs circle the house and look in. Then her husband Tom shuffles in on a frame. He is almost 90, and his palms are deeply pruned and creased. He came out from Chelmsford in Essex in 1930, he tells us, and he had only £5, which he used to buy his first small plot. 'I've been on this farm for

70 years, and I've produced a thousand tons of maize each and every year I've been here. This land was bush before I came.' Peta asks why his farm is called Danbury Park and the old boy starts crying. 'Because I came from a village near Danbury,' he says. I am afraid that at this point I feel a bit overwhelmed myself. This is his land: he planted it; he developed it; he bought it, and there is not a damn thing anyone can do to help him protect it.

The old man is British, or 'British Empire', as he puts it. He has a tray of medals earned by some uncle in the King's service. But the British cannot help him now. You and I may dream of some SAS operation to save the farmsteads, or some Essex-levied militia sailing up the Zambezi. It is not going to happen. The Bayleys' torture will go on for as long as Mugabe wants, and there are many people who deserve the blame. As Algy Cluff pointed out in these pages two weeks ago, there was a failure – on the part of the Commercial Farmers' Union and the British government – to see the importance of the land-reform issue. They should have done a deal with Mugabe before he started to combine land redistribution with the rhetoric of race hate. One might mention the EU, which disastrously pulled out its observers before the recent polling day.

There is Mugabe's single most important political ally, Thabo Mbeki of South Africa, who has signally failed to condemn the elections. The South Africans are effectively supplying the bankrupt Mugabe with free electricity. Mbeki could pull the plug on Mugabe overnight, just as John Vorster terminated Ian Smith. And then there is a host of other names which are cursed on the verandas of anti-Mugabe households. These are the white businessmen, who have connived, actively or passively, in keeping the mad old tyrant in power. No doubt Tony O'Reilly, the newspaper-to-baked-beans magnate, has long repented of Mugabe's visit to his Irish schloss.

A less abashed co-operator is John Bredenkamp, a former member of the Rhodesian rugby team and husband to ex-Miss Rhodesia, who was revealed last Sunday to be the 33rd richest man in Britain with a £720 million fortune and a home in Berkshire. Mr Bredenkamp is thought to be close to Mugabe, but especially to Emmerson Mnangagwa, the speaker of the Zimbabwean parliament and Mugabe's heir-apparent. Mr Bredenkamp's mining operations in the Congo benefit greatly from the incursion of Zimbabwean troops, which is a kind of joint-stock venture by Zanu-PF and its business friends. Has Bredenkamp ever raised his voice in protest at anything done by his chums? On the contrary. He is going round offering to buy up some of the most beautiful white farms, on the understanding that he can get the acquisition orders lifted. Then one might mention another Zanu-PF crony, called Billy Rautenbach, who is wanted by Interpol. And then there are the really big players, the ones who should have had the guts to speak out, but who have kept silent. Prime among these is Anglo-American, the giant South African conglomerate, which is now supposed to have a good liberal conscience.

Anglo has vast investments in Zimbabwe. It could easily turn the screws on Mugabe. But when some Zimbabwean human-rights activists went to call on Philip Baum, Anglo's head honcho, to ask for modest financial help, he told them not now, not ever. It is true that Anglo-American has not publicly declared in favour of Mugabe. But it has done nothing to remove him. It could have made it clear, for instance, that its workers would not be penalised for striking in protest at Mugabe's breaches of democracy. It did not.

We now have a Zimbabwean Milosevic, a man using the themes of race hate and land; a man so egotistical that he is prepared to ruin the country to keep himself in power. Like Milosevic, Mugabe is illegally deploying security forces to conduct and abet racially motivated pogroms. We went to war, in Kosovo, on behalf of the KLA, who later turned out to have links with the al-Qa'eda network. What are we doing for these British people, weeping and terrified?

But now the policeman is back outside the old couple's front door, and we are being asked to go. I take down some phone numbers for Bobs, friends she wants me to ring in Hampshire, and the name of some medicine she needs for her shakes. As we walk back out of the compound, surrounded by the youths swinging their chains and sticks, Peta is magnificent.

'If you were my son,' she says to one yob, as we reach the gate, 'I'd bend you over my knees and whack you.' At once the visored one, Spike Lee, gets angry; and since the gate is still locked against our exit, I don't like the look of things. 'If you were my f—ing mother,' he says with an imperfect command of logic, 'you would not be my f—ing mother.' At last we get out, and my nape crawls as we turn our backs on the gang. One of them shouts after us, 'Only black people allowed here now.' Twenty years ago, before this kid was born, Zimbabwe had among the best race-relations in Africa. One man has filled these minds with violence and hate, and too many people have stood by while he has done so.

Our strategy so far has been to bellow at Mugabe from afar; but he has no difficulty in turning purple-faced British denunciations to his advantage. Might it not be time to direct our wrath – and penalties – at his silent white collaborators?

There probably is, alas, a clash of civilisations, and it is very largely about feminism. I am proud to say that Polly Toynbee copied this piece almost exactly.

What Islamic terrorists are really afraid of is women

So we're going in. In the next few days, our boys will be taking on the Taliban, and we must all pray they succeed. Let them winkle him out of his cave. Let them blast Osama bin Laden's arms dumps and blitz his followers, and carpet-bomb the Khyber with pineapple chunks, to appease the civilians, and then, and then . . . er: nobody seems sure what happens then, because this is a war against terrorism unlike any other.

We have had our own such war for the past 30 years, and we know that it is accompanied by a stately hypocrisy. On the one hand, we do our best to catch them, or sometimes just shoot them. On the other hand, we secretly talk to them and give them what they want. We invite them first to Cheyne Walk, in 1973, and eventually to Downing Street. My dear Gerry, my dear Martin, what would it take to get your lads to stop blowing us up? A ministerial Rover? Done. The end of the RUC? Say no more.

The trouble with the war against Islamic fundamentalist terror is that the terrorists themselves have no interest in talking. Bin Laden calls on his followers to kill all infidels. Then, he says, the killers will go to heaven. There is not much room for negotiation there, not even over tea at Number 10. We are not only horrified by the actions of the 19 suicide killers; we are still baffled, two weeks on.

What is it really all about? What is the true well-spring of this rage? We have all read that these crazed young men resent America for supporting Israel; that they believe the sufferings of the Iraqi people are excessive; that they hate

353

their own corrupt regimes, especially in Saudi Arabia, and blame America for backing them. None of these geopolitical reasons, I am afraid, quite does the trick, for me. There must be some deeper offence to their pride.

I think it is to do with their sense that they are representatives of a culture under siege. They fear that American morals and values will take them over, just as Coca-Cola and McDonald's have conquered the Earth. And what is the biggest single difference between their culture and Western culture? That's easy: it's the treatment of women.

Not all Islamic societies are equally sexist. You may not believe it, but the Turks gave women the vote before the British did. But listen to the casual bias of bin Laden's address to 'brother Muslims'. Look at the wacko women's gear that the BBC's John Simpson wore when he smuggled himself into Afghanistan, a sort of blue tent with a letter-box hole for the nose.

This is a world where women are lashed for adultery; where little girls are denied education; where female teachers are sacked; and where women are kept from elementary health care. Mohammed Omar, the Taliban leader, says that mingling men and women is Western and decadent, and leads to licentiousness. To call these views medieval is an insult to the Middle Ages. And yet they are held, with varying intensity, across the Muslim world.

In Kuwait, the country for which we fought, they recently decided against giving women the vote. As one enlightened Kuwaiti MP, Ahmad al-Baqer, put it: 'God said in the holy Koran that men are better than women. Why can't we settle for that?' The Kuwaiti tribunes later had a debate on the Sydney Olympics, in which a fruitcake called Waleed al-Tabtabaie called for the banning of women's beach volleyball, on the ground that it was 'too sexy and indecent'.

In Kano, Nigeria, the Muslims banned female soccer. In Dhaka, Bangladesh, women have been banned from working for NGOs. A Malaysian minister recently announced that any kind of skirt is an invitation to rape. Iranian magazines may not show unveiled pictures of Monica Lewinsky, or any other woman who has had sexual relations with President Clinton. The imam of a mosque in Fuengirola, Spain, one Mohamed Kamal Mostafa, has just published a handy guide to when you may beat your wife. Only hit the hands and feet, he says, using a rod that is thin and light. Of course, it's all grotesque. It's nutty. But these prejudices are so deeply held by Islamic fundamentalists that they will die to preserve them.

They look at America, and they see a world full of spookily powerful women, such as Hillary Clinton. So terrifying have been the advances of Western feminism that her ludicrous husband can almost be expelled from office for having a sexual liaison with an intern. The Muslim fanatics see denatured men, and abortion, and family breakdown, and jezebels who order men around. It tempts them and appals them and, finally, enrages them. Mohammed Omar says that 'only ugly and filthy Western cultures allow women to be insulted and dishonoured as a toy'. What he means is that only the West allows women to be treated as equals.

Now, there will be plenty of British conservatives who think these Taliban chappies run a tight ship, women's lib is not an unalloyed blessing, look at all these poofters these days, and so on. There are even ex-feminists, such as Germaine Greer, who will take a perverse pleasure in announcing that women can look very beautiful in a veil.

These points may or may not be valid, but they are essentially irrelevant. Female emancipation has been the biggest social revolution since print. In trying to resist it, the Muslim fanatics are establishing themselves as doomed cultural Luddites. Let me say what the Left cannot say, since it chokes on the contradictions of its position, at once feminist, and yet relativist.

It is time for concerted cultural imperialism. They are wrong about women. We are right. We can't have them blowing us up. The deluded fanatics must be helped to a more generous understanding of the world. Female education is the answer to the global population problem. It is the ultimate answer to the problem of Islamic fundamentalist terrorism.

The hunt for Osama.

We should try bin Laden first

Suppose you are one of the lads from Bravo Two Zero. You're up there in the frigid wastes of Tora Bora, and all around you is the devastation wreaked on the al-Qa'eda positions by the daisycutter bombs. It is a terrifying lunar landscape of rock splintered by TNT, littered with blood-spattered clothing, kettles, tins of food, and the mortal remains of the Arab terrorists.

And then, like the soldier in the Wilfred Owen poem, you find yourself stumbling into some dark tunnel full of corpses; and suddenly one of those bodies rises before you, and, as the poet puts it, lifts distressful hands as if to bless. You look into those dark eyes, and at once you know the man.

His turban may be askew and his cheeks grimy; but this is he, the face that launched a thousand air strikes, the ultimate objective of the war on terror. It is Osama bin Laden, badly injured, and against all predictions, he is trying to surrender. The man who encouraged demented young men to take their own lives is making a pitiful attempt to save his own.

What do you do? Do you blow him away? You could sort of accidentally squeeze the trigger and pow, no more bin Laden; and if you did, there is hardly a person in the West who would condemn you. To be sure, there would be long editorials in the *Guardian*, denouncing the shoot to kill policy of Her Majesty's Armed Forces, and John Pilger would accuse you of being a war criminal.

But almost every other well-adjusted member of the human race, on hearing that bin Laden had been whacked accidentally-on-purpose by the SAS in a mountain cave would conclude that it could not have happened to a nicer guy. Amid the general jubilation, there would be profound relief, in Washington and Whitehall, that a major diplomatic and military problem had been snuffed out with a single bullet. But it might be that you could not bring yourself to take a life in this way.

No matter how angry you might feel, and how vividly you recalled the events of September 11, you might think, as you raised your rifle to point at his chest, that British soldiers are not taught to murder unarmed people in the act of surrendering. You might suddenly be overcome with feelings of compunction, and dim memories of the Geneva Convention.

And if you were afflicted by such scruples, you would have my sympathy. Of course, it would be the neatest solution if the terrorist maniac were to be dispatched in the coming days, whether by an M16 carbine or a 10-rupee jezail. But it would not be the best or most satisfying outcome. Bin Laden should be put on trial; not in Britain, but in the place where he organised the biggest and most terrible of his massacres, New York.

He should be put on trial, because a trial would be the

profoundest and most eloquent statement of the difference between our values and his. He wanted to kill as many innocent people as he could. We want justice. It was a trial that concluded the tragic cycle of the *Oresteia*, and asserted the triumph of reason over madness and revenge.

There are those who worry that a trial would give him the chance to grandstand. They say that putting bin Laden in the dock, week in, week out, would merely boost his status as a martyr, and that the Arab 'street' would rise up in revolt at his treatment by the West. Well, there are already plenty who see him as a martyr and hero. It seems just as likely that a trial would expose the cruelty and emptiness of the man, the muddle of his beliefs, the mushy-minded chippiness of his politics.

Osama bin Laden is not a modern Socrates, a sage whose self-defence can be expected to shame his accusers and echo down the ages. He is both sinister and ludicrous at once, and a trial would expose that. If it is really true that a trial would provoke a revolt in the souks, then that is a small price for showing the souks how we in the West obey the rule of law.

Fair enough, say the opponents of a trial; but how can you be sure that we will get a conviction? What if it becomes the OJ bin Laden trial, a grotesque pantomime of top-dollar human rights lawyers, trying to pull wool over the jurors' eyes? To which one can only respond that the evidence was pretty good on September 11 that bin Laden was responsible for the massacres. It is now, thanks not least to the bragging of the man himself, over-whelming.

It seems inconceivable, if bin Laden were produced in a New York court, that he would not be convicted of murder. Yes, say the opponents of a trial: but what of those jurors? Would not they and the judge be potential victims of bin Laden's suicide squads? To which the retort is that if the safety of judges was the paramount consideration of the judicial system, there would never be any trials of Mafia goons. The whole point of the exercise, the whole point of the war against terror, is that we believe in due process and the upholding of civilisation against barbarism.

All right, say the opponents of a trial: but how can you possibly send him to America, where they have the death penalty? It is true that there is currently an absurd ruling, which seems to mean that we could not send him from Britain to America without securing an undertaking that he would not be killed. That does not apply, however, in the event of our capturing him in Afghanistan, where British forces are expected to turn him over to the Americans without any such agreement. Yes, they probably would fry him, if we hand him to US troops. But I wouldn't be prostrate with grief; and at least they would try him first.

As an embattled President bombs Baghdad in 1998, a Gulf War veteran reflects on our earlier failure.

We blew the chance to finish Saddam

So, that's it. Mission accomplished. Saddam has been 'degraded' to the satisfaction of Washington and London. He's been 'attrited', in the magnificent word of Colin Powell.

Hundreds of cruise missiles costing $1.3 million (£812,000) each have blown up bits of Baghdad real estate. The Iraqis are burying their dead, tending their injured and generally going around with the dustpan and brush.

And who comes on the radio to tell his people they have been heroes? Not him again? Not Old Walrus Moustache?

Hasn't he had the decency to implode with shame at the destruction he has brought on his country?

The West sent half a million men to wage war on this fellow eight years ago. Here we are again, at the end of another campaign, and he's still vowing the mother-in-law of all revenges.

Why do we always seem to let him off the hook? We can trace the error, perhaps, to Feb 28 1991, the day the Gulf War effectively ended. Col Mike Vickery remembers it well, and with frustration.

For three days of intense fighting he had led his 53 Challenger tanks of the 14/20th King's Hussars north from Saudi Arabia into Iraq, and then east into Kuwait, crushing bunkers beneath the treads, killing and taking prisoner thousands of troops in what he calls the 'application of a serious amount of violence'.

Then, 35 miles west of Kuwait City, they were stopped.

'It was "End Ex", as we say – the end of the exercise. There was a great deal of shock among my soldiers that we hadn't defeated Saddam at all, and then we found out he was turning around and beating up his own people. There was shock and disgust.'

What checked his advance was the furore following the bombing of Highway 6, or the 'Turkey Shoot', as it became known. As the Iraqis fled north on the road to Basra, they were shot up.

In reality, it now looks as though many of the vehicles had already been abandoned. But to the media – deprived of Western casualties about whom to wax indignant – it was an atrocity. Gen Norman Schwarzkopf came under immediate pressure from Washington to cease fire.

'That precipitated the end of the war,' says Vickery. 'That sort of thing is bad PR and PR counts for a lot.'

The trouble was that Saddam was by no means a spent force. 'He's a lunatic, but he's a splendid chess player. He fed us all his pawns while he deployed all his smarter pieces round the back, and very few of them were taken. They were to become his power base after the war.'

The Allies could have destroyed those forces without breaking their United Nations mandate, he believes. 'The UK division could have gone straight on. We could have got ourselves poised and barricaded him in the Basra pocket. That is something we could have done and we didn't do it. We didn't want to carry on and slaughter innocent Iraqis. We wanted to finish the job.

'I would have very much liked to have stopped him killing the Marsh Arabs and the Kurds. It was a scandalous mistake to allow him to keep his helicopters. He said he needed them for peaceful operations and he used them as gunships.'

He also believes Saddam should have been made to surrender in person at Safwan airfield.

Vickery does *not* believe that the Allies should have gone on to invade Baghdad. 'In good old-fashioned imperial terms, you have to take it over and run it, and none of us was prepared to do that.'

He believes simply that far more could have been done, legitimately, to demolish Saddam's hardware and to foster opposition. 'I regretted the lack of support for the dissident elements who may well have been told – I am walking on eggshells here – that we would be supportive.'

Vickery is now a defence consultant, and has spent his Saturday shooting, with greater accuracy than Iraqi anti-aircraft guns, he says, though less than a cruise missile. He supports the latest operation, and no, he doesn't believe Clinton started a foreign adventure in the hope of getting out of trouble at home. 'It hasn't, and he knew it wouldn't,' he says.

For a cavalry man, Vickery has surprising faith in the bombing. 'These Cruise missiles are one-window-in-a-building accurate. The Iraqi casualties are staggeringly few, considering what has been dumped on them.

'What is very much the coming thing is the bloodless war.' He even defends the term 'degrade', and takes it to mean reducing an enemy's threat by a certain percentage.

'But what you can't do is win a war and take ground and hold it with planes.' The bombing has not been value-less, but it has been 'a limited war', he says. 'There was a question in the Sandhurst exam about whether there can be a limited war. This is it.

'I don't think it'll lead to his downfall. It'll prevent him from reassembling this sort of weapon for a while. They can rebuild, and it'll take them a long time and cost them a large amount of hard-earned money, but I don't believe that will defeat Saddam or destroy his wish to do whatever he wants.'

We had a chance to do that eight years ago, and we blew it.

I see the arguments for getting rid of Saddam, but wonder whether the Weapons of Mass Destruction business is a red herring.

Saddam must go but don't lie to me about the reasons

The brutal reality of the American electoral cycle means that Saddam Hussein must be gone by 2004. That is when George W. Bush is up for re-election.

Given all that Dubya has now said about 'regime change', he cannot possibly present himself to the Ameri-can people if the Butcher of Baghdad is still in office, waving his pearl-handled revolver and making insulting remarks about the Bush family. Never mind the oil, or the potential boost to the American economy, or the security issues: that is the paramount reason why there will be a war sometime between now and then.

It is also a brutal reality that Britain's global role is to do more or less what the Americans want, in order to achieve maximum 'influence' in Washington. You can quibble with this cunningly supine approach, which the Foreign Office also uses in Brussels; but it has been followed by every British prime minister since Suez, and Blair is no exception.

If I am right that Bush's electoral fate is now inextricably linked to Saddam Hussein, and if Blair is unlikely to let a chink of daylight between London and Washington, then it follows that America and Britain will in the near-ish future launch a violent attack on Iraq.

If we know the Pentagon, there must be a very good chance that this will be an outstandingly successful and stress-free war, with computerised drones queueing up over Baghdad and Basra to pulverise the relevant silos and barracks.

There must also be a risk, however, that the war will not only involve the deaths of many innocents, but will also cost the British taxpayer considerable sums. The latest figures suggest our bill could be £5 billion, which is almost as much as Labour blew on foot and mouth. That is why it is so important to persuade the public to snap out of their current curmudgeonliness.

With 65 per cent currently opposed to military action, one can see why the Government goes to such lengths to pretend, for instance, that there is a link between Saddam Hussein and the al-Qa'eda network.

At every key moment in the Iraq drama, there is a little Whitehall-generated drum-roll of alarm about a terrorist threat in London. Last week, the Americans declared that

Iraq was in material breach of UN resolution 1441. The war came closer! And offstage, as if by magic, government sources muttered about anthrax on the Tube, smallpox in the water supply, etc.

It is a cynical and ludicrous attempt at Pavlovian conditioning. War in Iraq! Terrorist threat! War in Iraq! Terrorist threat! On it will go until the poor mutton-headed public believes that only the first will obviate the threat of the second.

It is a belief for which, alas, there is no evidence whatever. Try as he may, Blair has been unable to link Saddam with September 11, and we have no good grounds for thinking a war on Saddam will make future al-Qa'eda attacks less likely.

Which brings us to the other grounds for war: the weapons of mass destruction, and the Keystone Kops of the UN fossicking around hopelessly in their search for evidence.

This week Blix and co continued their Cook's Tour of the Mesopotamian Rustbelt, sniffing around a milk factory that has already been blown up twice by allied forces, in 1991 and 1998. They confirmed that, as a producer of milk, the factory was pretty washed up. They did not, it seems, find any weapons of mass destruction.

That's not good enough, say the Americans. Washington, and London, want Baghdad to *prove* that it has no weapons of mass destruction, which is a singular demand. Suppose you accuse me of having an illegal weapon in my house. You may refuse to believe me. That is your right.

But how on earth am I supposed to prove that I don't? Produce a few non-certificates for my non-revolver? It is up to you to prove that I do have a revolver under the floorboards; and that is why it is utterly demented, now that Saddam has let the weapons inspectors back in, that

364

Blix and co are blithering about, without any decent intelligence to back them up.

If Washington wants our support for military action against the possessor of these weapons, then the world needs to be convinced, as soon as possible, that they are there. That means assisting Blix in distinguishing anthrax from fermented goat's milk. And if America won't help, then the whole business starts to smell worse than one of these devastated desert dairies.

If we are really concerned about the weapons of mass destruction, then let the UN process work itself through, and if Blix finds something, and Saddam won't destroy it, then by all means let's send in the stealth bombers and the cruise missiles and the B52s, and let's do the job ourselves. If I had an illegal revolver in my house, I could hardly object if the police decided to burst in and put it beyond use.

I could hardly protest, especially if they had been waiting for months on my doorstep, in ever increasing numbers, and had given me ample warning of their intentions, and every opportunity to dispose of the thing myself.

But I think I might feel hard done by if the police decided that, in order to accomplish this end, it was necessary to blow up my house, and kill me and many of my relatives. That sense of injustice would be all the greater if they had no real proof that I had the wretched revolver in the first place.

It may be that there is a very good case for getting rid of Saddam without any of these tiresome pretexts about terrorism and weapons of mass destruction. The world would unquestionably be the better for his removal.

Perhaps America should be encouraged to go around making appropriate adjustments to the geopolitical scene. Many of us would be prepared to listen to such a case. But it would help if someone started to make it honestly.

The fear, the squalor ... and the hope

We could tell something was up as soon as we approached the petrol station. There was an American tank parked amid a big crowd of jerrycan-toting Iraqis. Unusually, the soldiers were down and walking around, guns at the ready. Then I heard shouting and saw the Americans using their carbines like staves to push back some of the customers, who were evidently trying their luck. Just then a black sergeant near me started shouting at an Iraqi. 'You, I've told you to get away from there,' he said, swinging his gun round.

The Iraqi appeared to be a phone technician, with pliers and a handset. He was standing before an open relay box, up to his ears in wire, and trying to repair some of the damage that has left Baghdad for three weeks without telephones, electricity, and in some places without running water and sanitation. The American repeated his command; and again. Still the Iraqi did not move, while others vehemently and incomprehensibly tried to explain what he was doing. Then the American seemed to lose his temper.

'Let me put it this way, buddy,' he shouted, lifting the gun to his shoulder and aiming at the Iraqi's head from a distance of a couple of feet. 'If you don't move, I'm going to shoot you!' At this point, since it did not appear out of the question that there would indeed be a tragedy, I am afraid that I intervened. 'I say, cool it,' I said – or rather, croaked. Three pairs of US army shades turned on me, and a couple of American guns waggled discouragingly in my direction.

There is gunfire the whole time in Baghdad. It barks around every street corner. Every night is enlivened by the rippling and popping, as if someone were tearing a sheet a few feet away. Within the space of the last half-hour, I had slunk past a ten-year-old with an AK47 over his shoulder, chewing the fat with his dad in the door of the shop. Just five minutes ago I had flinched when another shopkeeper cocked his automatic in my face to show how he dealt with the plague of thieves. But in my three days in Baghdad, this was easily the scariest moment, and the one time I really wished I had bothered with the flak jacket kindly loaned to me by Fergal Keane of the BBC. 'You!' screamed an American, whose stitched helmet name-tape proclaimed him to be Kuchma, blood-type A neg. 'Who are you? Go away! No, wait, give me that,' he said, shaking with anger when he saw my camera. 'Give me that or I will detain you.'

I refused; but it was only a couple of minutes before Kuchma and I had calmed each other down. He explained to me the huge pressures his men were under, trying to keep order in a city with no recognised authority, a gun under every Iraqi pillow, and with only a fraction of the troops necessary. I apologised, as we shook hands, for accidentally interfering with his work. I gabbled some congratulations on the amazing achievement of his men and the rest of the American forces.

It wasn't just that he had the gun and I didn't. I meant my congratulations, and I still do. Like everyone in Baghdad, Kuchma asked what the hell I was doing there. I went partly to satisfy my curiosity, but mainly to clear my conscience. I wrote, spoke and voted for the war, and was hugely relieved when we won. But owing, no doubt, to some defect in my character, I found it very hard to be gung-ho. My belligerence never burned with the magnesium brightness of, say, Mark Steyn.

It was troubling that we were preparing war against a sovereign country that had, so far, done us no direct harm. And the longer Blix and co. fossicked around in search of weapons of mass destruction, the more cynical I became about the pretext. If you took it that the WMD business was just a rigmarole, an abortive attempt to rope in the French and others, there was only one good argument for violently removing Saddam Hussein from power; and that was not just that it would be in the interests of world peace and security, but that it would be pre-eminently in the interests of the Iraqi people.

It was, therefore, a piece of utilitarian arithmetic. You had to weigh the disasters of war against the nightmare of life under Saddam. You had to set the misery of old Iraq against the uncertainties of a free country. That is the calculation; and it would be quite easy to construct a powerful case for believing that the exercise has been a disaster. You don't need to be Robert Fisk. You just shut one eye in Iraq, and look around you.

As we drove into Baghdad from Jordan, I saw some sights familiar from Kosovo, like the way a smart bomb deals with a motorway bridge: the writhing steel reinforcements twisted like spaghetti; the concrete shaken free as if it were plaster. But about 50 miles away from the city, in the neighbourhood of Ramadi, it became obvious that this was a much, much bigger deal than Kosovo. The tanks were not just neutralised; they were frazzled and oxidised, and in some cases they had flipped their lids – with the gun turret blown right out – like a biscuit tin. Cars had been crushed like balls of paper, and chucked over the side of the bridges. In every cock-eyed anti-aircraft gun, in every useless and deserted gun emplacement, you could read the humiliation of the Iraqi army.

We drove past the Baghdad Museum, which has still not recovered the Warqa vase and the 300-kilo bronze Akkadian king, and which every Iraqi believes was looted with the collusion of the Americans, or the Kuwaitis, or both. We went by a shopping centre flattened by bombs, as the vast buttocks of an American security guard might accidentally squash a cardboard box of cornflakes on the front seat of his Stingray. My interpreter pointed out the Ministry of Irrigation. Irrigation is the word. The thing was fuller of holes than a watering can.

But it is not the Americans who have done the worst damage to Baghdad. Weeks after the invasion, buildings are still burning, not from missiles but from the looting. Most of the shops are shut. There is glass everywhere, and rubbish all over the streets, because there are no municipal services; and there are no municipal services because civic order has broken down. Little Japanese pick-ups scoot by, laden with copper wires uprooted from the streets; and the very same looters shake their fists and complain that there is no electricity. Like every other reporter in Baghdad, I have done dozens of vox pops, shoving my notebook under the noses of passers-by, virgins to this procedure, and canvassing their opinion on the traumatic change we have made to their cityscape and their political arrangements. With my interpreter, Thomas, I went down to Sadr City, formerly Saddam City, where two million Shiites live in scenes of unremitting squalor, with markets petering out and starting up again on the wide, tank-friendly streets.

'Hello there,' I asked Hamad Qasim. 'How is it for you? Are you happy that Saddam has gone?' The djellaba'd shepherd chopped the air with his hands, as if brushing a fly off each ear, and said, 'We lived for 35 years under oppression and we are very happy that the Americans are here.' He then tried to sell me one of his malodorous brown ewes for $50. Others thought his words needed amplification. 'The Americans have come and purified us [Thomas's translation] from Saddam, but until now we have seen nothing from the Americans,' shouted another man, and the mood of the crowd became more assertive as, finding my Arabic inadequate, they engaged in choleric altercation with Thomas.

369

'Where is our gas, our electricity? They just make promises!' And as they grew more emphatic in their views I buttoned up my jacket and we found ourselves retreating to the car. A skinny man in a waistcoat stuck his nose through the window. 'I have no job. I have no money. There are gangsters everywhere shooting people. If this goes on,' he cried, flapping his waistcoat in ominous demonstration, 'I will make myself a suicide bomber!'

Those are the kind of words that terrify men like Kuchma, the harassed marine at the petrol pump, and which tempt them to blow away someone who might be a phone-repair man, but who also might be about to set something off. Two and a half weeks after toppling Saddam, the American forces are pitifully ill-prepared for the task of rebuilding the country they conquered with such brilliant elan. Behind the scenes, under their breath, Iraqis are starting to make comparisons with the former regime. 'When the last Gulf war ended,' said Thomas, whom I suspect of being a bit of a Baathist, 'it took only a week before Saddam restored everything.'

Yes, agreed Mohamed, his colleague, you needed two Saddams to run this country. 'Your William Shakespeare has written in his novel *Julius Caesar*,' said Thomas, rolling his eyes and waving his finger, 'a country with a tyrant is better than a country with no leader at all.' Indeed, said someone else, Saddam may have been a thug and a killer, but at least he had a policy on law and order. Somehow, perhaps because we have so far failed either to capture him or to produce his moustachioed corpse, the shadow of the dictator still hangs over this town like a djinn. Where is he? What happened to him?

Some say he was seen at the Adamiya mosque on the day that American column sliced through Baghdad's pathetic Maginot Line. Some say he is holed up in Ramadi, the badlands to the west of town which fought on for six days; others that he is being ferried between the many households prepared to give him hospitality. I'll tell you where he is not. He is not at the bottom of that enormous hole made by the US air force in the posh district of Al-Mansour, when they had a tip-off that he was having a working dinner with his henchmen. He may indeed have been at the Al-Saab restaurant, a fine establishment that gave me a topflight Shoarma and chips, but the bomb landed about 100 metres away from the joint, doing it no damage whatever. There were twisted bedsteads, snatches of curtain and other remnants of four civilian houses. But there was no Saddam.

It was theoretically his birthday on Monday (actually, no one knows when he was born, in the miserable village of Ouja near Tikrit; like everything else in his life, Saddam swiped his birthday from someone else), and everyone was gripped by a delicious paranoia that he would pop up, like some awful Saddamogram, with a special birthday commemoration. Almost all his images have been shot up, or defaced, and Mohamed, my driver, was very happy to join in, jumping up and down on a fallen statue. But the image is still there, on every corner, the grin still visible beneath the bazooka holes.

It is obvious why the name Saddam is still potent, and can still, incredibly, be spoken of in terms of grudging respect; and that is because no one else has taken power, at least not in the way that Iraqis appreciate. A charming Foreign Office man briefed the international press on Monday night, flying in and out on a lightning visit with his minister, Mike O'Brien. He sat on a desk in his salmon-pink tie, blue shirt, chinos, and twirled the toes of his brown brogues. Asked about law and order, and the creation of a new government, he said we were on a 'process' or a 'journey' in which he hoped the Iraqi police would shortly start to do the job themselves.

371

So far the Iraqi police are finding themselves unavailable for work, no doubt owing to heavy looting commitments. The Americans roll by in their Humvees, or sit behind their shades and their razor wire. They do not have the numbers to mount foot patrols; they have abandoned any attempt to confiscate the guns of the population, since it is a bit like trying to confiscate all the cannabis in Brixton. The result is that they do not control the streets. No one does. Iraq in 2003 will be studied for generations by anyone interested in power, and the emergence of authority in human society. Into the vacuum have flooded competing hierarchies – religious, military, secular – and a hilarious range of political parties, already exhibiting Monty Pythonesque mutual loathing.

Saddam's palaces are now controlled by the Americans, and I was repeatedly frustrated in my attempts to gain admission. But there are plenty of other looted palazzos, formerly belonging to Baathist kingpins, and all sorts of people seem to be in charge. A sign outside the home of Saddam's half-brother, Watban Al-Tikriti, proclaimed that it was now the headquarters of the Democratic and Liberation party. What were their political aims, I asked the shuffling men who allowed me in. They grinned. The charter of the Democratic and Liberation party is to liberate, in the most democratic fashion possible, the possessions of Watban Al-Tikriti.

Then I went to the villa of Tariq Aziz, in a hopeless attempt to emulate David Blair and find some documents incriminating Western politicians. My fingers clutched greedily at some papers scrumpled outside; and – yes! – they were indeed communications between Iraq and a foreign power. They were letters from the Swedish ambassador, dated 1982, complaining about the mugging of his au pair, and registering the import, to Baghdad, of a Ford Capri. I decided not to trouble the *Telegraph* copytakers. Apathetically overseeing me was a group called 'The Military Liberation Force of Officers'. Their aim, they said, was to purge the army of corruption.

They might as well have had 'looter' tattooed on their foreheads. I went to the next looted palace, formerly owned by a Baathist vice-president. Yet another gang was in charge. 'We are a new party but we do not want to give you the name,' said a raffish, amply constructed fellow. Oh, all right, I said, what is the name of your leader? 'He is a religious man. I do not want to give his name.' I see, and what does he want? 'He wants a government.' What sort of government? 'He wants a patriotic government. He wants freedom.' These are some of the Shias who make up 60 per cent of the population, who were repressed by Saddam, and the people Thomas, the Christian Baathist, fears most.

Everyone has seen the pictures of the nutty head-cutters of Karbala. But what makes the Shia clerics dangerous is their appetite for power, and their shrewd understanding of how to get it. The leading mullah in Baghdad is the evocatively named Mohamed Al-Fartusi, who has already been arrested once by the Americans. On Monday night the coalition convened an extraordinary meeting of all those who might have a political role in rebuilding Iraq. There were perhaps 250 in all, including 50 sheikhs, tribal leaders in full headdress; there were Iraqi intellectuals who had suffered under Saddam, and there were émigrés who had come back to help.

But there was no Fartusi. Not only had he not been invited; he would have boycotted the proceedings anyway. Nor was he available for interview when I turned up at his mosque. But as you studied the crowd at his gates, begging for arbitration from the holy men on questions of usury, theft or divorce, you could see why Thomas the Christian feels so threatened. They want to close down the booze shops, he said. They are mediaeval, he said, and he is exactly right. Sharia law means that there is no separation between church and state. The clerics are doing the job of the civil courts, and in the absence of any other authority their influence will surely grow. And who is there to rival them?

No one thinks much of Dr Ahmed Chalabi, whose Free Iraqi Fighters are in the pay of the Americans. For a couple of days Baghdad had a Chalabi-backed mayor called Zub-eidi. Unfortunately, his first act as mayor was to loot $3 million-worth of TV production equipment, and the red-faced Americans put him under arrest on the charge of 'exercising power that wasn't his'. So who does have power? Not Jay Garner. 'Who's Jay Garner?' asked one marine, guarding the building in which I was told the pro-consul resided.

Power is being contested on every corner, between Shia moderates and extremists. It is being fought for by umpteen Kurdish parties, Assyrian parties, secular parties. Of course there was something absurd about the conference organ-ised by the Americans, the endless jabbering of groupus-cules under a mural of a semi-naked Saddam repelling American jet bombers. There was a priceless moment when Mr Feisal Ishtarabi could not remember whether his party was called the Iraqi Independent Democratic party or the Iraqi Democratic Independent party. But does it matter?

There was also something magnificent about the process. It was a bazaar, a souk, in something the Iraqis have not been able to trade for 30 years. It was a free market in politicians. In a word, it was democracy. Sooner or later there will be elections in Iraq; and no, funnily enough, most people do not think that the Shiite extremists will sweep the country, or that government will be handed over to Tehran. There will be no more torture victims, like the man who showed me the ivory-white sliced cartilage of his ear, cut off by Saddam to punish him for deserting from the army, or the stumbling old man who claimed his three sons had all been killed by the Baathists.

If there are any weapons of mass destruction, the good news is that they will not be wielded by Saddam or any group of terrorists. And since it is time to put the good news into our utilitarian scales, here is a statistic that you should be aware of, all you Fisks and Pilgers and Robin Cooks, who prophesied thousands and thousands of deaths. I went to see Qusay Ali Al-Mafraji, the head of the International Red Crescent in Baghdad. Though some nametags have been lost, and though some districts have yet to deliver their final tally, guess how many confirmed Iraqi dead he has listed, both civilian and military, for the Baghdad area? He told me that it was 150, and he has no reason to lie.

Of course it is an appalling sacrifice of life. But if you ask me whether it was a price worth paying to remove Saddam, and a regime that killed and tortured hundreds of thousands, then I would say yes. What do you see now when you walk past Iraqi electrical stores, which are opening with more confidence every day? You see satellite dishes, objects forbidden under Saddam. One man told me he had sold ten in the last four days, at between $200 and $300 a go.

Snooty liberals, and indeed many Tories, will say that this is vulgar and tawdry, and make silly, snooty jokes about the poor Iraqis now being subjected to *Topless Darts* and Rupert Murdoch. What such anti-war people don't understand is that the Iraqis are not only being given their first chance to learn about other countries. They can now learn about their own. They can now watch channels not wholly consecrated to the doings of Saddam.

There have been terrible mistakes in this campaign, though those who followed the cataclysm at the Baghdad

Museum may be interested to know that, when I went there, three big boxes of artefacts were being handed over, having been recovered from the looters. I suppose that, with 170,000 objects stolen, there was a slight glut in the market for cuneiform seals, no matter how old.

As George Bush gave his speech on Tuesday night, I happened to be watching it with three Iraqis. When he said that 'the windows are open in Iraq now', meaning that people could talk without fear for their lives, they laughed and banged the table. I can imagine the anti-war lot in Britain, with their low opinion of Bush, also laughing at his folksy rhetoric. But when I asked the Iraqis what they thought of the speech, I found I had completely mis-understood their laughter.

'We agree with Bush 100 per cent,' said one, and they all passionately agreed. Really? I said. 'Yes,' he said. 'We are free now.' Iraq has huge problems, including colossal debts. It is barely governable. It would be unthinkable for America and Britain to pull out. But he says that his country is now free, and that, to me, is something that was worth fighting for. Saddam may be a ghost, but that is all.

MANNERS AND MORALS

People tend to tie themselves in knots these days trying to explain what Conservatism is. Are we libertarian, authoritarian, vegetarian or rotarian? Should we be a little bit Rastafarian now and then? Here, in these articles, is how I think we should be: free-market, tolerant, broadly libertarian (though not, perhaps, ultra-libertarian), inclined to see the merit of traditions, anti-regulation, pro-immigrant, pro-standing on your own two feet, pro-alcohol, pro-hunting, pro-motorist and ready to defend to the death the right of Glenn Hoddle to believe in reincarnation.

Alcohol is good for you

'Waiter, my cabernet sauvignon is being drunk by someone else,' said the dark-haired young woman opposite – whose card now reveals her to have been called Carolyn Panzer of the Portman Group of seven big British drinks companies – looking accusingly in my direction. Somehow, by the third course of the lunch given by a new and wonderful society called 'The Case for Moderate Drinking', things had indeed become muddled up.

It is a vintage Strasbourg scene. In an alcove of the members' dining room in the Euro-parliament, the windows have steamed up against the cold air outside. The *huissiers* in their black tail-coats and gold fobs glide about, settling Europe's representatives at table: here a Belgian Green, there a former SS Stormtrooper.

About 20 MEPs, and the half-familiar faces of assorted Euro-consultants and lobbyists, have gathered to celebrate the self-evident proposition that alcohol is good for you. Before us, for starters, is a scrummy *chiffonade de la laitue* with prawns and cooked oysters, garnished with a large indeterminate crustacean.

It had been a hard, dry morning of lectures on the medical evidence supporting 'moderation', here taken to mean consistent but not excessive spending of money on alcohol. Now was the time for the practical. One young blond man's face is so suffused with the *'Bienfaits de la Moderation'* that he is the colour of a letterbox.

Now, the *chiffonade de la laitue* could mean anything as far as I am concerned – probably French chef for lettuce leaf. Actually, it turns out to be a delicious sort of patty stuffed with boiled greens. The roar of the company dies a little as the sea creature is broken up and sucked dry, and a toast is drunk to the 1988 chardonnay.

This is also terrific, and has apparently been made by my left-hand neighbour, an energetic, deep-voiced, turtle-faced Californian in his sixties. 'We only make very high quality wines,' he says. 'They have their own style and character, but they have helped to set the pace for wine-making worldwide.'

It suddenly becomes apparent that I am sitting next to a colossus of the wine world, and had better get with it. This is Mr Robert Mondavi, as in Robert Mondavi of the

Napa Valley, California. What, apart from the fame of the members' restaurant, brings him to the Strasbourg Euro-parliament, home of lost causes?

About two years ago, Mr Mondavi became concerned at the neo-puritanism that was sweeping the United States and the world. His father, an Italian American, made his money during prohibition by exporting grape stock all over the United States, so that ordinary householders could ferment their own wine. But those profits were nothing to the serious wine business that Mr Mondavi had conducted in the Napa Valley.

The pinot noir arrives, also made by Mr Mondavi, and we analyse the growing global tide of intolerance. In France, they have just passed the Loi Evin, which restricts advertising to mere representation of the bottle and how the wine was made; the 1990 Mammi law has imposed sponsorship restrictions in Italy, and tighter controls are planned in Spain, Luxembourg, Denmark and Belgium.

This lunch in Strasbourg is the culmination of a world tour to campaign for the right to drink – moderately. 'They are taking away our freedom of choice and expression. We want education, not control,' says Mr Mondavi.

Who are They? Our host intervenes with an amazing fact. This is Mr Peter J. Duff, chairman of the morning's symposium, Director of the Robert Mondavi Alcohol Initiative and European Consultant to the Wine Institute of California. He reveals that the huge financial resources of Saudi Arabia are being poured into the coffers of the growing world temperance lobby.

'The Koran states that the drinking of alcohol is a sin, though you can drink in the next life. They want to destroy alcohol,' he explains. It seems there is evidence of heavy Arab influence in the World Health Organisation, the UN body which last year decreed that world alcohol consumption must fall by 25 per cent. More hatefully yet, the WHO concordat mentions alcohol in the same breath as drugs.

Some Westerners seem to be involved. There is a man called Dr Craplet in Paris, whose name is savoured richly around the table: 'ha ha ha . . . only a little one!' And there is a man called Dr Derek Rutherford, who has drawn up the obnoxious 'Alcohol Charter for Europe'. But Mr Duff points out that they are in a minority. 'Where do they get their money from? If you read the names, these are not European or US names,' he says. They are Arabs . . .

The only way to fight their reverse crusade is with science, and that is why this morning's key speaker has been Dr Agnes Heinz, now sitting two away from me. She is a Director of Nutrition and Biochemistry at the American Council of Science and Health. (Why is it that this sort of job is always done by very good-looking women in their thirties, anthropologists, palaeographers, gorilla experts, etc? Is it some concession to Hollywood?)

Dr Heinz's talk was a piece of scrupulous scientific balance. There was a downside to alcohol, no doubt about it. But the message of hope stood out like a beacon for us all: 'The liver is an enormous recuperative organ . . . moderate drinkers live as long or longer than abstainers . . . alcohol can prevent coronary heart disease.'

What! Alcohol staves off heart attacks? It seemed worth pursuing this with Dr Heinz at lunch, as the Napa Valley Cabernet Sauvignon arrived. Yes, it is true. Researches at Harvard have concluded that those who drink wine have a 25–40 per cent less chance of sustaining a heart attack. In addition to relieving stress, alcohol helps build the vital, life-giving HDL, the High Density Lypoprotein. This is useful in some way, though Dr Heinz smiled bashfully, indicating that I was unlikely to understand exactly how.

Anyone who has seen journalistic colleagues return to their desks after three pints of beer and seven whiskies, and produce perfect copy in 20 minutes, or fellow students taking finals so drunk that they cannot push their spectacles up their noses, will have an instinctive understanding of the benefits of HDL. As she says herself, it is 'multifactorial'. Myself, HDL works the other way. After this particular lunch it produces a contemplativeness so deep that not even the dramas of the Euro-parliament debate can break it.

Riches have become the bad dreams of avarice

Seldom in the history of the British middle classes has there been such unanimous fury. Rarely has this nation known the same degree of moral outrage on the part of the many against the few. In certain quarters, you merely have to breathe the words 'top people's pay', 'share options', 'bonuses', 'executive pension rights', or 'Cedric Brown' to watch your friends' eyes pop in reflexive disgust.

Those who would normally consider themselves enthusiastic supporters of enterprise show the irrational righteousness, on this subject, that one imagines marked the witch-doctors smelling out corruption on behalf of Chaka the Zulu. Wrinkling their noses, they point at the boardrooms of Britain. See, they say, a coterie of mutual backscratchers determined to treat each other right, irrespective of the fate of junior ranks, voting each other stupendous handshakes and pay-offs, even if – sometimes, it seems, *especially* if – the firm is on the verge of ruin.

Almost every day bears new statistics stoking public wrath. Like announcements of wills, the newspapers publish details of what has become known as Boardroom Greed, the noughts streaming across the page: we learn that Lord Alexander of Weedon is to receive a £100,000 bonus from the NatWest Bank, that the executives of the privatised utilities stand to make £100 million, one way or another, among whom one might cite Mr John Baker, chief executive of National Power, who luxuriates in a £675,000 profit on his options.

His voice quivering with Calvinist contempt, Gordon Brown, Shadow Chancellor, bangs on the same point, day in, day out. City editors fulminate against the practices. Committees are set up to wring their hands over the question. Former Tory MPs such as Sir Anthony Beaumont-Dark warn the Government that the level of anger now eclipses that felt against the unions in the 1970s. If any issue has cooked the Tory goose at the next election, we are told by pollsters, this is it.

So against this tide of collective hysteria, is it not urgent that someone should take a stand? My friends, I appeal for calm. I appeal for logic.

Perhaps there is a legitimate case for discontent with the actions of the privatised utilities. It is hard to deny the general perception that men like Cedric Brown, the chairman of British Gas, have been able to swell their pay packets by becoming monopoly purveyors of life's essentials, while reducing costs by sacking thousands of employees. But this self-enrichment by a handful of utility barons has, in the view of the public, contaminated the motives and reputations of everyone earning more than £100,000. Or shall we say £50,000? Where does it end?

At the risk of an excessively colourful comparison, one is reminded of the rage whipped up by Stalin against the kulaks. Hardly anyone, not even Left-wing charities, escapes in this great smelling-out of perks and privileges. Yesterday, we learnt that Mr Pierre Sane, the rather underpaid francophone boss of Amnesty International, was in trouble with his subordinates for receiving an extra £3,000 per year for keeping his children in French-speaking education in London.

What has come over us? Are we experiencing some kind of communist backlash? Are the Levellers abroad again? If I asked you: 'Is there anything wrong with making money?' you would say: 'No, of course not, don't be so silly: it all depends *how much* money, and how you make it.'

But no matter how many Greenbury Committees the City sets up to study the question, there remains only one way of settling how much executives are worth and that is to leave it to the market. These people are, by definition, worth what they are paid, no more and no less. Even in the case of the privatised utilities, gas, water and electricity, where the market is rigged, you cannot entirely blame Cedric and his kind for their remuneration. They are there to make money for the shareholders. Provided they achieve that, it will be in their genetic make-up, as businessmen, to take their chance to squirrel something away in advance of what now appears the inevitable victory of Tony Blair and Labour at the next election. If anyone is to blame for high salaries in the utilities companies, it is the regulators, men like Professor Stephen Littlechild, and the Government, who, deliberately or not, underestimated their profitability.

Blaming Cedric is like getting angry with a dog for wanting to chase rabbits. And think it possible, gentle reader, that Cedric and his kind may be doing some good. When they rise before dawn to spend their long day thinking about making biscuits or selling gas, we cannot exclude the fact that these chief executives are adding value to their companies. It is understandable, in a way, this middle-class urge to scratch your neighbour's Rolls-Royce. It has spread with the recession, among those in the negative equity trap, who have been forced to take their children out of prep school, who have felt the pinch at Lloyd's. What goads them most is the disparity between, for instance, the pay rise of 173.7 per cent for Mr Keith Orrell-Jones of Blue Circle, and the 21.5 per cent for the company's staff. As Incomes Data Services testifies, the gap between the incomes of chief executives and middle management has widened fast in 1979 to 1995. Managers' pay went up 409 per cent, chief executives' 645 per cent.

In its spleen, middle-income Britain has fallen for an absurd redistributive fallacy, as if lopping a few noughts off Lord Alexander's bonus could make a difference to NatWest's customers. We seem to have forgotten that societies need rich people, even sickeningly rich people, and not just to provide jobs for those who clean swimming pools and resurface tennis courts.

If British history had not allowed outrageous financial rewards for a few top people, there would be no Chatsworth, no Longleat. The stately homes of England would never have been built, nor much great art commissioned. There would be no Nuffield Trust. Yes! Had a certain Quaker family not profited enormously from making chocolate there would be no Rowntree Foundation ... The point, surely, needs no labouring.

In the same way, and to make the face of his particular brand of capitalism acceptable, Cedric might in time sponsor a poetry prize, or endow a professorship in physics. Perhaps he will. Let us keep our fingers crossed. In the meantime, though, we should avoid confusing a genuine moral affront with the politics of envy.

Rights and Duties

One sometimes wonders whether the fire has died in the belly of the Parliamentary Labour Party. One wonders how they can contain themselves, those ex-miners, those shop stewards, those thin-lipped lawyers, as they watch Tony Blair drift off to the Right in search of Tory raiment. He has sent his son to a grant-maintained school. He has rewritten the sacred text of the Labour Party. He has given a lecture sponsored by the *Spectator* in which he banged on about Responsibility with a capital R. Yet from the Labour Left we hear not a squeak of protest. They appear to have lost the power of speech.

Perhaps it is just that they are content to watch the media chew again the supermasticated question of whether or not a change of leader might increase Tory chances of winning the next election. Perhaps they feel they need only wait for power to drop into their laps. Or perhaps there is a further reason why Labour's rank and file bite their tongue: that they can't quite believe their luck. The Left, I would guess, is secretly astounded at how the middle class, and especially the Right-wing media, have allowed themselves to be gulled by the new Labour leader.

Just listen to the credulous yippees of these last few days. Blair is applauded on all sides for apparently resuscitating Duty. He is said to be dragging Labour away from the idea of what we think society owes us, and back to the Victorian concept of what we jolly well ought to do by way of mucking in. All hail 'Responsibilitarianism'! Someone the other day suggested that Blair's moralising approach evoked Lady Thatcher. Well, we may all be forgiven for hungering for a change of government. And we hacks are professionally obliged to come up with paradoxical headlines, such as Blair is the New Thatcher or Freddie

Starr Ate My Hamster. But it breaks my heart that we should acquiesce so happily in our own deception.

Consider more closely Blair's new Clause Four formulation, that 'the rights we enjoy reflect the duties we owe'. This is suggestively phrased. Blair appears to imagine a sequence of nice equations, beginning with 'Your right to life: your duty not to kill' and continuing through 'Your right to chew gum: your duty not to stick it under the seat', and so forth. In fact, the balance between rights and duties is rather different. These days a 'right' is usually a legal entitlement, often costing taxpayers' money. Duties, on the other hand, are thought of as moral obligations, but with no compulsion attached other than the prickings of conscience. Rights and duties may sprout together, as Blair seemingly believes, like dock leaves and nettles. But it is not too obvious to point out that modern Britons are much keener to avail themselves of their rights than they are to perform their supposedly corresponding duties, just as they are keener, broadly speaking, to handle a dock leaf than a nettle. Smokers frequently prefer their right to light up to their duty to the health of others. Sufferers from ingrown toenails, as we discussed recently on this page, are sometimes quicker to exercise their right to call an ambulance than to think about their duty to those in genuine emergency. Some of the unemployed would put their right to benefit ahead of their duty to look for work.

The paradox and shame is that this rights-first culture has been greatly encouraged under the Tories. Contrary to its rhetoric, this government has presided over an explosion of rights and entitlements of all kinds; not just more spending on old entitlements, but on new entitlements as well. One might cite the Children Act of 1989, which gave children rights against their parents. One might mention the Disability Discrimination Bill, which the Tories brought forward in January, with its destructive costs for industry. One might mention, as a specimen charge, Mr Major's decision to update Child Benefit even for the richest families. Overall, the budget of the welfare state has risen by an astonishing 75 per cent *in real terms* since 1979. No wonder the Tory Right is furious and disappointed with Tory rule, and wishes it would end. The wretched truth, though, is that Labour, at least in this respect, would be far worse.

Tony Blair may have reintroduced Labour to 'duty', but he cannot ignore Labour's constituent interests, who remain dedicated to expanding 'rights' of all kinds. Not even Mr Blair has been able to erode the unions' conviction that we all have a 'right' to a minimum wage. Mr Blair is also fully committed, the instant he reaches Downing Street, to accepting the detailed entitlements of the European Social Charter: minimum holidays, minimum weekly rests, paternity leave.

Both the minimum wage and the Social Charter would palpably destroy jobs. And what is Labour's answer to unemployment? Everyone with an interest in the pressures impending on Prime Minister Blair should read *Tribune*, the organ of the Labour Left. In this week's issue Mr Roger Berry, Labour MP for Bristol Kingswood, has a wheeze for promoting the 'right' to work. He has worked out that to devise employment for each of the one million long-term unemployed, perhaps in fretwork or making macramé placemats, would cost a mere £20,000 per head. That is 'only' £20 billion on the budget, says Mr Berry, who is *Tribune*'s economics correspondent.

Labour will scrap the few improvements that the Tories have made to the welfare state, such as the Jobseeker's Allowance, which is intended to prevent people remaining in the dole queue without trying to get a job. Labour will abandon Tory efforts to build up private pensions, exposing future taxpayers to the crippling cost of paying for our old age.

Worst of all, Mr Blair's concept of 'duty' is, on careful analysis, perverse. Far from leaving responsibility to individual volition, he appears to want local authorities to have more powers to interfere, over noisy radios, dangerous dogs or truant children. That is not duty; it is legislative coercion, and a familiar Labour nostrum. Sitting in their ranks behind Blair, Labour MPs know that this new talk of duties is merely covering fire for the extension of rights, and, consequently, spending. Hence their ominous complacency.

The rest of us, meanwhile, should realise that sand is being thrown in our eyes. The way to improve British society is not to attempt to enforce 'duty' through new and interfering legislation. It is to take the billhook to the great accreted thicket of expensive and often universal rights and entitlements.

Sardines gutted as Socrates comes in on the rebound

The French philosopher and footballer M Eric Cantona was sitting alone in the changing-room, meditating on his intellectual role models. He thought of Descartes. He thought of Camus, the fiery French existentialist goalie to whom he had been frequently likened. Most of all, he thought of Socrates. No, not the famous Brazilian mid-fielder of that name who flourished in the late 1970s, but Socrates of Athens, reputedly the wisest man in the world.

Like Socrates, he brooded, he had been falsely accused of corrupting young minds by his example. Like the Athenian, he had been misunderstood by society. Yes, you could say, he, too, was a martyr to philosophy. If this had been another age, mused Cantona, he might have been forced to drink hemlock. As it was he had barely escaped a jail sentence, and owed his freedom to a judge on appeal. He was pondering deeply the unfairness of his commuted punishment of 120 days teaching football to children, when, as if from nowhere, a pug-like man appeared, wearing a beard and swaddled in white linen.

'Socrates!' exclaimed Cantona, starting from his reverie.

'Ah, Cantona,' replied Socrates. 'I have just come from the market-place, which is in a ferment, believe me. The sophists cannot agree what to think about the decision of Judge Ian Davies to overturn your 14-day jail sentence at Croydon Crown Court, and everyone is repeating your brilliant apophthegm – let me get it right: "When the sea-gulls are following a trawler it is because they think the sardines are going to be thrown into the sea." It excited me so much that I went out to buy *La Philosophie de Cantona*, newly published by the Ringpull Press. Great stuff, I am sure.

'As I have said before, our city-state will not be justly ruled until all the football-players are philosophers and all the philosophers football-players. I have to say, though, that some cynics are unconvinced by your claim to profundity. Would you mind, therefore, if we engaged in argument, and tested this assertion that you are a philosopher, and not, as some others would have it, an impostor?'

CANTONA: By all means.

SOCRATES: You will have to guide me, for it is some time since I hung up my boots. But I think we can take it that the skill of a footballer lies in kicking well?

C: Certainly, O Socrates.

S: But a skill can be abused. Is the proper function of a sharp pruning-hook to prune vines or is it to puncture car tyres?

C: Why, to prune vines, of course.

S: And is the proper function of a footballer to kick balls, or does it lie rather in kicking people?

C: Assuredly, it is to kick balls.

S: And you would agree that the difference between kicking a ball and kicking a person is one of intent? When you kick a ball, it is not, I think, to damage the ball in what one might call its ballness. But when one kicks a person, it is to hurt the person's person, and that was your intention towards Mr Matthew Simmons, 20, fan of Crystal Palace, was it not, against whom you launched yourself, studs-first?

C: We have been over this, and as judge Davies pointed out, the provocation would have taxed a stoic.

S: Tell me, Cantona, what did Mr Simmons say that was so insulting? My friend Thrasymachus says he merely urged: 'Go and have an early shower, Cantona!'

C: How typical of you to feign ignorance, Socrates. As you know, he called into question the sexual preferences of my mother.

S: By Zeus. And was there any substance in his assertion? My dear fellow, I merely ask. Life without questions is life not worth living. It is just that, as a philosopher who does not play football, I wanted to understand the strength of your feeling.

C: Suppose, O Socrates, that you had just lost a complicated argument with Gorgias about the Nature of Love, or the Being of the Beautiful, or whatever, and as you were leaving the symposium, an ignoramus shouted: 'Get away, Socrates, you couldn't argue your way out of a paper bag!' How would you feel?

S: Hmmm.

C: Anyway, no one would expect a custodial sentence if, for instance, they took a vague kick at someone outside a pub. It is absurd. You cannot single a man out for special punishment just because he is famous.

S: Yes, I see. That is your central point: that when the Croydon magistrate Mrs Jean Pearch gave you a two-week jail sentence, she was unfairly victimising a famous man. So let me put my question another way. What is the goal of football?

C: The goal is, um, to score goals.

S: So the goal is the goal. Very good. And yet I am sure you would agree that there are other goals as well. I was watching Bolton Wanderers v Liverpool last night with Glaucon and Adeimantus and I reminded them of Bolton men gone by, of Nat Lofthouse, the 'Lion of Vienna', and his extraordinary goals in 1958 . . .

C: Forgive my interruption, Socrates, but I do not see where all this is leading.

S: I wanted to remind you of what we used to call the Corinthian spirit. Even you have said in your collected works that 'Football is the most beautiful of the arts.' You did say that, didn't you?

C: Yes.

S: What is the purpose of art, Cantona, other than mere self-expression? Surely art is intended to educate and to produce feelings of admiration.

C: I suppose so.

S: And do we not educate our children by example? If a man utters a profanity, is it worse or better if his children are with him, or does it make no difference?

C: Why, worse, of course.

S: And if a man steals, is it worse or better if he is a leading banker and responsible for maintaining confidence in the financial system, or is it just the same?

C: Um. I do not like the direction of these questions, Socrates.

S: And if a man runs and does a kung-fu kick while millions of people are watching, including children who venerate that man, and who have posters of him on their walls, is that the same as a man who lets fly an abortive kick in the dark outside a pub? I would think, and many people in the agora would agree with me – though not all – that the man has a special duty to restrain himself, no matter how severe the provocation.

There is a further point. Suppose Mr Simmons had run down from the stands and kicked you? What would have been the result. He would have been incarcerated, whereas you will be allowed to earn £10,000 per week while doing your community service. You may be a philosopher, Cantona, with your talk of sardines. But it seems we have proved that you are also a thug.

C: So it seems, O Socrates.

S: And you should have been locked up.

C: If you say so, Socrates.

Let in the Hong Kong Chinese

One could almost hear the splutter in the voice of the Tory MPs as they gave their opinions to news agencies yesterday of the bombshell from Hong Kong. 'It is unacceptable to the British people,' frothed Mr David Wilshire, whose constituency takes in Heathrow airport, 'to let in one more, let alone three million!

'My response and the response of my constituents is that Britain is full up,' he said, as though he were the proprietor of the Hotel Great Britain. Michael Howard, the Home Secretary, appeared on breakfast television to wave aside the suggestion by Chris Patten that the Government should grant rights of residence to the Hong Kong Chinese. 'There is no question of that,' he snapped.

And no sooner had Mr Howard slapped down Mr Patten than Mr Jack Straw, his shadow, popped up. Would

Labour, traditionally the party friendliest to immigrants, sympathise with Mr Patten? One hardly needed to ask. For this is New Labour, and Mr Straw was quite as convinced as Mr Howard that there were No Vacancies here. Indeed, he taunted the Home Secretary and invited him to make clear what, exactly, constituted Tory policy on immigration, given the amazing proposal by the distinguished former party chairman.

The view of Tory MPs and of the Government is that Mr Patten has, as one MP put it, flipped his lid. He seems to have forgotten, they say, that we are in the run-up to an election, and immigration, like tax cuts, is one of the few high cards in a Tory government's hand. In recent months Mr Howard has begun to flutter this card.

'Crackdowns', to employ the depleted jargon of the Home Office, have been mounted against illegal immigrants spongeing off the state. Employees have new incentives to inform on colleagues they suspect of being here under false pretences. Fraudulent asylum seekers are to be weeded out with more zeal. The process is under way. Only 825 people were granted refugee status in 1994. All those of us who resent being mobbed in the Tube by bogus Romanian gipsies will offer a discreet hurrah. And this Tory enthusiasm for control is not merely political tactics.

The reality is that no country in western Europe is able to open its doors to substantial immigration; nor should it. But in the din of slamming doors, and bolts ramming home against putative yellow hordes, our politicians are drowning an important question. We need a rational debate about whether Mr Wilshire is right in shouting 'Full!' through the letterbox.

This argument has nothing to do with the national 'duty' to the people of Hong Kong, or whether Sir Geoffrey Howe ignobly washed his hands of the colony in 1984; nor are we concerned, here, with what Mr Patten's real agenda may be – a subject Graham Hutchings discusses on another page. Dame Lydia Dunn may or may not be right to say that this is a 'moral issue'. All that is not to the purpose. Our question here is whether the admission of affluent and well educated Hong Kong Chinese might or might not be in the economic and social interests of the country. I do not mean three million such arrivals; no one believes that so many would come; but, shall we say, several tens of thousands, in addition to the 50,000 heads of families who already have the option.

It is not too trite to say, first, that the evidence of economic history, from ancient Greece to modern America, is in favour of immigration. Historians attribute the vigour of the Greeks to the commingling of the Mediterranean 'Peoples of the Sea' with the peoples of the Thracian landmass; and America's extraordinary ability to create jobs is attributable in large part to migrant labour. If some Hong Kong Chinese came here, moreover, they would not be the first settlers to energise Britain, and to invigorate her population. My colleague Simon Heffer was originally a Jute; that is to say, he traces his ancestry to immigrants from the Danish peninsula of Jutland, just as others trace their descent from Saxons, Normans, Celts, Huguenots and others.

You might say, well, that was rather a long time ago; and that the experience of more recent immigration from further afield has been less happy. Partly, I might agree, though one could point out the ways Commonwealth immigration has enriched our culture, providing this country, not entirely trivially, with one of the fastest men on Earth, and, in our curry-houses, the nation's most popular way of dining out. But if you went further and said there was 'no room' for a few thousand, or tens of thousands, of Chinese; that this was an over-built island, then I would say you were wrong.

Like much of western Europe, Britain faces a demographic quandary. In the words of a recent UN review, the populations of EU countries are 'melting like snow in the sun'. In order to replenish the population, the average British female of child-bearing age should be producing 2·1 children. As it is she is producing 1·8. As Professor John Simons of the Centre for Population Studies at the London School of Tropical Medicine testifies, we are becoming what Durkheim called a 'pathological society', showing the feeblest desire to reproduce.

No one knows whether this is caused by the fecklessness of the modern British male, or by women's liberation; or whether it is because divorce has become too easy. But demographers are agreed that in the medium term, that is by 2025, the population will begin to fall. Even more alarming is that this will be accompanied by a sharp rise in the dependency ratio: the number of pensioners who must be supported, in tax, by each worker. Meanwhile, the one section of the population which appears to be booming is that represented by Ms Sue Simcoe, currently costing the taxpayer £10,000 per year for having five children by three fathers, and who now has two more offspring on the way.

We face a choice. We can either follow Mr Wilshire, slam the door, and rely on the children of Ms Simcoe to pay our pensions. Or else we could have a policy of selective admission of immigrants, based on a property qualification and a willingness to work.

I once shared a classroom with a Hong Kong Chinese called Rayner Cheung. I don't think Rayner will mind me noting that there was one week when he came top in every single subject; not just maths and science, which was bearable, but also in Latin, Greek, French, History, and, yes, English. Matters were set right in following weeks. But it still rankles.

I am not suggesting for one minute that the Hong Kong Chinese, or any other immigrants, be admitted in numbers sufficient to make up the demographic imbalance. All I say is that discriminating use of immigration could not hurt us, and could have economic benefits. All it requires is a willingness to discriminate.

Thoughts on the ruin of Aitken

In ancient Greece they liked to curse the 'origin of evil', that seemingly innocuous event that started the ineluctable chain of causation that led to the downfall of some great man, the beginning of some war. Woe, woe, the chorus cries in Greek tragedy. If only Argo had never been built, Medea would never have killed her children. If only Paris had never stolen Helen, Achilles and Hector would still be alive, and thousands of doughty heroes with them.

Woe, cries the chorus of Tory elders, as they behold the awful comeuppance of Jonathan Aitken and the Tory party; if only Michael Howard – or, more accurately, his junior, Charles Wardle – had not shown such scruples; if only Mohamed Fayed and his brother Ali had been given British passports!

For then the owner of Harrods would never have gone to the *Guardian* with his tawdry tales, the Tories would never have been cursed with 'sleaze', Tim Smith would still be MP for Beaconsfield, poor Sir Robin Butler, the man who 'cleared' Aitken, would not have so much egg on his face, Neil Hamilton would not have been exposed as an alleged handler of brown envelopes, Christine Hamilton would not be a housewife superstar, Cash for Questions would have been a pilot quiz game, Ian Greer the lobbyist would still be plying his merry trade at Westminster, the children of

Britain would not be having nightmares about Peter Mandelson coming to get them if they don't eat up their greens, and dear, dear John Major . . . John Major would still be in power!

The Tories would have won the election! Thrice woe. If only the Tories had not crossed Fayed, the wrathful merchant of Alexandria, groan the chorus, the Tories might have escaped the Pharaoh's revenge, the tragedy might have been averted. Such is the counterfactual history of the past few years. Yet one has only to put it that way to feel uneasy.

Suppose it were possible that the great Tory disaster was not determined in other ways. Even if we could go back in time, pacify Fayed, snuff out 'sleaze', would that have been any better? The trouble with counterfactual history – in spite of the fascinating new book by my erstwhile colleague Niall Ferguson – is that it so often seems to rob events of pattern, proportion and symmetry.

To abolish the wrath of Fayed would have been cheating, tampering with what in retrospect can be seen to be a perfect historical cycle. There is something in the story of Aitken, and, yes, of the Tories, that is both vastly suggestive and comforting. Take Aitken first.

It is a plot that has everything: brilliant, engaging Old Etonians, exotic Yugoslav heiresses, illegal arms exports; television stations; Cabinet red boxes – the sensation is scarcely dimmed by the fact that Mr Aitken lost Thanet South at the last election – all thrown away in a full-blooded, old-fashioned *ruin* of 19th-century proportions, and now a proper Lucanesque flight from the country aboard a private jet, it seems, to fool the tabloid papers, with Inspector Knacker of the Yard already puffing in pursuit. The last we heard of the tall, pin-striped former Chief Secretary to the Treasury, he was in 'the Americas'. One imagines that reporters are even now paddling up the

Orinoco or quizzing the suspiciously well-spoken short-order chef in San Diego, California; and now news reaches us, perhaps brought in a cleft stick by some piccaninny from the steaming Mato Grosso, that he has resigned from the Privy Council. And we nod. It could not have been otherwise. It *should* not have been otherwise.

This was a man, as it will be pointed out ever after, who was willing to put his innocent teenage daughter in the dock, to ask her to perjure herself, and thereby to put her very liberty at risk. We may not think him quite as 'despicable' as the editor of the *Guardian* claims to do. But there is a touch of Darius Guppy about him, to take an example from my own generation, a Walter Mittyish refusal to face up to reality, and an inability to sort out right from wrong. Let us put the best possible construction on events in the Paris Ritz on Friday, September 17, 1993.

The most favourable explanation is that it was all On Her Majesty's Secret Service. It was all – wink, wink – in the national interest. The defence procurement minister needed to be alone with the chaps in tarbooshes because a certain Levantine touch was required, which might have shocked his Private Secretary at the MoD. Mr Aitken might try some such explanation if and when he returns. It won't wash. At the very least he was in breach of ministerial guidelines, to say nothing of the allegations that he attempted to procure prostitutes from among the good ladies of Kintbury, or the question of what he did or did not know about the arms exports of Bmarc to unsavoury places in the Middle East.

Like all tragic figures, Aitken was the author of his own downfall, and like most tragic figures, there was at least an initial dash of greatness, if not quite of heroism. Aitken may not have been a particularly brilliant Chief Secretary to the Treasury. But he was a man of considerable attainments, the author of a book on Nixon fat enough to mend a broken bedspring, possessor of some fancy houses in Lord North Street and in Kent. With his status went hubris.

Here was a man so sure of himself that he was prepared to stick his head in the lion's mouth of a libel action against the *Guardian*. It was the madness, the Ate, of those whom the gods wish to destroy. As Dr Robin Kirk, the principal of the Inglewood health hydro, said: 'I think he's slightly insane, he doesn't follow the normal behaviour of people like you and I would do.'

Then, inevitably, came peripeteia, or reversal, that shattering moment when he read the docket produced by the British Airways investigator, Wendy Harris, which proved that his wife was in the wrong city, like the moment when Oedipus discovers what he has known all along, that he married his mother. And then there was nemesis, flight, ruin, the national nodding over the cornflakes, the sense that the will of the gods has been fulfilled, the fear and pity excited in the populace by the spectacle of this great crash. Bent is the bough that might have grown full straight, we mutter to ourselves, and withered is Apollo's laurel bough, as we put down the newspaper and ask our wives to pass the marmalade.

And what is that feeling, that tiny smug satisfaction? It is catharsis: the sense of cleansing, purging, of rightness, a smaller version of the same emotion that so many in this country seem to have felt at the end of the 18-year cycle of Tory rule. After the heroic achievements of the early years came the arrogance of too long in office, the slip-ups, the 'sleaze', until, even among those who accepted intellectually that the Tories had the best case to govern, there was such a yearning for them to leave the stage that on the night of May 1 the brutal forces of democracy smashed the Tories so violently that even Labour supporters may have felt some sympathy for John Major. In the morning came the feel-good factor, otherwise known as catharsis.

That is the basic drama of politics. Politics is a constant repetition, in cycles of varying length, of one of the oldest myths in human culture, of how we make kings for our societies, and how after a while we kill them to achieve a kind of rebirth – as Tony Blair would put it, new life for Britain. Some of the kings are innocent; indeed, some of them take away the sins of the world. Some of them are less innocent, like Mr Aitken. It doesn't really matter. They must die.

Moments of moral choice

You're in the car with your secretary after a party and trying to effect a ticklish exit from your parking place when, damn it, you bump the car ahead. Some bawling French brat has been squashed in his pram and his father's cutting up rough. You're a former Tory minister and you foresee all the embarrassment of being breathalysed, and suddenly, though you perhaps don't realise it, you're in one of those positions where you've got to do the right thing.

You must work out in a flash whether it is more sensible to stay and face the consequences, or whether it might not be quite as prudent, since you can see that the kid is perfectly all right, to drift off down the pavement. In that instant, the depths of your character stand to be exposed. Depending on how you behave, a lifetime's cultivation of respectability can be made to seem hollow.

Looking back afterwards in shame at these moments of moral apocalypse, we can all work out what we should have done. If we had our time again, we would not hesitate. The lucky ones are those who can spot the ball early, who can see at once that they are in a genuine left-or-right, yes-or-no moment of moral choice, without having the position pointed out to them afterwards by the press: 'You liar! You coward!' The lucky ones also divine instantly that a cover-up will be impossible.

It takes skill to recognise these moments, because the decisions, when they are required, are required with such urgency. It is difficult to keep a clear head when you've driven off the bridge at Chappaquiddick in the middle of the night, and the water is closing around your head and you have to order your priorities: save self; save pretty blonde co-passenger? And you then have to work out whether to deny all knowledge of Mary-Jo Kopechne in the hope of protecting your political career, or whether to do the right thing and come clean.

These decisions take skill, also, because most of us have so little practice. Contrary to the impression given by various theories of moral philosophy, modern urban life is not an endless series of bifurcations between right and wrong. We might waver for a second or two before chucking a pound coin to a man selling the *Big Issue*. But perhaps because of the giant apparatus of state control and welfare that cushion our society, most of us, thankfully, find it hard to remember the last serious moral dilemma we faced.

Indeed, the drama of Sir Nicholas Scott, the former Minister for the Disabled, is really the stuff of fiction. In essential respects the episode resembles the famous opening scene of Tom Wolfe's *The Bonfire of the Vanities* (which itself owes something to *The Great Gatsby*). For the embarrassment of the former Tory minister and his secretary, read the agonies of Sherman McCoy, the Master of the Universe (Tom Wolfe's hero), and his female companion, and the little accident in the Bronx that transforms their lives. In fact, these moments of revelatory moral choice are so rare that they sometimes have to be confected by those who wish to dig out the underlying character.

401

One thinks of the cash-for-questions affair, in which MPs faced an artificial dilemma offered by the *Sunday Times*.

It is because these moments are so rare – or at least so rarely come to light – that they are so illuminating and important. What the inquiry by Lord Justice Scott tells us above all is that even the most experienced Cabinet minister can be prone to the same mad self-delusion as Teddy Kennedy or Sherman McCoy: that they can do the wrong thing and get away with it.

For any of the Cabinet ministers concerned, the moment of crisis, of decision, may have come like this: he is sitting up late doing his red boxes at home, his eyes pricking with fatigue and the whisky not helping, deciding whether or not to sign these curious papers, these Public Interest Immunity Certificates. He knows that both options are bad. If he allows certain documents to be produced in court, that will expose embarrassing modulations in the Government's embargo against Iraq.

On the other hand, if he signs the 'gagging order', he must know that he will be frustrating justice and that innocent men may go to jail. That is the choice at the heart of the Scott Inquiry. Never mind the sophistries of Mr William Waldegrave who, admittedly, seems to have produced an odd syllogism: 1) All change in policy on Iraq must be approved by Downing Street. 2) Downing Street did not approve the change of policy. 3) Therefore there was no change of policy.

At the end of all this, I would guess we are likely to forgive Waldegrave, who took a First in Greats and knows about Wittgenstein, for saying there can be a change which is not a change. Most reasonable people would accept that on sensitive matters of Middle East policy the entire diplomatic minuet need not be played out on the floor of the Commons. No, the moral dynamite is in the question whether Mr Henderson and his fellow directors of Matrix

Churchill should have been faced with jail to spare the blushes of the British Government.

Unlike Sir Nicholas Scott on the pavement, these ministers had plenty of time to think. The amazing thing is that – and I should be surprised if this is contradicted by Lord Justice Scott's final report – they all, in varying degree, flunked the test, Clarke, Garel-Jones, Rifkind, Lilley, Baker. Heseltine may have shown the sharpest appreciation that this was a moral dilemma (or rather, that it would look terrible if it got out), an occasion for thinking ahead, and thinking straight. But even he signed the gagging orders.

What is even more amazing is what these ministers now say in mitigation: 'Lyell told me to sign it.' 'It was for the judge to make the decision to waive the certificates, not the minister.' There may be other excuses for the actions of these £65,000-per-year decision makers, with their vast powers of regulation, their armies of civil servants to do their bidding; these people whose entire profession and expertise is to select options not just for themselves but for millions of others. But they cannot say that they had no choice.

Who'd want to be a Tory MP these days?

You have to wonder why anyone should want to replace them, these great men now giving up their seats. Hurd, Baker, Renton, Biffen, Walden; yes, and more widely across the Tory benches, it is as if the old boys are waking up with a start, glancing at their watches and realising they have been there for about 25 years, and Good Lord! it is time to collect their K and make way for a younger person. As local Conservative associations begin casting around for candidates, one ponders the unceasing miracle of the party's regeneration.

For it is a miracle that anyone should want to embark on the struggle to power, with that rather expensive weekend at the Slough Marriott with a hundred other keenies wearing their names on their lapel badges, there to be catechised by the examining panel for the slightest sign of Euroscepticism, and thence, assuming you pass, to begin the humiliating crawl towards the Palace of Westminster. It is a common prejudice in that building that there has been no worse time in Parliament's history to try to become an MP, and not just because of the Conservatives' likely fate at the next election.

'There's no money,' says George Walden, who has just issued a fairly dyspeptic explanation for his reasons for standing down at the next election. By 'no money' he means that the salary stays at a measly £32,000 per year, and one sees his point. 'There's no sex,' he goes on; by which he means not just no illicit sex, but not even blameless difficulty with girls, not with impunity.

Listen to Walden, O ye generation of thrusters. Heed him well. Your private life will indeed be taken away from you and pushed back through your letterflap one morning in the italicised innuendo and non-sequiturs of journalism. As a result of this drip-drip-drip denigration, the public now conceives there is something ribald in the very concept of a male Tory MP. 'People don't respect you as much as they used to,' says one member Eeyoreishly. 'It used to be something to be an MP. Oh! An MP! Best table in the restaurant, that kind of thing. Now they just snigger.'

You must resign yourself to inhuman patterns of work, small offices, sometimes overbearing secretaries, a phenomenal mortality rate, almost certainly assisted by beer and boredom. Under a rule devised in 1885, debates continue after dinner until ten o'clock, and, indeed, sometimes last all night. The job, in general, is increasingly like being an MEP without the travel, or the Strasbourg food.

And at the end of it all, my friend, you must prepare for failure. All political careers end in tears, said Enoch Powell. He might have added that a good many parliamentary careers hardly get going. It is a regular complaint that there is no such person in Britain as a successful non-ministerial parliamentarian. Apart from Bill Cash, Frank Field and one or two others, few backbenchers establish themselves as independent figures, respected for their mastery of a certain issue. Therefore, you must spend years oiling up to the whips, in the hope of securing a Red Box, or even attaining the bogus rank of PPS; and heaven help you, as Geo. Walden points out, if you show anything approaching independence of thought.

Consider Mr Iain Duncan-Smith, one of the brightest of the 1992 intake. Because Mr Major continues to punish this sage for his doubts about the Common Market, and has refused to promote him to ministerial office, Mr Duncan-Smith is likely to have to wait until the party gets back into office – in, what? five, ten years? – before he has a sniff of power.

Did someone mention power? Hah. Above all, at least according to the Walden analysis, the job has shrunk. Britain is relatively poorer, and less important in the councils of nations. Power is seeping away from the House of Commons. The sovereignty of parliament is now disputed with the judiciary, and above all with Brussels; which may explain why so many Tory MPs have fastened on 'Europe', as an object of resentment.

When Patrick Cormack stands up to talk about Bosnia, he is heard respectfully, with only the most discreet rolling of the eyes. But no one believes that it matters much what he says. The continent of Europe does not hang on the words of a British MP, as it did when Gladstone took a dim view of human rights abuses in Naples or Athens. Far from twanging their braces and surveying the horizon, MPs complain that they are treated as glorified social workers. 'My constituents ask me about their marriages? What am I supposed to do about their marriages?' says Eeyore. To cap it all, Lord Nolan now hovers over everything like some puritanical bird of prey, ready to snatch the tiniest crumb of financial consolation from their lips.

Why, to repeat our original question, would anyone want to do it? There are many layers of gratification. There is vanity. In almost all of these MPs, I think, though, there is at least a tiny grit of an instinct to public service. Probably most of us should be gently dissuaded from becoming an MP, just as we should be dissuaded from writing a novel. But, as with writing a novel, there is a thousand to one chance that you will hit the jackpot. There is a chance that you will have a role, like Mrs Thatcher, or Norman Tebbit, or Nigel Lawson, in briefly shaping the destiny of the nation. The only place to do that is in the upper reaches of government.

That is why beneath them, as they prepare to depart, Cranley Onslow, John Biffen and the rest can already hear the drumming roar of Young Men in a Hurry, desperate to take their places. We are fortunate, in a way, that so many relatively good people are prepared to risk the tears and disillusion with which their careers will undoubtedly end.

The nation is lucky that so many relatively bright people will not be happy unless they are able to haul themselves to their feet at 3.15 on a Tuesday, with the square eyes of a select band of BBC2 viewers upon them, their pate burnished by Trumpers, waistcoat flatteringly tailored, and say, 'May I ask my Rt Hon. friend to what he attributes his great gifts of leadership?' That is still an honourable

406

ambition. Without politicians, after all, there would be no political journalism.

Calling out ambulances by mistake

It was no one's fault. But somehow matters became a little out of hand the other night. The two-year-old was running a temperature, and by the time the nanny had been on the telephone to the doctors and discussed whether to bring her to surgery in the pushchair, and after what must have been some fairly confused conversation, an ambulance was for some reason despatched to our house.

I think of the cost of that operation: two infants and two au pair girls, roaring through the traffic on the rainy Holloway road, siren wailing, while hundreds of drivers heading back to St Albans and Welwyn Garden City made way, doubtless wondering what manner of stricken patient might be within. The mix-up occupied the attention of an ambulance crew for at least three quarters of an hour, when, somewhere nearby, there might have been a stroke victim waiting for that same ambulance.

At the hospital, I became uncomfortably aware of the radiant health of the child. I felt, frankly, a prat. I remembered that in living memory I had written a long blast against those who call out ambulances without good cause. So you can imagine that I was much struck to read the words of Sir Duncan Nichol, the former NHS chief executive, who has said that the only way to solve the service's long-term funding problems is 'increased private expenditure through, for example, an extension of user charges and patient co-payments'. Good point, Sir Duncan.

Why should I not be charged, say, £50 for that inglorious episode, a fraction of its real cost? Why not even a tenner or a fiver? As Sir Duncan has said, the NHS budget strains at its seams. There is no reason why we should pay for people to have tattoos removed from their bottoms. It seems reasonable that the middle classes should be required to stump up for non-essential services they can well afford. Mr Rodney Walker, former chairman of the NHS Trust federation, is also bang on the nail when he says that in the future the NHS should be for those who are genuinely sick, and for the elderly.

There is a moral point. If NHS services continue to be free in this way, they will continue to be abused, like any free service. If people have to pay for them, they will value them more. Above all, there is an economic point. In a very modest way, this extension of private funds into the NHS would help the Chancellor's straitened circumstances. The Government's borrowing figures for August show that this year's budget deficit is likely to be about £28 billion, about 4.6 billion more than forecast.

Yet somehow, as we all know, Mr Clarke faces an absolute political imperative to cut taxes in the November Budget. The only proper way to do that would be to cut spending. Mr Clarke is reported to be contemplating a public sector pay freeze. But public sector pay has already been frozen. Across Whitehall, orchestrated rows are breaking out about whose budget will be cut, with various unlikely characters taking turns to play tough cop and soft cop.

No sooner does John Major announce a Chequers meeting to launch a new Tory onslaught upon the welfare state, than sources close to Mr Lilley point out the difficulties, namely that this will penalise the very erstwhile Tory voters whom the Government must win back if it is to have any chance of winning the next election. William Waldegrave, the Chief Secretary, makes minatory noises about the way Gillian Shephard has been demanding more money for education. And then a leak appears from the Department of Education, warning that without more money state schools will have to close.

Mr Lilley's people admit that consideration has been given to a modest little plan to cut maternity benefit and transfer the responsibility to employers, with a potential saving to the Government of £450 million. The following day, the idea is reportedly squashed by the Prime Minister, not least because it fits rather oddly with Government ambitions for a new bonfire of burdens on business. And when Sir Duncan Nichol makes his case for encouraging more of us to spend their own money on health care, Stephen Dorrell takes immediately to the airwaves to assure us that people's access to health care will not be decided by the size of their wallets.

We have an impression of fervid activity, of voices raised in debate, of symmetrical threat and response. The end result is likely, of course, to be neutral. The reality is that no big spending cuts can be expected from the Government in the lifetime of this parliament. It is just not something one does, not 18 months before an election. Tax cuts there will indeed be this November. But they will be found by raiding the £7 billion contingency reserve, or fudging the payback of the PSBR, or some other such device.

Therefore they will be short-term tax cuts, matched by inconsequential cuts on spending. And the reason why there will be no serious spending cuts is that the Government would not dare make a substantial change to middle-class entitlements under the welfare state.

To return to my dilemma with the ambulance: there is no practical reason why I should not be charged for allowing my family accidentally to use an emergency vehicle as a taxi. There is a political reason: I will not be charged for the ambulance because politicians dare not take away from the middle classes the benefits they have accrued under the welfare state. For the same reason they will not take away all the other instruments of universal provision such as child benefit, disability allowance, and the rest. It is greed on our part, and cowardice on theirs. Now, to break the cycle, where do I send the cheque?

Nation of curtain-twitchers

If I were an immigrant, there is one main reason why I might feel alarmed by Michael Howard's plan to sniff out illegal workers in the office and factory. It is not that the measure imposes an extra burden of bureaucracy on employers, though it probably does. Nor is it that the measure is necessarily racist, though it may prove to be so, and is certainly designed to suggest as much to those who approve of racism.

Nor, again, is the latest Howard 'crack-down' demonstrably hysterical. Perhaps the Tories are right to say the country is being 'swamped' with illegal workers of all hues; though one would have thought the economy benefits from cheap labour vacuuming our hotel rooms, and doing so, moreover, without defrauding the benefit system, since the mere act of signing on exposes them. No, the reason for distrusting the measure is that it accelerates progress towards what one might call a Nark's Culture; by which I mean a Britain in which neighbour informs anonymously against neighbour, and in which the state encourages him to do so – sometimes financially.

In the new Michael Howard era, immigrants will be vulnerable not just to bosses who may wish to discriminate against black faces, but to the malice of their fellows, who may wish for whatever reason to see them gone; and who have only to lift a telephone or whisper privily to achieve their end. These *corveaux* of the workplace will have a new way of spreading misery, and without any necessity to ensure that their allegations are true.

The state has always relied on sneaks: the Inland Revenue, Customs and Excise and Maff will all tell you that most fraud is uncovered through tip-offs. But so far as I am aware, the State has not hitherto incited such people. Already, in certain parts of the country, the Department of Social Security pays Post Office workers a tenner a time if they shop a benefit fraudster. Following the roaring success of the scheme, Peter Lilley has just announced that he wants to go further. A hotline is being established, with a toll-free number.

The next time you see that fellow on Incapacity Benefit hitting the tennis court or giving aerobics classes, just pick up the phone and relax as he gets his comeuppance. In a way, this is to the good. As the DSS explains, benefit fraud is costing us all a fortune. According to a lately completed survey, about £1.2 billion is ripped off from Income Support alone. The Government itself admits that the total lost in fraud is about £3 billion; heaven knows what the true figure is. And there is nothing wrong in itself with bearing witness anonymously against another.

If you saw a hooded man with a gun breaking into the next-door house, you might not challenge him, for fear of being shot. But you would be quite right to pick up the telephone to call the police. There seems no reason in principle why people should not be urged to inform against all law-breakers. My only question concerns the practical effect of this mass delation on people and on communities. In Scotland recently I talked to a couple who had just built their own house. A neighbour who had suffered a heart attack and had time on his hands offered to rally round, unpaid, on the site. He gave advice.

Now and then, they told me, he passed the odd brick.

Alas, the neighbour was spotted by person or persons unknown, who tipped the wink to Mr Lilley's agents at the DSS. They swooped. They demanded to know how he could be fit to pass bricks, and yet claim Invalidity Benefit, as it was then called. Perhaps this helpful neighbour was indeed a fraud. Perhaps he deserved to be humiliated. But – and this is the point – he had no idea who in that small Scottish village had ratted on him.

His life was poisoned; and the same is happening across the land. As any lawyer who has prosecuted benefit fraudsters will tell you, they have almost all been nailed by sneaks. I don't think it is too much of an exaggeration to say that we are starting to live in a kind of Vichy society, a world of curtain-twitchers and whisperers, which has institutionalised the kind of behaviour which would be punished at school by ostracism, if not debagging. The root cause of this rising national urge to Tell Sir All is not an increase in the natural dishonesty of the British people. It is largely that the expansion of welfare tempts good people to break bad rules.

With £90 billion circulating through the tax and benefit system, and with one in three households receiving a major benefit, Beveridge's plan has become like the Common Agricultural Policy. People feel silly, indeed irresponsible towards their families, if they pass up their chance to take a slice of the enormous communal pie, especially while everyone else is doing the same. The logical answer might be to apply free market principles, and attack this irrational system of subsidy, the excessive disbursements that warp honest people.

As Adam Smith pointed out of a different set of bad laws: if there were no excise duties, there would be no smuggling, at least of legal substances. And if there were no smuggling, there would be no tell-tale tits, no poisonous atmosphere of doubt and recrimination. The difficulty, of course, is that at this stage in the electoral cycle, the Government is in no position to cut the welfare state. It will not happen; and we will slip further and further into a mire of cheating and sneaking.

One thing could be done, though, to end malicious informing. We may reluctantly accept the need for Mr Lilley's fraud hotline, and perhaps also for Mr Howard's plans to persecute illegal immigrants. But I propose a small modification which might serve as a deterrent to those who make miserable the lives of others without good cause, by bearing false witness, or witness they do not positively know to be true. Anyone who uncovers anyone else falsely testifying against another should, without delay, dial the new Sneakline. Do you know a mendacious sneak? Sneakline is on 0171 538 5000. Ask for me. Do call.

Killing deer to save them

All the warning we had was a crackling of the alder branches that bend over the Exe, and then the stag was upon us. I can see it now, stepping high in the water, eyes rolling, tongue protruding, foaming, antlers streaming bracken and leaves like the hat of some demented old woman, and behind it the sexual, high-pitched yipping of the dogs. You never saw such a piteous or terrible sight.

In that instant we would have done anything to help the stag get away. I think we vaguely shouted and flapped our arms, but too late. In a trice, the stag had been brought to bay by the hounds, almost at our feet in the meadow. And then a man with an ancient-looking pistol, a bit like a starting gun, blammed it in the head and they cut it open in a kind of laparotomy.

I remember the guts steaming, and stag turds spilling

out on to the grass from within the ventral cavity. Then they cut out the heart and gave it to my six-year-old brother, still beating, he claimed ever afterwards, or still twitching, and he went dancing home singing: 'We've got the heart! We've got the heart!' So we cooked it up with a bit of flour, and the German *au pair* girl left the next day.

No, you don't need to tell me that hunting with hounds is cruel. We don't need some report by scientists to show that the animals suffer 'stress'. No one looking at that deer could deny that this was a sentient being in the extremity of suffering. This wasn't the stopping of some Cartesian clock. This was savagery, and that is the case for banning hunting, stated as forcefully as I can – and it isn't enough.

When the 80,000 or so marchers for the preservation of country sports arrive in Hyde Park tomorrow, they will have my support, and I think Labour is mad, after its enormous success in winning over so many former Tories, to make an enemy of such a large slice of rural Britain by going ahead with a ban.

You may think it odd to take this line, having been exposed to the full horror of a kill and never having hunted myself; and, indeed, some of the pro-hunting points seem weak. There is the argument from inconsistency, which says that every day we kill thousands of cows in wretched circumstances, and moreover this fellow Mike Foster, the MP for Worcester tabling the Bill, is a competition angler, who yanks hooks out of the cheeks of fish, and the faster he yanks, the better he does. Why should he ban hunting? Such a ban, the argument runs, would lift but a pebble from the mountain of man's inhumanity to dumb brutes. As so often with arguments from inconsistency, this is not quite the knock-out point it seems. Just because we are unable to stop all cruelty to animals, this is no reason why we shouldn't be able to stop some. Medicine cannot end all human pain. That is no reason to abandon medicine.

Then there is the argument from tradition. Hunting has been going on for a long time, part of the warp and woof, says this argument. You can be in some hellhole hotel, the Khyber Pass Marriott, and, like Stephen Glover's, your eye can alight on a hunting print in the breakfast room, and suddenly you're bathed in Rupert Brookeish emotion about a body of England breathing English air, washed by the rivers and warmed by the sun of home. Well, that is good as far as it goes. But then plenty of traditions have been dispensed with: slavery; male-only suffrage; absolute monarchy; and you'd have to be pretty reactionary to want them back.

And then there are some good arguments for keeping hunting. There is the simple argument from liberty. This is an ancient freedom. To take away people's freedom to do something they have always done is serious; and when it appears that hunting is to be banned by those who have no standing in the matter, the New Labour types who want to 'make a statement' about the kind of Britain they believe we should live in, without any thought for the effect on rural employment, or point-to-points, or gymkhanas, or tourism, then it is an odious interference.

And it is especially odious when, as so often, the antis do not really appear to be actuated by concern for the animals, but by disgust that people should enjoy hunting, mixed in with a healthy dash of class prejudice. If you want evidence that this is largely about class, look at the proposed Labour amendment to protect footpacks – which still rend the fox in pieces – but ban the toffs in pink.

The argument from liberty alone would probably be enough to make me want to keep hunting. But it is not the strongest argument for protecting the Devon and Somerset stag-hounds – and I pick the staghounds because those are the ones I have observed the closest and which are, in the popular imagination, even more brutal than the fox-hounds. The best argument in favour of keeping them is that hunting is best for the deer, as Dick Lloyd, the historian of Exmoor's deer, has shown. Ted Hughes set out the case beautifully last week.

The number of deer has fluctuated over the past 350 years in direct correlation to the success of the hunt. From early times, the deer were protected for baronial hunts, and the chief threat came from the resentful Saxon farmers. The deer population flourished until the Civil War, when the hunt's protection was removed, and by 1660 the red deer was almost extinct in the West Country.

After the Civil War, the hunt was revived under the auspices of the North Devon staghounds and recovered to about 200 deer. When the North Devon staghounds folded in 1825, the deer population again collapsed, falling to about 50 by 1850, most of them peppered with gunshot. And then the Devon and Somerset Staghounds was set up.

Farmers took part in the hunt, the staghunt became part of the farming way of life, and the deer were systematically protected. Since then, North Devon and Somerset have become a kind of free-range deer park, and the population of red deer has climbed to 2,500 according to the 1995 census, far more than ever before. When the huntsmen say that the population would fall dramatically if the hunt were abolished, that seems demonstrable on the evidence of history. Deer are already shot by farmers. If they were no longer valuable for a hunt, they would simply become pests which could be turned into meat. They would go.

Another time we were up on the moor and we came across the hunt, the cars parked up against the hedges. Standing on the roof we saw the deer, its coat more blond than red in the sun, going fast and well ahead of the hounds. We cheered as it jumped one hedge, and then another and then we saw it still going fast towards the sea, antlers disappearing over the brow of the hill. Afterwards we found out that the stag had indeed escaped, and we were thrilled. But that did not mean we were against the hunt. Apart from anything else, without the hunt, there might be no deer.

They're only jealous, Bill

Frankly, I never much liked the look of Bill Clinton: a bit too blow-dried, too much ghastly phoney sincerity. Many of us would be perfectly prepared to believe that he and Lady Macbeth did indeed bump off Vince Foster, make an illicit killing in cattle futures, cream off millions from a shady property deal called Whitewater and run cocaine out of Mena airport, Arkansas.

For all I know the Internet conspiracists are right to think he is virtually an executive director of Murder Incorporated, with the blood of Waco and Oklahoma City on his hands. But in the matter of Monica Lewinsky, and what is now called the Oral Office, he deserves our full support.

Oh it's not the sex, says everyone. It's the *lying*. Yes, well, lying is grave in a Commander-in-Chief. If he has perjured himself, he may be finally winkled out of the White House. The lovely Monica may indeed have a dark blue semen-stained dress in her possession that she has been saving for the Impeachment Ball; though it seems at least conceivable that she is lying her head off, a star-struck booby trapped in a fantasy malevolently encouraged by others.

'I've been lying all my life,' she says on one of the

tape-recorded conversations with Mrs Tripp. That goes, as m'learned friends might say, to her credibility. But let us for the moment accept that Bill is cornered.

He's gone pink with bogus rage and denied any 'sexual relations'. There is no wiggle room now, no scope for cunning retrospective biblical exegesis to the effect that – sensitive readers avert their eyes – oral sex is not sex. Hillary Rodham, with her icy cool, has appeared on break-fast television to offer support (in exchange for heaven knows what pound of flesh from her husband). The hostages have been given to fortune. The trap is set.

But if and when the trap is sprung, and the Clintons are caught, what will their lie have been about? It wasn't as though Congress had been deceived about selling arms to Iran to fund the Contras – which was straight duplicity in a matter of state, whatever you happen to think about the net effect of Col Oliver North's operation. It was about Zippergate, Tailgate, Fornigate.

It was about whether something more than friendship flowered between the President and an unmarried woman. It was a lie about sex, the kind of lie we try to avoid, but which we would all admit is sometimes justifiable, even, God knows, desirable.

Why *on earth* should the affair itself be of public impor-tance? What rubbish to suggest that it might somehow impede the President in the conduct of his duties. We are endlessly bemoaning the way British politicians are slaves to their red boxes. If Clinton is able to lead the Free World, without any noticeable disasters, while simultaneously having a fling, one can conclude only that he must have prodigious powers of organisation.

Some have implied that the President coerced Miss Lewinsky. What tosh. The more footage we see of the pair together, the more obvious it is that she transpires at every pore with lust to be noticed by the 'big he', as she calls him. The more we learn about how she used her Blue Pass to hang around outside the Oval Office in a low-cut dress, the more one is inclined to sympathise with Clinton's predicament.

He may have a bad case of satyriasis. He may have made an unwelcome pass at Paula Jones – immediately retracted – but it doesn't add up to harassment of women. Indeed the feminist lobby in America is maintaining a deafening silence, mainly because Clinton has been such a battler for abortion and other feminist causes, not least the $21 billion he announced last night for childcare; and it is the Right that is driven, preposterously, to denounce him as a monstrous philanderer, an ogre, a predator upon innocent womanhood and sundry other nonsense.

Partly this is mere opportunism. Some Right-wingers may not really think the alleged liaison matters, but any excuse to dish the Clintons will do. Other Right-wingers genuinely think that Clinton's Oval Office carryings-on are appalling, and that they vitiate his entire presidency. The same argument is used in Britain, in the case of everyone from David Mellor to Robin Cook, and it needs to be tackled head-on.

Extra-marital sex is said to be of immediate political relevance, and not just a matter for the couple concerned, because it is said to expose a basic treacherousness, 'If-a-chap-can-lie-to-his-wife . . .' etc. Oh really? Is Gladstone to be condemned, because of what we now know about his weird work with prostitutes? Was Thomas Jefferson a failure as a President, because he had an affair with a slave-girl? Does it really *matter* what Palmerston got up to with women in Hyde Park?

Then we are told that, in an age of mass media, such behaviour 'sets a bad example'. Governments are increasingly worried about the state of marriage in this country, the evaporation of old taboos. Around us we see unmarried

419

mothers pushing buggies containing children who will grow up with no father, and who will have no idea how a man should behave, who will be more likely to be drawn to delinquency and crime.

How can we expect these young people to recover their sense of shame, or to value the family, if at the apex of their society they see politicians behaving like goats? Or that at least is the argument of those who denounce any kind of sexual impropriety in politics; and to see how fallacious it is, you have only to imagine what would happen if the mullahs were successful.

Suppose every politician in Britain and America were as blameless and happy in his marital conduct as John Redwood, to pick a name at random. Does anyone think a bunch of uniformly virtuous politicians would make the slightest difference? Of course they wouldn't. The decay of marriage, the rise in illegitimacy, are far more directly traceable to female emancipation, unemployment and the vast welfare state, which so often supplants the role of the husband. The press wilfully muddles the issue, feeding on public prurience and jealousy.

Yes, jealousy. We know why these politicians are so attractive to young interns. It is because they have power, and *we* gave them that power. We want to delimit the consequences of electing them, to stop them enjoying the attentions of the likes of Miss Lewinsky; and how snivelling and short-sighted that attitude is.

We believe it is our democratic right to insist that Clinton and Cook have no mistresses, when it is nothing whatever to do with us. So politics is trivialised and turned into hell for so many of its practitioners. I say to Clinton: Bill, you may be a gangster, but you appear to have balanced the budget. Nato expansion is proceeding. America remains the only superpower. Washington airport is about to be renamed after Ronald Reagan. You cannot be called a total disaster and, in respect of Monica, I'm rooting for you, if you see what I mean.

Why Tony worships in the Temple of gammon

My hand hovered above the leg of lamb. In that instant, I had a sickening sense of what I was doing. Here I was, in Sainsbury's in Taunton, preparing to buy a leg of lamb from a supermarket. There, in the chilled meat section, round about aisle three, my conscience convulsed, and it hit me that only the previous evening I had been vowing, *vowing* to myself, never to buy meat from a supermarket again.

The night before, I had been on the roof of Exmoor, listening to a farmer who had been driven to the desperate extremity of shooting his sheep rather than lose money trying to sell them. He had been hammered by the madness of the BSE regulations. Pork and beef were in such super-abundance that the market for lamb was in free-fall.

And above all, he and his fellow hill farmers were being imperially screwed by the cartel of the big supermarkets: Sainsbury's, Tesco, Asda, Somerfield, Safeway. These five now sell some 70 per cent of meat in Britain. Their buyers call the shots in the livestock industry, inciting farmers to join their 'producers' clubs' and then using their domi-nance, as the only buyers, to drive down the price.

That haunch of cling-wrapped meat, which I had so glibly thought to slam in the trolley for Sunday lunch, and which J Sainsbury was offering to sell me for £7.45: how much had J Sainsbury paid the poor suicidal producer? About an eighth of that amount. The supermarkets and their agents are now buying lamb for 76.5p per kilo, and selling it for £8.01 per kilo. In the 50th year of their existence, the supermarkets have become commercial and political bully-boys. They control agriculture. They dictate what we buy, and where we buy it. No politician dare stand in their way.

With their amazing distribution systems, the super-markets are forcing British vegetable growers to go toe to toe with sub-Saharan Africa. When Cornish farmers came up with some perfectly delicious but yellowish cauliflower, the supermarket cauliflower chiefs said No, and 100 acres were ploughed back into the soil. Assisted by the *laissez faire* policies of successive governments, the supermarkets have built their great brick cathedrals outside town centres. Bustling butchers and grocers have been replaced by slot machine joints, frequented by forbidding youths. The market-place, the forum, the agora, the centre of every community since civilisation began, has been ripped out and transplanted to a car park in the middle of nowhere. Employment, inevitably, is reduced; and to cap it all, they are ripping us off.

Staple foods are 20 per cent more expensive in British supermarkets than in France; and a German professor yesterday revealed how a representative sample of 38 products from Tesco in Cambridge was 55 per cent more expensive than in a local grocer's in Kassel, Germany. All these thoughts, or at least some of them, flashed through my mind as the hand hovered above the chill cabinet.

And then I looked at my watch, and realised, Good Lord, that I had to pick my family up from the station in 10 minutes. In went that leg of lamb, and then, let me tell you, I gave that trolley some welly. In the space of about seven minutes I bought £83 worth of food and wine, took the tricky corner between household cleaners and babycare with all the ruthless daring of Schumacher on the Monaco hairpin, screeched through the chequered flag of the check-out, and had I not been in such a rush, I might have reflected that supermarkets, in a hotly contested field, excite the British to their highest pitch of humbug and hypocrisy.

Of course we hate them, in a way, for what they do to farmers and to town centres. But deep down, we love them, too. We love them for being so quick, so handy. We love the way we can shop on Sunday in these temples of gammon, marvelling at the 20,000 exciting lines that are now stocked in major stores. Maybe there really are some people who yearn for shopping as it was in the old days, when mothers and their children would spend Saturday fighting their way out of the old-fashioned, overcrowded butcher's and into the pullulating haberdasher's.

Maybe it would be lovely to go back to the age I dimly remember, when shopkeepers knew their clients, and gossip was exchanged, and there was a sense of community. The trouble is, there is just no evidence that this is what we really want. No sooner is a supermarket built, than people cynically desert their wheezing old grocer, and take to their cars. The supermarket question, in short, encapsulates the central dilemma of modern politics.

When Nicholas Ridley and John Gummer gave permission for the out-of-town shopping centres, they were following one of the two contradictory strands of Tory thought: the instinct to let the market rip, to let people decide how to run their lives, to give them choice. What they neglected was the classic Tory concern for the old way of doing things, for the little platoons, for communities. It is an unresolved tension.

We cannot disinvent the supermarket, and would not if we could. All we can say is that there are aspects of their current dominance which are legitimate political concerns. They should *not* be allowed to crush small farmers by using their cartel strength to drive down the price at which they buy; and they should *not* be allowed to rip us off by inflating the price at which they sell. The Office of Fair Trading has shown what they are up to. Will the Government act?

Will it hell. It is a measure of Blair's opportunism that before the election, Labour policy was to be generally against new shopping centres. To the dismay of Frank Dobson and Michael Meacher, there was then a meeting in Blair's office, organised by John Mendelson, one of his advisers, and the supermarket barons. Labour policy on shopping centres 'matured' to a studied neutrality. Mr Mendelson has now left Mr Blair's office to set up the LLM lobbying company, briefly hitting the headlines during the Dolly Draper lobbygate affair, and numbers Tesco among his clients.

Tesco has given many millions to the Millennium Dome. Lord Sainsbury of Turville is a generous private donor to Labour, and is now a government minister. Somerfield sponsored the dog tags at the Labour Party conference. Labour has all but completed the selling of its soul to big business; and here, one would have thought, is a theme for William Hague and the Tories.

It is not simply a question of bashing the supermarkets, but of sticking up for the consumer, and for rural Britain. It is helping the underdog. It is the British way. Who better to lead the attack than the chairman of Asda and deputy chairman of the Tory party? Come on, Archie. Never mind the profits. Think of the people.

Defence of Glenn Hoddle

So the martyr perishes. Farewell Hod, old bean, as the believers in Pythagorean bean-reincarnation say to each other. Your mistake was not to make some injudicious remarks about karma.

Your mistake was to deny you had said 'them things' and to cringe before the appalling tide of tabloid-whipped hysteria and government-inspired political correctness. Oh Hod! Some of us were still praying, hoping, that you would figuratively stick two fingers up to the Prime Minister and stand by your wacky beliefs.

You have a right to believe them. You have a right to repeat them. Insulting though they may be, they do not come near the limits that a modern democracy places on freedom of speech. It was odious and disgraceful that the Prime Minister should have joined the hue and cry from his lime-green upholstery on the Richard and Judy show.

From the spring of next year, the European Convention on Human Rights will be written into British statute, protecting freedom of religion and expression, under articles nine and ten. If I were Hoddle's lawyer, I would advise him to hire Cherie Blair and sue Tony immediately in the Court of Human Rights in Strasbourg. What is the material difference between the case of Hoddle, who thinks the soul of his grandam may haply inhabit a bird, and Salman Rushdie, the Rugby-educated wordsmith?

Like Hoddle, the author of *The Satanic Verses* caused huge offence to an important and vocal minority in this country. Like 'Glennda', the gloomadon-popping Rushdie had a controversial take on religion. Consider the difference between the treatments of the two heretics.

Rushdie is championed by virtually everyone. The Muslim world is aflame, British contracts are torn up, public treasure is lavished on the protection of the provocateur, and yet we all of us stout-heartedly defend his right to thumb his nose, for hundreds of scatalogical pages, at Muslim holy writ. And when one former Spurs star cum God squadder ventures one half-baked, ill-thought-out and virtually incomprehensible opinion about reincarnation, what happens?

The Pharisees and the Sadducees of New Britain line up to call for his instant execution, including, nauseatingly, the Prime Minister. What accounts for this difference? Why is it one thing for Rushdie to hold offensive views about Islam and quite another for Hoddle to hold offensive views about reincarnation? The Muslims, after all, took far more offence than the 'disabled', as they are so patronisingly called.

It boils down to this. Hoddle is not a trendy liberal author from an ethnic minority who frequents the salon of Harold and Antonia. Hoddle is a white middle-class male with a taste for snakeskin shoes and towelling socks. He is barely literate, my dear, and above all not much good at winning football matches. He is therefore fair game and, in common with other people in the eye of the PC cyclone, he has absolutely no idea how to defend himself.

Take another man being forced to cut short his career amid jeers and boos from the crowd, Sir Paul Condon. Yes, there were grotesque failures in the Stephen Lawrence murder case. They may well have originated in racism. The officers who were called on to investigate his death jumped to the wrong conclusions, possibly from a racialist mindset. But it is as if the PC brigade, having punched this hole in the Metropolitan Police, having forced this admission, is swarming through to take over the entire system.

There has been a whiff of the witch-hunt as the Lawrence road-show tours the country, demanding confessions of racism from senior officers, and excoriating those, like Sir Paul, who are not prepared to defame their entire force. If, in a few years' time, you were to ask a member of the public: 'Who killed Stephen Lawrence?', the answer would probably be: 'The police.'

Am I alone in wondering whether a sensible attempt to find justice for the family of Stephen Lawrence has given way to hysteria? But of course that is a thought-crime these days. For years the Right thought it had PC on the run, by identifying and ridiculing the phenomenon.

Too late, folks. PC has won. Look at the top brass in the Armed Services, jargon-bound slaves to correctness. In each case there is a bashfulness, a reluctance to fight back, and an instinct to apologise. What they do not understand, they who mumble guiltily before the kangaroo courts of PC, is that, unresisted, the affliction leads to madness. Look at the example of America, where the disease is now raging full-blown.

On the front page last week in Washington was the news that the mayor of that city had sacked David Howard, one of his officials, for using the word 'niggardly', in respect of his proposed administration of a fund. That was not how his hearers, both of whom were black, took it. They thought it had something to do with nigger, and Howard was sacked, like Hoddle, *simply because offence had been taken.*

'I immediately apologised . . . I would never think of making a racist remark. I regret that the word I did use offended anyone,' Howard said afterwards. He might have been indignant. He might have protested and demanded immediate reinstatement, saying that it was absurd to sack someone for a simple lexical misunderstanding.

But no: the presumption of guilt was upon him. He was denounced by the lobby groups, and he grovelled, even though the attacks on his character were quite unfounded.

Some groups do not apologise or bow to political correctness. In Ulster, the Orangemen are so used to being the whipping-boys of polite opinion that they are long past caring.

Others have only just woken to the rules of engagement with our new masters. The best example is the Countryside Rally, the hunters and shooters who suddenly realised that they were in danger of extinction from the politically correct majority. We saw something we had never seen before: Middle Britain marching on London, and in high rage. That march was organised by an American who understands the weapons that must be used in the *Kulturkampf*.

If political correctness is not resisted, it will go on and on and on, becoming more and more irrational: silencing one man's religious beliefs, forcing another to 'confess' to his racism; and unless they are resisted, Mr Blair and the Labour Government will ride the hysteria of the crowd whichever way it takes them.

I wish Hoddle had fought on for his right to share his faith, publicly, with about a billion people on this planet, however curious we may think it. I wish more people could see how opportunistic was the bullying of the Prime Minister. But if his martyrdom has mobilised anyone against the PC tyranny, then it has not been in vain.

Call to raise the speed limit

Have you ever driven very fast on a motorway? I have. As the motoring correspondent of *GQ* magazine, I have sometimes attained velocities which are incompatible with my new status as a tribune of the people.

Not so long ago, I found myself at the wheel of a Ferrari Maranello Testadicazzo, or some such name, whose dashboard boasted it to be capable of 220mph, which, as my six-year-old worked out after much coddling of his intellect, is more than three times the national speed limit. Did you get that? Three times! Powee! If I'd really put the pedal to the metal, I'd have gone through this planet's event horizon and found myself in the middle of next week.

Who on earth needs a car that fast, you will ask. Who needs to bust out of the comfortable old corset of the 70mph restriction? Well, all I can say is get out on to a road near you, baby, and look around. It's you. It's me. It's everyone.

If you see anyone who is obeying the law, apart from the odd motorised rickshaw, please give me a ring. The national speed limit is, *de facto*, 99mph, because everyone knows that you lose your licence at 100mph. The law of the land is disregarded by good people, held in contempt by Middle England, and scorned by no less a person than Jack Straw, who saw fit to scream through the sound barrier when he was Home Secretary.

Oh, we'll sometimes make a passing stab at legality. If there's a police car on the road, we'll all slow down to a theatrical 70mph, and cluster round the cops like guilty sheep around a sheepdog; and for an interval we'll keep pace, dawdling politely along, until we feel the proprieties have been observed, and when we have nosed a couple of hundred yards ahead, we give it some welly and show the law a clean pair of heels. And what do they do? What can they do? Nothing. They haven't the time or money thoroughly to enforce a law that no longer reflects the power and safety of modern cars, and, above all, no longer reflects the custom of people who, broadly speaking, have a care for the interests of themselves and others.

The same point can be made, of course, about cannabis, which is now a subject of lively debate in the Tory party. Isn't that, by the way, just one sign that the Tory party is the coolest, chic-est and most happening place to be right now?

I appeal to all members of our nation's yoof who may be reading this article to get with it, join the Tory party, help lower the average age from 67¾, and come break dancing with Peter 'Tosh' Lilley and Charles 'Rastaman Vibrations' Moore, the apostles of liberty.

Forget about Tony Blair and his ghastly pretence at bourgeois values. Get with the Tories, who really understand about bourgeois values and how they may be changing. If you were to go to any great national festivity this summer – a regatta, for instance – you would see the flower of England's youth assembled. And if you were then to ask them all to turn out their sock drawers, and their handbags, and their pockets, you would find a fascinating harvest of objects looking faintly like desiccated hamster droppings which, on analysis, would prove to be Peruvian skunk or Colombian gunk, or whatever.

As the police have told me and anyone else who is interested, they cannot possibly enforce the letter of the law as it is currently framed. They can't bust all these people, and bring criminal proceedings against them, any more than they could arrest everyone who is speeding on the M40; and yet they naturally do intercept some abusers, which makes the application of the law seem uneven and therefore unfair.

Now there is an argument for living with such imperfection, and it is one that I have tended in the past to accept. There may be some laws, such as those on speeding and controlled substances, which are not there to delineate a precise boundary between what you may and may not do.

It may be that they are there to act as a kind of cultural drag-anchor, a tug of conscience. The 70mph speed limit may be regularly exceeded, but the mere fact of its existence survives as a whispered reproach to the motorist, and discourages him from being truly reckless. In the same way, cannabis may be smoked everywhere, but the fact that it is still technically illegal serves as an assertion of society's basic disapproval of drugs.

As bans, both laws are hopeless. But they are not meant to work as exact interdictions; they are attempts at mass psychological conditioning. The herd has crashed through the fence, and is busily grazing the forbidden pasture. But the animals do so a little bit nervously, and with a vague sense of restraint, because they know that some of them, sometimes, could still feel the cattle prod of retribution.

That argument, as I say, has tended to satisfy me in the past. I wonder, though, whether it really works. We pay the police to enforce the law, not to engage in a game of bluff with the motorist and the cannabis-user, in which the policeman's bluff is almost always called.

The speed limit is 10mph too low. It bears no relation to the speed motorists actually use, when, as Alan Judd points out in this week's issue of *The Spectator*, fewer people died on the roads in 2000 than in any year since records began in 1926. There were 3,409 deaths last year and 4,886 in 1926, when there were only 1·7 million cars on the roads.

Yes, cannabis is dangerous, but no more than other perfectly legal drugs. It's time for a rethink, and the Tory party – the funkiest, most jiving party on Earth – is where it's happening.

Indian elephant piece

The elephant shuddered beneath me, and when I say shuddered I mean he positively heaved. He chugged, in out, in out, like an old Route-master bus about to expire, waved his dappled trunk, sprayed us with trunk snot, and gave an elephantine whinny. And if you could have seen the goad the mahout was using, you would have seen why.

This tool was about 6lb of forged steel, filed at one end to needle sharpness, and the blunt bit was now being thudded repeatedly into the top of the animal's warty, black-haired, double-domed pleistocene bonce, bonk, bonk, bonk, with the force of a navvy laying a rail.

Me, I didn't complain, because you don't try to back-seat drive an elephant. What is more, I was enjoying the ride, fantasising in my howdah about trampling mogul infantry. But the thought flashed across my mind, as the beast swayed on, and we undulated on top of his vast hips, that all this might soon be banned; not just the goadwork, but perhaps even the elephant routine itself. One day the global blender will complete its work, and western values will penetrate every aspect of Indian life. By New Year's Day 2013, I prophesy, there will be a campaign to stop the use of steel goads on elephants.

There may even be calls to end the custom of sawing their tusks, daubing their foreheads with paint, and allowing them to carry six heavy tourists up the hill to the Rajah's fort. There will be a parallel campaign to stop the clonking of poor deaf cobras with flutes by cross-legged men trying to persuade them to 'dance'; and all will be funded not just by the widow's mites of animal-lovers in Dorking, but by the Indians themselves. Borne by television, western values are seeding themselves everywhere. Many wonderful things will bloom, but some fine things will also be lost.

There could be no better education in the difference between Indian society and western society than to spend the past six days immersed in the preparations and rituals of a vast double wedding. The Indians take it very seriously, this business of being a family member. In India, families are big, not just because the Indians are enthusiastic reproducers of Indians. They stay in intimate contact with relatives who would be, in British terms, quite distant. They ring up. They pay calls. They endlessly confabulate. There is no word for a brother-in-law, or sister-in-law, or a cousin. Everyone is either a brother or a sister.

Looking at this intricate set-up, I found myself mentally contrasting the big American bestseller of last year, which described so well the atomised western family. Jonathan Franzen's *The Corrections* relates the wretched struggle of Ethel, an elderly woman, to convoke her small, scattered family for one last Christmas. Her husband, Albert, has incipient dementia. All three of her adult children know it would mean the world to her if they could be bothered to show up. Franzen paints a gloriously realistic picture, a kind of inverted Norman Rockwell, of their selfishness, their evasions, their instinct for self-gratification. There's one thing worse than the spoilt 11-year-old who refuses to go to Grandma's, and that is the yuppy father who gives way, because the child has made his 'choice', which must be 'respected'.

All these things – casual deprecation of blood ties, endowing children with premature sovereignty – would be thought appalling by Indians; and so would the way we treat our old people. Many good, honest Britons are furious these days to find, in middle life, when they have their own children to look after, tuition fees to pay, pensions and mortgages to worry about, that the state will not do more to help them look after their elderly parents.

Most Indians, on the other hand, would be amazed at the idea. They don't put old people into homes in India, even among the vast and growing middle classes. It is not just a question of repaying the benefits of nurture. Anything else would be a breach of family obligation. None of this is to say that there is something intrinsically superior in the traditional Indian reliance on the family, or that it is necessarily pernicious to create a taxpayer-funded safety net.

It is all too easy, in fact, to see how we have allowed the state to encroach as the family has retreated. The state looks after us, in ways that families cannot. It legislates on such matters as health and safety, and anyone touring the delapidated and precipitous Rajput fortifications of Jaipur could happily wish for a visitation from the most high-minded Dutch-Belgian hygiene inspectors or Scandinavian child protection units. The state does not disapprove of us, or maddeningly insist on judging us by the standards of our nearest relatives. The state does not fuss and cluck, or start weeping if we fail to wear the tie it bought us. The state does not demand any token of reciprocal love, or even of respect. The state just gives us the money.

The state is not oppressive, or claustrophobic, or feud-riven, in the way that a large family can be. It is not the state that is the model of the greatest criminal organisations, in which a code of honour co-exists with terror, and a rule of silence among outsiders. It is the Family. These may be among the reasons why sophisticated western folk have come to prefer the ministrations of the state to those of their relatives.

You might also say that the welfare state deprives people of genuine warmth, and a genuine sense of the need to look out for others, and also deprives them of a great deal of their hard-earned cash. Perhaps, to judge by a paper I bought for 150 rupees, the Tories will one day return some of the cash that is currently being wasted. That is not my point.

My only point is that the Indians stand to lose some good things, as well as gain some good things, if they approximate themselves to our ways, and not just their immemorial skill in making an elephant move in the right direction.

PERSONALITIES

What an odd business it is, the big feature interview. In a sense it is an illustration of the rebalancing of power in Britain, in favour of the media. In France or America, you can still read interviews with politicians or celebrities which consist of reverential Q and A transcripts. British readers, with their jaded palates, want something stronger. They want the revelations, the confessions. They want the sudden grabbing for the hankie. That is why the British hack approaches his interviewee with what is sometimes a frankly treacherous smile.

The interviewer fawns, he beams, he keeps one eye on the little red light on his taperecorder; and then he pounces. If you want a perfect example of the disingenuousness of the modern interviewer, consider the episode of Martin Bashir and Michael Jackson. When the programme was broadcast, it appeared to be a remarkable indictment of whacko Jacko's approach to fatherhood, with the implication that Bashir thought his subject more than slightly weird. But the pop star then turned the tables, by producing the out-takes. These showed the simpering journalist apparently with tears in his eyes congratulating Jacko on his parenting skills, and generally sucking up in a disgusting fashion.

It is because interviews involve these betrayals that PR men have become ever more ruthless in handling them: sitting in, cutting in, turning off the tape, and so on. Journalists, in response, have become ever more ratlike in their cunning. In principle, of course, I am on the side of the hacks.

After all, journalists have to turn these maunderings into something readable, and it is sometimes very difficult, faced with a great dumper truck of verbal gravel, to pick out the pebbles for the mosaic. For my own part, I have always tried to be faithful to the drift and mood of the conversation, even if there is a lot one must necessarily cut. I also tend to like my subjects, though Chris Evans and I were probably quite relieved when our game of golf was over.

Jimmy Goldsmith

The riot police have silenced the students outside. The crowds press in at the back. The water trembles in the glass on the podium as the compère steps forward in the conference hall in Rennes, Brittany, and a quiet falls on the thousand people, fanning themselves with campaign literature 'And now!' he says into the mike. 'Zhimé Gol'smees!' For it is he.

Yes: the billionaire ecologist, the former owner of Marmite, the founder of *Now!*, the Sir Jams Fishfingers of *Private Eye*, one of the truly extraordinary capitalists of his generation, is about to give the most important stump speech so far in his first attempt at elective office.

As the people of Rennes clap him to the stage – old Breton women in elasticated knee-length tights, young shiny-faced students from the university – the TV cameras track his white head bowed in concentration. Some of the journalists are already sympathetic. 'He's the billionaire with the beautiful eyes,' a woman from *Le Figaro* whispers. '*Il aime la femme avec un F majuscule!*' she adds, having spent some days trailing him across France.

And the questions form again in the mind: why is he doing this, a man who has everything – two national identities, three concurrent families, eight children and an estimated £880 million in personal funds? Will he really be elected to Strasbourg, mother-in-law of parliaments? Why does he seek such an honour? And will the burghers of Rennes approve the Anglo-French Midas who has struck fear into the boardrooms of Europe and America?

Back in Paris, the day before, Goldsmith sets it all out. We are in rue Monsieur, a half-timbered house with a grassy stableyard once belonging to the brother of the king of France. Birds twitter through the open French windows as I try to pump him about where this is coming from, and where it is going.

What I want to know, and what I think we in Britain want to know, is whether this could be a prelude to the general emergence of Goldsmith the politician; not just in France but even in Britain, the country that has sometimes treated him so caustically.

As the world remembers, Sir James Goldsmith mystified brokers by liquidating all his assets, down to his house in New York, in the summer and early autumn of 1987. And when, sure enough, the markets melted on Black Monday, October 19, in New York, London and Tokyo, he was left with the reverence of his peers and about one billion dollars.

Since then he has been husbanding it, taking a punt on gold, doing I know not what. 'Money is a tool, not a religion,' he says now. But a tool for what? A tool for taking things a bit more gently now that he is 61 with a mild case of diabetes, requiring a man to carry medicines for him in a hold-all wherever he goes?

A tool for adorning Montjeu, his château in Burgundy, or for jetting off to Cuixmala, his 18,000-acre Eden on the Pacific coast of Mexico, complete with support village, crocodiles and animals from John Aspinall's zoo?

Or is it, also, Sir James, a tool for a new career in public life?

'All that has happened was wholly unplanned. I'd been trying to re-establish my anonymity.' Re-establish? 'I'd had anonymity until I was 20,' he avows, delicately reminding one that it was at 20 that Goldsmith first made the front page, eloping with the Latin beauty Isabel Patino, Bolivian tin-mining heiress, and sending her poor father in a Benny Hill-style pursuit around the hotels of Scotland, with much of Fleet-Street in the rear.

From that moment, via Isabel's death in childbirth a few months later, to the selling of his interests to Hanson and others by 1990, he has seldom left the consciousness of news editors. Anonymity was at last returning, he claims, when in 1992 a French female TV producer rang him out of the blue.

He made a one-hour programme. He spoke on an issue that was troubling him. He called for a referendum on Maastricht.

Since then, with gathering fervour, he has given public vent to his obsession with Europe and world trade. At the risk of slick, journalistic analogy, he seems to see the Brussels bureaucracy with the eye of a corporate raider. Overmanned, excessively diversified; in need of returning to its core businesses; if necessary, in need of breaking up.

His Goldsmith Foundation, it is no secret, has helped leading Tory Euro-rebel Bill Cash in his fight in London. He sponsored William Rees-Mogg's doomed attempt to foil Maastricht in the English courts. Then he was

440

approached by the Vicomte Philippe de Villiers, a smooth, aristocratic right-wing Gaullist of royalist tendencies. Would he join L'Autre Europe, his anti-Maastricht 'list' for this month's elections. In February he accepted.

This is no mere philanthropy, mind you. Goldsmith is No 2 on the list and, with L'Autre Europe riding at between 5 and 7 per cent in the polls, French political analysts say his chances of striding the lush brown lobbies of Strasbourg are better than evens.

Now he lays into the treaty in the fluent drawl, with the slightest hesitation over his Rs, of a man used to dominating the kind of dinner parties that are attended by Henry Kissinger. Speaking French, the language of his mother, Goldsmith is said to have *un petit accent*. Speaking English, though, the language of his father, he also has an accent; modulated since Eton into something else, not foreign, not exactly mid-Atlantic; perhaps it is just *rich*.

'Sovereign power has passed to 17 unsackable and unelected commissioners, the greatest transfer of power in peacetime, and it took place under a system of organised secrecy. That is not me,' he adds, quoting Claude Cheysson and Jacques Delors to the effect that there was a deliberate attempt to keep the public in the dark. Maastricht is a recipe for centralisation, for vast, corrupt, Italianate spending on construction projects. Above all, it will sanctify global free trade.

Nothing quite prepares one for the charm of Goldsmith. His laugh is booming, conspiratorial. I had always imagined a burly tycoon. In fact, he is tall and gangly. Today he is wearing a grey suit with a white handkerchief in his breast pocket, tapering brown half-brogues and a gold tie, the same one, I think, in which he was photographed for the cover of *Time*. He deploys his erudition, including quite detailed knowledge of the Maastricht Treaty's articles, to persuasive effect.

But on this point I object. It seems a bit thin to say that Maastricht's article 3a enshrines free trade any more than the Treaty of Rome. And anyway, isn't free trade a good thing?

He leaps up, taking from his pocket a disc of red amber, the one that Aspinall gave him and which he uses to stave off the desire to smoke.

'It's a disaster of incredible proportions. Its one of the greatests crimes of the 20th century.' Listen, he says, circling a marble inlay table. Four billion people are being brought on to the world market, thanks to Gatt. Already, since the British introduced freer trade to the Community in 1972, French unemployment has risen by 800 per cent, while GDP has grown by a mere 80 per cent.

He cites a recent World Bank report on the global free exchange of goods and labour: the developed will get poorer and the underdeveloped countries will not get richer.

But look, I say, what about the consumer? What about economic efficiency? Why shouldn't people be able to buy cheap garments from China?

'F*** Chinese underpants!' he explodes. 'Let me explain to you that the world is not all about the price of Chinese underpants.'

But is it not futile, I say, to try to construct a little, transient, protectionist moat around Europe? Won't it eventually burst, with even more deleterious consequences for industry and employment?

'A little moat!' he retorts. 'The largest free market in the world, 350 million people rising to 500 million.' To allow free access for Asian goods, he says, is 'just like bringing in immigrants. These people have been separated by politics, lack of technology, lack of capital. Why not take it a bit further? Allow them into your house! Why don't you bring them in! Invite them in!'

All right, then, I say, what about the welfare of the Third World paupers; what about their right to haul themselves up by their bootstraps and earn foreign exchange. What else do they have in their slums but the chance to make use of competitive advantage?

With a roar Goldsmith is on his feet again. For a moment he seems genuinely angry. Not only do the British have an incurable delusion about free trade, but I have also misunderstood Ricardo's theory of comparative advantage. 'I am sorry. I am sorry. It is impossible to talk to you, because you . . . I must stop.'

But of course, he does not stop, continuing to map out his world view, from the half-life of plutonium to the 24,000 strains of potatoes, for more than an hour.

At present, to be sure, he sounds like a voice in the wilderness. Most other businessmen think he is wrong to call for protection. But the reader should know that it is in the teeth of precisely such unanimity that Goldsmith has an amazing knack of being proved right.

One fellow tycoon describes Goldsmith coming into his office in 1970 and warning that the oil-producing countries might soon conspire to drive the price up to $50 per barrel. One thinks of the way he borrowed $660 million to revamp Grand Union, an ailing chain of American super-markets, and was vindicated.

Mainly, one thinks of him getting on the telephone to his friends in the summer of 1987, warning them that the price of yachts and executive planes was too high, and to get out while they could.

Goldsmith's father, Major Frank, was MP for Stowmar-ket. Major Frank's political ambitions were thwarted by anti-German feeling in the First World War, and he went on to become one of the leading hoteliers of France. Jimmy, say his supporters, has never lost interest in British politics. This is the man who had dinner in the 1970s with Edward

443

Heath, was knighted by Harold Wilson and whose name has even been mentioned in connection with running Conservative Central Office. So: cometh the hour, cometh the man?

Absolutely not, apparently. 'In the UK I can see zero opportunity, because there is no party I could join.' What about the Tories? 'First, I would not be selected. I certainly would not. Secondly, I would be under a hierarchy I disapproved of.

'In England, how can you vote for anything except one policy, because it is the same policy, Conservative, Liberal or Socialist?' He then says, in words that Mr Major might do well to heed: 'The mould has to be broken. It probably will be. The press has a role to play, for the very simple reason that, as there was no opposition, the press had to be an opposition.

'I don't exclude the possibility of a split in the Conservative party. I don't exclude the possibility of a total revolution in the Conservative party, a complete change of guard.'

If he is right, and the revolution comes, I have little doubt that Jimmy Goldsmith will be, at the least, its quartermaster. If one thing, though, appears to keep him from these shores, it may be a reluctance to undergo England's inevitably prurient scrutiny of his triple ménage: with Ginette, the French woman he married after the death of Isabel; with Lady Annabel, former wife of club owner Mark Birley; and with the French journalist Laure Boulay de la Meurthe, said to be the main woman in his life these days.

'I have no doubt that culturally the way I like to live is more compatible with modern French standards. I am talking about the way I lead my life, which I do according to my own standards, and that is acceptable to the French, who are not interested in other people's lives.

'I am not suggesting one system is better than another. One suits me better than the other, and frankly I am uninterested in other people's sex lives. Perhaps they'd make me jealous.'

I remember at school my friends and I deeply admired Jimmy Goldsmith: the way he had been expelled and went on to make a billion while we clocked up our ritual academic distinctions; his semi-Muslim concept of marriage; his ecological concerns, shared with his brother Teddy. We were too young to remember the Goldenballs case, or where right and wrong lay in the battle with *Private Eye*.

Having met him, I can see why he is assumed to be faintly bonkers, just as Lady Thatcher is assumed to be faintly bonkers. Perhaps he is ruthless, perhaps erratic; perhaps his pessimism is linked, psychologically, with his enormous material success. But he seems to have a vision, intelligence and breadth of understanding quite alien to the present strain of British politicians.

And he impresses the people of Rennes, too. They have mainly come to hear Philippe de Villiers, whose toffish populism recalls Oswald Mosley. But they clap Goldsmith like thunder when he tells them about the relative wages of a Frenchman and a Vietnamese. The stifling air has given way to a downpour, and as the Goldsmith bandwagon vanishes into the night to board his private jet from Rennes back to Paris, the discussion goes on as the crowds file out.

They are all demagogues, says Morgan Leroux, a medical student. 'Protectionism leads inevitably to fascism,' he explains.

But Anne Boutheon, 21, another student in a little lacy top, believes she has heard a visionary. 'He is not just thinking about the elections. He has a long-term view. It is up to us to spread the message,' she says.

445

Ken Clarke

One could swear there is something deliberate about the way one of the scuffed brown shoes has its lace undone; something calculated in the uninhibited convexities of his frame; the frequent laugh that gurgles from his merry face. And when he vanishes to an antechamber to slick back his hair for the photographer, it is, perhaps, a sign of the underlying self-possession that has made him among the most durable of modern politicians.

For the followers of political Wisden, the Treasury is Ken Clarke's seventh department of state. Along with Malcolm Rifkind and Lynda Chalker, he is the longest continuously serving minister since Lloyd George; and you don't survive that long in British politics by tactlessness alone. He is the bull in a china shop who is actually rather careful about the china.

'You're not going to talk about Europe,' he says with an air of mock dread. People are so obsessive about the subject, he complains. We both chortle. Of course I am going to ask him about Europe. But first, how does he propose to save the next election?

Will he guarantee to cut taxes in the next Budget, assuming there is one? He has a way of drowning his opponent by repeating the word he happens to be stuck on.

'I, I, I had this disagreement with the Conservative press, or what used to be the Conservative press, last autumn. I don't think the fortunes of the Government entirely depend on us producing enormous tax cuts for the population.

'To offer tax cuts purely as an electoral bribe, I, I think underrates the intelligence of the electorate. In fact the electorate is rather cynical about us, and it does not want to have the Government behaving as though just giving them big tax cuts before an election entitles the Government to be re-elected.

'I want to offer the public the prospect that any tax cuts we have made will last, and that there may be more to come if we're re-elected.'

'What do you mean bribes?' I say, feigning outrage at this sensible answer. It's our money, isn't it?

'It's our money, it's our money. That's right. The Government should restrict the extent to which it takes away people's own money. But first you control the Government, then you make tax cuts.'

Yes, but are you as macho about budget-cutting as you should be? John Major and William Waldegrave, the Chief Secretary, seem to think government spending could fall to 35 per cent of GDP. But Mr Clarke was lately reported to believe 40 per cent was the minimum in a civilised society.

Get away, says Clarke. 'I was the guy who *set* a 40 per cent target in the first place. I've had the three toughest public spending rounds I think since the war, in getting down to the 42 per cent we're at now, and still falling.

'So I don't personally regard myself as the last of the big spenders', chuckle, chuckle, chortle. I try a different tack with this One-Nation Tory. What, I ask, is the difference between you and Tony Blair?

'Between myself and Tony Blair?' He leans back. Clarke thinks he's rumbled the point of the interview. I'm out to paint him as a Lefty.

'Firstly, my instincts for a market economy, my instincts for a deregulated economy; my instincts for a flexible Labour market; my instincts against the power of the vested interest lobbies, have always set me well apart from anyone in the Labour Party.

'If he's a One-Nation Tory, I'm a monkey's uncle.'

According to Clarke, Blair would never have taken on

the vested interests of the nurses, the police, the doctors, the teachers. He is proudest of the NHS reforms and attributes his success to 'strong convictions and, ha ha ha, probably an excessive self-confidence'. Self-confidence is right. Whence does it come?

'My self-confidence? I suppose it comes from the process of having done it for a long time and being reshuffled a lot, and learning from one's mistakes.'

Ken Clarke was born in Nottingham in 1940. His father was a pit electrician. His grandfather was a communist. 'He was a very formidable character, my mother's father, a very, very nice man, a communist and not remotely a Marxist, who fell for the Uncle Joe Stalin bit.

'The only newspaper he would take in the house was the *Morning Star*. He said it was the only one you could believe.'

And did his upbringing ever trigger any Left-wing impulses? 'Yes, but only at school. When I went up to university I joined all the political parties because everybody did. I wasn't sure what political party I had any allegiance to when I arrived.'

The Cambridge Tory mafia which Clarke joined was characterised more by ambition than Right-wing fervour. But he was reactionary in his way. For instance, he voted against women joining the Union, of which he was President. 'I now think that was a mistake,' says Clarke. 'If the Garrick club had a vote now on the admission of women, I'd vote for them.'

I tell him that in Edwina Currie's latest bonkbuster he is portrayed as Bampton, the pot-bellied, cigar-puffing Health Secretary from the Midlands, conventionally married with two children. Bampton is a cynical sexist who lets the heroine down. Let's take these charges of Currie in order.

Pot-bellied? That's Clarke. 'Do I look like a man who goes to an effort to keep fit? I enjoy robust good health', says the man who was a wonderful, walking reproof to the nannying tendencies of other Health Secretaries. 'My outdoor activities are the occasional good long walk and bird-watching'.

Cigar-puffing? Check.

Conventionally married? Well, Clarke's wife, Gillian, an exceedingly clever medieval historian with an auntyish appearance, is not exactly an Edwina Currie heroine, but the Clarkes are said to be devoted to one another. The Midlands? Yes, that was where Clarke practised as a barrister for 16 years.

Two children? Spot on, Edwina. Now both married, the Clarke children were educated in good One-Nation Tory fashion, leaving their state primary schools at 11 for the independent sector. 'I went through the same process Mr Blair is supposed to have gone through, but in my case there was no hypocrisy or crisis of conscience,' he says.

And what about these allegations of sexism, Mr Clarke? Did you let Edwina down when, as a junior minister in your department, she issued her *fatwa* against eggs?

'Yes, she has a grievance against me over the eggs saga – even though I was about the last member of the Government to argue that she shouldn't be driven out over it. I tried to defend her.

'She, she, she criticises me now for telling her to stop making public statements, but the reason I did that was she kept repeating the original error. She says it is sexism. That is rubbish, absolute rubbish. Well I don't think I'm remotely sexist. I don't think anybody in the world would regard me as sexist.'

But Clarke has far more powerful opponents on the opposite end of the party: the men of the New Right – no names, no pack-drill – who see him as the last and most dangerous exponent of what used to be called 'wetness'.

'If you ask me to answer my Right-wing critics, who I

am told do regard me as a sort of slightly worrying character, I regard it as baffling,' says Clarke. 'Because I regard myself as someone who's followed a very straightforward approach of being a market economist, and a fairly orthodox one.

'Some of today's Thatcherites are not in my opinion the real thing. I'm not going to name names. But people who proclaim themselves Thatcherite now hold views which were not the views of the Thatcher Government. Ten years ago, when the health reforms were at their most difficult, I was regarded as a very Right-wing, rather thug-like, Conservative.

'So it's Europe,' he says almost sadly. He brings it up, not I. 'People have got this curious idea that if you're Europhile you're Left-wing and if you're Euro-sceptic you're Right-wing.

'I don't regard myself as a federalist and never have. I believe in a union of nation states,' he says. No, Mr Clarke. But the issue is the single currency, of which you are emphatically in favour.

'I am sympathetic to the idea,' he says, though he enters the usual caveats about achieving economic convergence. 'I think if it happens it will matter a lot to us whether we're in or out.'

A fellow cabinet minister says if and when the moment comes, Clarke will lead a splinter group of 40 Tories who favour a single currency. That moment may never come. But if it does, the great thing about Ken Clarke is that we know exactly where he will stand.

Clare Short

Whoever handles Clare Short's PR does a fine job. The advance billing was becoming positively wearisome. Everyone who heard I was going to meet Labour's transport spokesperson seemed to go into a kind of fit. Oh, Clare! My dear! 'You'll love her!'

'You'll fall in love!' It was her crusty glamour, apparently. Her gipsy charm. So authentic, so real. She's not at all like her public persona, I was assured.

I was told to forget about how the tabloids try to portray her as Killjoy Clare, the grim-jawed persecutor of the tit-and-bum merchants, the militant, childless, snaggle-toothed Fenian feminist of the hard Left. And, of course, the more I was urged to sit back and enjoy the Clare Short experience, the deeper the iron entered the soul.

One does not like to be schmoozed. We hacks are desperadoes, professional cynics. We do not lightly allow our prejudices to be brushed aside. So I entered her office in No 7 Millbank determined to uncover the Stalinist harridan within; an hour later I left in a state of rout.

She took my coat. She brushed my arm. She laughed with a great throaty cackle at my excuse for being late (no trains to King's Cross from Highbury), which delighted the transport spokesman on the eve of her cunning announcement about how Labour intends to buy back the railways without, supposedly, spending a dime.

And it was when she plied me with coffee in a mug bearing the insignia of Emily's List, the ginger group for getting women into politics, that I remembered my mission.

Thanks largely to Clare Short's lobbying of John Smith, Labour muscled another 35 women on to its candidates' list. The European Court has lately banned the practice for flagrant sexism; yet if Labour comes to power, they can expect about 90 female MPs in the party alone.

When you listen to the Commons in the next few years, don't be surprised if the baying has gone up an octave. Starting from tomorrow night, the BBC will be giving us a taster of the coming feminocracy with a series called *Ladies of the House*, featuring Voortrekkers such as Barbara Castle and Gillian Shephard.

Clare Short stars in the first programme. The question, though, is whether she will be rewarded in person for her pioneering work. Will she, like them, make it to the Cabinet?

For if she has one engaging characteristic, it is a failure to watch her mouth. The word in Westminster is that the Blairocrats were none too chuffed by her recent performance on the *Today* programme. The hard young men say she was slurred; forgivable, one might think, since it was not yet 8am.

Rumour tells of a feud between her and Brian Wilson, an able and sharp-suited Scot who understudies her at transport and is said to be nipping at her heels. And popular though she is in the parliamentary party, it has not been forgotten that she did not vote for Blair in the leadership election.

So come on, Clare, what do you think of this Pied Piper turning you all into an SDP Mark II?

'We've got a good working relationship,' she says in her Birmingham voice.

Aha. Not soulmates, then?

Actually, says Clare, she recognises in Blair the same sense of moral indignation which, she says, is her own motivating force. 'Because he's glamorous and pretty and good at soundbites, he can look more synthetic than he is. I go for the firm interior rather than the glitzy exterior.'

452

Very well, then. What about Harriet Harman sending her child to that grant-maintained school? We saw on television how that got up her nose. New Labour cracked open, and Old Labour came bubbling through.

'In reality I was saying, I don't know all the facts, and that I was not going to sit here and pontificate about Harriet's choices.'

Okay. Now that you know all the facts, what do you think?

'Well,' she says, 'I am not going to sit here and pontificate about Harriet's choices. I have my views.'

Now if she had been a real Blairite, Clare would have worked out some weaselly formula exculpating Harriet Harman for her sin – using an educational option officially anathematised by Labour policy. She would have found some way of blaming the Tories.

But she didn't. Her views were written all over her face, which, while we are on the subject, is far more handsome than it appears on television or in most photographs; her hair and skin seem vaguely lustrous, though when the photographer comes, she claims, somewhat against the evidence, to have a spot on her chin.

She's honest, Clare Short. She left the Catholic Church at 16 because she thought it was silly to say people shouldn't use contraception. She recently found herself in piping hot water with the Blairocracy, when she was deemed to be in favour of legalising cannabis. As she now explains on the cannabis front: 'What I should have said as a member of the Shadow Cabinet is that this is a matter for Jack Straw, and I gather this is not his view at the moment . . .'

Er, it's not his view *at the moment*? How often does he change his view?

She laughs like a gurgling drain. The flexibility of Jack Straw's opinions on law and order is a subject for Left-wing Labour despair. 'Sorry! It's not his view, full stop.'

The outlines of authentic Old Labour are beginning to emerge. Given that Blair may yet face a schism in his own party on the single currency, she is embarrassingly honest, too, about European monetary union.

Clare has nothing against currencies circulating freely: 'I remember when I was a child, we went on holidays in the west of Ireland, and you could buy ice-cream with your Irish money or your Birmingham money.'

But EMU fills her with old-fashioned Left-wing dread. 'The Maastricht criteria are so deflationary that they would drive Europe into the most terrible recession with the most dreadful social and economic consequences if it goes too fast. For countries that are economically less successful now, it could entrench them into a second-rate position in the EU, and Britain could be in that position.'

Clare Short was born not quite 50 years ago in Dudley Road Hospital, Ladywood, Birmingham. Her family is Irish, and she is an instinctive supporter of the republican cause. 'My father came from Crossmaglen, three miles north of the border, in the bandit country of South Armagh.' (For bandit, read murderer, I suppose).

'My family come from an area which straddles the border, and the border is irrational in that area. My father, who was a brilliant guy, felt very deeply about it, very hurt, very angry that they'd drawn this line in his country, and I grew up with that. That affected our world view.

'We grew up thinking that the British empire wasn't a good thing, and that it was a good thing that India gained its independence and that slavery was abolished.'

Do you really mean to say the empire wasn't a good thing?

'No, it wasn't.'

The British empire ended slavery, though; no one else.

'The British empire helped to *organise* slavery.'

Well, I say, it was the native rulers of West Africa who invented and also helped to organise slavery.

'It was the black African kings who had feudal friends in Europe. They both organised slavery,' says Clare, and our discussion on slavery ends with a nil-nil scoreline.

'It all depends where you come from,' she goes on. 'My ancestors were depicted historically as ape-like creatures. There is a "mass" rock near the village where my ancestors came from, and I go there because I have got aunts who are getting older and more precious. The rock is where my ancestors went for mass because the Brits were persecuting them for practising their religion.'

Clare Short has had a hard life in many ways, not least witnessing the slow and miserable death of her husband, former Labour minister Alex Lyon, from Alzheimer's disease in 1993. But she seems to be one of those school-of-hard-knocks types whose temperamental reaction is to stand up for the underdog.

In that same group she would put the poor, the old, the PLO, the IRA, and aspirant female politicians. I ask her, finally, why it is so essential to have more women in the House of Commons. Is the place really so disreputable?

She admits that the Commons can have great moments of theatre, such as Mrs Thatcher's resignation speech, or Sir Geoffrey Howe's attack on Thatcher . . .

Or Michael Howard's demolition of Jack Straw?

'Ye-e-,' says Clare, and then catches herself. 'Well, I wasn't there for that,' she says diplomatically.

But she says the problem with the Commons is that it's full of Billy Bunterish males, all going yah-boo. 'It's second-rate grot,' she says.

Women would be more reasonable, she says. They speak their minds. 'I don't think women are of superior moral quality to men. But we tend to be outsiders, and that's where being less sleazy comes from.'

But will women always be less sleazy than men? 'Oh, I think if 100 years from now, women are as much part of the institutions of power as men, they will have equally undesirable characteristics.'

So if you get your way, I say, we are all doomed to endure the transformation of the Commons from a bearpit into a touchy-feely Finnish-style seminar with everyone sitting in the round and being careful not to disagree.

'People like you create such distortions because you find the idea of women being as bright as men terrifying,' she says. 'Well don't worry!' and she laughs so much that the idea seems almost benign.

Harry Wu

Next time you have a cup of tea or, who knows, pull on a pair of silky Chinese underpants, think of the word Lao-gai. 'I want to see this word appear in every dictionary in every language in every country,' says Harry Wu.

Laogai is the Chinese equivalent of gulag. It means reform through labour. You wouldn't think it to look at the 59-year-old Wu, sipping his coffee in his business suit in the penthouse of a London hotel, with his full head of black hair and the healthy glow to his skin. But he has spent the best years of his life in hell.

He was born in Shanghai in 1937, and that was when he made his first two mistakes. He was a Catholic and he was bourgeois. 'My father is a banker, a very good friend of the Keswick family. The communists want to destroy the bourgeois class, and you cannot practise religion.'

He made his next serious mistake in 1957. 'I'm a student and the 20-year-old captain of the baseball team. In my class meeting I say the Soviet invasion of Hungary violates international law. They tell me – your opinion is not a flower, it is a poisonous weed. You are a counter-revolutionary Rightist. You are finished. You have to confess and make a self-criticism.'

Wu objected. What, he asked, was the point of Chairman Mao's new policy, Let A Hundred Flowers Bloom? 'They said, You are attacking the party. My crime was slight but my attitude was bad.'

His difficulties dragged on until he was framed for the theft of 50 yuan. In 1960 he tried to escape. That was his fourth mistake, and he paid for it with 19 years in forced labour camps.

Harry Wu is now the world's greatest expert on the Laogai. The Chinese government says it has 1.2 million people in such prisons – giving China a slightly smaller per capita prison population than Britain. Wu says there are 1,115 camps containing up to eight million people. He calculates that they produce at least 120 items, from tea to plastic flowers to diesel engines, regularly sold to the West.

There will be those who say there is nothing wrong, per se, in buying the product of convict labour. Do British lags not stitch mail bags and make dolls' houses? And reading Harry Wu's book, *Trouble-maker*, it is clear that his cause has been taken up by those, such as American unions, who have half an eye to protection against Chinese goods. The question is what kind of people are kept in these camps, and in what circumstances. Wu worked in 12 camps, including a chemical factory and a steel mill.

During the 19 years in which his youth was stolen and his family persecuted, he was tortured; he was never allowed to see his girl-friend again; he suffered a broken back and other injuries; he was kept in solitary confinement measuring 3ft by 3ft by 6ft.

He was taught to survive on frogs and rats; he saw his

friends die of dysentery in the fields; when he fell asleep standing up he was woken with the blow of a rifle butt.

He was released at the age of 42, following the death of Mao, and fled to find relatives in California. But on clandestine missions back to China, he has substantiated his claims about the Laogai, which have been independently attested by human rights organisations.

He has proved the existence of a trade in kidneys and corneas from prisoners executed for the purpose. Now he emanates cold anger at the complaisance of the West.

'Five months ago Mr Henry Kissinger said there was no fundamental contradiction between the US and China. Well, I'm very interested by that. China is a dictatorship. The US is the world's number one capitalist democracy. Mr Henry Kissinger, what are you talking about? The West has sold China capitalist values, stock market, copyright, paying bills on time. But they have not sold the Chinese fundamental human rights.'

Won't democracy and freedom prove uncontainable, as economic reform gathers pace? Wu is only partly optimistic. 'There is no denial that China is changing. We have a 1.3 billion labour force, double-digit growth rates. You see new buildings, improving living standards.

'So many Chinese travel abroad, plus there will be the integration of the Hong Kong Chinese next year. They will be like a six-million virus killing communism and encouraging political and religious freedom.

'But the country is still fundamentally lawless and entirely controlled by the communists.'

The problem, he says, is not really ideology. 'Communist ideology is finished. Chinese culture is the basement, the soil. It is very good for these dictatorships. In Confucius there is nothing about democracy or human rights. Everybody has a position, and it's been the same for the last

2,300 years. The brainwashing applies to the whole country.

'They are like frogs at the bottom of the well – isolated. The frog asks what is the sky? The circle at the top of the well. They believe it. They are mentally destroyed.'

Wu plays down comparisons with Solzhenitsyn. The Laogai are not the Arctic gulag, and Deng's China is not the same as Stalin's Russia. But the regime is nonetheless abominable.

Instead of admitting China to the World Trade Organisation, with Most Favoured Nation trading status, she should be shunned, he says. In the years he has been in California, he has done China spectacular political damage. He receives repeated death threats.

Still he goes back incognito to find out more, most recently in 1995 when – the story of *Trouble-maker* – he was arrested and imprisoned for six weeks, despite his US passport.

Will he go back again? 'Even if they have three million military, and 1.5 million police. I don't have a pistol but I will go. Not to make trouble is impossible.' As Socrates said.

Buthelezi

He was black South Africa's last best hope. He was the venerated Zulu chief who campaigned against apartheid and for the release of Nelson Mandela.

He was championed by Western conservative leaders as the man with true compassion for the poor blacks, who saw that sanctions would not work, and who rejected the armed struggle.

And in the sweep of history, there are those who say he

will go down as the big loser; the man who saw the prize
– the leadership of democratic South Africa – awarded
amid global acclaim to the man who had been imprisoned
for his role in a terrorist conspiracy.

By the end of the apartheid regime, the Zulu leader's
moderation looked perilously like collaboration; members
of his Inkatha movement appeared to have been in cahoots
with the white security forces: and his own leadership was
implicated in the bloody feuding between Inkatha and the
African National Congress.

Marginalised by the new ANC government, routinely
outvoted in cabinet, he might perhaps be forgiven, at the
age of 66, for accepting the verdict of history, and conced-
ing the fight.

But if you are the Nkosi of the eight million Zulus, if
you are the great-grandson of Cetewayo, if the blood of
warriors courses in your veins, you do not just give up.

This Wednesday Chief Mangosuthu 'Gatsha' Buthelezi
is contesting the local elections in Kwa-Zulu Natal, and
yesterday his cavalcade was sending up dust round
Durban, as 20,000 turned out to hear him.

This time there are none of the leopard-skin accessories,
the winged head-gear and lion-claw necklaces. This campaign has mobile phones and Ian Greer Associates, the
London political consultants.

For this campaign, the underlying message is still that
the Zulu nation deserves a measure of autonomy, and that
President Mandela has reneged on a promise of international arbitration. But this time the rhetoric goes beyond
Zulu nationalism.

The Chief has returned to the free-market liberalism he
adopted during the age of apartheid, and his theme is that
South Africa is now approaching political despotism and
economic disaster.

He sets out all his ideas in the Intercontinental Hotel,

Hyde Park Corner, overlooking Buckingham Palace Gardens, where he has made a one-night kraal to attend the birthday party of John Aspinall, the zoo-keeper and honorary Zulu.

Buthelezi's state is kingly, his entourage standing in silent respect while he changes in his bedroom, reappearing with a goose-motif tie and a faint whiff of cologne.

He is faintly reproving, in his husky voice, when I try to fast-forward some of the history of the ANC-Inkatha feud. 'We shouldn't get there quickly Mr Johnson. I think this background is important . . .'

For he wants me to know that he has nothing personal against Mr Mandela, who is making a state visit to Britain on July 9.

'I have had a relationship with him for about 40 years as a friend. We were both in the ANC, and I would say without boasting that there is no one who campaigned harder for his release.

'One must try to be balanced and say that President Mandela suffered for the struggle. For 27 years, which is a big segment of one's life, he was in jail.

'But all of us now cannot look at why he was jailed, but at the fact that for 27 years this human being was deprived of his liberty.'

The trouble, says Chief Buthelezi, is the way that the sainted one is leading the country: not just the Left-wing ideology that has led to a sharp fall in the Rand, a 73 per cent rise in the professional exodus, and which the magazine *Business Day* says has set South Africa 'firmly on the road to banana-republic poverty'.

There is a more sinister resemblance, both to the old Soviet Union, and the old South Africa. 'There is a tendency to develop towards some kind of autocracy,' he says.

Does he mean a one-party state?

'Absolutely. One has to understand that the media is

461

biased, even more than here. It gives the picture that everything is rosy in the garden.

'But in the alliance of the ANC, you've got the ANC, the South African Communist Party, and you've got the Congress of South African Trades Unions.

'People tend to overlook the Communist Party in South Africa because it hasn't got a big following. But its influence is beyond its size, because right up to the Cabinet there are communists, and that is why, even though as a government we have agreed to restructure and privatise, they are totally against it.

'The influence of the Congress of Trades Unions is actually unbelievable, unbelievable. In fact, one might say children are nowadays beginning to wonder who is the president, because when they go on strike, the president goes out there and supports them publicly.'

There was even a 'no lock-out' clause written into the constitution, he says.

I ask what investors are supposed to make of all this, and he checks himself a little. He is after all a cabinet minister on foreign soil, when 50 per cent of his people are unemployed.

'I can see that there are lots of people who want to come to help us, but I can see why if I were in their shoes, I would also hesitate.'

It is exactly as he always said in the age of apartheid: South Africa depends on foreign investment, and 'as my old friend Baroness Thatcher once put it, you can't buck the markets'. But is he not himself partly to blame for the instability, for setting on the Inkatha thugs who have a shared responsibility for the 15,000 dead since 1985? That, naturally, he denies.

Buthelezi is now more powerful than for many years. He is in no hurry to follow De Klerk's whites into opposition.

But the next elections are in 1999, and if ANC-led South

Africa sinks into an Albanian morass, he will not hesitate to say, I told you so. 'I am not saying my party will remain in the government forever.'

F W De Klerk

As ye sow, so shall ye reap. Once the Afrikaner discriminated against the black man on the grounds of his colour. Now the boot is on the other foot, and the deposed leader fights for the rights of his white tribe, even of its guttural tongue.

'Afrikaans is the only one of our 11 official languages where something is being taken away,' complains F W de Klerk. 'There has been a reduction of airtime on TV; Afrikaans medium schools are under pressure from the ANC.

'They are trying to implement a melting-pot theory and they are reducing Afrikaans from where it was, co-equal with English, to the status of other indigenous languages.'

Only the other day, he says, the ANC education minister made a 'very threatening speech' with regard to the language policy of Stellenbosch, the oldest Afrikaans university in South Africa.

Once F W was the all-powerful president of white South Africa; thousands at his bidding sped (or, he maintains, in the case of some of the more zealous members of BOSS, the Bureau of State Security, not at his bidding). Now he finds himself shorn of his jet, exiled from the tint-windowed cavalcade, out of power, and closeted in a windowless conference room in the Holiday Inn, Cambridge, where he has been addressing undergraduates.

A single overhead light glows on his pate, and the smoke spirals up from his endless cigarettes. I feel rather like the

Truth and Reconciliation Commission, poking under the flat rocks of the old regime. De Klerk has apologised for the sins of his once-mighty National Party. 'We have gone on our knees before Almighty God to pray for His forgiveness,' says the strict *gereformeede* Calvinist. It cuts no ice.

Under the chairmanship of Archbishop Desmond Tutu, South Africa's new masters are using the commission to exact humiliation. 'On the last occasion I was treated as if I were in the dock,' he says.

'I was subjected to a form of cross-examination by an advocate working for the commission, which evoked a highly critical response even from newspapers which have no great love for me.

'Archbishop Tutu clearly transgressed the provisions of the law in attacking my party's integrity.' He wants Tutu to give an unqualified apology. He wants the insolent lawyer sacked.

He believes there is an 'imbalance in the Truth Commission, in the time, energy and money spent'. All the fire is concentrated on the white regime, and none on ANC terror.

One feels like saying, my dear old Boer, what did you expect? Frederik Willem de Klerk is the heir of Verwoerd and P W Botha, a man who was once seen as a hardline defender of 'separate development', or apartheid. When he became president in 1989, he warned that he would not 'reform himself out of power'. And yet that is just what he did.

In the early 1990s he was the Gorbachev of Africa. He sprang Mandela. He dismantled apartheid. He shared the Nobel Peace Prize. He established one man, one vote. And now he is paying the price.

Mandela never accepted the Swiss-style constitution he proposed; and last year, fed up with being marginalised, de Klerk quit the government. He must have known that this would happen, that the minority tyranny of apartheid would be followed by the majority tyranny of black rule.

He can hardly be amazed that the Truth Commission has taken on the Orwellian flavour its name suggests, or that it is being used in a partisan way. So why did he unleash these forces? Was it principle, or did he realise that the gig was up for white rule, that dark thumbs were about to close on the National Party's windpipe?

'I never had a Damascus Road experience when it suddenly dawned on me. The policies of separate development failed, because of demographic and economic realities. I decided we cannot build a future on injustice if the end of that injustice is not in sight,' he says, neatly wrapping both motivations together.

Now he wants to rebuild the National Party, down to 20 per cent in the last election, into a serious opposition: free-market where the ANC is statist, and promising to tackle the appalling level of violence.

He wants a true multi-racial party for 'all the moderate, religious, hard-working South Africans'. He is proud that more than 50 per cent of his voters are 'persons of colour', but to achieve a breakthrough he will need far more than the 600,000 black votes he attracted last time; and some say it's time for F W to make way for a younger, blacker leader – a suggestion he rejects.

'At the moment there is a very adamant insistence that I should stay on,' says the 61-year-old.

Has he any regrets? 'No. With hindsight, all the major decisions I'd have taken again. Here and there I'd have followed a different strategy, but the major things – the unbanning of the ANC, the release of Mandela, the implementation of a very tight programme of reform – I'd have done all over again.'

He rises and holds out his hand. 'Everything of the best

to you,' he says, in the words of a man more used to speaking Afrikaans.

Peter Thomson

Now this could go horribly wrong. There he is, in the front row of the congregation; the same iron-grey thatch, the same beatific grin.

For months the Rev Peter Thomson has been jovially rebuffing my requests for an interview and, in deciding to come unannounced and watch him in action in his church, I know what I am risking.

I could be denounced from the pulpit – if there was an operational pulpit in St Luke's, Holloway – or perhaps worse. I shudder to recall how, as a junior assistant master in the outdoors school of which Peter was head, I watched him take giant, brooding adolescents from his Australian homeland, gorged on plate-sized steaks, slam them up against the clapboards and shout: 'I'll go clean through you, pal!'

He may be a compelling theologian; he may be 60. But he once played Australian Rules football for St Kilda and, in case you fail to grasp the implications of that achievement, it means he is meaner than a junkyard dog.

And the reason I take this risk is that Peter Thomson is the one man who understands what, if anything, is at the heart of new Labour. He not only witnessed Tony Blair's conversion to Christian Socialism. He inspired it.

When Tony Blair speaks in Blackpool tomorrow, we will all – if it is anything like last year's speech – remark on his boss-eyed, quasi-messianic certainty of purpose. Anyone who knows Peter Thomson, or who has heard him preach on 'love', will know where he gets it from.

Just over 20 years ago, Peter was a post-graduate student at St John's College, Oxford, where Tony was an undergraduate. Somehow, at some point, whether over a few tinnies or a mug of coffee, Thommo was the midwife of Blair's spiritual and intellectual enlightenment. Blair has said so himself.

They remain fast friends. Last Christmas, the Blairs stayed with the Thomsons on their farm near Merrijig in the Victorian alps. This spring, Peter announced he was coming to Britain because – or so the polls suggested – something big was about to happen to his old mate and Peter wanted to 'be part of it'.

Now Peter has found his ministry in north London and there he is with Helen, his wife. And, when we have finished holding hands in a circle for the blessing, he turns, spots me and, mercifully, his blue eyes bulge and a great smile breaks over his prehensile, snaggle-toothed face.

'How the hell are you?' says the vicar of the Blairite revolution. We all have coffee. While Peter says 'G'day, Sheba', I notice that the congregation is young and middle class.

'There's a lot of 30-something media types here,' says Peter, and then, instead of toughing me up, he launches into the role he sees for his protege in changing British politics. We start with John Macmurray, the Balliol philosopher to whose prolix works Peter introduced Blair at Oxford.

I find Macmurray like a mixture between Marje Proops and Aristotle on the sex life of the cuttlefish. But he goes down big with Blair. Unlike most 20th century British philosophers, Macmurray is into matters of the spirit.

Blair has given several interviews about his faith and I ask Peter whether religion is one of the buttons new Labour seeks to push. In his speeches, Blair advertises himself as the man who can bring the moral dimension back to politics, as if offering spiritual and political renewal.

He agrees about the religious bit. 'I don't know this man Mawhinney but what the heck did the Tories think they were doing with that poster?' he says, meaning the one with the demon eyes. 'That didn't persuade anybody. The moderate voter isn't going to buy it.' According to Peter, the Tory campaign was at least partly inspired by a desire to neutralise this spiritual dimension which Blair manages, however unfairly, to claim more easily than the Tories. But surely Toryism, as currently practised, is just as compatible with Christianity as new Labourism?

'They make it pretty hard sometimes,' he says. 'There used to be a Tory concern for welfare. I don't mean just the welfare state but for the poor, the people at the bottom of the heap. What the hell happened to all that?' The way Peter sees it, the Tories can either go off to the Right and say that the poor 'aren't our problem'; or else they can stay and become a 'new liberal party', fighting Blair for the middle ground and even attacking Labour from the Left.

Hang on a minute, I say, what are we supposed to make of new Labour? If they are just Tories in drag, why not stick with the Tories? 'What we used to be useless (he uses a stronger expression) at in the Labour Party – now I'm not a Labour member, never have been but I've always been that way inclined – was this whole business of being down on the spirit of enterprise.

'It was all about trying to level down,' he says. So what about now? I ask. Does Blair still believe in helping the underdog? 'There's no way he's not into that,' he says. But where is he going to find the money? 'It's all to do with your attitude, deciding it's going to be managed more efficiently.

'Think what he's done with this party. It's amazing. It's not Mandelson or Ali Campbell running this party. It's Tony Blair.'

It is remarkable. But the central enigma seems unresolved. If he is not a socialist, what is the difference between him and the Tories? If he is, where does the money come from?

Ah, says Peter, in his most ominous remark: 'You think there isn't enough dough to go around. There is enough dough.'

David Trimble

David Trimble is in the middle of explaining that the IRA will never go away – didn't Martin McGuinness say so himself? – when he breaks off. 'Oh hallo!' he exclaims. For a vision has appeared, a cherub, or possibly a seraph. 'Come on in,' beams the leader of the official Ulster Unionist Party; and then Sarah Trimble, aged four, is scampering to his lap.

She strikes one pose, then another. Anyone would think she had done it before. The scene is so heartwarming that one almost forgets to be cynical. Aaaah! the gingery choleric Trimble, the grim-faced, bowler-hatted, orange-sashed victor of the Drumcree stand-off; see how he melts.

You might choose to believe that it was pure fluke that Mrs Trimble happened to be driving by after picking her daughter up from school; or you might think that there was an element of calculation. And if there was, then it would be hardly surprising in a man who must think through every move.

With the Government's majority now flickering on empty, Trimble's moment is at hand. One long evening in the next weeks there might be a confidence vote, and if Trimble's troops tramp into the Opposition lobbies, that would be it. Not for the first time in history, the pivot of power is here in Glengall street, hard by the Europa hotel, in the schizophrenic city of Belfast.

Trimble is on cracking form, so happy with the position he keeps wheezing with laughter. 'I sit in the tea-room and the Tory back-benchers come to ask if there is anything I want, heh, heh, heh! Of course they're pulling my leg. To a large extent I'm hoping the situation of actually having to make a choice doesn't arise; but if it does, we are not going to shy away from it.' But what will the Unionists *do* with the Government's jugular pulsing beneath the sword? Thumbs up? Or death to them?

'I have got to be careful to answer that question in such a way as to give no hint as to what I will actually do when the time comes,' he says, and gives another cackle. But he points out that his men have voted against the Government on crucial issues – like VAT on fuel. The truth is David Trimble doesn't give a toss about the fate of the Tories – this fast-talking barrister will do what is best for the Unionist cause.

The Trimbles came out here from Northumberland about 300 years ago, the name being a variant of Turnbull. Young Trimble became active politically when the Troubles began in the late 1960s; and he is an admirer of Brian Faulkner, the last Prime Minister of Northern Ireland. In Dublin they say Trimble's dream is to follow him and that he will go down as the 'de Klerk of Northern Ireland'.

'Oh, I would much rather be the Mandela, absolutely, de Klerk was the leader of a minority group that was frustrating the democratic rights of the majority.

'In Northern Ireland there is a minority group frustrating the rights of the majority and it's called Sinn Fein. Mandela got 70 per cent of the vote – Gerry Adams isn't going to get that.'

But if Northern Ireland is to remain part of the United

Kingdom, how are the nationalists to be appeased? Trimble swears it can be done. It involves an assembly with limited powers, and some North-South co-operation on social and economic issues.

'We all know that this is the general ballpark area. It's frustrating that people are not yet getting down to the nitty-gritty. Part of the difficulty is that Sinn Fein, parts of the Irish foreign affairs department and parts of the SDLP still have the primary objective of a united Ireland.'

Isn't the trouble that the Catholics are breeding faster? 'The projections are that, sometime in the middle of the next century, there will be no majority, in religious terms.

'It'll be even stevens. But the important thing is voting intentions, and the number who are prepared to endorse a united Ireland has actually been dropping.' He cites Northern Ireland's standard of living, 25 per cent higher than in the Republic, the lower taxes and better public services.

He paints a picture of Catholic families sitting in the Falls Road, watching *Coronation Street* and with Manchester United football satchels. 'We are living in a British culture. Social mores are conservative but we are living in what is fundamentally a liberal state compared with the claustrophobic social morality that exists in the Republic.'

So which British party do you trust more to keep this happy Union? The argument is if Trimble pulls the plug on the Tories, and there followed a big Labour victory, he might be vulnerable to some Clinton-Blair initiative, especially if the IRA stage another of their bogus ceasefires.

'Blair is no softie,' he says, 'but we don't know whether he will be pointed in the right direction.

'We'll take each issue on its merits, and if and when there is a confidence motion then we'll look carefully to the interests of those we represent. Heh, heh, heh.'

Tony Benn

Aargh. I almost popped out of my skin. 'It'sh down here,' says a voice and there is a faint whiff of tobacco. And I boggle because there appears to be a head sprouting from the brickwork at my feet, the silver head, the cartoonists' beloved eyes and pipe that all my life have stood for the same set of ideas.

How typical of Anthony Wedgwood Benn not to live in this house in Holland Park Avenue but in the basement flat, a bit like being Viscount Stansgate but giving up the title.

He leads the way into his study, full of bits of once-high technology, a pipe-shaped model of Big Ben, tributes from Left-wing organisations and a deep arm-chair. 'Would you like some tea or coffee?' he asked, and as I look at his trim 71-year-old form I think of the billion cuppas, the muggas, the pintas that have allegedly preserved his vigour, the tannin tanning the Benn innards like some Aztec formula.

I go for the tea. Soon he is back with a tray, launching into a virtual soliloquy.

'Well I've lived a very long time 'cos I was brought up in a political home, I mean, Ramsay MacDonald sat me on his knee and I've looked at Labour leaders in a funny way ever since,' he says, off the starting block before I have barely asked him a question. And on it goes in a lisping cataract as he expounds his theory of what really happened in the twentieth-century. The insight hit him – Pow! – about 20 years ago when, for such is Benn's instinct for charm, he says he bought a *Daily Telegraph* historical wall chart. 'And at the top it had the words: *the first part of the 20th century was the advance in political influence of the industrial working class*. If I take my life and divide it in half, the first half was the enlargement of the power of ordinary people.'

But in the last 40 or 50 years market forces have counter-attacked against the advances of democracy. And here he figures we must be soulmates, for nothing, says Benn, has been as anti-democratic as Brushelsh; the bureaucrats who tried to stop him nationalising North Sea oil, who tried to put the kibosh on his plans for industrial subsidy.

'The first time I went to Brushelsh I felt like one of those Angles who paraded before the Emperor in Rome. I think politicians in the West are now maharajahs of the new raj of money. The maharajahs were allowed to remain as long as they did the will of Queen Victoria, and we are allowed to remain as long as we abide by the requirements of international capital.'

When Thatcher went against Brussels she was doomed. '"No, no, no" did for her, just as the markets did for Labour in 1976 ... I feel I'm witnessing the progressive extinction of representative democracy.' There is something so hypnotic about his discourse that only now and then one realises with a start that he has completely cut the moorings of fact.

For instance, Benn at one point is explaining that the British have always been ruled by foreigners. 'Julius Caesar arrived in 55 BC and brought a single currency and they stayed until AD 610 when the 7th Legion had to go back to Masada.' Eh? I say. I thought the Jewish wars were in AD 17? It's a bit like Benn's theory of 20th-century history. It's hogwash, but it sounds so seductive because it is based on a half-truth.

Of course he's right to say democratic politics have often impeded the free market. As the franchise has widened, politicians have tried to win the votes of more and more people by spending more and more money, whether taxing or borrowing. That is why the state has taken and spent an increasing part of the nation's wealth as the century has gone on.

But when Thatcher fell over Europe, that was hardly because she opposed the free market. The Europe of Delors, Mitterrand and Kohl was in many ways *anti*-free market. Benn has ignored this simple point in his desire to make the facts fit the theory. The wonderful thing about Tony Benn is that he still believes that British manufacturing industry could have been 'the best in the world' if he'd been allowed to lubricate it with the entire receipts from North Sea oil. He reminisces fondly about Meriden, the ludicrous workers' co-operative he invented in a doomed attempt to revive the British motorcycle industry.

I've always wanted to meet Mr Benn, and now I understand the mixture of sweep, vision and nuttiness that inspired his followers and kept Labour in the wilderness. Of course, he's scathing about New Labour. He is, though, full of hope. If Blair is elected, he believes it will not be long before the great public desire for a change wells up, as it welled up over Dunblane. 'I think the pressure will build up for a fairer society.'

Well, I wonder. His real problem is not that the free market has stifled democracy. It is that democracy has rejected Bennery. Not that he minds. 'Really I have no chip on my shoulder. That must be very apparent to you. If I did, I would be able to open a fish and chip shop.'

Frank Bruno

It was always possible things would get rough when I went to interview the former heavyweight champion of the world. OK, so he's Uncle Frank, the nation's favourite rear-end of a pantomime horse. He's the gentle giant, know what I mean 'arry, the dedicated family man.

But he's still 6ft 3in of chestnut-hard menace, with a

punch likened by the Royal College of Nursing to being hit by a half-ton car. And he is not in the sunniest of moods when he finally leaves the tint-windowed muscular Merc where he had been having a long, agitated conversation on his mobile. He grasps his close-cropped bonce.

'I don't need these anxieties in my head,' he tells the person who had agreed that Frank could be consulted on the issue of the hour: what was it like when he went the distance – the distance of two and a half rounds – on March 17, 1996, with Tyson, the former World Chomp? Is it true, as Bruno is reported to have said, that those steel gnashers also closed on a piece of Frank?

He's standing in a school theatre, where he's doing some television work, and still talking to his hapless minders when he suddenly says, *basso profundissimo*: 'Why are you looking at me like that, Mr Johnson, brigadier? Are you trying to suss me out?' Gracious no, I say, noting that the peripheral vision is phenomenal from those big, ironical brown eyes. And it's ding ding, round one of one of the shortest interviews in history.

Mr Bruno, Frank, I say, it always strikes me as amazing that you can do such violence when you're obviously so pacific in temperament . . . He starts a kind of Ali patter, shuffling in his cool blue suit and snakeskin bootees. 'I'm no nicer than you, no nastier than you, I've got the same arms, same legs' – he reaches down to prod my legs and squeeze my biceps – 'the only difference is I'm black and you're white.'

And then his fists are up, giving me a chance to see his jewellery real close, the doubloon on his ring, the watch, everything scabbed and crusted with diamonds.

'Are you going to tell me that when I hit you, you're just going to say *(falsetto)*: "Oh stop that, old bean"? Are you going to be that nice to me? When you do your job you do your job. It's survival. I'm doing a job to make a living for my family and myself; lock me up if that's a crime.'

It's time to close in. Tell me about when Tyson bit you, I say. Apparently this is a low blow. 'I don't like to get involved in boxing questions. I'm not giving no exclusive interviews. Boris, what I'm trying to say to you man is that I wasn't there at the Tyson thing.

'I don't know whether you're kinky and you like that sort of biting thing. I'm not kinky. Tyson he come up and give me the elbow, things like that, but he won fair and square and at the end of the day he's got to be punished, he's got to be stopped. I haven't got time for these loaded questions. I'm not sitting on my backside drinking beer and saying I rocked Tyson once, and if that's a crime lock me up again.'

And now the seconds are crowding into the ring. 'You've had 20 minutes,' says a frightening looking man with a very short haircut. Have I? According to my watch, it's more like five.

'Relax, man,' says Bruno. 'Don't get out of your pram.' And now the former world champion has extended his 82-inch reach and he's got me in a playful headlock. At least I assume it's playful. 'Relax, Mr Boris brigadier,' he says, massaging my neck muscles with his thumbs like a man preparing to ease a Champagne cork out of the bottle. 'You're getting all tense here. I don't want to give no exclusive,' he says. It's all right, I gasp. I don't want an exclusive, really and truly.

And then ding ding, a man in shorts and various girls with clipboards demand an end to this degrading spectacle, saying I've taken up far too much of Mr Bruno's time. He's got to get on with the serious business of being a roving reporter for ITV, before appearing in the Spice Girls movie. I'm seriously out of my depth here.

But Uncle Frank relents, waving them aside. 'I'm trying to be as nice as possible,' he says. 'I don't want to tell you to go to the toilet and have a vindaloo,' and the interview staggers on for a few more seconds. He thinks Muhammad Ali was the all-time greatest, Bob Marley the greatest musician, and no, he's not planning a come-back.

'If you gave me all your money, all your mother's money, and I can tell you've got a lot of money, I wouldn't go back. I've made enough corn . . . There you are Mr Johnson brigadier. I've given you more than just a few crumbs, I've given you a loaf.'

And then for Uncle Frank, the warhorse-turned-circus horse, the man who rocked Tyson, it's back to the shaded interior of the Merc, for a long gesticulation on the car phone.

Chris Evans

There is panic when the call comes through. For two years, the features department has been lobbying the ginger binger for an interview, and then – jackpot: not only will Chris Evans consent to see us – he will give *The Daily Telegraph* a game of golf!

The multi-millionaire proprietor-star of Virgin Radio is ready to plug a new television series called *Tee Time*, and he requires a partner. Just when he is needed most, Bill Deedes, the paper's answer to Arnold Palmer, is in Sudan.

Someone, anyone, is needed to play golf with Evans. Have you ever swung a club in anger? the features impresarios ask and, like a fool, I say yes.

It is when I arrive with George, a *Daily Telegraph* features executive turned caddy, that it dawns what we are letting ourselves in for. In the car park of the Buckinghamshire Golf Club, an official looks ruminatively over our Fiesta.

Uh-oh. There are Rollers and Beemers here, but no Fiestas, and I have a sense of impending doom. This man

Evans once humiliated an employee on air by reading out the details of his expenses fiddle. He said Anthea Turner should be kicked in the teeth. What will he say when he twigs the quality of his opposition?

'Are you going to change?' asks the chain-smoking PR, Patrick Keegan of Freud Communications, looking incredulously at my trousers. It's all right, he says at length. 'Chris won't mind. He's not at all precious. He's easy-going and generous.' Pathetically, we ask what Mr Evans would like to discuss with us.

'Golf is his big love,' says Patrick, Our Man In The Navy Corduroy Suit, as if to say: 'Keep it to golf, my son, and you'll be all right.' The woman in the Buckinghamshire Golf Club shop speaks of Mr Evans with reverence, and all at once it hits me where I have seen all this before.

It's pure James Bond. The shrubs, the scurrying minions, the golf club built by the Kajima corporation of Japan which has a vaguely oriental atmosphere – something, no doubt, to do with the samurai swords on the walls – and lowering over it all, the impending arrival of the man of power, the tycoon-golfer.

In the mind's ear, I hear Shirley Bassey: 'Goldfingaah! The man with the Midas touch! He's just too much!' He's turned his blatherings to gold. He's paid £85 million for Virgin Radio, and they say it's worth twice that now. He's ranked 668th in the *Sunday Times* top 1,000, with £30 million to his name, he has just won yet another Gold at the Sony Radio awards and – Omigosh . . .

Just as Evans arrives, wearing his baseball hat, a mere one and a half hours after the appointed tee-off time, I notice that the PR bumf says he is a 'junior member of the professional golfers' association and an ex-golf shop assistant'. This is bad.

The last time I played golf was at school when one Major Morkill expelled me from the course for using only one club. 'There you go, making excuses already,' says Evans. 'It's all in the putting. What's your handicap?' I am tempted to reply: 'Wooden leg and glass eye.'

Evans insists on showing us the Kajima corporation's shower rooms, equipped with three-legged milking stools: apparently, Japanese businessmen like to hunker down for a really good go at the toes.

We walk towards the first tee and I try to contain my anxiety. Japanese businessmen fly over here just to play golf, says Evans. 'It's cheaper than playing in Japan. The presidents of Mitsubishi and Toyota play here, and they take no prisoners.' He played here recently with Gazza, the footballer. 'Gazza had never played before, but he was a natural. He beat everybody.'

As we reach the first tee, Chris and David Granger, the producer of the golfing series, announce that they are playing a game called camels, starfish, snakes. You are a camel if you land in a bunker, a starfish if you land in the water, a snake in the rough.

The stakes begin at 12½p and mount in geometrical leaps to thousands of pounds. George, the *Telegraph* executive-cum-caddy, declines to bet on my prowess.

David goes first, thwacking it very nicely, and then it is the turn of Evans. He's wearing Oasis-style Adidas trainers and green army-surplus fatigues. He is much taller than I had imagined – 6ft 2in, with greying temples – and he bends artistically at the knees, leaning into the shot.

There is a professional sounding clack. 'Good shot, Chris,' says David the producer. Unless I specifically say otherwise, David has a very high opinion of Chris's golfing ability, which he is not shy of expressing. Now it falls to *The Daily Telegraph*.

'You want a five iron if you haven't played since school,' Evans says. George hands me a putter, which Chris kindly intercepts. He finds me the right tool. *Whack.*

I am in the rough, and the grass has swallowed the Titleist. David finds another from his bag, and it seems a good idea to move the interview along before being banished again by the authorities. In America, recently, I was listening to Howard Stern, the supreme shock jock. Does Evans model himself on Howie?

This is a *faux pas*. 'A lot of people compare me to Stern, which is so wrong. We are both the most talked about DJs in our country.' It seems that the difference between them, in the view of Evans, is that Stern relies on shock tactics, Evans on talent.

Chastened, I fall back into the abject role of Goldfinger's golfing pal. I paint a picture of his triumphs: the Jags, the Aston Martins, the fling with Kim Wilde, the show called *Don't Forget Your Toothbrush* he invented and franchised around the world, the triumph at the BBC, where he boosted Radio One's ratings by a million.

What will you do now that you have achieved everything? 'Well, I haven't achieved anything,' he says, arriving on the green after a spell in a bunker. 'Good shot, Chris,' says David.

Evans and I are now putting, and it becomes clear that putting is a serious problem. The *Telegraph* ball zooms from one side to the other, as though over a billiard table. An aerial map of the strokes would look like a spider's web. At last, we both get sufficiently near to be given the hole, and Evans continues his self-analysis.

'I am trying to look over the mountain and let everyone get on with climbing it. I am trying to look over the other side,' he says. Aha! I scribble the quote, and as we launch into the second hole, my spirits begin to rise.

Evans is not, in the literal sense, a big hitter. 'I'm very weak,' he says, and indeed, our shots from the tee are not dissimilar.

'Nice one, Chris,' says David as the megastar's second

heads for the green, and then – shame and despair. I square up, swing violently, and instead of the ball, a large chunk of Buckinghamshire floats through the air, followed by several smaller clods. The ball trickles a few feet.

Evans retrieves the divots. My next two shots are like hitting the top of an egg. The ball spangs uselessly a few yards at a time; and then Evans does a wonderful thing. He gives me a piece of advice.

'Always swing through it,' he says. 'You're trying to hit it.' And do you know, he is right. 'I talk a great game,' says Evans as we move on. By now, though, three golfers behind us are signalling a desire to play through, and we sit down in the rough.

It is a balmy day; high clouds, soft sun, and Evans seems happy to talk. Others have excavated his past – the father who died of cancer when he was 14, the working-class upbringing in Warrington, the £150 a week job as a Tarzanogram, the way he wangled himself a job on Manchester's Piccadilly radio. But never mind the past; what about the future? Where is he on that mountain he mentioned on the green?

It seems that, in fact, he's not at the top. He's just having a breather, while everyone else scrabbles vainly on ahead. 'If you have the luxury of stopping – having other people do things for you – you can look around and look into the future,' says the 32-year-old. 'That's what Rupert Murdoch does. He thinks about the future.'

There it is again! I can hear Shirley Bassey singing the theme tune of the great tycoon. All we need is David to play Oddjob and decapitate someone with a bowler hat.

So what aspect of modern life does Evans propose to dominate next? Books? Film?

'It's not about that. Books have been done before and feature films have been done before. It's quite easy to turn the media upside down, but nobody has ever done it before. I was really angry after the Montreux television festival. This is supposed to be a ground-breaking weekend, and the BBC people came back after getting completely trolleyed in Lake Geneva, and the biggest headline was that they have re-signed Dawn French and Jennifer Saunders.'

The full horror of this is not obvious. Even more puzzling is his objection to drunkenness. What about his friendship with Jimmy Five Bellies, the benders with Gazza? 'That's my style. I enjoy drinking too much, but I think it's quite bad for me.

'I've been so drunk I haven't been able to pronounce my name or give my address to the taxi driver. I had to move from Kensington Park Road because it is difficult to pronounce.

'Arundel Gardens is easier. Pont Street is a piece of piss. Try Prison Officers Association when you are drunk. No chance, absolutely no chance.'

What about drugs? 'I smoke the odd spliff. I don't have a problem with that. I've been cornered by people talking about nothing for an hour with their noses six inches from your face. Now, I know to walk away, because they are on coke.

'I have been offered coke millions of times; but I've never taken it because I am not interested. A lot of people who work with me take it, but I don't think it does them any good.'

Just then, Patrick comes tripping across the sward in dark glasses. He pretends to be worried about an appointment I have in London, but the real reason is obvious.

Another golf cart has drawn up some way off. Our time is drawing to a close. We can see the *Sun* snappers, with lenses the size of milk churns.

'One more hole,' says Evans, sensing perhaps that I need to salvage some golfing pride; and on the way, he describes his cultural life. He is famously a man from the post-literate age. He used to boast that he had read only three books, including *My Family And Other Animals* by Gerald Durrell, and *Lady Boss* by Jackie Collins, but the tally is rising. He's stuck into *Sophie's World*, and Jeffrey Archer gave him his latest in the hope of securing Evans's support in the race to be London's mayor.

'I said, "I can't give you my support while Ken Livingstone's involved," and he said, "I think Ken's going to drop out pretty soon".

'*I'd* be a great mayor,' he adds, and then qualifies this quickly. 'But I don't think I'd know enough.'

It is time for the last tee-off. Whoever is the god of golf – Hercules, I suppose: he had a club – took my elbow, and good heavens, the ball soared from the tee to the green in one.

'Look at your pitch, mate,' says Evans, pointing to the impact hole with real delight. 'We're so intimidated, aren't we? That will be a birdie – one under par.'

If only it were. The match ends, and we reflect what a genial chap Chris Evans is, though, funnily enough, he's not that good at golf; unless – ghastly thought – he was only being polite.

Kelvin MacKenzie

Health warning: this article should not be read by those of a sensitive disposition, or by anyone having breakfast.

It is only a couple of hours since the coup. The radio station has barely capitulated and already Kelvin MacKenzie is firing on all cylinders. In fact, he's fired three senior executives already, and seems frightfully bucked by the experience.

'It's only 20 past four,' he boasts, meaning there's plenty more firing time left in the day. You may never have heard of Talk Radio, a so-far unsuccessful attempt to mimic the speech-only programmes of America and Australia. But if anyone can justify the £24.7 million he has just spent on a business losing £8 million a year, it is Kelv; because any journalist would admit that he is a master of his trade. He is the privately-educated wordsmith who reduced newsrooms to jelly with his sarff London bawl.

His name stands, in some eyes, for all that is coarse, brutish and base, and yet his reign at the *Sun* yielded such gems of the sub-editor's craft as 'Gotcha' (the sinking of the Belgrano), 'Hop Off You Frogs' (the lamb war), 'Up Yours Delors' (plans for a single currency) and 'Freddie Starr Ate My Hamster' (speaks for itself, I think). 'It's highly unlikely that the editor writes the headlines,' says Kelvin modestly. 'He takes the credit for the ones that go down well and, with the ones that go down badly, someone has to be dismissed at once. The headline "Paddy Pantsdown"; was written by the picture editor, but I don't like to reveal these things because it affects my after dinner speaking price, hur, hur.'

Kelvin took the *Sun* to the height of its political influence, as John Major discovered on Black Wednesday, Sept 16, 1992. 'He said, you know (imitates John Major), "Heh, exciting day, how are you going to play it?" This was 7.30, quarter to eight, and interest rates had been going up and down all day like a whore's drawers – no, you can't say that in *The Daily Telegraph* – like Ron Davies's trousers. So I said, "Look, I've got a bucketful of * * * * on my desk and I am going to pour it all over you" and he said "Hmmm, you are a wag". Which showed me that he was totally out of touch with ordinary people and the danger of Prime Ministers having relations with tabloid editors, because in the end the one loyalty an editor should have is to his readers.'

Doesn't he regret any of his rubbishings and monsterings? 'No, absolutely not. All those guys who employ PRs to give one image of themselves have virtually no defence. They all live in these great big houses and all the rest.'

And what about the not-so-famous, such as that man who glued himself to the lavatory seat. Did he deserve such humiliation? Kelvin hoots. 'He went into the bathroom and thought he was getting some haemorrhoid cream, and for some reason it was superglue and he glued the cheeks of his **** together, and it took half an hour with a hacksaw and half of Derbyshire Infirmary to help. That was raised by Joe Ashton MP, and the point was that the guy was quite happy to talk about it.'

What about the children he sent crying home from school? His mood subtly alters. 'Are you all right? Did you have a long lunch, Boris? Crying over what? Perhaps their parents should have thought about that before they did it. Lots of people, including me, get tubloads poured over them.'

Actually, *Sun* victims have one modest consolation. Kelvin himself appears to have undergone a mid-life crisis, and disappeared to the West Indies with a girl. At which point he was 'fronted up' by another tabloid. 'Well, what could I say, what could I do? The *Mail on Sunday* were doing their job. There was a young lady who was euphemistically described as not my wife, and that's fair enough. You can hardly complain.'

There were more serious goofs, like the *Sun*'s handling of the Hillsborough stadium disaster, and the libel of Elton John. But MacKenzie survived. After 12 years he took his pungent gift of innovation to Sky and then to Live TV, famous for topless darts and the News Bunny.

Now he has pumped his entire savings into Talk Radio. 'When I told my wife she didn't say anything except, "I'm not moving house and I'm not living in a semi in Whit-stable."'

A man from Apax, a venture capital outfit that is funding Talk Radio, puts his head round the door. 'I'll be back in a minute,' says Kelvin. 'I've got to sack him.'

As I leave, our photographer is striving for the most flattering angle. 'It does look a bit chinny,' he says, indicating the MacKenzie dewlap. 'I'm not surprised,' says Kelvin. 'There's a lot of Chardonnay gone into that.'

Dancing with Ulrika

The ancients believed that sometimes a goddess or nymph would descend from Olympus or Parnassus or some such top address, and, finding a horny handed goatherd, reveal to him the secret of a key advance in human civilisation: the notes of the musical scale, bee-keeping, wine-making, and so on.

They further held that this goatherd, regaining the power of speech after the shock and beauty of the epiphany, would spread the word among his fellows. Think of that antique peasant, my friends, and you will understand the feelings of this hack.

First they hooted, the cackling crows in the office when the idea was discussed. Then you can imagine the blank, hostile jealousy when the sensational news came through from Ulrika's people. Not 90 minutes, old son, they said, white-lipped. Not you and her, cheek to cheek. Naaah, they said.

And yes, as the Weekend team stood in the graffitied murk of the Ministry of Sound, run by the ever so slightly terrifying Jamie Palumbo, we were none too sure that the visitation would really take place. In the anterooms of the

'Ministry', a *boite de nuit* in Elephant and Castle, board-room meetings full of black polonecks were charting a course of world domination.

The vulpine figure of Palumbo himself could be seen in a raised glass-walled office, greenlighting new discos in Manila and Vientiane. The clock advanced. Our hearts sank.

Then, when we had all but given up hope, the metal door clanged. Somehow the shades of the discotheque seemed to melt in bashful awe as she approached. The janitors ceased their sponging of the begummed and butted floor. 'Hello, lovely Boris,' said Ulrika, with the easy familiarity of Athena addressing Odysseus, and her teeth lit the room like a lamp.

Bowing low, I led her to a special disco place in the heart of Palumbo's darkness, called the VIP bar. A tape machine was turned on and began to spool silently. She looked at me. I looked at her. There was nothing for it.

You know the problem. Or if you've forgotten the embarrassment, it's coming up again in the next couple of months. Yup. It's time to get that party hat on, get those shirt tails out, get legless and get on down.

It's not that all men are bad at dancing. It's just that most of us are. Our strategy is to shuffle ambiguously, until the Rolling Stones come on, at which point we do a kind of vertical squat-thrust, like Gianni de Michelis, the 18-stone former Italian foreign minister and global authority on Milanese discotheques; and having raised ourselves about six and a half inches, we come down with enough violence to rattle the parquet, were our descent not checked by the ingrown toenail of the nice woman in the expenses department.

Or else we stick out a tentative foot. We jut our chins. We wiggle stertorously down into a squatting position, whereupon our pants split. That, frankly, exhausts our repertoire, and that has been good enough for me; good enough, that is, until a month or so ago, and I realised that times have moved on.

It was in Nice, and I was doing my Denis Thatcher routine at a conference of European lawyers, hoofing it, as one does, in the Negresco ballroom. All of a sudden I realised that everyone was doing the same thing. Out of the jumble a phalanx had been formed. Cummerbunded QCs, chaps who spend their days explicating article 85 of the Treaty of Rome in Luxembourg, were touching their elbows and wobbling their bellies with perfect synchronicity, and then, as one, shouting in Spanish.

Someone later told me it was called the *Macarena*. Apparently Al Gore, the catatonic Democrat, is an accomplished exponent. Even Newt Gingrich can do it. Try as I might to keep up out of the corner of the eye, I was nowhere. I blushed. I stammered.

It was like being suddenly invited to chip in to a seminar on particle physics. That is why, for the sake of all of us easy skankers, kibe-gallers and toe-squashers, we begged Ulrika for a lesson. She could tell us, we reasoned, what challenges chaps like us face this festive season.

To my astonishment, in an act of golden-hearted charity that one might liken to Brigitte Bardot's compassion for some stricken donkey or condemned mutt, she consented. The former Rear of the Year, she with the Red Devil tattooed on her left buttock, the woman opinion polls say most men would like to sleep with, agreed to come down from her Olympus – in Datchet, I think – and give us, the Hopeless Ones, the gift of the dance.

So we waited ominous seconds for the music to begin. She observed that it was parky in here. Those Ministry of Sound tycoons don't waste money on fuel, I agreed, my breath hanging awkwardly in the air.

'I've got cold hands,' she said, blowing on them, 'but a

warm heart.' Now there were drums. It sounded promising. Aha, yes: Sympathy For The Devil. The Stones. No problemo. Up. Kick. Down. Kick. 'No, no,' said Ulrika. She wanted something else, and soon it was procured.

Whooh. I wonder why. Whooo. He's the greatest dancer. Ulrika did something oriental with her neck, causing her head to move along her shoulders in a kind of smooth Thunderbird click that only my mother-in-law can surpass.

I wonder why. Whooh. That I've ever seen. Another problem about dancing: what on earth are you supposed to say? You think of some banality, and bellow it, and she says 'What?' and then you try again, and she says 'What?' and by the third or fourth go, you've rather lost heart in the thing you were going to say.

So I asked Ulrika, did she, er, go to many clubs and raves and that sort of thing? 'Do you come here often?', she shot back, with a mellow laugh. I ventured to compliment her on her long black leather coat, a sort of SS commandant's dream.

've have vays of making you dance,' she said, looking appraisingly at my style. 'Boris,' said the former weather-girl and all-purpose comedian-cum-megastar in warm, understanding tones, 'the whole thing is about absolute freedom of the body.

'You can do things you can do on the dance floor that you wouldn't do in the office. You can afford to push back the boundaries of your sexuality.' Now she was like an oscillating osier in a warm, wet, wind.

'Think snake,' she urged. Perhaps because it was so nippy in Palumbo's dungeon, my efforts were if anything a shade more lumpy and disjointed than normal. 'Slow down,' she advised. The problem was partly in the shoulders, she diagnosed, and partly in the legs.

'Think sssexy,' said Ulrika, running her hands over what

her fellow metmen used to call her frontal systems. By Zeus. Now she was undulating like a Sikh Queen approaching the divan of her moaning king, before bumping him off with a draught of khat or ghat or whatever.

Or perhaps she was, indeed, a snake, a leather-coated mamba hypnotising a gerbil. Inspired by a distant memory of rugby warm-up exercises, I started to rotate what I believed to be my pelvis.

Ulrika was polite. 'In dancing, you should use your greatest asset, which in your case is your face,' she said. This seemed uncommonly civil. 'When we get to the really sexy tune, you'll want to be telling everything with your face.'

Aha. The sexy tune, eh? I was all set for that one. By now, Ulrika had taken her coat off, and it was obvious why Palumbo didn't bother with the heating in here. When the place is stuffed with semi-nude teutonic tourists, as it apparently is every weekend, it must become an inferno.

But for some reason the next tune was a species of techno-jangling House or Garage or Carpark, and Ulrika wasn't having it. 'That is for people who've taken some tablets,' she said. Followers of Ulrika will know that she can drink a pint of lager in one, but pills are not for her.

While someone rootled for a new tape she walked over and read the Sports section of the *Daily Telegraph*, or, to be more exact, an analysis of the latest infamy perpetrated by her man, Aston Villa's Stan Collymore. This Collymore, you will recollect, is the brute who tendered his resignation from the human race when he struck Ulrika in a Paris bar, just because she was showing everyone else her lager-drinking trick. The amazing truth, according to the tabloids, is that Ulrika still feels affection for Colly. This cowardy Custard. This big girl's blouse. It would have been tactless to bring the subject up. But her continuing devotion to the Colly must be rated one of the mysteries of evolution.

'Huh,' she said, after absorbing the truth about Collymore's foul, and its part in Villa's defeat. She set her jaw in an unreadable line. Whatever her inner thoughts, the tutorial seemed to gain momentum after that, as Sister Sledge came on with the new theme tune of Tory social policy.

'We Are Fam-i-LY!' She took me by the middle and we leant backward together, a bit like the cover of that old Madness album. 'You're collapsing,' she said, which was quite wrong. Perhaps the odd bead was by now dewing the brow, but the legs were as tungsten girders. Pretty soon, I must confess, it would have been good to have that old slow number; and what man in my position would not have conceived the same hope, if only for the sake of a breather? *Honi soit qui mal y pense*, that's the motto.

But, no, there was no let-up from the lactic-acid build-up in the legs. 'Night fever, Night fev-AAAH,' sang the Bee Gees. 'Pout, pout!' said Ulrika, showing me how. 'That's part of the flirting. It's communicating without sending memos.' Indeed, I assented, composing the features into a cast-iron pout.

'You look like an orang-utang,' she said, indulgently of course. Things must have started to look a bit more systematic because Eleanor, the photographer, shouted, 'No, Boris, not so close!' and I sprang away like a startled frog.

'I would say closer,' said Ulrika, with what can only be called supreme sportsmanship. Struggling to get my mind back to the question of office parties, I asked her advice for damsels pursued, as they will be in the coming weeks, by corpulent executives of middle years. 'Outdance the bastard!' said Ulrika, showing her pace, and now she was doing something complicated with her arms.

Stop! In the name of love! said the song, and she imitated a policeman holding up traffic. *Before you break my heart!* and she quickly made a snapping motion with both fists, and then drew a picture of a heart in the air. Disco kings have since told me that this is a well-known dodge, but to my joy it came pretty easily, and soon we were two minds with but a single thought, two hearts which beat as one . . .

'That's the kind of song where you can make your feelings very well known to someone,' she said, and her blue eyes locked on mine. And then for one brief, flame-like moment that somehow seemed an eternity there on the floor of the Ministry of Sound, we came together and . . . Relax, relax, everyone. I made that bit up. Take it easy, Stan. Easy there, boy. Anyway, we *Telegraph* hacks, it is well known, are expert in the arts of self-defence. The wretched truth was our time was drawing to a close.

'We're not doing a slow number?' she asked, with what sounded pretty convincingly like disappointment. We were not.

'It needs more than one session,' she said. If that isn't politeness on a heroic scale, I don't know what is. So, my fellow rugcutters and curvetters, what did Ulrika teach me, apart from 'Think snake'?

At the end of our session she had given instruction in 'the cauldron', in which you make a stirring motion, while moving your body at half the speed. Very tricky. There was the 'Nefertiti and Akhenaton', where you imitate an Egyptian frieze with sideways-on jabbing motions of the arms. And there was the ever-popular 'shelf-stacker', in which you pretend to heave six-packs from the floor to waist height.

Schooled in those, none of us will ever seem inadequate on the dance-floor again. Such was the revelation from on high. She was gone, Terpsichore or Melpomene or some other muse, convincingly disguised as a Swedish wunder-frau, back to Olympus or Parnassus or Datchet, or at least back to her prowling limo outside.

Soon she was talking happily on her mobile, and waving to us as we trudged on blistered feet back to our ploughs at Canary Wharf. Actually, she said she was off to see her osteopath. It was completely coincidental, she said.

Robert Harris

As we cross the foot-bridge and see the house he laughs lightly. 'Rumours of its opulence are greatly exaggerated,' he says. Surely not.

What a vision. Here, rolling immaculately down to the Kennet, is the sward where Blair rests his weary limbs, where Mandy sports on a summer afternoon. There the XJS squats butchly on the gravel: all trophies of Robert Harris's coruscating pen. Within is Gill, his wife, assorted staff, and one of his three children.

He's the Labour answer to Jeffrey Archer – and what a withering retort he is.

I speak as one who has been kept awake by *Archangel*, his latest bestseller. We mere journalists, we who are as he once was, grind our teeth as we contemplate not just his success, but the elegance, the neatness of his creativity. Why didn't I dream up this yarn of a brilliant-but-bibulous British history don (Norman Stone) discovering something spooky beginning with S in the Russian north?

In the study, Harris explains that Stalin came to him in a dream. 'There was this sense of violence crackling round him, though he was quite friendly.' History does not relate what Stalin said to Harris. But we can guess. 'Good work, Comrade, with your what-if-Hitler-won book, *Fatherland*.

$1.8 million for the US rights alone! Not bad. Six million copies sold of *Fatherland* and *Enigma* combined, and now Mel Gibson has bought the rights to *Archangel*. But, Tovarish, now is the time to achieve power! Socialism needs you ... ha ha.'

And with a horrible cackle the Georgian melted into the Kintbury night. Shaken, no doubt, by this epiphany, the 41-year-old Harris is changing tack again.

He is the son of a Nottingham printer, and 'born into the Labour Party'. He went to the local school in Melton Mowbray before going to Cambridge, where he managed to edit the university magazine and be president of the Union. He has scaled the summits of hackery. He has done the novels. Now he's trying to be a New Labour media tycoon, prising the *New Statesman* from Geoffrey Robinson's grasp.

The other week he wrote a column in the *Sunday Times*, which might have been called My Friend Mandelson the Martyr. Pah, he said, pressing the smelling-salt-soaked hankie to his nose. He was appalled at the way dear Peter had been treated. For the first time, he felt ashamed of his profession. They were a bunch of 'skinheads'.

'Ere, said the rest of us, 'ow come you're calling us skinheads, Mr Fancypants? Think you're too good for us now, just cos Tony Blair's yer best mate?

'I don't knock the media for one second for getting the story,' says Harris. 'The column was written on Boxing Day morning,' he says plaintively. 'But the idea that I shouldn't even put in a word for the poor old sod [Mandy] honestly never even occurred to me. I took the view that my name had been linked with his in the good times and it would have been morally weak to dissociate myself.'

Indeed. Harris it was who first tempted Mandy to error. He took him into a high place, Notting Hill, and showed him the fleshpots of west London; at one point, Harris was going to buy the house for him.

For better or worse, something has happened to Harris the Hack. He has become a New Labour figure. 'Politics,' he says, 'has become like late 19th century France, all about who is sleeping with whom. Society hostesses strut across the stage. It is like *Vanity Fair* – there's this extraordinary group of people.'

He detects a whiff of puritanism in some of the Mandy-bashing. 'Oooh!' he says in mock horror, 'his £1,400 chair. They [the critics] are the new Bolsheviks.'

But surely there's a kind of logic in feeling cheesed off with people who put up your taxes, when they are cushioned from life's realities by Robinson's millions? 'Huh,' he says, 'maybe Labour has made some marginal difference in tax. But not as much as John Smith or Healey would have made.'

So what ethic does he have in mind for the *New Statesman*, bible of Britain's sandal-wearing wheat-germ scoffers? The Staggers, which drones on about 'the Third Way', loses £500,000 a year, while *The Spectator* has double the circulation and makes a profit. He wants the *Statesman* to be a pleasure to read, he says, 'but those very characteristics which render people Left-wing render them reluctant to be seen having a good time'.

'Moneybags', as Harris is affectionately known, is writing the biography of John Le Carré, with whom he bears some comparison, and has a contract to write three more thrillers. This dabbling in hackery and politics is only 20 per cent of his life, he swears. 'I don't want to keep opening a paper and reading something about me and my life-style and my friends.' But 20 per cent of him does.

Jenny Agutter

Phwoar, we said, and who can blame us? It was hot. The end of term video was *American Werewolf in London*. Jenny Agutter appeared on screen, and, let me tell you, she went down big with her 12-year-old audience.

We stamped. We cheered. We toasted her with orange squash and Nice biscuits. And that is why, decades later, when I am slumped before some zoo-like late night discussion show, and there she is, tip-tilted as ever, I feel a sudden spasm, a memory of those pent-up feelings. Even Glenda Jackson's Stalinist features melt in the penumbra of her charm.

Jenny Agutter is talking passionately, persuasively, and – good grief – according to the caption on the screen, she represents 'Transport 2000' the anti-car think-tank. Wouldn't it be grand, I muse, if someone like that could be persuaded to appear on the back page?

Wouldn't that be the stuff to give the troops? So imagine my feelings when, the following day, she actually rings back, within 10 minutes. 'It's Jenny Agutter,' she says melodiously, her surname scanning like Agatha rather than a piece of road drainage; and barely two hours later my cab has groaned through south-east London, and here we are in the cosy parlour of her newly done-up Camberwell schloss, she in her lacy white shirt, black waistcoat and flowery skirt. Yes, who can forget how she took off her red knickers in *The Railway Children*, and waved them at the train? This event is seared in the memory of the boffins of Transport 2000 because, she admits, it inspired them to ask her to be a patron, and to speak in their cause on TV.

'In truth, I have always loved trains,' she says, and speaks fondly of travelling from Waterloo to Camberley, where she was at school. Indeed, it would be a mistake to think that Jenny Agutter is just lending her name, on the strength of being a Railway Child.

So volcanic are her feelings that if a car should go past her at speed in Camberwell, 'I stand and shake my first, or stand in the road to slow them down.' Paragraphs bubble from her lips as we sit in the gloaming, ideas for 'diamond lanes', and car pools. She denounces the 'hideous' school run, and wonders why supermarkets cannot lay on buses like Ikea in New York.

She is about to set off for Cornwall and points out that a first-class return costs more than a transatlantic flight. She asked Glenda Jackson why the Government subsidy could not go towards cutting fares, rather than boosting Railtrack's profits. 'She gave a very complicated reply,' she says.

'Why will people stand waiting for a taxi for 15 minutes when they could have walked in that time?' Why, she wants to know, can't the staff on public transport have some sense of where they are, instead of thinking of stops as blobs on the line in a white desert? And as her fervour mounts, it suddenly hits me: there are two great themes to the art of Jenny Agutter. They are environmentally-friendly transport, and nudity. You will remember her sensational role in *The Eagle Has Landed*, where she rides a horse to the beach, and then takes her clothes off. Then there was *Equus*, in which horses play a key part, and in which she also took her clothes off.

Then there was *Walkabout* which, I gather, involves a lot of walking about with no clothes on. We have already discussed *The Railway Children*, and her bloomer-removing approval for public transport. In fact, we've covered the first key theme of her oeuvre, transport, pretty well. We've got to the core of the problem: viz, that if you do succeed in persuading a large chunk of the public to stop using their cars, there will come a point when people will suddenly notice that the roads are nice and clear and, hey presto, traffic's back.

By this stage, well, I am mentally trying to formulate a question on the other aspect, you know, the nudity business and am finding it quite tricky (and so would you) when clunk, thunk, dunk ... Uh-oh.

A very large blond man comes in to the room.

'Hello,' he says challengingly and thuds down a big black briefcase. I say, idiotically: 'I'm just taking the chance to grab a quick interview with your wife.'

'Well,' says Johan Tham, the proprietor of the Cliveden hotel, 'I'll just take the chance to grab a quick drink.' He crashes into the kitchen, pours a glass of white wine for Jenny and himself, and heads upstairs.

'I don't use public transport,' he announces, at the door. 'Never'. In fact, he has an Audi A8 with an engine of no less than 3.7 litres. Somehow, perhaps because Johan can be heard on the phone upstairs, I never get round to the no-clothes-on business. But who cares?

Buoyed up with the pleasure of meeting her, I leave determined to do my bit. This means walking some way to the bus stop. After quite a long wait in a dodgy-seeming area a bus arrives, shudders to a standstill, and a sign says 'Not In Service.' After a while another bus arrives, and ... to cut a long story short, I get a cab.

RIP Alan Clark

The thing about charming people, the catch, the downside, is that the greater their charm, the more painful it is when, almost certainly inadvertently, they say something that is in some way wounding. There I was in the Committee

Corridor of the Commons. It was the day of the 1997 Tory leadership election.

Here came Alan Clark, swaying down the corridor with his lizard-hipped gait, eyeing the pustulent throng of lobby correspondents through narrowed, amused eyes. 'Alan!' I cried, since we were, so I imagined, on good terms, or rather, we enjoyed the treacherous chumminess of journalists and politicians.

I had once interviewed him fairly sycophantically, with lots of stuff, which I stick by, about how he was arguably our greatest diarist since Pepys, and how he could detect a bogus Bellini at 50 paces and a bottle blonde at 100 yards. The article had drawn attention to his power and originality as a historian; and he had once, in public, been embarrassingly kind about me. And so, fortified by this vague sense of matiness, I hailed him there in the corridor, surrounded by my friends and colleagues in the Lobby.

'Alan,' I said, and asked him a wholly reasonable question, a question we had been asking every one of the smirking Tories who came and went from Room Five, after voting for William Hague or Ken Clarke.

'Who are you going to vote for, eh?' I asked. And then he slowly turned that dolichocephalic skull with its woolly iron quiff, and around me I could feel the crowd of journos tense over their notebooks, since Clark was an unknown quantity in this question, and he gazed at me briefly in a saurian sort of way, and he spoke, this belletrist, this curling-tonged epigrammatist, this adornment of the English language; and do you know what he said? He said: 'Sod off,' though he managed to fit about five syllables into the word 'sod'; and I must confess that I felt ever so slightly crushed.

Yes, I thought, of course he is right: I should set about sodding off immediately. Off is exactly the direction in which I should sod. That, I thought, as all the other hacks gurgled with pleasure and my ears turned pink, is a jolly good piece of advice from Mr Clark to an impertinent journalist. All of which serves no purpose other than to prove how frail our egos are and, in that key respect, of course, Clark was the same as the rest of us, only more so.

When you think of the cultural impact of Alan Clark in 1990s' Britain – as great as that of his father in another decade – you could not solely attribute his popularity to his diaries. These were, as everyone has said, a kind of masterpiece; not because of the lascivious stuff, the studied indiscretions about the bouncing globes of girls on trains, and the Red Box winking at him in the luggage rack above.

Clark's achievement was to produce a melancholy and absorbing thriller, in which he understood the central role in politics of failure. He takes us through his worship of Margaret Thatcher, his craving for approval, his pathetic, spaniel-like attempts to get into the Cabinet; and then, symmetrically, we see the comeuppance of that rare woman who has refused to go all the way with him, and to whom he remains devoted – particularly devoted – in the hour of her political extinction.

Those diaries reached a vast readership; they made politics interesting to people who would not normally bother with the *Today* programme; but they don't, in themselves, explain the impact of Clark. To understand his success, you have to grasp what was happening to the entire male sex, or at least its British representatives, in the pathetic post-feminist uncertainties of the 1990s.

Here was a man, just like the readers of *GQ*, *Esquire*, *Loaded* – all the reassurance-craving magazines that have sprouted in the past 10 years – who was endlessly fascinated by the various advantages and disappointments of his own gonads. He was interested in cars; he had Bentleys, bulging with tinplate testosterone; he had Rollers and Aston Martins and special chickwagons for arriving at *The Spectator* party; and in that respect, of course, he perfectly echoed the hedonistic juvenile vroom-vroom obsessions of anyone who reads a lads' mag.

He even went so far as to share with the former editor of *Loaded* magazine an unhealthy interest in Nazism, or at least in the style of the Nazis; though Clark, naturally, was more outré. He seemed to share the autarkic tenets of Nazi economics, and would, had he ever been allowed to by Mrs T, have pursued a Goldsmithian agenda of agrarian self-sufficiency and protectionism.

Like the readers of the modern lads' mags, wondering vaguely what to do with themselves now that women seem so keen on running the world, Clark also exhibited a certain insecurity. Behind all that ostentatious boasting about sex, there must have lurked, one assumes, an element of self-doubt. Above all, like the ideal *Loaded* reader, he had a selfish side to him.

He dumped his colleagues in it over Matrix Churchill, and some of them have not forgiven him. He was loyal to John Major, after he had made the mistake of giving up his Plymouth seat in 1992, but that may have been because he wanted to get back into the Commons. He was certainly not loyal to William Hague when he re-entered in 1997.

My last visual memory of him is watching him break ranks over Kosovo, shaking with anger as he attacked the bombing of a 'Christian' country. That was Clark all over: provocative, brilliant – but carrying you just further than you wanted to go. There were many reasons for finding fault with the Kosovo war, but not that we were backing Muslims against Christians.

And thinking of selfishness, and party unity, we come to his successor in the Royal Borough of Kensington and Chelsea. It would be good for the Conservative Party, and good for Michael Portillo, if he were the man. Let us hope he 'allows his name to go forward'. It will work, though, only if he sticks to Hague like glue, if he expends all the devotion on the party leader that Clark expended on Thatcher. The last thing the Tory party needs is another scene like the one we have mentioned in the Committee Corridor, or another defenestration to be secretly recorded by whichever political diarist has the nerve to follow in the footsteps of Alan Clark.

Martin McGuinness

What a place, I think to myself, as I arrive at Stormont. You drive up past the enormous lawns, and the great bronze statue of Carson, the Unionist leader, waving defiance, and everywhere you look there are signs of the British imperium: the vast ghostly pediment fringed with marble palmettes, the ceilings painted eggshell blue, and terracotta and silver; the lion, the unicorn, and *honi soit qui mal y pense*; the red despatch boxes; the Speaker's Chair, the dedications to those who died for king and country. But if you keep going down the marble corridor, and up about three flights of stairs, you will come to something rather odd. 'Crinniu ar siul bain usaid as an doras eile', barks the notice on the door, in what one takes to be a Gaelic demand for privacy.

Behind it sits the blond-curled and sweatered form of a man who has spent his entire adult life engaged, as he confirms, in a programme of terror, whose objective has been to destroy British power in Northern Ireland. He has almost succeeded in chopping the Royal Ulster Constabulary; he has brought about the release of hundreds of terrorist prisoners; he is on this very morning conducting a war of words over whether the Unionists have the right to insist on the Union flag flying from this building where, if and when the executive returns, he will once again serve as education minister; and he has done it without renouncing violence, or even causing a single weapon to be handed over.

Some see Martin McGuinness as a cherubic grandfather and fly-fishing fanatic, a man of religious conviction who rose to the leadership of Sinn Fein/IRA through his manifest integrity, and who has just persuaded them to make the huge concession of offering their weapons for inspection. To others he is the *capo di tutti capi*, the godfather of the IRA, a pale-eyed killer. In the words of the IRA historian Kevin Toolis, 'no other living person is a greater threat to the British state'.

He welcomes me with great friendliness, and his charm perhaps partly explains the chronic weakness of the British government in dealing with him. On the wall is a poem about the death of Mairead Farrell, and a child's pencilled scrawl in praise of Sinn Fein.

What's it like being dwarfed by these emblems of British rule? How does it feel to come to work every day under the salute of Carson, to be a member of the British government? 'No, I'm not actually – uctually – I don't swear an oath of allegiance to anyone other than the people who elected me.' This is still part of the UK, isn't it? 'Well, the British – the Bratash – tell us it is, but we want to change that.' Come on, Martin: are the salaries of your officials paid for by London or by Dublin? 'Obviously the salaries are paid for by the executive and by the considerable subsidy that comes from the British government.' And might you not have a car and a driver, paid for by us, the British taxpayers? 'No "might" about it. I will get one. I didn't want a BMW. I didn't want a Mercedes. I just wanted a car that would be adequate and would not be over the top or anything like that.'

What was the best bit about your eight weeks in government, before Mr Mandelson closed down the assembly? 'I announced the largest school-building programme ever in the North of Ireland, £72 million for building new schools.' And I bet it was a pleasure to spend British money, eh? I ask the man who drew the dole while trying to smash British rule. 'Yeah, ha ha ha,' he laughs.

It is amazing. The butcher's boy from the Bogside is campaigning against the 11-plus, which he failed himself. He's tough on EU integration. 'We're anti a common European army, that's what we're anti,' he says, and chuckles at the thought of a Sinn Fein–Tory agreement. He's in and out of Downing Street; he's penetrated the highest levels of the British establishment; he's bombed his way to power. Don't you feel a sense of triumph, I ask him. 'Triumph? Why? You have to understand that we are Irish Republicans. What we want to bring about fundamentally is an end to British rule in the North and the establishment of a 32-county republic.'

Martin McGuinness's mother was from Donegal. His father worked in a foundry. The second eldest boy in a family of six children, he had his first experience of sectarian prejudice when he tried to get a job with a local garage; when it emerged that he had been to a local Catholic school, the interview ended. He was at the battle of the Bogside in 1969. In 1971, as 'officer' commanding the Derry Brigade of the IRA, he set about blowing the heart out of his own city. Of Londonderry's 150 shops, only 20 were left standing by the time he and his comrades had finished.

Then, on 20 January 1972, there was Bloody Sunday. According to an intelligence source codenamed Infliction, McGuinness fired the first shot, from a tommy gun in the Rossville flats, which prompted the Paras to return fire. 'That has since been repudiated by British soldier after

British soldier who has given evidence to the tribunal.' But you were there? 'I was on the march, yeah, like thousands of others.' But you did no shooting on that day? 'That's all nonsense.'

Actually, Sean O'Callaghan says that Infliction is wrong, and that McGuinness is telling the truth. Huh, scoffs McGuinness at the idea of support from O'Callaghan, a senior IRA man in the republic who became an informer, and saved many lives. If Sean says it's the truth, it must be a lie, he says. 'What a remarkable person to be quoting to me. He's got himself in an awful predicament. I am sure it must be painful for anyone born in the island of Ireland, even in a place like Kerry, to be effectively domiciled in a place like England.' This sounds like gangster talk. Why should Sean be afraid? 'I mean if he walked down the main street in Tralee, I wouldn't give tuppence for his ability to get from one end to the other.' Sean O'Callaghan says he had dozens of meetings with you to plan terrorist operations. 'I used to have meetings with him? I think I met him once or twice in Sinn Fein HQ in Dublin, but, I mean, Sean's the past.'

After Bloody Sunday, the British state in Northern Ireland was under siege. In 1972, 500 people were killed, including 150 members of the security forces. In a panic, Willie Whitelaw flew the Provos to Paul Channon's house in Cheyne Walk. I wonder whether that was when McGuinness first sensed the irresolution of the British state? 'At that stage I was 21 years of age and never in a million years did I expect that I would be part of a delegation to meet with, effectively, British ministers in London. It was a totally unreal experience for me.' McGuinness only spoke once, clashing with Whitelaw about Bloody Sunday. The talks produced nothing. The bombing and the killing went on.

I try to explain why, as a child, I came to loathe the

505

IRA and why it seems so monstrous that terror should be rewarded. 'But if you were to apply that logic fairly and honestly, you would have to admit that the British security forces have used terroristic methods in the last 30 years.' Oh come off it, I say, and he reverts, as usual, to Bloody Sunday. 'I come from a city where 14 people were killed by the British army, and many others were wounded. Now outside of those deaths in that city alone, dozens of people were killed by the British army.' But how can you say that those heat-of-the-moment shootings were morally commensurate with what your organisation did to thousands of innocent civilians, in Ulster, and in Warrington, Manchester, Birmingham? 'I believe that the people of Derry believe the opposite of what you believe, and that is a huge problem for you.' He suggests that I have a sentimental pride in the British army, and repeats his experience in 1969, when the army started to shoot his friends. 'You have to imagine the impact that has on an 18-year-old kid from the Bogside.'

When I last met McGuinness five years ago it was in his flyblown HQ, at Cable Street in Londonderry. I asked him if he had ever been a member of the IRA, and he denied it, so I put the question again.

'I have never denied that I was a party to the resistance against the British government in the North during the last 30 years. I've always been very open about that.' So you'd stick by what you said in January 1973, in the Special Criminal Court in Dublin, after you had been found close to a car filled with 250lb of explosives and 5,000 rounds of ammunition? I read it out: 'I am a member of the Derry brigade of Oglaigh na hEireann and am very, very proud of it. We fought against the killers of my people. Many of my comrades were arrested, tortured or killed. Some of them were shot, while unarmed, by the British army. We firmly and honestly believed we were doing our duty as

Irishmen.' There is a long pause. McGuinness grunts and says, 'I am not ashamed of anything I have done in the past.' Did you ever use violence? 'Everyone uses violence. British soldiers use violence.' Were you responsible for anyone's death? 'I think we're all responsible for people's death.' By firing a bullet from a gun? 'Paisley has fired verbal bullets which have caused people to fire guns.' Do you have the blood of anyone on your hands? 'We all do, we all do. We're all responsible. If you're asking me, for example, in the course of the resistance to the British military in the siege of Derry, did I throw a stone that hit a soldier in the head and took blood from him, or did I throw a petrol bomb at a member of the RUC, or did I ever fire a shot that killed a soldier, you know, what's the point? What's the point of it?'

The point, I suppose, is to find out whether you're still a killer, or whether it's all behind you? 'I don't think David Trimble would be meeting with me if he didn't think we were for real,' he says, and nor would Blair or Clinton. But you did return to violence after the 'ceasefire'. I remember the Docklands bomb. 'Well, that was an IRA bomb; it wasn't a Sinn Fein bomb.' Sean O'Callaghan says you must have known about it. 'What credibility does someone have who has been out of Ireland for 15 years?'

So is the war over? 'That question has been raised by the rejectionist Unionists.' Look: your organisation has a bad record of blowing people up. Is the war over? He starts another answer, about how you have to judge people as you find them, so I cut him off. Is the war over, yes or no? 'The answer is that I don't believe the IRA are ever going to say the war is over because the Unionists make that demand.'

Martin McGuinness will not allow himself to be portrayed as the loser; why should he? And yet I come away better understanding why successive British governments have decided that, in spite of his past, he is the man they must deal with, and who, with Adams, holds the key to peace. In the long struggle of wills, he won, and the British government connived in its own defeat. The best hope now – and of course it is morally bankrupt, but not wholly despicable – is that the 'peace process' should grind on, the executive return, and Martin and his kind lose their instinct for terror, and discover the delights of spending taxpayers' money on schools, and riding in Rovers paid for by the state he would destroy.

Roy Jenkins

It's all right, it's all right, says Roy Jenkins, wreathed in smiles as he stands on the landing and watches me puff up to his Notting Hill flat. 'One of the advantages of your being late,' he says, handing me some champagne, 'is that I have now written 580 words today, even though it has been a rather *mouvementé* day.'

Well, phew, I think, as we sit down. If I have allowed Roy to add a few lines to his oeuvre, which stretches from *Purpose and Policy* (1947) via his 'storming' (T. Blair) life of Gladstone to the present biography of Churchill, then I cannot be wholly in disgrace. What energy, I think, as I gaze at Lord Jenkins of Hillhead, who already has at least six inches in *Who's Who*. He was the first leader of the Social Democratic party, and is the holder of the Order of European Merit (Luxembourg), the Grand Cross, Legion of Honour of Senegal (1979), the Legion of Honour of Mali, Order of Charles III (Spain), Hon. D.Litt. Glasgow and holder of gongs from Berkeley to Bologna, Chancellor of Oxford University and Lord High Everything Else.

There used to be a club where right-wing fogeys would

meet to make the famous Jenkins hand-purse gesture, which has been likened to an aristocrat fondling the breast of a passing peasant girl. They would stick their noses into glasses of claret and say things like, 'It has a lively velleity.' They used to use the word 'rancour' a great deal, pwonounced as Woy would pwonounce it, and laugh immodewately.

At least, they did until three years ago, when it emerged that they were not alone; and that the president, chairman and secretary of the Roy Jenkins Appreciation Society is Tony Blair. It was Roy, you will remember, who pointed out that the 20th century was the Tory century because the Labour party and the Liberals fatally failed to unite, and it was Roy who sowed in Tony's mind the notion that this century should be the liberal century. Now we are three years into the Project; and, though Roy gives credit to Labour for its achievement in education and in fighting child poverty, he is plainly disappointed.

'There are times when governments slightly lose their touch, and this government is going through one.' The reform of the Lords does not impress him and he speaks of a 'shoal of not very distinguished nominations. Even if you leave out some of the more rococo edges of Harold Wilson's lavender list, I think they were better nominations than this lot.' He's not happy that fox-hunting has been shunted up the political agenda. 'I'm not a great fox-hunter. I'm not a fox-hunter at all, but I believe even more strongly that, if people want to do it, why the hell shouldn't they do it?' He'd like to see a more libertarian Home Office, which reminds me of the consistent liberalism running through his own politics.

He was the home secretary who began to relax the laws on homosexuality and who abolished the death penalty. On his watch divorce and abortion were both made easier. His dictum – that the 'permissive society is the civilised

509

society' – made him a hate-figure for right-wing frothers. 'I do not regret any of the liberalising measures I introduced in the 1960s, nor do I think anybody in the Tory party would want to object except as part of fulminating at large . . . It was typical of Mrs Thatcher's attitude to the death penalty that she always said she was in favour of it, but never tried to persuade anyone else to be in favour of it.'

But what does he think of the continuing pressure to push back the boundaries of conventional morality? What about gay marriage? There is a pause. 'I haven't applied myself greatly to that,' he says, beaming, then adds: 'I don't think it is worse than a lot of marriages that actually take place.'

All these anxieties are nothing, of course, next to his preoccupation with Europe. EC Commission President Jenkins revived the Exchange Rate Mechanism, and is one of the honoured ancestors of the euro, and he feels strongly that Blair should show more of a lead. He still regards the Prime Minister as a 'very agreeable companion', and enjoys talking to him, but cannot understand why he will not begin the crusade to scrap the pound. 'I have told him many times, and I have written to him, too. It is a fallacy to believe that you can pay out the rope and let the other side make all the running, and then believe that after the election you can suddenly convert the public in two or three months.

'Blair is the most committed European prime minister since Ted Heath, *au fond*, but he has misappraised the position,' he says. It is no good trying to suppress the discussion, as Gordon Brown suggests. 'Our only previous national referendum was in 1975. Yah. I was president or whatever it is called; chairman. The polls were nearly as bad as they are at the present time. They weren't quite as bad, but there was certainly a substantial majority against, at least 60–40.'

The debate was helped, of course, by the comparative qualities of the rival camps. On one side: Tony Benn, Peter Shore, Barbara Castle, Enoch Powell. On the other: Jenkins, and his lieutenants, Heath, Whitelaw, Carrington, Jo Grimond. 'I remember making a bad-taste joke at the dinner after we won. I said, I think one of the reasons we won was that we looked as though we were well-fed men who had done well out of the CAP ha ha . . .'

Jolly funny, but not a line I think Blair would be advised to try in the present condition of British agriculture. So why doesn't Blair go for it? What is Gordon Brown up to? Lord Jenkins agrees that it is partly a Whitehall squabble, in which Brown wants to show that he is master of the euro policy.

'Brown's a great man not only for his own turf but for other people's turf as well.' Would he say that Brown is brighter than Blair? 'Blair thinks he is. He says Gordon has a brilliant intellect.' Roy concedes that his favourite pupil has a 'second-class mind', not that there's anything wrong with that, he hastens to say. 'You remember Walter Lippmann's view of Roosevelt: second-class intellect. By which I think he genuinely meant second-class, not third- or fourth-class. I mean he didn't mean it entirely disparagingly – far from it. He meant second-class intellectually and first-class in temperament, and the second is more important than the first. A very shrewd remark.'

We then have a discussion about which prime ministers received first-class degrees: 'Wilson yes, Anthony Eden yes, though it was in oriental languages ha ha. Gladstone had several first-class degrees, in classics and then in mathematics as a *bonne-bouche*. Balfour yes, Hume no. What did Thatcher have? A 2:2?' I point out that they weren't divided in those days, and he agrees that she probably had a perfectly good second.

Which brings us to Oxford, and Gordon Brown's

speech, which, he says, 'has not enhanced my view of Gordon Brown'. 'He had a singularly ill-chosen target. The medical examiners of Magdalen are a very progressive body of men, and the phrases he used – the old-school tie, the old-boy network – it was absolutely farcical. If he had wanted to launch a great attack, I would have thought his alma mater, Edinburgh, was a better target, since it has more Etonians than Oxford at the present time.

'I got into Balliol 62 years ago from a most awful school – no, I mustn't say that, but talk about an ordinary grammar school, as Lady Jay did! It was a very, very minor school, with very little good teaching.' And his point is that he doesn't, as Oxford's Chancellor, want any more interference. 'There should be no question of governments, or agents of governments, deciding which individual should or should not be admitted to university. It would also be intolerable that someone should be excluded on the grounds that they are from a privileged school.'

But isn't Oxford already being bullied by this government? Doesn't the Higher Education Funding Council already attach money to specific admissions programmes for this or that minority?

'I am not a great fan of HEFC. The more independent Oxford can be of HEFC, the better.' I wonder whether he is disappointed that Blair has failed to dissociate himself from Brown's remarks.

'It's very difficult to dissociate yourself from a chancellor, especially one as powerful as Brown.'

So will Tony get an honorary degree? 'No, not now.' Has this row made an award more difficult? 'Oh yes, certainly. It nearly came up in his first year, but we've rather lost our nerve about politicians now. I got one in 1969, but I'd never have got one now.'

What about giving one to Lady Thatcher, as a final

rebuke to Tony and Gordon for their class war? 'I don't think she'd accept it, and it's passed its time.'

Alas, my time with Lord Jenkins has also passed. He has a couple of engagements, and then 'I have to go to the House of Lords and appear in the Chamber and get my money. It's a most discreditable thing,' he chortles. No, I say, after half a bottle of champagne: money well earned, in my view.

The day Woy threw a wobbly

What I like to look for are the moments
Which seem to show us as we really are,
And whip aside the gauzy little garments,
The smiling clothes we use to hide the scar.

The quiet German starts to rage and quiver
When bumped off the last flight back to Berlin.
The politician drove into the river
And left the girl to breathe the water in.

The gentle dope-fiend sitting in Row A
Could jump an Arab gun-arm in mid-air.
The nicest of the siblings bursts out, 'Hey!
He's got more sweets than me, and it's not fair!'

The clouds roll back, the mask falls off, and so it
Was one autumn afternoon when, boy,
I saw a famous charmer really blow it.
His name, you'll be amused to know, was WOY.

Though some were better, none was grand as he,
For all the grander men were long since dead.
He chancelled Oxford's university,
The noble Roy, Lord Jenkins of Hillhead.

He founded Europe's monetary system.
He led the SDP and broke the mould.
He aimed at stars and even if he missed them,
And even if his party's dead and cold

That hardly takes away from his achievements
And now upon the face of that great man
There writhed a mix of loss, desire, bereavement:
Someone had left him off the seating plan!

For forty years we've had a certain notion
That Jenkins was as smooth as smooth can be.
He salved your problems with his verbal lotion,
The incarnation of urbanity.

He shunned the vulgar language of extremes
For discourse ever svelte and politic,
Suffusing either side with frog-like beams
That made his foes seem rather small and thick.

His style was so unutterably grand
That Woy might just as well have been an earl,
And when he spoke he pursed and furled his hand
As if to cup the bosom of a girl.

He bent his smile on almost everything.
Each sinner felt its civilising rays.
He stopped the judges sending men to swing,
And plugged the cause of those who swing both ways.

Whatever deed he did, he did it nobly,
So when across the room I heard a noise
I never dreamed that WOY could throw a wobbly
Or sit up in his pram and chuck his toys

Two hundred guests had slipped into their places
And now the roar descended to a hum
As all alike began to stuff their faces
Yet Jenkins had no seat to park his bum!

The throng knocked back its opening glug of claret
As when a mighty engine changes gear.
I looked again, and, no, I couldn't bear it:
Still no chair for Woy to plonk his rear!

His eye caught mine. He scythed around a table.
My nervous system flipped to panic mode.
He grabbed my arm as hard as he was able.
The beaming frog became a scarlet toad.

No prize that Britain offers the ambitious
Eluded Jenkins' energetic grasp,
But now that grip was positively vicious,
And now that languid drawl became a rasp.

His crinkling eyes had prawned all out of shape.
He boggled at me bleakly like a killer.
His salon arms he raked like some vast ape.
Did I say ape? Scratch that! He was WOYZILLA!

Vibrating like a thunder-smitten oak
Or like a rocket on the launching-pad
He hissed and spat the words: 'Is this a joke?
Because if so, it's VEWY, VEWY BAD.'

Just when I thought that he must have a fit
And pop a small capillary in his brain
An honoured place was found for him to sit
And look! The beam stole slowly back again

But if his rage had lasted just a minute
That parting of the curtains was enough
To glimpse his soul – or something deep within it,
Some pretty adamantine, tungsten stuff.

I understood how WOY had worked all hours,
Gone whoring after London's poshest wives,
Then whacked your croquet ball into the flowers,
And churned out thumping books on great men's lives.

Like opening up the bonnet of a car
To find the coiling tubes of the machine,
These moments teach us how we really are
And show the human animal within.

He wanted to be treated like a toff
And yet that wasn't why he was so sore.
He feared he would be cheated of his scoff.
For acting on both fears I liked him more.

He fought for both his stomach and his rank,
A fight for luncheon fitting his degree.
His fight was just. Without it, let's be fwank,
Where would we be? Where would this country be??

Ghazi Algosaibi, the Saudi ambassador

'No, no,' says the Saudi ambassador, 'this is how you do it. You cannot lift your arm above the shoulder, and you must do it sideways.' He moves alongside, a big man with a faint resemblance to Leon Brittan, and makes a thwacking motion. Meet Ghazi Algosaibi, 62, a poet and author, the Arab world's leading envoy to London, who has recently earned not just a personal rebuke from Jack Straw, but the demands of the Jewish Board of Deputies that he be expelled from the country.

Mr Algosaibi recently wrote an ode to a suicide bomber (which prompted the rebuke). In the last two hours, in the lacquered mudéjar comfort of his Curzon Street embassy, he has been fluently denouncing the West. He has attacked cultural imperialism, bashed Bush, hammered Sharon, and now, as a coda to a virtuoso performance, he is giving a short tutorial in the virtues of lashing.

'What would you rather have? Thirty lashes or three years in prison?' he demands, swishing away. On the anniversary of 11 September, and with a new war impending, it seemed useful to hear the opinions of our most valued and vital Arab ally.

What will he be doing on Wednesday the 11th? Will the flag be lowered? Um, he says, they have this thing about lowering the flag. It has the name of God on it. It seems the embassy has no real plans to mark the anniversary, which is perhaps not surprising, given that 15 of the 19 hijackers were from Saudi Arabia. Why was that, by the way?

'The answer is easy,' he says. 'It was much easier to get a visa for a Saudi.' But let's face it, Ghazi (as he asks me to call him), bin Laden has Saudi support, doesn't he? 'Please don't kick the ambassador out of London for saying this, but if you go around the Muslim world, you will find the vast majority of people will support Osama bin Laden, and this is more tragic than the attack itself. Why would such a crime like this find such support, not just on the streets of Riyadh, but on the streets of Turkey, the streets of Tunis, the streets of Britain?'

But why is he so strongly supported?

'That comes to the question of why people hate America. And people definitely do hate America, because she is the superpower. All countries have different reasons, but in the Muslim world there is one issue with America, and that is Israel.'

Look, I say, I just don't believe that 15 Saudis are going to take their own lives in that way, purely because of Palestine. He plays ferociously with his amber worry beads. 'You have to be an Arab to understand the Palestinian cause, just as you have to be Jewish to understand the Holocaust. The impact that the Palestinian problem left on the Arab is something that is beyond the understanding of anyone who is not an Arab. It really ignited memories of the Crusades.'

But come off it, surely the problem of Palestine has been largely caused by abominable Palestinian leadership. 'If you want me to tell you that Yasser Arafat is the worst leader in history, I have no problem with that.' Then why does the Ambassador to the Court of St James make the odious analogy that Israeli occupation of the West Bank and Gaza is 'far more severe than anything the Germans did'?

Ghazi says that he is the victim of a 'dirty trick' of misquotation. He never meant to connote the Holocaust; he was merely referring to other aspects of Nazi rule – curfews and suchlike. And anyway, he says, 'Sharon is much worse than Hamas. He has more lethal rockets and he is killing more civilians.' He produces a sheet of figures.

'There have been 2,283 Palestinians killed between 28 September 2000 and 19 June 2002. Did Hamas do that? We are talking about the killing of civilians. That is what terrorism is. Why, when it is done ruthlessly and efficiently by a state, is it not called terrorism?'

Surely Israel's answer, I say, is that there is no moral equivalence between the intentions of a terrorist, and the authorities who are trying to pre-empt the suicide bombers ... 'I don't see the moral equivalence,' he interjects, 'because what Sharon does is much worse. Have you been brainwashed? Have you been intimidated by Lord and Lady Black? Sharon engineered the intifada and the repression. These are people who have been living all their lives in misery.

'When I was a little boy in Bahrain in 1948 [when he was eight], I was going on the street and demonstrating. I didn't say down with America, I said down with Britain, because Britain gave Palestine to the Jews and it didn't belong to them.'

And that, he says, remains the problem. I wonder. Doesn't bin Laden also loathe the corrupt and despotic Saudi monarchy, the 4,000 princes, the hypocrisy? 'No, no, that's just what you guys write. Bin Laden is going to do this no matter what. He's a maniac. We rescinded his nationality in 1994, and the human-rights organisations were up in arms. We always warned you against him, and we made sure no money went to him because we realised he was a danger.'

What about the $200 million the Saudis allegedly gave him, as a bribe to take his operations off home soil? 'We didn't give him a penny. He went to his family and said, give me my share, and he was given his share of his father's inheritance. You could not take that away from him at that time, so he took away $50 or $60 million, yes.' So you are telling us that bin Laden's grudge against the world is all about Israel, and nothing to do with the Saudi regime? Would these demented suicide bombers really have been produced by a democracy?

'Democracy is a Western phenomenon,' he explodes. 'If you look now and say 142 governments in the world have elections, that's a disgusting lie. If you exclude the West, there are no democracies. . . .'

Well, hang on, I say. 'Tell me, tell me!'

What about parts of Africa? 'But these countries have Anglo-Saxon elites. You take countries like Afghanistan and Saudi Arabia. They have been isolated from the world. There is instant coffee, instant tea, instant wine, but there is no instant democracy. Democracy requires many things. It requires a middle class, civil society, judicial process. I mean, come on, now, Churchill was ordering the troops to fire on the suffragettes in 1917.

'I think we should work towards a system where people run their own affairs, but you cannot impose it from the outside. Look at what is happening in Afghanistan. The famous committees on Evil are back, and yesterday there was a ruling against female singers on TV. In Saudi Arabia, or in any tribal system, if a girl marries outside the tribe there is war.

'In Saudi Arabia, a lot of people refuse to mention the name of their daughter. Some friends of mine wrote to me to invite me to attend the wedding of Ali and "our daughter". I wrote back, saying, "Does your daughter have a name?" When women were forced to have a picture on their passport, more than 20,000 of them handed back their passport. When I was a minister, I suggested that women should be allowed to drive. It was the women who protested.

'If someone thinks the proper punishment of a murderer is execution, why should you or I interfere? We are not talking about a couple of banana republics, with all

520

respect. We are talking about 1.3 or 1.4 billion Muslims. Are you or I going to convert them? If you had a democracy in Britain, you would have the death penalty tomorrow, especially after the death of those two girls. I have made a study of it,' he says, rootling around for another pamphlet.

'Nobody in Saudi Arabia wants a secular state. They believe in their religion.' Oh, by the way, what is the position on alcohol, here in the embassy? 'I am not going to answer that question. I am not a Catholic and you are not my confessor, but who said Muslims do not commit sins? Has it not occurred to you that what goes on in this country is abhorrent to Muslims?' Yes, but remind me, what is it that Muslims find abhorrent? 'First of all there is great jealousy, of the financial and military power of the West, the gap between rich and poor. There is a common perception that the wealth of the West is the result of looting colonies.

'I have always said that this is not sustainable. I have always said you should not hate the Jews.' But now, he says, these feelings are ever stronger, and encouraged by American behaviour. 'I am worried because we are talking about a nation, a country, which is almost gripped by mass hysteria. This struck them where it hurt most. Even Pearl Harbor was nothing like this. Someone hit the Pentagon. They are just stunned, and looking left and right for revenge. Now we are getting these military courts in America, and holding people without trial. It is almost like what happened to the Japanese interned during the war. The American psyche is unlike the British psyche. You are in many ways more lackadaisical. You have two prime ministers almost killed, and you say, Oh well, some things are fated, some are not. The Americans say, We are going to go and get them.

'And then most Muslims are looking at the Americans and saying, My God, are only the Muslims terrorists? What about Oklahoma? Or the Basques? Then the President says there are going to be actions against 60 countries. That is terrifying. What is the rational explanation for hitting Iraq? I don't understand it. Nobody understands it. I think Bush is obsessed with hitting Iraq, like Eden with Nasser. Eden was convinced that Nasser was another Hitler.'

But isn't Saddam like Hitler? 'No, no,' he laughs. 'Hitler was able to conquer 90 per cent of the civilised world as we know it. Saddam cannot do that. He is hemmed in.' Isn't his regime brutal? 'What is brutal? How many civilians did the Americans kill in Vietnam? Half a million? One million? Are you now avenging angels? Once you finish with the dictators, then you go to the regime which does not allow women to drive; and then to the people who cut off hands and the people who circumcise. What is this? The Lord of Hosts couldn't manage that! What are you going to achieve in Iraq?'

Change the regime, I say. 'Why? I think Sharon is a monster. Why don't they get rid of Sharon?'

So Saudi Arabia will offer no help? 'Of course not, and I say that as a friend of America, because I believe it will backfire. I am sure America can do it, militarily. The Baghdad In, Baghdad Out option will work. Three or four weeks' bombing, and you get rid of Saddam, and then what? Are the Shias going to become suddenly buddy-buddy with the Sunnis? Are the Kurds going to forget their separatist tendencies? Are you going to inherit a safe seat in Basra South from Michael Heseltine?

'I don't know what is going to happen next, but I know that Dubya is going to hit Iraq, and it is going to end up a tragedy. I think Blair will do what he did in Afghanistan – a token participation that will not really offend anybody; more like moral support.' And no Saudi help whatever?

'As things stand now, no.' No use of bases? 'No. The feeling in the Middle East is so overboiling that I hate to think what is going to happen. We will do our best to keep the oil price steady. If it wasn't for Saudi Arabia, oil would probably be double its price now. Tomorrow if we cut our production by two million barrels, the price would go up to $35 a barrel.

'Everybody attacks Saudi Arabia, because it is the personification of everything a Western journalist hates.' As he is speaking, there is a ping on the embassy loudspeaker, and a muezzin starts summoning the faithful. 'It is privileged, Muslim, reactionary, and it suppresses women. Whatever I do, I don't like to bullshit anyone, because I don't like to be bullshitted myself. I am becoming like President Bush. I am becoming paranoid.'

Shortly after giving the last interview, Ghazi Algosaibi was unexpectedly repatriated to Saudi Arabia. I cannot say whether or not his move was in any way connected with the article. What I know for certain is that huge numbers of people, day in, day out, are traduced by journalists. In spite of all our efforts to target our weapons, to check for balance and accuracy, and to make sure that we are basically fair, it is a terrible fact of journalism that it involves collateral damage. To anybody out there who feels he or she has been undeservingly monstered and I stress undeservingly I sincerely apologise.

AFTERWORD

I want to leave you with a final consoling thought. It is true that all journalists are endowed with these terrifying weapons. Sometimes they use them well, sometimes not. But they are never individually quite as powerful as they think. All journalists, after all, are locked in a bitter and ceaseless struggle with each other, a competition to get it first, to say it best, to mint the phrase that catches the taste of the moment.

They are, in other words, just part of that growing and all-encompassing free market system which I observed in 1988 and 1989. The free market destroyed communism because Adam Smith's invisible hand was better than collectivism at supplying lipstick to Bulgarian women. In the same way, the institutions of the free media – newspapers, magazines, the internet, radio and TV stations – are just broking houses in the gigantic bourse of public opinion. They are traders in news and views; and like all traders, they can be caught out by someone who is prepared to be original and daring.

They may all decide at once to dump a stock, and the results can be awful, especially if that stock happens to be you. But because it is a free market, there will always be someone ready to buck the conventional opinion, ready to buy when the market is low. Let us say that a charismatic Princess dies tragically young, and the whole country is convulsed with mourning. There will always be at least a few columnists happy to make a few caustic cracks, of a just-what-the-hell-is-going-on variety. If the nation decides that the Dome is a dump, there will be some journalist who will immediately test the market in Domes, and write a piece saying how wonderful it is.

If the conventional wisdom is that the war in Iraq will be over in days, someone will instantly prophesy that it could take months. Every day, every minute, the media is investigating the market in every possible proposition. They test the appetite of other journalists, who have to decide whether or not to take up these views. Ultimately, all these wares are for sale to the public. It is true that the media can to a large extent condition the public's appetite. But if for too long they supply them with an outdated product like dud Bulgarian lipstick a hidden gap in the market will be created.

If someone spots that gap, and starts to offer another stock, there will be one of those tipping points. Suddenly, everyone will stop selling and start buying. To take an example close to my heart, it has long been the conventional media wisdom that a certain political party is pretty washed up, hopeless, and has not much chance of winning the next election. I could urge you to wonder about that opinion. I could urge you to buy, buy, buy a blue chip stock that has been recklessly undervalued. But that might try your patience; and anyway, it is another story.

Acknowledgements

My journalistic debts are too numerous to mention, but I would like a special medal to be struck for Benedick Watt, who spent time ploughing through my oeuvre, and who is largely responsible for this selection.

I would like to thank the *Daily Telegraph* for their kind permission to reproduce the following articles:

Snails are fish – 8/11/89
Major signals softer stance on EU unity – 24/4/90
Thatcher alone as EU votes for single currency –
   29/10/90
Eurocondoms – 8/5/91
Wider still and wider, but where will Europe stop? –
   15/01/92
Danes vote to scupper Maastricht – 3/6/92
Lamont fails to save pound – 17/9/92
Labour leadership contenders – Blair ahead – 9/7/94
The Kamikaze Squad – 18/3/95
So much for the pen and dagger men – 5/7/95
The 'new' gospel – 4/10/95

Early Learning Centre climbing frame – 21/4/98
Going on *Have I Got News For You* – 8/11/01
Euro MP in a tizz over fizz – 26/7/89
Weapons dealer found murdered – 24/3/90
Hurd warns EC of US anger at Gulf response –
5/12/90
MEPs squabble on the sidelines – 23/1/91
After Mitterrand nothing much will change – 19/12/94
The birth of the euro – 16/12/95
A bacillus at the heart of Brussels – the end of the
Commission – 17/3/99
Blunkett and Le Pen – 25/4/02
Droll diplomat finds his place in history – 28/10/96
Scandal in the wind as Elton strikes a chord – 7/2/98
George Dubya Bush – 15/2/99
Flying a Scudbuster – 17/2/99
Good on you, Bush baby: you go ahead and tell 'em –
5/4/01
Bianca Jagger – 21/7/97
Blair and Clinton – will Bill let Tony down? – 14/5/99
Arkan – 31/5/99
Incompetent swatting from above the clouds – 2/6/99
Milosevic under fire for accepting American terms –
5/6/99
The Serbs will blame us and they will have a point –
9/6/99
How the Serbs were turned into a nation of victims –
16/6/99
Zimbabwe – we won't do anything for them – 17/4/00
What Islamic terrorists are really afraid of is women –
27/9/01
We should try bin Laden first – 13/12/01
We blew the chance to finish Saddam – 21/12/98
Saddam must go but don't lie to me about the reasons –
26/12/02

Riches have become the bad dreams of avarice – 27/2/95
Rights and Duties – 27/3/95
Sardines gutted as Socrates comes in on the rebound –
  3/4/95
Let in the Hong Kong Chinese – 25/9/95
Thoughts on the ruin of Aitken – 25/6/97
Killing deer to save them – 9/7/97
They're only jealous, Bill – 28/1/98
Why Tony worships in the Temple of gammon –
  14/10/98
Defence of Glenn Hoddle – 3/2/99
Call to raise the speed limit – 12/7/01
Indian elephant piece – 2/1/03
Jimmy Goldsmith – 4/6/94
Ken Clarke – 4/3/96
Clare Short – 17/4/95
Harry Wu – 11/11/96
Buthelezi – 24/6/96
F W De Klerk – 9/6/97
Peter Thomson – 30/9/96
David Trimble – 13/1/97
Tony Benn – 3/3/97
Frank Bruno – 14/7/97
Chris Evans – 12/5/98
Kelvin MacKenzie – 6/11/98
Dancing with Ulrika – 28/11/98
Robert Harris – 11/1/99
Jenny Agutter – 26/7/99
RIP Alan Clark – 9/9/99

I would like to thank the *Sunday Telegraph* for their
kind permission to reproduce the following articles:

Heseltine catches EEC's eye – 8/4/90
Delors plan to rule Europe – 3/5/92

Blair takes middle road to 'New Europe' – 25/5/97
Delors is no shepherd to Chaplain – 21/7/91

I would like to thank the *Spectator* for their kind permission to reproduce the following articles:

The French empire of Europe – 8/6/91
The making of a president – 7/12/91
Heseltine v Portillo – 6/8/94
Mr Blair has learnt a valuable lesson – 18/3/95
Who was fibbing – the Old Blair or new? – 29/4/95
Who *are* all these people? – 30/9/95
The permanent secretaries are preparing to demonstrate
    their permanence – 21/10/95
American revolution – 13/11/99
Congratulations it's a Belgian – 31/7/93
We few, we happy few – 23/10/99
Huh, I thought. Double Income, No Kids. That's what
    we have here. Bastards. – 18/3/00
One Nation – 8/12/00
Interview with William Macpherson – 6/1/01
In defence of Wodehouse – 25/9/99
Virgil's message for the Middle East – 7/4/01
London house prices – 26/3/94
Road testing the bodyguards – 11/12/93
Arthur interrupts me in Boobtropolis – 22/1/00
After You Helmut – 1/8/92
The public conscience of Douglas Hurd – 17/4/93
Bill Clinton is right – 10/6/00
The cowardly whites who help Mugabe – 13/4/02
The fear, the squalor . . . and the hope – 3/5/03
Alcohol is good for you – 9/11/91
Moments of moral choice – 10/6/95
Who'd want to be a Tory MP these days? – 29/7/95
Calling out ambulances by mistake – 23/9/95

Nation of curtain-twitchers – 28/10/95
Martin McGuinness – 20/5/00
Roy Jenkins – 24/6/00
The day Woy threw a wobbly
Ghazi Algosaibi the Saudi ambassador – 7/9/02

I would like to thank the *Guardian* for their kind permission to reproduce the following article:

'Am I guilty of racial prejudice? We all are' – 21/2/00

I would like to thank *GQ Magazine* for their kind permission to reproudce the following article:

The iron-on lady – January 2003